As a place to die, to dispose of the physical remains of the deceased and to perform the rites which ensure that the departed attains a 'good state' after death, the north Indian city of Banaras attracts pilgrims and mourners from all over the Hindu world. This book is primarily about the priests and other kinds of 'sacred specialist' who serve them: about the way in which they organise their business, and about their representations of death and understanding of the rituals over which they preside. All three levels are informed by a common ideological preoccupation with controlling chaos and contingency. The anthropologist who writes about death inevitably writes about the world of the living, and Dr Parry is centrally concerned with concepts of the body and the person in contemporary Hinduism, with ideas about hierarchy, renunciation and sacrifice, and with the relationship between hierarchy and notions of complementarity and holism.

Death in Banaras

THE LEWIS HENRY MORGAN LECTURES 1988

presented at
The University of Rochester
Rochester, New York

Lewis Henry Morgan Lecture Series

Fred Eggan: *The American Indian: Perspectives for the Study of Social Change*
Ward H. Goodenough: *Description and Comparison in Cultural Anthropology*
Robert J. Smith: *Japanese Society: Tradition, Self, and the Social Order*
Sally Falk Moore: *Social Facts and Fabrications: "Customary Law" on Kilimanjaro, 1880–1980*
Nancy Munn: *The Fame of Gawa: A Symbolic Study of Value Transformation in a Mussim (Papua New Guinea) Society*
Lawrence Rosen: *The Anthropology of Justice: Law as culture in Islamic Society*
Stanley Jeyaraja Tambiah: *Magic, Science, Religion and the Scope of Rationality*
Maurice Bloch: *Prey into Hunter: The Politics of Religious Experience*
Marilyn Strathern: *After Nature: English Kinship in the Late Twentieth Century*
Byron J. Good: *Medicine, Rationality and Experience: An Anthropological Perspective*

Death in Banaras

JONATHAN P. PARRY
London School of Economics and Political Science

CAMBRIDGE
UNIVERSITY PRESS

Published by the Press Syndicate of the University of Cambridge
The Pitt Building, Trumpington Street, Cambridge CB2 1RP
40 West 20th Street, New York, NY 10011-4211, USA
10 Stamford Road, Oakleigh, Victoria 3166, Australia

First published 1994

Printed in Great Britain at the University Press, Cambridge

A catalogue record for this book is available from the British Library

Library of Congress cataloguing in publication data
Parry, Jonathan P.
Death in Banaras / Jonathan P. Parry.
p.   cm. – (The Lewis Henry Morgan lectures 1988)
ISBN 0 521 46074 3 (hardback). – ISBN 0 521 46625 3 (paperback).
1. Funeral rites and ceremonies, Hindu – India – Vārānasi.
2. Death – Religious aspects – Hinduism. 3. Cremation – Religious
aspects – Hinduism. 4. Vārānasi (India) – Religious life and customs.
5. Hinduism – Customs and practices.   I. Title.   II. Series.
BL 1226.82.F86P37   1994
294.5'38–dc20   93-31990CIP

ISBN 0 521 46074 3 hardback
ISBN 0 521 46625 3 paperback

Dusra rin
For André, with affectionate respect

Contents

Illustrations

Plates

Figures

Maps

Tables

Foreword

Jonathan Parry delivered the Lewis Henry Morgan Lectures on which this book is based at the University of Rochester in April 1988. This marked the twenty-sixth year in which the Lectures were offered to the public by the Department of Anthropology at the University of Rochester. The thirty-second Morgan Lectures will be delivered in March 1994.

The Lectures serve in part as a memorial to Lewis Henry Morgan. A prominent Rochester attorney as well as a founder of modern anthropology, Morgan never found it necessary to accept a formal academic position. Nevertheless, he was connected with the University of Rochester from its beginning. A major early benefactor, he left the University money for a women's college. He also left it his manuscripts and library. Until the creation of the Morgan Lectures, however, the only memorial to him at the University was a residence hall wing named in his honour.

The Morgan Lectures, the published volumes as well as the public lectures in Rochester, also are the site of a complex series of intersecting and overlapping conversations. Most importantly, of course, the Lecturer addresses other anthropologists and scholars in a variety of allied fields on his or her own behalf. The Lectures also provide an opportunity for the Department – undergraduates, graduate students and faculty alike – to engage in close interaction with scholars working on a wide range of problems in our discipline, many of which we cannot hope to represent in a single department. Ideally, their work challenges as well as complements our own. Through its selection of Lecturers, the Rochester Department of Anthropology is able to convey its sense of the growing points of the discipline as a whole. Here our audience is both local and international, anthropological and interdisciplinary. First through the public lectures in Rochester and then through the published volumes, the Lectures serve as a forum in which scholars from a variety of disciplines and members of the public may meet to discuss matters of general as well as academic interest.

As Maurice Bloch and Parry noted in the Introduction to their edited volume on *Death and the regeneration of life*, the anthropology of the symbolism of death has had a chequered history. Prominent in the Victorian anthropology of J. J. Bachofen, J. G. Frazer, Robert Hertz and Jane Harrison, the analysis of mortuary symbolism largely disappeared from view in the work on social morphology that predominated in the middle of the twentieth century. The topic has returned to prominence in the last decade or so with the renewed anthropological interest in systems of thought.

Jonathan Parry has had a particularly important place in the resumption of anthropological work on the symbolism of death. *Death in Banaras* brings to a conclusion a line of analysis first opened in a series of articles and chapters that have generated considerable anticipation. In addition, to the Introduction to *Death and the regeneration of life*, co-authored with Maurice Bloch, these include 'Ghosts, greed and sin: the occupational identity of the Banaras funeral priests' (*Man*, 1980), 'Death and cosmogony in Kashi' (*Contributions to Indian Sociology*, 1981) and 'Sacrificial death and the necrophagous ascetic' (*Death and the regeneration of life*).

Death in Banaras focuses on the priests and other sacred specialists who serve the enormous numbers of mourners and pilgrims who are drawn to Banaras from throughout the Hindu world. A clear and coherent descriptive analysis of the rituals performed by these specialists, their exegeses of those rituals and their ideas concerning death, and of the ways in which they organise their 'business', the book is at once more particular than an account of mortuary rituals and soteriology in Hindu South Asia and larger than a case study. This is death *in Banaras*, modern India's pre-eminent pilgrimage centre and a preferred place to die. A city of just over 700,000 persons, Banaras confounds conventional theories of social and cultural change. The 'traditions' discerned in India's villages are not attenuated by the forces of modernisation, but instead appear in particularly striking form. It is especially in urban centres such as Banaras that the traditions of contemporary India are invented and reproduced. Here, too, in Parry's striking phrase, death is 'big business'. The choice of Banaras as a fieldwork site and of mortuary rituals as a research topic reflects a fine sense of the processes of cultural production at work in India.

The framework of *Death in Banaras* is comprised of an introductory chapter, three substantive parts and a concluding chapter, itself largely ethnographic. In addition to sketching the overall argument of the book, the Introduction notes a special feature of the material on which it is based. As Parry puts it, the practitioners with which his book is concerned are 'propagandists' as well as ritualists. They are experts in the production of ritual exegesis and of commentary on exegesis, perfectly willing to 'extemporise' on questions that have no standard answer. If, as they rather frequently aver, they are rogues, they certainly are lively and witty rogues, worthy participants in a work of anthropology.

The two chapters that comprise the first substantive part of the book examine the relationship between Banaras and death. Chapter 1 is concerned with the ways in which the city is represented in its sacred literature. These are the conceptions of space and time and of the relations between death and (re)birth that sustain the pre-eminent place of Banaras and its ritual specialists in the Hindu world. Chapter 2 traces the history of Banaras as a pilgrimage centre and sketches the scale and shape of the contemporary 'business'. Adopting the perspective of an outside observer, which in this case seems remarkably close to the backstage voices of the ritual specialists themselves, the chapter argues that the traditions of Banaras are, in fact, produced and reproduced in the rituals performed by and for the thousands of pilgrims and mourners.

The second substantive part of the book is concerned with the 'business' of mortuary rituals. Chapter 3 deals with the ways in which various categories of ritual specialists allocate opportunities to serve their patrons. Chapter 4 is concerned with the manner in which priests are remunerated, focusing especially on the ideology of the gift and on the fierce bargaining that pervades the interaction of priests with their clients.

Part III turns to a close analysis of a variety of mortuary rituals and associated exegesis. Chapter 5 is concerned with the rituals surrounding the disposal of the body, especially cremation and immersion. Cremation is a kind of sacrifice. It reproduces the cosmogonic sacrifice of Vishnu at the centre of the representations of Banaras as a sacred space and results in the rebirth of the deceased and of the chief mourner. Chapter 6 focuses on the series of rituals performed in the days, weeks and months following the disposal of the body. Chapter 7 examines rituals attendant upon 'bad death'. The bodies of those who die 'bad deaths' are immersed rather than cremated. The souls of these unfortunates are thought to become unsatisfied and dangerous ghosts who may possess the living. The rituals analysed in chapter 7 are intended to diagnose cases of spirit possession and exorcise the victims.

The concluding chapter turns to the Aghori renouncers whose ascetic practices are meant to 'conquer death entirely by escaping from the endless cycle of rebirths'. The practices of the Aghoris 'are peculiarly extreme', but, in addition to describing the end of death in Banaras, Parry uses this material to confirm his analysis of the ritual services offered to the vast majority of householder pilgrims and mourners. Extreme and everyday, the two sets of practices are informed by the same set of ideas.

Parry's lucid analysis of the symbolism of mortuary rituals and of the organisation of the funeral and pilgrimage trades forms a compelling narrative. It surely will become required reading for those interested in topics as diverse as death and death rituals, pilgrimage, exchange and occupational hierarchies. Refreshingly, Parry is content to let his ethnography speak for itself. He abstains from any extraneous theoretical claims, though it must be admitted that in these postmodern times this in itself amounts to a theoretical claim about the capacity of ethnographic writing to represent reality. This is not to imply, however, that Parry's work will be of interest only to South

Asianists or to those interested in the particular topics he treats. On the
contrary, running through his analysis are several arguments of very broad
sociological interest.

In order to put these arguments into context, it is useful to recall that Parry
was a student of Edmund Leach and that he belongs to the generation of
anthropologists who began doing research in and writing about India in the
mid to late 1960s, just as Louis Dumont's enormously important structural
synthesis, *Homo hierarchicus*, was published in French and translated into
English. These scholars held contrasting positions. For Dumont sociological
analysis began with systems of values. In the Indian case, he emphasised the
principle of hierarchy, the hierarchical interdependence of purity and
impurity, and the ways in the values of ritual hierarchy encompassed and
rendered residual the brute facts of power. Leach, of course, accorded
considerably more importance to considerations of power and is famous for
arguing, in *Political systems of highland Burma*, that ritual actions may be
understood as symbolic statements about the distribution of power in the
social order. Parry has managed to remain faithful to both models. The
tensions between their positions plays a productive role in his work.

Perhaps this appears most clearly in his references to Marshall Salhins and
the notion of practical reason. Such references run throughout Parry's
discussion of the business of death in Banaras, especially the rota systems that
allocate opportunities to serve clients among ritual specialists (e.g. pp.
115–17) and the bargaining over the value of the 'gifts' (*dan*) presented to these
specialists (e.g. 139–48). It appears, too, in his persuasive attempt to reconcile
the sacred text's concern with salvation with his own and Peter van der Veer's
perceptions of the crass competition and exploitation that pervade the
relations among ritual specialists and between the specialists and their clients
in pilgrimage centres such as Banaras and Ayodhya (pp. 119–22), perceptions
that are shared by the priests among whom Parry worked. Van der Veer sees
the proper function of the pilgrimage system in Ayodhya as collapsing under
the pressures of democratisation and economic change. Salhins, on the other
hand, rejects the notion that cultural forms are determined by 'practical
reason', arguing instead that utilitarian interests are shaped by culture. Parry
regards both positions as oversimplifications. In his view the apparent
venality of the Banaras ritual specialists is 'over-determined . . . the product
of a complex interplay between culture *and* practical reason'.

The same tensions inform Parry's important insights concerning the
principle of hierarchy. One of these concerns the relations between Dumont's
principle of hierarchy and McKim Marriot's concept of the individual. These
concepts have been seen by their authors as mutually exclusive alternatives
and generally have been received in that way. Parry, however, proposes an
ingenious reconciliation of these analyses. This reconciliation turns upon
what he shows to be an essential feature of rituals, namely that they must first
recognise what they subsequently devalue. In other words, if Hindu mortuary

rituals are to re-enact convincingly the creation of a holistic social order that instantiates the hierarchical opposition of purity and impurity, they also must represent the world as a place in which that order is threatened by a looming chaos. The 'law of the fishes', the notion that the little fish of the social world are constantly in danger of being eaten by the big fish, is one such image of chaos. Representations of the persons as a dividual, continuously open to change and decay through interaction with others, is another. From this perspective, the Hindu conceptions observed by Dumont and Marriot are not competing truths, but rather 'ideologies in the Marxist sense' (pp. 112–15). Each relies upon the other for its persuasive power.

Parry also argues that Dumont's principle of hierarchy itself must be modified, at least in Banaras. Dumont sees the pure and the impure as mutually dependent. The Brahman priest requires the services of the low castes just as the low caste requires the services of the Brahman. Like C. J. Fuller, who also worked in a major religious centre, Parry argues that the high status accorded to ascetic renouncers has separated holism from hierarchy. The inferior acknowledges his or her dependence on the superior, but the superior is acknowledged by both parties as an autonomous entity who does not require the services of the inferior. The idea that this transformation of the values of hierarchy is influenced by the values of the renouncer suggests that the relation between status and relative autonomy is likely to be quite general in India. At the same time, however, Parry is careful to keep in mind the varying ideological salience of alternative versions of Indian values in historically specific settings. This remains Banaras.

ANTHONY T. CARTER, *Editor*
The Lewis Henry Morgan Lectures

Preface

The fieldwork on which this book is based has been conducted at intervals over the past fifteen years. Some of this material appears here for the first time; some of it has been previously published in scattered articles, parts of which have been incorporated into the present text in a slightly re-worked form.

Research in Banaras was carried out between September 1976 and November 1977 and in August 1978, August–September 1981, March–April 1983 and April 1992. Though the last of these visits was extremely brief, it was long enough to establish that there had been some important changes in the previous nine years. As far as the subject matter of this book is concerned, two of these are particularly significant. Though I realise with hindsight that I should have anticipated the first, I was shocked to discover that a distressingly large number of my best informants, and most of the main protagonists to the disputes referred to in the early chapters of this book, had themselves died in the interim. New bones of contention have arisen on the *ghats*, and new factional alliances formed between rival groups of sacred specialists. The second striking change has been the opening of an electric crematorium at Harishchandra *ghat*, a technological innovation which has not only had a dramatic impact on the 'traditional' division of mortuary labour, but which has also led to significant modifications in the rituals which accompany cremation. Though I briefly report on some of these recent changes, the 'ethnographic present' to which this book primarily refers should be taken as the period between 1976 and 1983. The illusion of timelessness which so much in the mortuary rites is concerned to create is just that – an illusion.

In the long gestation of this book I have incurred a long list of debts – so long that it is impossible to acknowledge them all. Thanks must first of all go to the large number of friends and informants on the *ghats* of Banaras who patiently put up with my sometimes intrusive presence, answered my tiresome questions with an often delightful sense of humour, went out of their way to instruct me and offered me hospitality in their homes. The families of Rani Maharaj, Om Prakash and Krishna Pande, Lachminarayan Pande, Bholanath and Pomar Chaube, Dr Daya Shankar Pande and Muktanand

Chaube all have a particular claim on my gratitude. The quantity and quality of the data I was able to obtain, and my enjoyment of the fieldwork itself, were immeasurably enhanced by the extraordinarily able language instruction and research assistance I received from Virendra Singh and Om Prakash Sharma. Both of them have had the role of genuine collaborators in the project of this book, though I alone am responsible for its deficiencies.

David Pocock and Loki Madan originally gave me the idea for this study, and to both of them I owe thanks for much kindness and encouragement over the years. There is by now a large company of scholars who have worked on various aspects of Banarasi culture. I gratefully acknowledge the particular stimulus I have received from exchanges with, and the writings of, Chris Bayly, Diana Eck, Nita Kumar, Baidyanath Saraswati and Mary Searle-Chatterjee. Outside the not-so-little world of Banaras specialists, I am conscious of having particularly benefited at various stages from the help and advice of Richard Burghart, Audrey Cantlie, Tony Carter, Veena Das, Tim Dyson, Alfred Gell, Raymond Jamous, Murray Milner, Gloria Raheja, Marie-Louise Reiniche, Tom Trautmann, Peter van der Veer and Woody Watson. André Béteille, Maurice Bloch, Chris Fuller and Jock Stirrat require special thanks – both for many invaluable comments on embarassingly many versions of these chapters and for much moral support. Margaret Dickinson has suffered the birth of this book with even greater fortitude, and has been a constant source of encouragement and extremely acute comments. She and Kate shared the original fieldwork; and Kate and Joe have suffered from it being re-run at supper-time ever since.

The first period of fieldwork was supported by the Social Science Research Council, and subsequent visits to Banaras by the London School of Economics. Much of this book was drafted while I was a Fellow at the Netherlands Institute of Advanced Study, and I gratefully record my thanks to its Director and staff for the extremely congenial time I spent there. I also thank the University of Rochester for the opportunity to present the Morgan Lectures in which I was able to explore some of the data presented in this monograph.

Glossary

In transliterating Hindi words I have generally given priority to the way they sound rather than to the conventions of Sanskrit orthography. I therefore drop the final unsounded 'a' – to write, for example, *tirath-purohit* and *pret* (rather than *titratha-purohita* and *preta*). It has not, however, seemed sensible to apply this rule with pedantic consistency to terms which are extremely common in the Indological literature and in works on Hinduism, and which are more likely to be familiar to the general reader if conventionally rendered. I have, for example, preferred *Veda*, *Purana*, *dharma* and *karma* over the spoken forms *Ved*, *Puran*, *dharam* and *karam*. Indian words are pluralised in the text in the English manner by adding an 's'. When performed by the members of the specific 'caste' (e.g. Barber) – or 'sub-caste' (e.g. Mahabrahman) – with which they are associated, the names of occupations begin with a capital letter; occupations which are not associated with a specific 'caste' (e.g. exorcist) or 'sub-caste' (e.g. *panda*) begin with a lower case letter. Diacritical marks are used in the glossary, but not in the text itself. The glossary is primarily intended as an aid to the general reader, and includes only those words which occur several times and which have not been glossed within a few lines of each occurrence.

akāl mrityū	untimely death
akhārā	wrestling school; an ascetic order
āgnīhotrī	a householder who offers daily oblations to the three sacrificial fires
amāvasyā	the new-moon day of the Hindu lunar calendar
Antargrahī	the prilgrimage which circumambulates the innermost core of Banaras
antyeshti	cremation; literally 'last sacrifice'
artha	the domain of material and political advantage
āshram	hermitage or retreat; one of the four stages of life for a male Hindu: student, householder, forest hermit and renouncer

Aughar	*Mashān* the ghost of an Aghori ascetic who died in the performance of his terrible austerities
avatār	the incarnation of a deity (especially Vishnu)
bahī	a record or account book
Bhairavī yātnā	tortures of the god Bhairav inflicted on those who die in Banaras
bhakti	devotion, love (especially for a deity)
bhavānī	the ghost of an unmarried female
bhūt-pret	a generic term for malevolent ghosts
bīr	a 'hero'-ghost; the ghost of one who has died by violence in a just cause
brahm	the vengeful spirit of a Brahman who died a 'bad' death
Brahman	the supreme and transcendent reality that subsumes all oppositions within itself
chakra-pūjā	a secret tantric rite involving the use of the five 'Ms': *mans* (meat), *machchhli* (fish), *madhya* (liquor), *mudra* (parched grain or kidney beans) and *maithun* (sexual intercourse)
chaukī	a wooden platform
dāgīyā	'the one who gave fire'; the chief mourner
dakshinā	a fee paid to a Brahman priest for his ritual services; a supplementary gift added to the main gift of *dan* to make good any deficiencies in it
dakshināyan	the six months of the year when the sun appears to move south
dalāl	a commission agent; tout
damri	an obsolete unit of coinage worth one-eighth of a *paisa*; a Mahabrahman *pari* yielding one day's turn in the year is described as a one *damri pari*
dān	an unreciprocated gift which makes merit for the donor and/or rids him or her of sin
dhananjay	one of the five (or ten) types of 'breath' or 'wind', it pervades the body and is liberated from the corpse at the rite of *kapal kriya*
dharamshālā	a pilgrim lodge
dharma	religious and moral duty; righteousness
dhotī	a loin garment
dūdh-bhāt	'milk-rice'; the name of the meal held for close kin on the day after cremation
gaddī	throne; figuratively used for the ancestral property of a priest or merchant
gamchhā	cloth or towel, generally check
Gangā-putra	'son of the Ganges'; a title claimed by certain families of pilgrimage-priests

gāyatrī	*jap* repetition of the *gayatri mantra*
gāyatrī mantra	the *mantra* whispered into the initiate's ear at the time of his investiture with the sacred thread
ghāt	a segment of river frontage
ghātiyā	a sacred specialist who sits on the *ghat* to perform various ritual functions for the pilgrims and bathers; notionally (though not always in practice) a Brahman
guna	one of the three qualities or dispositions of all existent beings
gumāshtā	an agent or representative
Hazār bhāī	'the thousand brothers', a title claimed by certain families of pilgrimage-priests
hijrā	transvestites who sing and dance on the birth of a son
hom	fire sacrifice
jājmān	client (especially of a Brahman priest)
jap	repetition of sacred formulae or the names of a deity
jinn	a generic term for Muslim ghosts
jīvit-shrāddh	mortuary rites performed by, and for, a person who is still alive
Kali Yuga	the last and most degenerate epoch in the cycle of the universe
kamīn	provider of services for a high-caste patron
kapāl kriyā	the rite of breaking open the skull of the deceased on the cremation pyre
Kāshī khanda	the best known eulogistic text on Banaras
kar	tax; 'payment' made to the Dom at the time of cremation
karam kāndī	a Brahman ritual specialist
kārindā	agent; servant (especially of a Mahabrahman right-holder)
Kāshī-lābh	'the profit of Kashi' (i.e. the promise of salvation for those who die in Banaras)
Kāshī-vās(i)	'residence (resident) in Kashi' (applied to those who move to the city in anticipation of dying there)
khand	a division or section (of space, or of a longer literary work)
khīr	a sweet rice pudding
kīrtan	devotional singing/song
kshetrā-purohit	'an area-priest' (applied to certain south India priests who had the right to look after pilgrims but allegedly not the right to accept their gifts on the banks of the Ganges)
kund	a tank or sacred pool
kushā	a kind of sacred grass

Lāl Mohrīyā pandā	the pilgrimage-priest with the 'red seal' of the Raja of Nepal
laukik	popular practice (as opposed to that which is scripturally sanctioned)
ling	phallic emblem of Shiva
lok	one of the three worlds (heaven, earth and nether-world)
lotā	a small rounded metal pot
mahant	head priest or monk
māhātmya	eulogistic text lauding a particular place, time or deity
mantra	asacred formula or incantation
marī	a female ghost (generally said to be of Untouchable caste)
maruā	the ghost of a young child or aborted foetus
math	a monastery
mohallā	neighbourhood
moksha	salvation or liberation (especially from the cycle of rebirth)
mukti	salvation or liberation (especially from the cycle of rebirth)
Narayani bali	rite performed in cases of 'bad' death to rid the ghost of its ghostly condition
Nau kul sardār	'the nine chiefly descent lines' of the pilgrimage-priest community
neg	a presentation given in return for a ritual service
ojhā	an exorcist
pachchh	Mahabrahmans' rota system for allocating rights to serve mourners from the surrounding countryside
pān	betel-leaf, nut and associated condiments
panchak	a set of five lunar asterisms in which it is particularly inauspicious to die/cremate a corpse
panchak shānti	the rite of 'pacifying' the evil effects of a death/cremation during *panchak*
Panch-kosi	the pilgrimage which circumambulates the entire sacred space of Banaras
pandā	pilgrimage- or temple-priest
pandāgīrī	the profession of the *panda*
pārī	a shift or turn; the system of allocating rights to perform some office on a rota basis
paisā	the smallest unit of currency; money
payas dān	'the gift of milk' (offered to the Funeral-priest before his departure on the eleventh day)
pind	a ball of rice or grains offered to the dead; an embryo
pindā-dān	the gift of *pinds* to the departed

pishāch	a demonic being
pitr	an ancestor
pitri paksh	'the fortnight of the ancestors'
pralay	the dissolution of the cosmos at the end of each world cycle
prān	the vital breath
prāyashchitt	penance, atonement (but in Banaras the word is also commonly used for that which must be atoned for – i.e. sin)
pret	an unincorporated ghost
pūjā	worship (normally consisting of a series of offerings or services)
pūranmāsī	full-moon day; fifteenth day of the bright fortnight
pūranmāsī	full-moon day; fifteenth day of the bright fortnight
purohit	a Brahman priest (generally used for one with who there is a long-term relationship)
purushārtha	the four goals of human existence (viz. *dharma, artha, kama* and *moksha*)
putla vidhan	'the method of the effigy'; the construction and cremation of an effigy of the deceased performed in cases in which the corpse itself is not cremated
rāj ansh	'the kingdom's share'; a share in the gifts of pilgrims from Banaras State claimed by the Maharaja's pilgrimage-priest
Rām Līlā	festival during which events in the life of Lord Ram are enacted
Rūdrabhishek	anointment or bathing ritual performed for Shiva
sajjā dān	gift made in the name of the deceased to the Funeral-priest, and to the household-/ pilgrimage-priest
samādhi	the tomb of an ascetic; the ascetic's state of suspended animation within it
sandhyā	Vedic recitations which should ideally be performed three times per day
sankalp	a binding ritual resolution to gift away
sanskār	one of the sixteen life-cycle rituals which perfect and refine the person
sapinda	kin with whom one shares the same body particles
sapindīkaran	rite performed on the twelfth day after death at which the deceased is made into an ancestor
sattvik	disposed or conducive to purity and tranquility
Satya Yuga	the first of the four world epochs; the (golden) Age of Truth
sādhanā	ritual practice or discipline
shakti	power; energy

Shāstras	scripture; teaching (especially Dharmashastra – 'teachings about *dharma*')
shāstrik	scriptural
shraddh	rites performed for the dead
siddhis	supernatural powers or accomplishments
sutak	pollution caused by birth and death (can also be used of menstrual pollution and the pollution occasioned by an eclipse)
tapas(yā)	ascetic austerity
tīrath	place of pilgrimage; ford or crossing point
tīrath-purohit	pilgrimage-priest
tripindī shraddh	Sanskritic rite performed for those who have got stuck in a ghostly condition on a long-term basis
tulsī	basil (sacred to Vishnu)
uttarāyan	the six months of the year when the sun appears to move north
vaikunth	(Vishnu's) heaven
varna	the four theoretical classes of Hindu society: Brahman, Kshatriya, Vaishya and Shudra
vrishotsarg	rite for the deceased in which a bull is married to heifers, branded and set free to wander
yagya	sacrifice
Yamrāj	the Lord of Death
yamdūt	messenger of the god of death
zamindar	landholder

Introduction

As a place to die, to dispose of the physical remains of the deceased and to perform the rites which ensure that the departed attains a 'good state' after death, the north Indian city of Banaras attracts pilgrims and mourners from all over the Hindu world. This book is primarily about the priests and other kinds of 'sacred specialist' who serve them; about the way in which they organise their business, and about their representations of death and understandings of the rituals over which they preside. For obvious reasons, intensive anthropological fieldwork amongst the huge numbers of transient and socially heterogeneous pilgrims who visit the city is not feasible. Though I spent a good deal of time talking to mourners who had come from outside, the only bereaved families with whom it was possible to have any sustained contact were of local origin.

The priests who are at the centre of this book are not only ritualists. They are also 'propagandists' who instruct their patrons on the meanings of the rituals in which they are engaged, on the fate of the soul and on the soteriological significance of Shiva's city. As this suggests, exegesis on matters of ritual blooms in Banaras with a luxuriance of which ethnographers of remote rural areas might sometimes be envious. In my own experience of such a setting at least (Parry 1979), enquiries about the purpose of this or that rite commonly meet with the terse response that it has been ordained by the scriptures and handed down by the ancestors. Beyond that only the Brahman priest can say – and he is likely to refer the question on to another more knowlegeable than himself. In Banaras, by contrast, even non-priests often volunteer interpretations of complex and seemingly opaque ritual sequences; and the priests themselves are well used to pilgrims and mourners asking questions which are almost as ignorant – if generally less persistent – than those of the anthropologist. For most of his questioners the priest is an 'authority', and like many authorities he would sometimes sooner extemporise than reveal the limits of his knowledge. When the matter lies outside conventional priestly wisdom, the views he expounds are possibly his own quite idiosyncratic – which is not to say ill-considered – solutions to questions that have puzzled him also. The anthropologist's problem, then, is not a poverty of exegesis, but its profusion, improvisation and consequent diversity.

I have tried to avoid creating the impression that my informants inhabit a seamlessly systematic ideological universe by ironing out this diversity. To most people in most cultures much about death *is*, I assume, a mystery. Though priests have a professional stake in imparting the religious certainties, it is hardly surprising that the answers they offer are not without contradiction and inconsistency. But nor of course are these answers an amorphous hodge-podge of individual speculation. On many mortuary matters there is near unanimity, and where this is absent the variant interpretations tend to be patterned around a limited set of identifiable discourses. The challenge, then, is to make it possible to follow the melody without drowning out the discordant voices.

But this book is as much about death as a living as it is about the theological speculations that surround it. While other anthropological monographs which report on field research in one of the major centres of Hindu pilgrimage have tended to leave ritual largely aside in order to focus more sharply on the sociology of the sacred specialists (e.g. Vidyarthi 1961; Fuller 1984 and van der Veer 1988), I have chosen to write both about the social organisation of death and about matters of ritual and belief. A narrower coverage may well have resulted in a tidier and tighter account, but I believe that my choice is justified not only by the obvious fact that death in Banaras consists of both aspects, but also by the fact that the two kinds of data are often difficult to disentangle.

On the one hand, ideas about death and the dead are sometimes transparently moulded by experience of social life. For example, the reason why the malevolent ghosts of those who have died a 'bad death' are considered likely to pass from wife-givers to wife-takers, and to attach themselves to affinal prestations, is explained – I will argue (p. 235) – by tensions within the joint household which result from marriage, and by tensions between in-laws over the gifts which pass between them. Conversely, the social organisation of death may clearly reflect the ideas that people have about it. Different kinds of caste specialist are, for example, required to handle different aspects of the deceased. Death results in a polluting corpse on the one hand, and a marginal and malevolent ghost on the other. The first must be disposed of, and the second must be transformed into a benevolent ancestor. The Untouchable Dom funeral attendant superintends the cremation of the physical remains of the deceased; the impure and highly inauspicious Mahabrahman Funeral-priest accepts gifts in the name of the malign ghost whom he represents or even embodies, while a relatively pure Brahman performs this service for the relatively benign ancestor. In short, the division of labour only makes sense in the light of certain ideas about the state of the departed.

Nor again is it possible to understand the highly equivocal status of the Funeral-priests, the rather aggressive exactions to which they sometimes subject the mourners, or the system by which they allocate rights to serve them, without reference to the notion that they embody the malevolent ghosts of the departed (pp. 75ff). Though the Funeral-priest is a Brahman, he is to all intents and purposes treated much like an Untouchable. Through his importunate demands on the mourners he serves, he reveals not only his own nature, but also the greed and malevolence of the ghost he embodies (pp. 139ff). What appears to be a supremely 'economic' activity (ruthless bargaining over 'fees') turns out to have other layers of significance when it is properly located in its idealogical context. A way of exploring the market in a situation of chronic uncertainty (as the economic model of bargaining supposes), the demands of the Funeral-priest are also a dramatic representation of the claims of the dead on the living.

Rights to accept the gifts of the mourners are assigned to the individual Funeral-priest on the basis of a complex rota system which maximises the anonymity and transience of their relationship. Though I will show that this system also answers to practical reason, it is at least partly a consequence of a cultural logic which precludes the development of long-term hereditary relationships beween patrons and specialists of the sort familiar from the extensive literature on *jajmani* relations in rural India, and of the sort which obtain between the mourners and those who embody the incorporated ancestor. The choice of system, in other words, is closely constrained by the mourners' unwillingness to acknowledge lasting bonds with those who deal with the most polluting aspects of death (pp. 115ff). Once again, the social organisation of death reflects the way in which death is symbolically constructed.

Both the bargaining and the share system suggest a different point of rather more general sociological significance. In a devestating critique of the idea that culture is an epiphenomenon of 'practical reason' – that cultural forms are determined by utilitarian interest – Sahlins (1976) turns the tables by arguing for a symbolic determination of material life. This simple reversal is in my view unfortunate. In both of the instances I cite the social form appears over-determined. It is the product of a complex interplay between culture *and* practical reason. ∮ K

The first part of the book – 'Death and the city' – deals with Banaras's association with death and its transcendence. The opening chapter looks at this association from a religious perspective. Lord Vishnu created the cosmos at the beginning of time by performing ascetic austerities at what is now the city's main cremation ground. My argument is that the cremation rituals which are continually staged there are a kind of re-enactment of his cosmogonic austerities, and that it is this which accounts for Banaras's immunity to the degeneration of time and for the notion that the rest of space is contained within it. Chapter 2 shifts the focus to examine the city's association with death through the eyes of the outside observer. It provides a brief sketch of what is known about its history as a pilgrimage centre, and as a place to die and to dispose of the physical remains of the dead. The chapter concludes with an attempt to estimate the scale of these activities, and to trace the growth over the course of this century in the number of cremations staged there.

With regard to the city's most important cremation ground, we shall find that different accounts of its origins are invoked to justify the divergent positions taken in a dispute over whether corpses should continue to be burnt on the very spot at which Vishnu performed his austerities. What seems to me significant is that those who most forcefully championed one or other of these rival versions of its 'history' are widely assumed to have done so out of purely interested motives. Material acquisition is highly valued, and my informants often take an extremely down-to-earth – not to say cynical – view of human motivation, crediting others with the most far-sighted concern for egoistic advantage. Over the past two or three decades, the study of values has been a central preoccupation of the sociology of India. It seems to me surprising, however, that very little attention has been paid to the pervasive *idea* that material acquisition and self-interest are a mainspring of action.

Death in Banaras is very big business, and the second part of the book – 'Death as a living' – is concerned with the way this business is organised. Chapter 3 discusses the division of mortuary labour between, and the allocation of rights within, the various groups of sacred specialists who are in one way or another concerned with the disposal of the physical remains of the deceased, the posthumous fate of the soul and the purification of the mourners. Chapter 4 looks at the remuneration – ideologically construed as 'gifts' – which the priests receive, at the donors motivation for giving and their willingness to tolerate the importunate demands of the recipients; at the dangers – both physical and spiritual – which these transactions are held to entail for both parties and at the insistent haggling which accompanies them. How, in a more general sociological perspective, are we to understand the evils that these gifts embody? Given that the priest has often been represented as the epitome of Brahmanical purity, what are the implications of the position he is held to accept for our understanding of the caste order?

Chapter 3 makes the wider significance of ideas about material acquisition more apparent. However much they deplore the fact, most people seem to regard the chicanery and sharp-practice which surround the business of death as inevitable. But though the things of this world may be greatly desired, the single-minded pursuit of them is of course seen as antithetical to the highest values, and as subversive of the moral order of *dharma*. Left to run riot, acquisitiveness and self-seeking result in 'the law of the fishes', the Hindu equivalent of our 'law of the jungle'. Now what is particularly striking about the division of ritual labour I describe is the meticulous way in which shares are defined, and the endless elaboration of rules which are clearly intended to preclude competition both between and within the various communities of sacred specialists. The two phenomena are not unconnected. Regulation is such an over-riding concern precisely because 'the law of the fishes' is seen as such an imminent threat.

If the social order must be endlessly shored up against impending chaos, the same kind of problem confronts the person. In South Asian thinking – as the Chicago ethnosociologists have taught us (e.g. Marriott 1976) – a person's bio-genetic substance and his moral code of conduct are two aspects of the same thing. To a greater or lesser extent, all transactions involve an exchange of bio-moral qualities, and consequently transform the substance-code of the parties to them. By continually giving out and taking in particles of themselves, transactors are endlessly modifying their physical-cum-moral natures. By contrast with the Western concept of the individual as an independent and autonomous actor with a unique and unchangeable bio-genetic makeup, the South Asian construct of the person postulates a far more malleable and protean entity.

The obvious problem with this picture, however, is that it is not at first sight clear how it squares with our received wisdom that each person has a more or less unalterable caste identity, or how all members of the same caste can be assumed to have the same kind of bio-moral nature. But there is, I argue (pp. 112ff), a crucial sense in which these apparently contradictory ideas fit together. The construct of the person as a constitutionally fluid and volatile being provides powerful ideological support to the ordained order of caste interactions. Those who infringe these rules disrupt the precarious equilibrium in which their own personhood is as it were suspended, bringing upon themselves a degradation, debasement and even disintegration of the self. Once more, it is the chaos which lies round the corner that proves the necessity for the most disciplined regulation.

I argue, then, that both at the level of the social order and at the level of the person a central concern is to batten down the hatches against incipient chaos, and to impose some semblance of control on the contingency of events. But perhaps the most worryingly contingent event of all is death itself, and much of the ethnography presented in Part III – 'Death into birth' – relates to the attempt to deny its aleatory character.

Chapter 5 centres around the idea of the 'good' death as a voluntary renunciation of life, and of cremation as a sacrificial offering of the self to the gods. Sacrifice is a ritual wrenching life out of death. Through it both the world and the sacrifier are reborn. Cremation is consequently an act of creation, and the mortuary rites are shot through with the symbolism of birth and parturition. Liberated from its 'gross' body, the tortured ghost now wanders the earth in search of a new 'house' to inhabit. Chapter 6 describes how the chief mourner builds for it limb by limb a new body through the ritual offerings of rice-balls over the ten following days, and how this 'ghost-body' is subsequently dissected and merged with the bodies of the deceased's three immediate lineal ascendants. The marginal and malevolent ghost becomes a benevolent and incorporated ancestor, a source of future fecundity and prosperity for his descent line. But if 'good' death results in the biological and material reproduction of the deceased's descendants, 'bad' deaths result in barrenness and poverty. The afflictions caused by such spirits, and the way in which such afflictions might be cured, are the central focus of chapter 7.

To return to the matter of contingency, at the most general level the overall thrust of the whole sequence is to make death appear subject to human control, by – for example – representing it as an orderly evacuation of the body and an act of willing abandonment (pp. 158ff), and by denying that the uncontrollable moment of physiological arrest is the 'real' point of death. That point is rather re-defined as the instant at which the chief mourner releases the 'vital breath' of the deceased by breaking open his skull as his corpse lies burning on the pyre. The deceased 'dies' on the pyre through the deliberate actions of the survivors in a cremation ritual which is symbolically constructed as a sacrifice (pp. 178ff). Since every sacrifice is a kind of re-enactment of the original sacrifice which created the cosmos, cremation deprives individual death of its specificity by assimilating it to a timeless prototypical model. Consistent with this de-personalisation of the deceased is a striking absence from the entire mortuary sequence of any formalised recognition of his unique biography, or any celebration of his personal achievements. No memorials are normally erected in his name, and as an ancestor almost all traces of his individual personality are effaced (pp. 207ff).

In some cases, of course, the contingency of death is harder to suppress than in others – as for example when it has resulted from sudden accident, violence or epidemic disease. But following the logic of the previous paragraph, this must also be the case when the deceased does not constitute a worthy sacrificial offering to the gods – because, for example, his body has been corrupted by leprosy. Unfit for the cremation pyre, the deaths of such people do not readily lend themselves to being represented as a replication of some perfect primordial model. Other ritual measures are therefore required, and these include the construction of an effigy of the deceased into which his soul is then summoned. This surrogate body is then made to die. An 'untimely' and uncontrolled death is thus restaged as a controlled release of life; a body that was unfit to serve as a sacrificial victim is replaced by a worthier substitute that can now be cremated like any ordinary corpse (pp. 184ff).

Unless a complex sequence of supplementary rituals is properly performed, the spirits of those who have died a 'bad' or 'untimely' death are liable to afflict the living, whose pollution makes them particularly prone to possession (p. 232). In other contexts, disease and death itself are commonly attributed to impurity (and especially to an impure diet). Purity, then, does not appear to be the irreducible value that it is in Dumont's (1970a) picture of Hindu ideology. It is rather a means to an end, a crucial bulwark against death, decay and the disintegration of the self. As for the disorderly ghosts, the procedure for exorcising them essentially consists in placing them under the control of superior supernatural beings, and 'causing them to sit down' at some sacred site through the performance of a ritual over which a Brahman priest should preside. Order, it would seem, is a proper subordination to *hierarchical* authority.

The concluding chapter of the book concerns the ascetic's endeavour, not merely to control the contingency of death and to convert it into a source of future life, but to conquer death entirely by escaping from the endless cycle of rebirths. The ethnographic description relates to a small group of renouncers known as Aghoris whose ascetic regime involves intimate contact with death, corpses and the cremation ground. Though by the standards of most Hindu ascetics, Aghori practices are peculiarly extreme, I aim to show that the ideas which inform them are in fact quite conventional. The creation of the cosmos at the beginning of time is represented as a process of progressive differentiation out of an undifferentiated Absolute Being (*Brahman*) that contains all opposites within itself. What the Aghori aims at, I argue, is systematically to recombine these opposites and thus to recapture this primordial state of non-differentiation. By so doing he escapes from time and hence from the endless cycle of death and rebirth.

The values of the renouncer return me in my concluding remarks (pp. 264ff) to a theme that runs throughout Part III and that relates to the values of hierarchy. In Dumont's (1970a) model of the caste order, hierarchy is held to be inseparable from holism (the valorisation of the social whole), and thus from the idea of an indissoluble interdependence between the high and the low. Following Fuller (1988), I argue by contrast that there is a significant strand in the ideology which radically compromises the idea of a complementarity between them. The acknowledgement of interdependence is markedly one-sided. The inferior depends on the superior but the converse does not apply. Relative superiority is a matter of relative autonomy – a principle we shall discover in the way in which the expression of grief is structured by gender (pp. 152ff), in the logic of the mourning regulations laid down in the Shastric texts (pp. 215ff), and in the rituals concerned with the pacification of malevolent ghosts (pp. 245ff). Its apogee is clearly the autonomous ascetic, and my argument is that when his values are brought back into the world they spawn a discourse which de-couples the notion of hierarchy from the notions of holism and complementarity, a discourse in which the inequalities of the social order are by a strange irony legitimated by reference to the example of one who has renounced it. As all this goes to confirm, in writing about death the best the anthropologist can probably aspire to is the discovery of something about the world of the living.

PART I

Death and the city

1

Through 'divine eyes'

1.1 The scene of cosmogony

Kashi – the 'Luminous', the City of Light – is the pious Hindu's name for the sacred city of Banaras, now officially known as Varanasi.

> When Babylon was struggling with Nineveh for supremacy, when Tyre was planting her colonies, when Athens was growing in strength, before Rome had become known, or Greece had contended with Persia, or Cyrus had added lustre to the Persian monarchy, or Nebuchadnezzar had captured Jerusalem, and the inhabitants of Judaea had been carried into captivity, she had already risen to greatness, if not to glory . . . While many cities and nations have fallen into decay and perished, her sun has never gone down; on the contrary, for long ages past it has shone with almost meridian splendour. (Sherring 1975: 7–8; originally 1868)

> [The city's] present life reaches back to the sixth century B.C. in a continuous tradition. If we could imagine the silent Acropolis and the Agora of Athens still alive with the intellectual, cultural, and ritual traditions of classical Greece, we might glimpse the remarkable tenacity of the life of Kashi. Today Peking, Athens, and Jerusalem are moved by a very different ethos from that which moved them in ancient times, but Kashi is not. (Eck 1983:5)

Whatever their historical justification, from the perspective of the extensive eulogistic literature on the city which its priests and other sacred specialists invoke for the instruction of the pilgrims and mourners they serve,[1] such statements are but a bland understatement of a far more venerable religious truth. Kashi is as old as time itself. As the site of cosmic creation, it is the place where time itself began. As cosmogony is here a ceaselessly repeated event, its present time is also the primordial time of origins.

In this opening chapter I focus on the place of death in this 'divine vision' of the city. Those with the eyes to see know that Kashi is both the origin-point and a microcosm of the universe; that it stands outside space and time yet all space is contained within it; and that it provides for the attainment of all the four conventionally enumerated goals of human existence (the *purusharthas*): in life for the fulfilment of moral and religious duty (*dharma*), material and

11

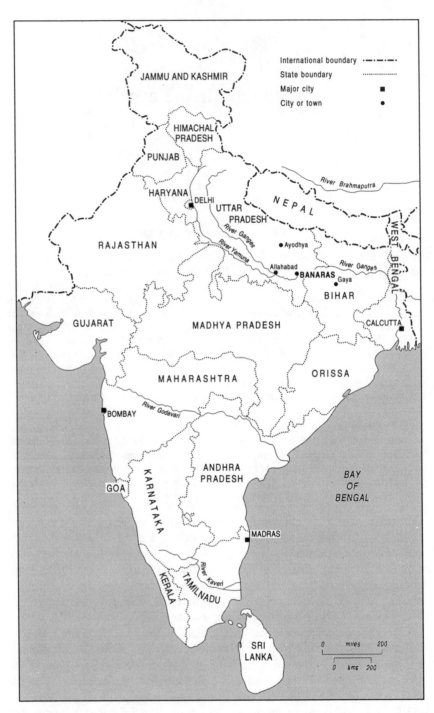

Map 1 Location of Banaras

political advantage (*artha*), and of the sensual appetites (*kama*), and – above all – in death for the attainment of salvation (*moksha* or *mukti*). The keystone of this symbolic construction, I argue, is death as an act of cosmic regeneration. It is the city's association with death that provides it with an immunity to the degenerative flow of durational time, and renews its capacity to encompass the rest of creation.

The celebrated *ghats* of Banaras are defined segments of river frontage between 30 and 200 yards in length. Most have been constructed to form a series of stone terraces and stairs running down into the sacred waters of the Ganges. Many are themselves important places of pilgrimage – none more so than Manikarnika *ghat*. Manikarnika is one of the city's most important bathing *ghats*, the focus of a wide variety of ritual activities, and – however pressed the pilgrim – a *sine qua non* of every pilgrimage. For present purposes, however, its most salient attributes are that it is not only the site of the sacred tank beside which Lord Vishnu performed his cosmogonic austerities, but also the site of the most important of the city's two cremation grounds. As I understand it, the conjunction is of crucial symbolic significance.

The *ghat* is located at a point roughly midway along the Ganges between the confluence of the Asi and the Ganges, which marks the southern boundary of the sacred city, and the confluence of the Varuna and the Ganges which marks its northern boundary (map 2). It stands at the dividing line between two equal divisions (*khands*) of the city – Shiva *khand* to its north and Vishnu *khand* to its south. While in India the cremation ground is generally on the periphery or outside the area of human settlement, in Kashi it is the city's focal point. Just as India is said to be the 'navel' (*nabhi*) of the world, and Kashi the navel of India, so Manikarnika is the navel of Kashi. As the site of creation itself, it is the very hub of the entire universe.

I paraphrase here the *Kashi khanda*'s account of cosmogony (chapter 26). This text is the most important in the whole corpus of 'praise' literature which eulogises the city.[2]

During the period of cosmic dissolution (*mahapralay*) all creation was destroyed and all was darkness. There was neither sun nor moon nor stars, no form or sense perception, and no cardinal points. All that existed was *Brahman*[3] which cannot be apprehended by the mind or described by speech, and which is without shape, name or colour or any physical attribute. This undivided one (*advaita*) desired to become two and accomplished this by his own divine play (*lila*). 'I [Shiva] am the material form of that immaterial *Brahman*. Oh Parvati, together we created the sacred area of Kashi.'

Wandering in this forest of bliss, Shiva and Parvati desired to create another being to whom they could hand over the burden of the whole [of the rest] of creation, which would leave them free to bestow 'liberation' on all who die in Kashi. Shiva turned his gaze full of nectar on his left side [i.e. Parvati] and a beautiful being was instantly created. This was Vishnu whose breath was the Vedas, through which he was omniscient, and according to which he was intructed to perform his task. Vishnu dug a tank with his discus and filled it with the sweat of the terrible

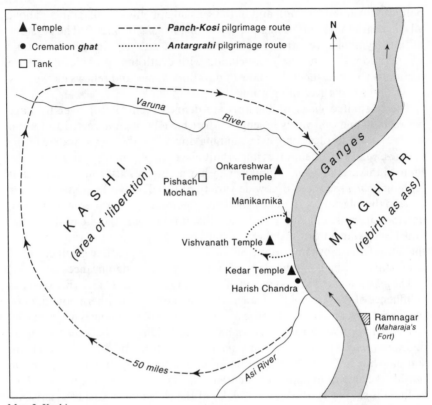

Map 2 Kashi

austerities he performed by its side for 50,000 years [in order to construct the universe]. At the end of this time Shiva and Parvati came there and saw Vishnu burning with the fire of his asceticism. Shiva was entranced, and with the violent trembling of his delight his ear-ring dropped off into Vishnu's tank, which Shiva decreed should thenceforth be known as Manikarnika ('jewel of the ear'). Aroused with difficulty from his austerities Vishnu was told to demand a boon. He requested that he should always behold the divine couple as at that moment; that he should take the form of a black bee perpetually drinking the nectar of Shiva's lotus-like feet, and that since Shiva's ear-ring had been studded with *mukta* (pearl), this sacred place (*tirath*) should confer *mukti* ('liberation'). Shiva agreed and added that for those who reside in Kashi it will always be the *Satya yuga* (the Age of Truth), the [auspicious] time of the summer solstice (*uttarayan*) and a festival day; and that pious deeds performed here will result in immortality.

Manikarnika, then, is the place where the genesis of the universe occurs at the beginning of time. But it is also the place where the corpse of creation will burn at the end of time (*pralay*). Kashi (in its entirety) is known as the 'Great Cremation Ground' (*mahashamshan*) because it is there that the five great elements which compose the world (earth, water, fire, air and ether) arrive as corpses (Kane 1973:4:627). Only the city itself survives this universal holocaust for it exists outside (normal/profane) space. At the time of cosmic destruction it becomes a light or halo in the sky; or – in the more robust idiom of my informants – is raised up above the general conflagration like an umbrella. But Manikarnika *ghat* is not only the scene of the genesis and dissolution of the world at the beginning and end of each cosmic cycle. It is also – I argue – the case that these cosmic events belong to a kind of eternal present and are perpetually reactualised on the *ghat*.

1.2 In and out of time and space

Kashi, then, exists in a time and space that is radically distinct from the time and space that pervades the rest of the world. But that is not to say that the city's own space is entirely homogeneous.

The circumference of Kashi is marked by the *Panch-kosi* pilgrimage route which at peak times – especially during *adhik mas* (the intercalary month that the Hindu calendar adds to every third year) – is followed by tens of thousands of pilgrims from the city and the surrounding districts. The journey of nearly 50 miles[4] is generally completed in five days. The essence of the *Panch-kosi* is that it is a clockwise circumambulation of the city such that the pilgrim always keeps the sacred area on his right. He worships in temples located to the right of the road (and which therefore fall just within the sacred perimeter) and performs his ablutions and bodily functions on the left. The route thus marks the boundaries of sacred space and of the area within which all who die are granted 'liberation' by Shiva.

One way in which space within this area is differentiated is on the model of a series of concentric circles which increase in sanctity as they decrease in size, and of which the outermost is the *Panch-kosi* pilgrimage route. In its most elaborate form we find a sequence of seven such circles, each described by a set of eight shrines dedicated to Lord Ganesh, thus making up the fifty-six conventionally enumerated Ganesh shrines of the city (Eck 1978:179; 1983:187–8). This elephant-headed and highly anomalous deity is the Lord of Obstacles and the Guardian of Thresholds who commonly appears on doorways or temple-gateways, who is worshipped on entry into or exit from sacred time at the beginning and end of all life-cycle rituals, and who in this context appears as the protector of Kashi's sacred space. At the focal point of the whole series is the most sacred and renowned of all of the city's temples, that dedicated to Shiva as Vishvanath – the Lord of the Universe. The pilgrim thus passes through seven protective rings in order to penetrate the sacred core of the city.

Not only the city however. The numerology equates it with the cosmos – the seven circles representing the seven layers of the atmosphere (Rana Singh 1986); the eight shrines round each circle guarding the eight points of the compass. What seems to be marked out, then, is the totality of space, at the centre of which stands the Lord of the Universe. Given the repeated equivalence we shall find postulated between Kashi and the cosmos, and between both of these and the human body, the whole scheme is moreover suggestively reminiscent of the yogic idea that in order to attain union with God, the adept's life-force must cross through the seven centres or circles ranged along his spine (Eliade 1969:241ff; Beck 1976).

A slightly different ground-plan is of a division into four circles, of which the outer and most inclusive is marked by the *Panch-kosi* route, and the inner and least inclusive by the *Antargrahi* ('inside the house') pilgrimage around the heart of the city. We will later see that, according to one theory, the fate of the deceased's soul depends on which of the four he died in.

Kashi is apart from the rest of space. Being really gold, the very earth on which it stands is different. According to the *Kashi khanda*, the city is not attached to the ground but is suspended in the sky, though this can only be seen by those with the 'divine sight' (*divya drishti*) of the *yogi*. It is popularly said to balance above the earth on the trident (*trisul*) of Shiva. As an elderly Funeral-priest explained it,

> Kashi was once just jungle. One day when Shiva and Parvati were sitting there, Shiva suddenly announced, 'O.K. Parvati ji, I am going to leave you for twelve years.' 'But Maharaj', protested Parvati, 'I always serve and worship you. How am I going to live without you?' Well, you know that God Shankar [i.e. Shiva] is *arbhangi* [one who follows his whims with truculent intransigence]. So Shiva said, 'No, I am going; it is my wish', and disappeared with a 'we'll see' when Parvati swore to find him before twelve years were up.
>
> Separately, both of them remained in this jungle. Every midnight Shiva would plant his trident in the earth, and stick Mount Kailash [his Himalayan abode] on top of it. All the gods would come there to sit and chat until morning.
>
> There was an old woman who lived in that jungle. Nobody knows what caste she was . . . On the very day before Shiva would have completed his twelve years' absence, she happened upon Parvati wandering alone in that dense and desolate forest. Parvati explained her plight, and the old woman promised to guide her to Shankar's court that night . . . So it came to pass that Parvati found the great god playing his *damru* [two-sided drum] with his left hand; in his right hand was his trident, and from his matted locks flowed the Ganges. Just as dawn was about to break, and Shiva was on the point of uprooting his trident, Parvati came up behind him and caught him by the wrist. 'Leave go', he ordered angrily. But Parvati refused. 'If I do', she said, 'and if you uproot the trident, then how will people in the *Kali* age [our present degenerate epoch] "swim across" [i.e. obtain salvation]?' 'Are you crazy?' asked Shiva. 'If I leave my trident here those people will profane (*apavitra kar dena*) Kailash; they will wash their arse-holes and spit in the Ganges, insult the gods and fuck in the temples. Is that a good thing?' 'Well', said Parvati, 'you should close your eyes and enjoy it, for everybody will be worshipping you. Just listen, don't look.' With that, morning came, the trident remained where it was and the gods were unable to leave.

The shaft of Shiva's trident is implanted below the Vishvanath temple, such that the temple itself stands on its middle prong. The two outer prongs support the Kedar temple in the extreme south of the city, and the temple of

Onkareshvar Madadev in the extreme north. These three temples give their names to three divisions (*khands*) of Kashi; and again we shall find that these are of eschatological significance, for it is widely held that those who die in Kedar *khand* are granted a more immediate and unconditional 'liberation' than those whose death occurs elsewhere. The three prongs are also said to represent the three *gunas* or 'qualities' from which all substance is composed, and the three 'worlds' (*loks*) of heaven, earth and the netherworld – once more equating Kashi with cosmos.

The gulf which divides the city from profane space is again underlined by the maxim that it stands *apart* from the three *loks*, the fourteen *bhuvans* ('worlds' of which seven are above and seven below), and the nine *khands* (regions of the earth). Kashi constitutes a tenth *khand*. Now clearly this formulation reiterates the theme of separation. But it also implies the notion of englobement. When, for example, the *Satapatha Brahmana* – one of the most venerable texts on sacrifice – claims that there are thirty-three gods and that Prajapati is the thirty-fourth, this is to be understood to mean that Prajapati 'is greater than the thirty-three gods and encompasses them and all other beings within himself' (M. and J. Stutley 1977:230). By the same token, Kashi is not only separate from, but is superior to, and contains the rest of space. Apart from the three *loks*, it subsumes them. Hence, not only do all the gods reside in Kashi, but so do all other places of pilgrimage.[5] There is consequently no need for its inhabitants to visit other sacred centres for they are present as physically identifiable locations within their own city. They are not only here, but they were created and will be destroyed here. Similarly space itself was given form in Kashi where the deities who preside over the eight directions were assigned their jurisdiction (Eck 1978). Since Kashi can be said to encompass the rest of space, the *Panch-kosi* pilgrimage is not just a circumambulation of the city but also a circumambulation of the universe.

But if Kashi is the cosmos it is also symbolically identified with the human body. The five *ghats* which are visited in the course of the *Panch-tirath* pilgrimage are sometimes explicitly equated with the five elements (*panch-tattva*) of which the body is composed. In popular thought the model which is most often suggested is that of the gross (physical) body (*sthul sharir*). The city is described as a prone figure with its head on the southern boundary at Asi, its loins at Manikarnika, and its feet at Varuna in the north. The *Kashi khanda* (chapter 55) would seem to suggest that this body is that of Shiva himself. In the literary sources, however, the postulated homology is more often with the centre of the subtle anatomy (Kashi is the spot between the nose and the eyebrows), or with the subtle body as a totality. On this last theory, the rivers Asi and Varuna at the extremities of the city, and a third river which flows through the centre, are identified with the three main veins of the yogic body – respectively with the *ida*, *pingala* and *sushumna* (Kane 1973:4:625–6; Ram Bachan Singh 1973:15–16; *Kashi mahima prakash* p. 36). This last is associated with the transcendence of duality and the achievement of *moksha* (Eck

1983:299). Synomyms for it are *brahmanadi* and *shamshan* (cremation ground); and it is significant that those of my informants who know this yogic theory generally identify the *sushmna* with the Brahmnal (= *brahmanadi*), a small rivulet of which there are now no obvious traces, but which is supposed to issue into the Ganges at Manikarnika. According to this identification, then, the central vein of Kashi's mystical body terminates at the cremation ground, equating it with the highest centre of the yogic anatomy.

As we have seen, one of Shiva's boons to Vishnu was that Kashi perpetually remains in the *Satya yuga*, the golden age of original time. All time is auspicious there, and not even the worst planetary conjunctions should prevent the pilgrim from setting out for the sacred city. Since it is always the *Satya yuga* in Kashi, the time in which it exists is immune to the degeneration to which time elsewhere is subject. It is said that there are three powers which can never enter its precincts: Yamraj (the god of death), *yamdut* (his messengers) and the Kali Age (the degenerate epoch into which the rest of creation has sunk). Time here does not so much run down as stand still. It remains as it was at beginning of things. Kashi is therefore free from the progressive decay and doomsday destruction to which our world is otherwise subject. Shiva's city thus takes on Shiva's own characteristics as the 'Conqueror of Death' (Mahamritunja), and as the only one of the gods who is truly indestructible (*avinashi*) and who survives the dissolution of the cosmos.

According to the doctrine of karma, all actions – sinful or meritorious – are held to have more or less inevitable consequences which the actor will harvest in this or future lives. Now although karma theory can be – and in popular thought commonly is – placed within the framework of cyclical time (by, for example, making the murderer suffer an appropriate fate at the hands of his victim in the next life) the doctrine would *a priori* seem to imply a durational notion of time flowing inexorably on into a future in which the actor will reap the fruits of his past actions. But in a timeless world actions have no future consequences; and this may perhaps help us to understand why people often talk as though the laws of karmic retribution are suspended in Kashi, where saint and sinner alike are equally eligible for release from the cycle of rebirths. If duration is denied, so too are the karmic consequences of conduct.

But this, of course, is only one side of a much more complicated picture. Karma doctrine is not completely abandoned; nor is Kashi's immunity to the insidious effects of time unequivocally upheld. The same informant who reaffirms the dogma that all time in Kashi is equally auspicious and belongs to the Age of Truth is likely to attribute the uninhibited venality of daily life to the exigencies of a degenerate epoch, and to be as fastidious as the next man about consulting an astrologer before scheduling his daughter's marriage. 'Where Kashi is, the Kali Age is not', says Sita Maharaj, only to admit ruefully that something of its 'influence' nevertheless 'falls' on the city, and that even here one who dies under an inauspicious lunar asterism (*nakshattra*) is unlikely to obtain the 'highest state'. In the Kali Age, people explain, the soil of Kashi no longer looks like gold to mortal eyes; the *ling* (the phallic emblem of Shiva) in the Kedar temple which was made of nine jewels in the *Satya yuga*, of gold in *Treta* and of silver in *Dvarpara* is now mere stone; and even the shape of the city has changed and contracted in size. Originally 84 *kos* (about 168 miles) and in the form of a trident, in *Treta* its perimeter shrank to 52 and became like a discus, in *Dvarpara* it was 32 *kos* and in the shape of a chariot, and it is now just 25 *kos* and like a conch shell. The change is so palpable that when an ascetic who had been meditating in a secret cave since the time of Lord Ram was disturbed by the rebuilding of Sindhia *ghat*, he opened his eyes, looked about him in dismay, exclaimed that the *Kali yuga* must have arrived, and disappeared into the Ganges. Even in Kashi, one is forced to concede, creation has been tarnished by time. It could hardly be otherwise, for here too the world is manifestly imperfect.

My informants were generally content to live with the contradiction between the notion that Kashi is preserved from the ravages of time, and the admission that even here time has taken its toll. But in many of their statements they nevertheless imply a resolution to it by suggesting that it is not Kashi itself which has degenerated, but man's ability to perceive it. The soil *is* gold, the city *is* suspended in space, and Shiva *does* wander in it daily; and if we cannot see all this it is because we do not have the 'divine sight' of the *yogi*. 'This Kashi', as Anant Maharaj explained, 'is like the sun behind the clouds. I know it is still there although I cannot see it.'

The more radical conclusion which is sometimes drawn is that this Kashi of bricks and mortar is not the real one. The real Kashi is in the heart, and this external one is merely an aid to its realisation. If this realisation is achieved, then there is no need to go to the physical *tirath* (place of pilgrimage), for it will come to the worshipper. Thus Shiva came to Kashi from Kedarnath in the Himalayas, and established himself in the form of the *ling* in the Kedar temple, as a reward for Rishi Mahandatta's devotions. As the popular saying has it: 'If the heart is good, the Ganges is in the [shoe-maker's] wooden bowl; if the heart is true, Mecca is in the shit-house.'[6]

But whether the real *tirath* is considered to be in the mind or on the ground, the overwhelming consensus is that the physical Kashi puts the worshipper in direct contact with the transcendental world. Transmission conditions between the sacred and profane worlds are – as it were – optimal; and the place itself is a kind of transitional zone between the two. The term *tirath* derives from the Sanskrit root signifying the idea of crossing over, and refers not only to a 'place of pilgrimage', but also to a 'ford' or 'crossing point'. It thus implies a literal and symbolic transition. The term *tarak* has the same etymological provenance (Eck 1983:332) and is the name of the *mantra* Shiva whispers in the ear of those who die in Kashi in order to enable them to 'swim across' and obtain salvation. In myth it is the place where the *ling* of Shiva is made to span the three worlds like a giant column, and thus to join the different cosmic planes (Eck 1978).

'A *tirath*', as one informant defined the term, 'is a place where you can settle to religious practice and immediately reap the fruits of it.' It is like sinking a well for water, he went on. In certain kinds of terrain you can dig and dig without success, while in others your efforts are almost immediately rewarded. Kashi belongs to the spiritual equivalent of the second. Meritorious actions performed there yield fruits a thousandfold greater than the same actions performed elsewhere; while such deeds performed during the *Panch-kosi* are magnified ten million times. The pilgrimage to Kashi is a sure way of expiating even such monstrous crimes as cow-slaughter, and it is said that all the pilgrim's past sins drop away as he crosses the *Panch-kosi* road. For such expectations there are impeccable precedents. When Bhairav chopped off Brahma's fifth head with the nail of his little finger, the skull clung irremovably to his hand, and until he came to the tank at Kapalmochan on the city's boundary, he was forced to wander the three *loks* in search of a means of ridding himself of the sin of Brahmanicide. Similarly, Ram and Sita performed the *Panch-kosi* in order to expiate the Brahmanicide of Ravana.

Kashi boosts the consequences of actions, with the result that merit performed here is powerfully magnified. But this quality is double-edged The repercussions from *sins* committed there are also heightened. According to the *Kashi mahima prakash* (chapter 22), such sins earn the sinner a lengthy spell as a *rudrapishach* (the most terrifying of demons). Popular tradition takes a more optimistic view by allowing them to be expiated on the *Panch-kosi*, the performance of which mitigates 'the sufferings of Bhairav' inflicted at the time of death (p. 29). Sins perpetrated during this pilgrimage, however, are recorded in the 'thunderbolt writing' of Vishnu – that is, they are ineradicable. A slightly more elaborate formula, much quoted by the Pilgrimage-priests (*pandas*), postulates a whole hierarchy of locations, the superior deleting sins of the inferior. Thus, those committed elsewhere are destroyed by visiting a *tirath*; those committed in a *tirath* are destroyed in Kashi; those of Kashi on the *Antargrahi* pilgrimage; those of the *Antargrahi* on the *Panch-kosi*, while the latter are written with the thunderbolt of Vishnu – unless, some *pandas* add, they are offered the gift of a cow at Manikarnika *ghat* as the final act of the pilgrimage. Since this last dispensation is in some doubt, the rules which should govern conduct on the *Panch-kosi* are particularly austere, for at all costs the pilgrim must avoid the merest hint of lust, anger and envy, or the unintentional destruction of the insects beneath his feet. The near impossibility of doing so, and the dire consequences of failure, are often casuistically invoked by the *pandas* themselves as justification for their own reluctance to undertake the rigours of the journey.

1.3 A full life and a liberating death

Not only does the sacred area contain the rest of space, but it also encompasses the four goals of human existence (the *purusharthas*). *All* are

fulfilled in Kashi (*Kashi mahima prakash*, chapter 64). Hence the desire for
salvation no longer excludes the politico-economic pursuits of *artha* or the
sensual pleasures of *kama*. When Brahma weighed Kashi against heaven and
the other *loks*, Kashi was heavier on account of the combined weight of the
purusharthas (*Kashi khanda*, chapter 30). Again an inscription outside the
main shrine of the Kedar temple claims that the *ling* bestows *moksha*, *dharma*,
artha and *kama* and that one who worships there will never lack grains. In
Kashi, Parvati frequently assumes the form of Annapurna whose very name
suggests her inexhaustible bounty as a giver of sustenance. She provides for
the physical well-being of the city's inhabitants, while her consort – Shiva –
provides for the salvation of their souls (cf. Eck 1983:161). Kashi is likened to
a huge store-house, and it is said (despite some rather intrusive evidence to the
contrary) that nobody ever goes hungry there.

Since tomorrow will provide for itself, the 'true' Banarasi whiles away the
day at the *pan* shop on the corner,[7] doing body-building exercises at one of the
city's innumerable wrestling schools, indulging his fancy for music or caged
birds, or merely sitting on his roof in a pleasurable hemp-induced haze of
bhang. A burping, pot-bellied, *pan*-spitting jocularity or a muscle-bound
devil-may-care assertiveness provide the predominant stereotypes for those
who work and live by Manikarnika *ghat*, rather than the morbid moroseness
one might perhaps associate with people who spend their lives in an
atmosphere perpetually permeated by the smoke and smell of the funeral pyre.
Their self-image is above all summed by the words *mast* and *phakkarpan*. The
meaning of the first is hard to capture adequately in English but conveys the
idea of an intoxicated joy and amusement at the divine comedy of the world,
while the second has the sense of a carefree eccentricity (cf. Sukul 1974:325;
Saraswati 1975:49; Kumar 1988:83ff). Both are pre-eminently characteristics
of Lord Shiva himself. Just as Shiva reveals himself in the nature of his chosen
city, so he reveals himself in the character of its inhabitants. It is tempting to
go further. If – as Kumar's (1988) study would suggest – an ultimate 'good' in
the Banarasi value scheme is a sense of freedom from constraint, then it is not
only Shiva who provides the role model, but also Shiva who is seen as making
it possible. In life, his city as a store-house of plenty assures freedom from
want; while in death, it assures an ultimate freedom.

As the much quoted Sanskrit tag proclaims, *Kashyam marnam mukti* –
'death in Kashi is liberation'. Those who die in one of the other six sacred cities
(*puris*) of India are reborn in Kashi, and thus enhance their prospects of
salvation next time round. Even the gods desire death here, and several
Puranic texts advise the pilgrim to smash his feet with a stone on arrival lest he
be tempted to leave for another *tirath* (Kane 1973:4:566–7). Although it is
close to where he lives, an old Dandi Svami ascetic of my acquaintance will not
so much as cross the Asi into the modern quarter of Lanka, for Lanka lies on
the wrong side of the sacred boundary, and who knows but that death may
overtake him there.

'Liberation' is granted to those who die within the sacred area enclosed by the *Panch-kosi* pilgrimage route. The course of the Ganges as it passes through Banaras is particularly auspicious – it flows from south (the direction of death and of the kingdom of Yamraj) to north (the direction of rebirth). The sacred city itself is built entirely on the western bank of the river, which forms one of its boundaries; while the eastern bank is known as Maghar and is an especially inauspicious place to die. The reason for this is explained by a number of myths which recount how the sage Veda Vyas attempted to establish Ramnagar on the far side of the river as a centre to rival Shiva's city. Jealous of his initial success, Shiva dispatched Ganesh to scotch the threat, and by various strategems Ganesh tricked the sage into writing in the scriptures that those who die in Maghar will be reborn as assess (cf. Sherring 1868:173). Since there is no gainsaying the veracity of these texts, the pious inhabitant of Ramnagar hopes to be spared time to move across the river into Kashi when death approaches.

Characteristically, however, there is a mitigation. According to some variants of the story, Ganesh had come to Vyas in the guise of one on his death-bed. When, having accomplished his mission, he then died, Shiva and Parvati were distraught at the prospect of such a rebirth for their son. What was written was written; but to it Shiva insisted on the proviso that those who die in Maghar during that particular month – the month of Magh – will obtain the same rewards as those who die in Kashi.

Conventionally there are said to be three different routes to salvation – the paths of knowledge, works and devotion. Although at first sight the dogma that 'death in Kashi is "liberation"' would seem to provide a fourth alternative, in fact this is not the case. Those who die here achieve gnosis at the moment of death when Shiva gives them the *tarak mantra*[8] which destroys the fruits of past actions 'as a single match burns ten thousand kilograms of cotton'. A vision of this scene was vouchsafed to Swami Ramakrishna Paramhams who – as he passed Manikarnika in a boat – saw the goddess Annapurna sitting with a corpse in her lap and Shiva bending over to whisper in its ear (cf. Sukul 1974:219; Vidyarthi *et. al* 1979:222). Shiva thus acts in precisely the same way as the Brahman who, by whispering the *gayatri mantra* to the initiand at the sacred thread ceremony, converts him into one of the Twice-born (Eck 1983:331). In the fullest sense of Hertz's phrase (1960:80), then, 'death is an initiation' with Shiva as the preceptor.

One way of ensuring that death is met with in Kashi is, of course, to take matters into one's own hands. We know that a tradition of religious suicide in pilgrimage centres goes back at least as far as the seventh century A.D. (Chaudhuri 1979:55; Bharadwaj 1973:76). The practice is sanctioned by the *Skanda* and *Padma Puranas* (Kane 1973:4:607), and is associated with several *tiraths* (Dave 1959:95; Chattopadhyaya 1937; Morinis 1984:297). Bishop Heber, who visited Banaras in 1824, described how every year:

Many scores . . . of pilgrims from all parts of India, come hither expressly to end their days and secure their salvation. They purchase two large Kedgeree pots between which they tie themselves, and when empty these support their weight in water. Thus equipped, they paddle into the stream, then fill the pots with the water which surrounds them, and thus sink into eternity. Government have sometimes attempted to prevent this practice, but with no other effect than driving the voluntary victims a little further down the river; nor indeed, when a man has come several hundred miles to die, is it likely that a police-officer can prevent him. (Heber 1861:168)

In the oral 'history' of my informants, however, this tradition of religious suicide is above all associated with the Kashi Karvat temple. It is significant though that here matters were supposedly not left entirely up to the pilgrim himself. It is said that in a less corrupt age a *karvat*, or saw, was suspended from the roof of the shrine and would spontaneously fall on those on whom Shiva chose to bestow his blessing. What this story reveals (and resolves) is a certain ambiguity in the attitude to religious suicide, which seems to smack of the victim's reluctance to submit himself passively to the divine will. The texts, as Kane notes (1973:4:604ff), are equally ambivalent and sometimes attempt to lay down stringent conditions under which such action is permissible. Certainly today, suicide in Kashi is regarded with equivocation, and some of my informants held that it is sanctioned by penalties ten times as severe as those which apply elsewhere. When, during my fieldwork, an old man tried to drown himself in the Ganges off Manikarnika *ghat*, the Boatmen promptly fished him out, and nobody I spoke to seemed to think that they had done his soul a grave disservice, or that their action revealed a want of faith.

But while the idea of travelling to Kashi in order to commit suicide is generally discountenanced, there is no question about the rewards which await those whose object is to die a natural death. We can distinguish between two broad categories of such people: those who have come for Kashi-*vas* ('residence in Kashi') and those who have come for Kashi-*labh* ('the profit of Kashi'). Kashi-*vasis* have moved to the city in order to lead the religious life during their declining years, and to await death with the confidence provided by the guarantee of Shiva's grace. Those who come to reap 'the profit of Kashi' are those who are carried here on their death-beds, the majority of them being catered for in one of several charitably founded hospices specifically intended for the dying.

Far larger numbers of corpses of those who have not been fortunate or deserving enough to die in the city are brought for cremation on the *ghats* – often from very considerable distances. Although the doctrine generally upheld as orthodox by the Brahman specialists is that it is only by actually expiring in Kashi that 'liberation' is achieved, many people maintain that cremation here is sufficient. In fact these two views are not entirely incompatible, for it is often asserted that the vital breath (*pran*) does not leave the body until the chief mourner cracks open the deceased's skull with a stave when the body has been half-consumed by fire. According to this theory, then, death does not occur at the cessation of physiological functioning, but during the last rites, and consequently all who are cremated in Kashi may be said to have died there (pp. 180ff).

An even greater number of bundles of ashes of corpses cremated elsewhere arrive in Banaras for immersion in the Ganges. The saying is that the deceased will reside in heaven for as long as any portion of his mortal remains is sanctified by Ganges water (cf. Kane 1973:4:243); for it is recalled that Raja Bhagirathi brought the sacred river to earth in order to inundate the bones of his forbears, and thus secure their immortality. As the Sanskrit verse proclaims: 'Those whose bones, hair, nails and flesh fall in Kashi will reside in heaven even though they be great sinners' (original quoted in Ram Bachan Singh 1973:20). An alternative theory is that those whose ashes are immersed in Kashi will be reborn in the city, with the implication that they will attain 'liberation' at the end of their next incarnation.

Ashes can be taken out into the river by boat from anywhere along the *ghats*. At present, however, cremation is confined to Manikarnika and Harishchandra *ghats*. Throughout most of this century, the former has been by far the more popular of the two, accounting for around three-quarters of the total number of corpses disposed of at the burning *ghats* each day (around eighty at the time of my fieldwork). As a result the funeral pyres burn uninterruptedly throughout the day and night at Manikarnika – a fact so palpable that my informants' constant reiteration of it seemed over-determined. Persons of real distinction are cremated right next to the footprints which Vishnu left at the very spot on which he performed his cosmogonic austerities; others to one side of the *ghat*.

Though in an admittedly weaker form, an association between cremation and cosmogony is again made with regard to Harishchandra *ghat*. Harish-chandra abuts onto Kedar *ghat*, and although at present a hundred yards or so separates the latter from the pyres of the cremation ground, I was frequently told that formerly there was no gap at all. Now the tank known as Gauri *kund* at Kedar *ghat* is commonly described as the 'original (*adi-*) Manikarnika'; and it is claimed by those associated with this part of the city that it was here that Vishnu 'really' performed his cosmogonic austerities, and that the Manikar-nika tank is merely a replica. In this way the Harishchandra cremation ground is also identified with the place of creation.

What the pilgrims and mourners who come to the *ghat* are far more likely to know, however, is the story of the righteous raja for whom it is named. There are several rather different textual variants,[9] but the following version (told by a Funeral-priest) is typical of the oral tradition of the *ghats*. Several of its most prominent themes will crop up again in subsequent chapters: in particular, a characteristic element of cynical self-parody in the portrayal of even a heavenly priesthood; and a stress on the vital significance of various types of prestation.

In the time of the *Satya yuga*, Raja Indra [the king of heaven] decided to perform a sacrifice and summoned the sage Vashishth to preside. But Vashishth sent word that he was engaged in an important *shraddh* (mortuary) ritual, and that Indra should invite somebody else. Accordingly, he called upon Vashishth's great rival, Vishvamitra.

Before Vishvamitra could get started on the sacrifice, however, Vashishth showed up at Indra's court having completed his previous engagement. This was a considerable embarassment as Indra now had two [notoriously rivalrous] priests to preside over the same ritual. Moreover, the sages had immediately started to squabble about which of them was the more knowledgeable. 'Well', Vashishth challenged, 'who is the most truthful being in the whole world? Tell me that.' Conscious of who was providing the gifts (*dan*) associated with the sacrifice, Vishvamitra unhesitatingly nominated Indra himself. But Vashishth stoutly insisted that it was Raja Harishchandra of Ayodhya. 'Having thrown the bone', Indra remarked to his wife, 'the two dogs quarrel.' The dispute, it was agreed, should be resolved by putting Harishchandra to the test.

So it was that Vishvamitra – in the guise of an impoverished Brahman – appeared to the raja that night in a dream. Being the king that he was, Harishchandra pressed him to accept *dan* of a thousand gold coins, and told him to demand whatever else he had need of. 'I require your kingdom', said the sage.

On waking, Harishchandra sent all his servants and soldiers in search of that Brahman; and when Vishvamitra was eventually brought before him, he made the *sankalp* [the binding ritual resolution] for the donation (*dan*) of all his possessions. But no sooner had the gift been gifted than Vishvamitra pointed out that 'on top of every *dan* there is a [supplementary] *dakshina*' [a gift or 'fee' which completes the original donation]. 'Where', he demanded to know, 'is that?'

Well, of course, Harishchandra had nothing left to give. So he set out on foot with his wife [Taramati] and son [Rohit] for Kashi. In order to realise the *dakshina*, he there sold Taramati and Rohit to a malevolent and grasping Brahman from the neighbourhood of Jangambari. In that house Taramati was put to grinding flour and washing dishes, was treated with unremitting harshness, and at one stage was even accused of being a witch who ate the livers of young boys. Meanwhile the raja had sold himself as a servant to Kalu Dom – the then Dom Raja. [The untouchable Doms are a caste of funeral attendants who preside over the construction of the pyre and the incineration of the corpse, and who levy a 'tax' – or *kar* – for providing the fire with which it is ignited.]

Piqued by his lack of success thus far, Vishvamitra one day turned himself into a snake and bit Rohit as he plucked flowers for the Brahman's *puja*. As her son lay dying, Taramati begged her cruel mistress to summon some man knowledgeable in the cure of snake-bite, shrewdly appealing to her self interest by pointing that if he died they would loose their original investment. But all her mistress could do was to kick her in the arse, and demand to know how Taramati proposed to reimburse them for their loss.

Thunder crashed all about her on that dark, rain-driven night when Taramati carried her son's limp corpse to the cremation ground where Harishchandra worked as a watchman. At first he did not recognise his wife and child through the murk; nor did he identify Taramati's grief-choked voice when she protested that she had no money to pay the *kar* on which he insisted. But even when a flash of brilliant lightning had illuminated his wife's features, and realisation had dawned on both of them, he resolutely refused to cremate the corpse until his master had received his due. 'Who is Taramati? Who is Rohit? This is my *karam* [work, destiny, *karma*]. Without the tax I cannot burn.' Now the one thing which Taramati still possessed was a ring which Raja Harishchandra himself had given her, and this she now offered as *kar*. But the Dom's perquisites also include a shroud off the bier. Rohit, however, had neither shroud nor bier; and again, Harishchandra was immovable. So Taramati began to unwrap her *sari* to offer the Dom in lieu.

Before her nakedness was revealed, however, a dazzling light appeared in the sky, and a heavenly aeroplane raining petals of flowers swooped down on the *ghat*. On one side sat the chastened Vishvamitra; on the other the triumphant Vashishth. The righteous raja and his rani were taken aboard; Kalu Dom clung on to the tail-plane and the three of them were carried off to heaven, where Harishchandra was offered – but declined – the throne of Indra. Rohit, who had been restored to life, ruled Ayodhya for many years as the true son of his truthful father.

1.4 The dialectics of 'liberation'

'Death in Kashi is "liberation"'. But what is 'liberation'? I employ the term as a rough equivalent for *mukti* or *moksha* (which are used interchangeably). The verb *mukt hona* means 'to be free of' – as in the phrase *rin se mukt hona*, 'to be free of debt'. The noun forms *mukti* and *moksha* thus commonly signify 'freedom' from some encumbrance. Tonsure, for example, is a procedure for getting *moksha* from sin; while the world gets *moksha* from the evil effects of an eclipse when it is over.

The problem starts as soon as one enquires what death in Kashi is a liberation *from*. The range of responses to this question is extremely wide. The commonest is that it is a 'cessation of coming and going' – that is, of rebirth. You no longer 'have to bear the pain of the womb', or have 'to wander between the 840,000 kinds of life-form'. But what kind of state this absence of rebirth is held to imply is highly variable and often only vaguely formulated. My theologically more sophisticated informants often claimed that it is a permanent extinction of the individual soul which is 'absorbed into the Universal Spirit as water mixes with water'. But a Funeral-priest with a reputation for being the most learned member of his community in such matters held that you become a star which eventually disintegrates into the five elements once your merit is exhausted. By far the most prevalent view, however, is that *mukti* entails a perpetual and sybaritic residence in heaven. As one informant – a man of apparently limited aspirations – put it: 'if you feel like a *rasgulla* [a variety of sweet] then one will appear before you'. Another visualised heaven as a kind of antithesis to the world of economics as defined by Lionel Robbins. In heaven, he said, 'the ends are few and the means are many. On earth the means are limited and the needs are many.'

The most knowledgeable *pandits* distinguish a hierarchy of four different types of 'liberation': *salokya* (residence in the same world as God), *samipya* (living in close proximity to God), *sarupya* (acquiring the form of God) and, the highest, *sayujya* (complete union with God 'as water mixes with water').

We have seen that the sacred area of Kashi is sometimes represented in terms of a model of four concentric circles, of which the innermost (marked by the *Antargrahi* pilgrimage route) encloses the area of greatest sanctity. In some of the texts this spatial hierarchy is made to interlock with the hierarchy of types of *moksha*, such that *sayujya* is attained only by those who die within the *Antargrahi*, and *salokya* – the lowest form – by those who die in the outermost ring bounded by the *Panch-kosi* road (Sukul 1977:39 after the *Padma Purana*).

Many people, however (*including* a number of prominent priests), interpret the doctrine that 'death in Kashi is a "liberation"'' as a promise of a happy and prosperous *rebirth* – a distinctly uncanonical view. A handful go so far as to repudiate explicitly the notion that it leads out of the endless cycle of existence on the grounds that if all the people who die in Kashi were regularly eliminated, the world would soon come to an end. Some are unwilling to say anything more precise than that 'from it one gets a good state'; and others combine these different theories – *moksha* means different things in different parts of the city. Those who die in Kedar *khand* are released from the cycle of rebirths, while those who die elsewhere are reborn 'in a good house'.

But whatever 'liberation' is, there is almost complete unanimity that all who die in Kashi get it. Shiva's grace is indiscriminately extended to all, whether they be Brahman or Chandal (untouchable), raja or beggar, dog, insect, Muslim or *mleccha* (foreigner). Not only is caste made irrelevant to one's prospects of salvation, but so too is karma. Here in Kashi Shiva bestows his blessing even on sinners, 'just as a mother takes a dirty child onto her lap'. The story is told of a certain Brahman who had lived the most infamous of lives and who was killed by a tiger. A vulture scavenged a bone from the corpse; and in mid-flight right over Kashi a second vulture tried to snatch it away, with the result that it fell into the Ganges below. Now at that very moment the messengers of death were dragging the deceased's soul into the most terrible of hells. But as soon as the bone made contact with the water, they were forced to release their victim who went straight to heaven (*Kashi mahima prakash*, chapter 22). Kashi, it is often said, is for he whose salvation can be obtained nowhere else. As the Sanskrit has it: 'For those who are ignorant of the revealed scriptures and the sacred traditions, who have abandoned purity and proper conduct, and for those who have nowhere else to go, for them Benares is the refuge' (quoted in Chaudhuri 1979:172).

We have earlier seen that in Kashi time stands still. What we are now in a better position to appreciate is that – according to the more orthodox view of *mukti* – it is not only the city which is outside time, but also all those who have died there. Death becomes liberation from time and impermanence. Shiva's city holds out to the dying the promise of its own, and his own, immunity to temporality.

Taken literally, it is clear that all this radically subverts a whole gamut of doctrines generally regarded as fundamental to 'orthodox' Hinduism. It not only implies a suspension of the laws of karmic causation, but also puts in serious question the significance of the sacerdotal function of the Brahman. The rituals at which he officiates becomes an irrelevance to the salvation prospects of his patrons. This conclusion is in fact drawn by many of the sacred specialists themselves, who will on occasion concede – or even volunteer – that in Kashi the mortuary rituals are merely outward form, and are not strictly necessary to the fate of the deceased's soul. The dilemma of the Banaras Brahman who makes his living out of the traffic of pilgrims and mourners seems to be this. If *mukti* is subject to the qualifications of karma, then the greatness of Kashi (on whose reputation his livelihood depends) is undermined, for it can no longer cater to the miserable sinner in search of a sure salvation. But if he insists that *mukti* is available to all regardless of their ritual conduct, then the Brahman declares himself redundant. Further, this same doctrine simultaneously constitutes an oblique challenge to the institution of renunciation, to the idea that an ascetic withdrawal from the world is prerequisite for salvation. It too is deprived of any ultimate significance, since for those who expect to die in Kashi *moksha* is attainable *without* abandoning the world, and is no longer incompatible with the sexual and material pursuits of the householder.

Even the position of the gods is subverted (as they themselves are quick to realise), for when all are liberated who will make them offerings? As a result they are not a little ambivalent about Shiva's munificence, and it is they who petition him to revoke his boon that a mere visit to the *ling* in the Kedar temple is sufficient qualification for *mukti*. Again it is in response to the representations of the gods that the Asi and Varuna rivers are instructed to prevent the grossest sinners from entering the city (*Kashi khanda*, chapter 30). Even Shiva himself is forced to recognise the problem. Exiled from Kashi during the reign of the righteous king Divodas, and abandoned by nearly all the gods who have been seduced by the glories of the city, he sourly reflects on the difficulty of commanding obedience when even death is without menace (*Kashi khanda*, chapter 52). The path of devotion (*bhakti*) as the pre-eminent route to salvation is again discouraged – the problem which apparently preoccupied the medieval mystic poet-saint Kabir when he insisted on being moved *out* of Kashi into Maghar on his death-bed. As his much-quoted verse explains, 'If Kabir dies in Kashi, what homage will he render Ram?'

Although nearly all my informants assert that 'liberation' is bestowed on all who die in the city, and although this would seem to abrogate the inevitability of karma, few of them maintain this position entirely consistently. Despite the complete eschatological significance to which such a theory condemns them, the mortuary rituals *are* (usually) performed; and – even though they died in Kashi – the souls of those for whom they are not are believed to wander the city as malevolent ghosts. Moreover, there is a natural reluctance to admit that the scoundrel gets off scot-free, and it is generally supposed that in some form or another he will be confronted by the fruits of his past actions. 'If you planted an acacia tree then how will you eat mangoes?' There is also the disturbing consideration that if literally everybody were eligible for 'liberation' in Kashi, the population of the world would soon be depleted, and the ordained order of things disrupted. 'If all the donkeys go to heaven, how will the Washerman live?'

The problem, then, is how to have it both ways: how to maintain the dogma that death in Kashi is *always* 'liberation' without abandoning the theory of the immutability of karma. For those who hold that the real Kashi is in the heart, there is of course no difficulty. It is by reaching the *internal tirath* that *mukti* is attained; and this can only be done by those who have escaped the bondage of desire. For others, however, the problem remains; and a whole range of possible resolutions to it are attempted.

One is to claim that retribution is exacted in *this* life. Sins will catch up on the sinner in the form of a lingering and gruesome end, or of a miserable existence before it. But a much more general solution is to propose that only those with good karma are privileged to die in Kashi.[10] Endless instances are given of people who had come to await death in the city, but who – on account of their insufficient accumulation of merit – expired on some brief expedition outside the sacred precincts. The tale of the Brahman reprobate, whose just punishment was rescinded after the vultures had dropped one of his bones in the Ganges, is matched by the parable of Dhananjay, the moral of which is diametrically opposed to that of the first story. Dhananjay was the dutiful son of a wicked mother. On her death he brought her ashes to Kashi for immersion; but owing to a whole chapter of accidents, they were stolen before he could complete the task. The lesson explicitly drawn is that even in Kashi karma cannot be cheated.

Even more frequently, however, the difficulty is met by postulating a period of expiatory suffering immediately after death and before the soul is granted 'liberation'. So, for example, it may be said that the sinner is condemned to a term as a demonic *rudrapishach*, or must pass through nine existences as a stillborn foetus. But the commonest and most elaborated theory is that he is first subjected to *Bhairavi yatna* – 'the sufferings of Bhairav', who is Shiva's ferocious and terrifying chief-of-police (*kotval*) in Kashi. The punishment is much less protracted than that meted out to those who died elsewhere, but is much more intense. The *Kashi khanda* (chapter 31) quantifies its severity as thirty-two times greater than that experienced at the hands of Yamraj. *Bhairavi yatna* is described as purifying the soul in preparation for *mukti* as gold is purified by melting it in fire. The punishment 'burns up the sins, after which the gift of Shiva is obtained'.

Given such a retribution, it might appear somewhat misleading to speak of the law of karma being 'suspended' or 'abrogated' in Kashi. This would be so were it not for the fact that the dialectics of 'liberation' are taken a step further. We have seen that, according to one scheme, Kashi is divided into three zones, or *khands*. Now even those who insist most stridently that sins must inevitably be paid for by 'the sufferings of Bhairav' are apt to claim exemption for those who die in Kedar *khand*. For them, it is held, 'liberation' is direct, immediate and unqualified. The inevitability of karma is thus once more subverted – on occasion only to be propped up again with the plea that it is exclusively those of exeptional merit who are permitted to die in this quarter of the city. Such submissions, however, bear the marks of an impromptu sophism with which even the sacred specialists themselves are not entirely comfortable; for it is hard to suppress the suspicion that not all the acknowledged soundrels who died here were really saints. The underlying contradiction cannot be so easily disposed of; and is perceived not only by the anthropologist but also by many of his informants.

1.5 Death and cosmogony

This belief that salvation is guaranteed to those who die at the pilgrimage centre is, of course, familiar from other world religions. Those who die at Mecca, Jerusalem or Compostella go straight to heaven (Turner 1975:105).[11] But in the case of Kashi the association with death and its transcendence is given a pivotal place in the sacred identity of the city; and my contention is that this association is inseparable from the set of sacred characteristics which I have outlined in the previous sections of this chapter.

At the outset we saw that Kashi is the place where the universe is created and destroyed at the beginning and end of each cosmic cycle. What I would now like to suggest is that at Manikarnika *ghat* this process is kept in perpetual motion by the constant stream of cremations which are staged there.

A recurrent theme in Hindu religious thought is the homology which is held to exist between the body and the cosmos (e.g. Eliade 1959:172ff). Kashi itself establishes a link between them, for – as we have seen – it is not only a microcosm of the universe, but also a macrocosm of the body. Body and cosmos are governed by the same laws, are constituted out of the same five elements and everything that exists in the one must also exist in the other (cf. Goudriaan 1979:57). Thus all the gods and the whole of space are present within the human body – a notion which is explicitly elaborated in the *Garuda Purana* (part 15), to which the Banaras sacred specialists continually refer. The homology is also one of the basic principles underlying the architectural theory of the Hindu temple, which is constructed on the plan of a cosmic man (Beck 1976); while many forms of worship involve a cosmicisation of the body of the worshipper (cf. Gupta 1979).

Body and cosmos are thus equated; and this would seem to imply a further equivalence between cremation which destroys the microcosm of the physical body and the general conflagration which destroys the macrocosm at the end of time (*pralay*). Etymologically, *pralay* is 'a process (*pra*) of melting (*laya*) [M. & J. Stutley 1977:231], but it is generally represented as a two-phase destruction by fire and flood resulting in a return to a state of complete undifferentiation. A corpse is similarly subjected to fire (through cremation) and water (through the immersion of the ashes) – in some of the Puranic texts an individual death being classified as *nitya* ('daily' or 'constant') *pralay* (Biardeau 1971:18, 76). According to these same sources, Shiva (as Rudra) presides over the conflagration phase, while Vishnu (as Narayana) presides over the deluge (p. 76).

Cosmic dissolution, however, is not only an end of the universe; it is also a beginning, a necessary prelude to a new world cycle and hence a renewal of time. Similarly, we shall find that cremation is not just a destruction of the deceased's body, but an act of regeneration through which he is reborn. So just as the world's annihilation by fire and flood is a precondition for its recreation, so the deceased is cremated and his ashes immersed in water in order that he may be restored to life. Since the body is the cosmos the last rites become the symbolic equivalent of the destruction *and rejuvention* of the universe. Cremation is cosmogony; and an individual death is assimilated to the process of cosmic regeneration.

It was by his prolonged austerities (*tapas*) that Vishnu created the world. *Tapas* generates heat, which is in many contexts represented as the source of life and fertility. Through the heat of his austerities the ascetic acquires a super-abundant sexual potency; through the cremation pyre the seven storm-gods are born (O'Flaherty 1973:109), and through bathing in the tank of Lolark in Banaras fecundity is conferred on barren women – the tank being sacred to the sun, the source of heat. Of a piece with this, Vishnu burns with the fire of his *tapasya* in order to create the cosmos at Manikarnika *ghat*. Cremation is sometimes explicitly described as a kind of *tapasya*, and certain of the texts clearly represent it as such (Knipe 1975:132). It is no coincidence, then, that the most celebrated cremation ground in India is also the scene of cosmogony. By entering the pyre here the deceased, as it were, re-fuels the fires of creation at the very spot where creation began.

That this association is symbolically meaningful is illustrated by Baikun-thnath Upadhyay's comments following his rendering of chapter 26 of the *Kashi khanda*. In recent years, he notes (p. 57), there has been a move to persuade the authorities to shift the burning *ghat* away from the centre of the city. But this, he argues, would be quite improper since it is *essential* that corpses be burnt by Charan Paduka on Manikarnika *ghat*, the marble sandals marking the very spot on which Vishnu performed his austerities.

Another way of developing the same argument would be to show that cremation is a kind of sacrifice (cf. Levin 1930; Pandey 1969:241; Knipe 1975:132–4; Das 1976, 1982:120–6), and that sacrifice is a re-enactment of cosmogony. With regard to the second of these connections, and to invoke a different account of the origins of the world, *every* sacrifice is held to replicate the primal act of Prajapati who produced creation by the sacrificial dismemberment of his own body: 'any sacrifice is . . . the repetition of the act of Creation, as Indian texts explicitly state' (Eliade 1965:11; cf. Zaehner 1962:57, Herrenschmidt 1978, 1979). Or, as Heesterman (1959:245ff) puts it, 'the sacrifice may be described as a periodic quickening ritual by which the universe is recreated . . . The pivotal place is taken up by the sacrificer: like his prototype Prajapati he incorporates the universe and performs the cosmic drama of disintegration and reintegration . . .' Prajapati is recreated 'in order that he may repeat the cosmogony and that the world may endure and continue' (Eliade 1969:109).

A proper elaboration of the first proposition – that cremation is a kind of sacrifice – will have to wait until chapter 5. Some preliminary indication of its plausibility is perhaps suggested by the fact that in the Sanskritised Hindi of my informants, cremation is *antyeshti* or 'last sacrifice'; that the manuals of mortuary practice regularly explicitly equate it with fire sacrifice, and that both are represented as resulting in rebirth. The ritual procedures described on both occasions reveal moreover some remarkable parallels – in terms, for example, of the preparation of the site, the treatment of the victim and the divine status it is accorded, the offerings to the fire and the idea of being engaged in an act of dangerous and polluting violence.

My argument, then, is that since cremation is a sacrifice, since sacrifice regenerates the cosmos, and since the funeral pyres burn without interruption throughout the day and night at Manikarnika *ghat*, creation is here continually replayed. As a result it is always the *Satya yuga* in Kashi, the beginning of time when the world was new. That it is because of the city's sacredness that people come there to die and be cremated is an obvious truism. What is less obvious perhaps is that the ideology itself implies that Kashi *is* sacred precisely because they come for this purpose, for it is death and cremation that keep the city at the navel of the universe yet outside space and time. It is no accident, then, that the scene of cosmogony is also the site of unceasing cremation; or that especially important corpses should be burnt on that very spot where Vishnu sat for 50,000 years alight with the fire of the austerities by which he created the world.

2

A profane perspective

While the last chapter was concerned with the 'divine vision' of Kashi, the present one views the city's association with death through the more literal – perhaps more jaundiced – eye of the outside observer. Divine eyes and Diana Eck's previously cited claim for an unbroken continuity stretching back to the sixth century B.C. notwithstanding, it seems that many salient characteristics of the city's sacred complex are of fairly recent origin, and that what is claimed to be *anadi kal se* – 'from time without beginning' – is commonly an invention of tradition of the last two centuries. Nor, of course, does this vision of a primordial world provide the only discourse available. When interests are at stake, another – and to the outsider more familiar – version of 'history' is invoked. Even amongst the sacred specialists themselves, the association between cremation and cosmogony discussed in chapter 1 may then become a point of contention.

2.1 By way of background

Banaras is located in the middle of the Ganges valley, roughly half way between Delhi and Calcutta and within half a day's journey of the other major north Indian pilgrimage centres of Ayodhya, Allahabad (Pryag) and Gaya. With a population of a little over 700,000 at the 1981 census, it is more than three times its size at the beginning of this century.[1] Relative to other major urban centres, however, its rate of growth has been sluggish. In 1891 Banaras was the sixth largest city on the subcontinent, but by 1931 it had slipped back to fifteenth place (R. L. Singh 1955:57). Currently just over a quarter of the population are Muslims, and extrapolating from earlier census returns somewhere between 15 to 20 per cent are Brahmans of one sort or another (this being the largest single caste category).

With its reputation for 'orthodox' Brahmanical Hinduism and its ancient tradition of Sanskritic learning, it is the Brahmans who set the dominant religious tone of the city. Despite its relatively small population, Banaras now supports three universities, each of which prides itself on a strength in Sanskrit studies and/or Hindu philosophy, as well as a host of *pathshalas* (traditional schools) devoted to transmitting under the tutelage of a Brahman *guru* a knowledge of the sacred scriptures and an ability to recite the Vedic *mantras*. Far more significant for the subject of this book than the small, though highly prestigious, class of Sanskrit pedagogues attached to such institutions, are the vast array of different kinds of Brahman sacred specialist who cater to the religious needs of the pilgrims, mourners and inhabitants of the city: Vedic chanters, Funeral-priests, pilgrimage-priests, temple-priests, and so on. This sacredotal class provides the ritual technicians of Sanskritic Hinduism rather than its theoreticians. It is they who actually conduct the rituals prescribed by the texts, who expound their meaning, and who in this sense mediate between the textual tradition and the theologically untutored.

Not that they could (by their own criteria) be described as prodigies of learning. Indeed their reputation for chicanery is at least as great as their reputation for scholarship. Though all of them are literate in the vernacular, only a small minority have any real command of Sanskrit. Though they learn to read, they do not on the whole learn by reading. The majority rely principally for their religious knowledge on the oral traditions of their communities, and secondarily on the religious pamphlets and digests in Hindi which are sold throughout the city. The Sanskrit *mantras* they recite have been learned by rote; they have little idea of their 'real' meaning, and some are reduced to inaudible mumbling and brazening it out with gobbledegook in the confident expectation that their patrons will never know the difference.

As well as its reputation for Brahmanical orthodoxy, Banaras also has a close association with a number of more heterodox traditions – with, for example, Buddhism, with the Kabir-*panth* (which claims spiritual descent from the medieval mystic poet-saint Kabir), and with the erotic devotionalism of Vallabhacharya (a medieval saint of western India who taught devotion to Krishna). It is also a major centre for a number of ascetic orders, and Sinha and Saraswati (1978:50) estimate that in addition to the numerous ascetic pilgrims, there were in the 1970s some 2,000 world-renouncers residing permanently in the city – either independently or (the majority) in monastic refuges. Though Shiva is its presiding deity, Banaras has for centuries been an important centre of worship of Vishnu and it was here that Tulsi Das is reputed to have completed his *Ramcharitmanas* (the best known version of the epic story of Vishnu's incarnation as Lord Ram). While the Raja of Banaras is an embodiment and representative of Shiva, he is also the patron of, and a major participant in, the most famous *Ram Lila* in India (*Ram Lila* being an annual enactment of the epic staged in villages and towns all over the country). Today at any rate, Shaivism and Vaishnavism coexist without conflict (Kumar 1988:80) – or better, for the ordinary householder there is no opposition between them.

It is further commonly claimed – both by the local intelligentsia and by outside observers – that Hindu/Muslim relations in Banaras are also unusually harmonious. Kumar describes them as 'exceptional' (p. 225). Not only is there a good deal of interdependence in the economic sphere (as most conspicuously in the case of Hindu silk merchants and Muslim weavers), but more importantly the lower classes of both communities 'share a similar life-style and ideology of work, leisure and public activity', with the result that 'those who define themselves as "Banarasi" have more in common with each other regardless of caste or religion that with their co-religionists elsewhere'(p. 226). Saraswati (1975:50) similarly observes that 'whether one is a Gujerati or a Tamil, a Sikh or a Moslem, a Brahman or an Ahir, he is first a *banarasi . . .*'.

Hindu/Muslim conflict, characteristically provoked by an alleged encroachment on the sacred space of the other community, nevertheless goes back *at least* as far as the middle of the eighteenth century (Bayly 1983:311).[2] Particularly bloody disturbances took place in 1809, during which sacra on both sides were attacked and desecrated, and a cow was killed on the *ghats* – in atonement for which

> All the Brahmans in the city, amounting to many thousands went down in melancholy procession, with ashes on their heads, naked, and fasting, to the principal ghats leading to the river, and sate there with their hands folded, their heads hanging down, to all appearances inconsolable, and refusing to enter a house, or to taste food. (Heber 1861:1:184; cf. Sherring 1868:194)[3]

In this century, the late 1930s was a period of almost continual tension. In one (relatively minor) incident in 1937, the *pandas* tried to deny Muslims the right to bathe in the Ganges at Lalita *ghat* (*Fortnightly Reports* 1937). Rioting seems to have been recurrent from the 1960s onwards. In the course of my fieldwork, the city was for several days under curfew in 1977 after a number of people had been killed (and many more wounded) in disturbances provoked by a procession to immerse the image of the goddess at the end of Durga *puja*; and conflict again broke out in the same area of the city during the *Holi* celebrations of 1983. More rioting followed in 1986 and 1991 in the wake of the Ayodhya mosque affair (in which Hindu 'fundamentalists' have attempted to re-claim 'the birth place of Lord Ram', the supposed site of which had become a mosque which was demolished by mobs in 1992).

Harmony, then, is a relative matter and the conclusion that communal relations in Banaras are 'exceptional' would appear to depend on a rather bleak assessment of what is 'normal' in other north Indian cities. Though on a simple body-count of those killed in communal rioting, Banaras might well be relatively peaceful, it is far from clear that this can be taken as an adequate measure of the state of inter-communal relations, let alone as convincing evidence of amity.

Despite the numerical and cultural significance of its Muslim minority, the Banaras of this book is an uncompromisingly Hindu city, for the mortuary complex with which I am concerned is almost exclusively presided over and patronised by Hindus. This has to be immediately qualified, however, by the recognition that (whatever its implications for communal harmony) there is

some evidence in the religious field for the kind of cultural commonality that is
stressed by Saraswati and Kumar. At the level of 'popular' religion, there is at
least a degree of 'syncretism'. Many lower-caste Hindus go as supplicants to
the shrine of the Muslim martyr Bahadur Shahid for the solution of problems
caused by the malevolent ghosts of those who have died a bad death (pp.
240–2); many lower-class Muslims visit the *samadhi* ('tomb') of a (Hindu)
Aghori ascetic for the cure of barrenness (chapter 8).

Nor should we forget that death and pilgrimage are extremely big business
in Banaras, and that for *all* its inhabitants much of the available employment
directly or indirectly derives from this business. Though any such figure is
bound to be arbitrary, Saraswati (1975:45) claims that as much as three-
quarters of the city's population is in one way or another dependent on its
pilgrimage industry. Certainly a great deal of the artisan production for which
Banaras is famous can be seen as a spin-off from its importance as a Hindu
pilgrimage centre. This is most obvious in the case of the brassware
production of images of the deities, articles for their worship and pots for
carrying home Ganges water; but it is also true of the economically more
significant luxury trade in silk brocades and other textiles which provides
employment for tens of thousands of predominantly *Muslim* weavers.
Demand for their products is to a significant extent sustained by the huge
numbers of visitors which the city attracts.

Certain neighbourhoods are overwhelmingly Muslim; others predominantly Bengali or South Indian. Banaras is a cosmopolitan city and contains
communities representative of almost every part of India. By the end of the
eighteenth century, it had 30,000 Maratha settlers out of a population that
could not have been in excess of 200,000 (Bayly 1983:137). In more recent
times the major influx has been of Bengalis, who currently account for about
one-fifth of the city's inhabitants and a much higher proportion of its
professional middle-class (Kumar 1988:217).

Banaras as a whole is subdivided into 351 neighbourhoods, or *mohallas* (R.
L. Singh 1955:37). In the past, *mohallas* seem to have jealously preserved a
good deal of local autonomy, making their own arrangements for street
cleaning and policing, and closing their gates at night. Some were, and a few
on the periphery of the oldest parts of the city still are, dominated by people of
a single caste or craft speciality; others were centred on a *haveli* (a noble
mansion) around which were clustered a more heterogeneous group of client
families (Heitler 1972; Cohn 1962; Freitag 1989b:18, 123). Although today the
inner city *mohallas* do not have this kind of social coherence, the neighbourhood remains an important focus of local loyalty and of many cultural and
leisure activities – wrestling schools, music clubs, *Ram Lila* and Durga *puja*
groups for example (Kumar 1988:81).

The neighbourhood which lies immediately behind Manikarnika *ghat* in the
heart of the old city is a complicated tangle of cobbled alleys (*galis*), many so
narrow that with arms outstretched one might almost touch the often

dangerously delapidated three- or four-storeyed buildings on either side. In the early morning, on festival days or when the city is more than usually full of pilgrims, this maze of *galis* becomes a kind of delta through which a milling, jostling river of humanity flows down in the general direction of the *ghat* – running the gauntlet of packs of mangy dogs snarling over scraps, of cows being shooed away by vigilant vegetable vendors, and of shopkeepers leaning out of their booths to spit scarlet betel-juice into an open drain below. A party of bewildered rural pilgrims file through the alleys, holding on to a sleeve here and an arm there lest they loose touch with each other, their group-leader periodically blowing a hunting horn or waving a flag so that any stragglers might know which way to turn. Mixed up with the pilgrims, daily bathers and early shoppers, coolies carrying wood for the cremation pyres stagger the quarter of a mile down from the main road under impossible loads precariously balanced on their heads. Temple bells clang; somewhere in the next *gali* Sanskrit verses are being chanted in unison; the tea-stall radio is playing the theme tune from *Jai Santoshi Mata*, and the endless hoarse cries of *Ram nam satya hai* ('Truth is the name of Ram') announce another party of mourners carrying their corpse down to Manikarnika on a joggling bamboo bier. Against this current, an emaciated elderly Brahman in a grubby *dhoti*, with a sacred thread across his bare chest and a *lota* (brass pot) of Ganges water in one hand, picks his way carefully back to his crumbling house, already purified by his morning bath and fastidiously trying to avoid brushing against those who pass by in the other direction.

Squeezed out onto Manikarnika *ghat* through this network of alleys, the pilgrim comes upon the wide sweep of the river and the emptiness of Maghar beyond. Immediately below him, down towards the water's edge, four or five pyres are at various stages of incineration, and a couple of waiting corpses have been parked with their feet in the river while the chief mourner is berated by the Dom, or the family Barber haggles with the wood-seller. An Aghori ascetic – whose discipline offers a living commentary on the transience of bodily existence – wanders casually over to a more or less extinguished pyre, smears his torso and arms with ash, picks out a live ember to light his *chillum* (clay pipe), or pilfers some charcoal and fragments of wood on which to cook the food he eats out of the human skull which is his constant companion and alms bowl.

To the outsider what is most striking about this scene, however, is the vibrant life that, seemingly impervious, goes on all about: boys flying kites, the pious performing their daily ablutions in the river, hawkers calling their wares, and muscular men and youths devotedly perfecting their bodies in one of the two wrestling schools (*akharas*) that are located not a hundred paces away from the burning corpses. One is single-mindedly engaged in countless press-ups and sit-ups; another effortlessly swings a stout wooden club with a solid head of rounded stone the size of a football from shoulder to shoulder – as though he were himself the god Hanuman limbering up to dispose of the demon army of Ravana. A third achieves yoga positions that seem to defy all physical possibility, while others – their daily regimen fulfilled – lounge in the shade of a tree, being massaged, preparing a concoction of the narcotic *bhang* or parting their hair and curling their moustaches in front of a broken fragment of mirror.

2.2 'From time without beginning'

> It is . . . a common reply which one receives, on inquiring the date of any given shrine, that it is without date, and has always existed. (Sherring 1868:47)

In fact, however, hardly any buildings in Banaras pre-date British control of the city by more than fifty years or so. But Kashi's antiquity is not, of course, in question. Excavations on the Rajghat 'plateau' – now largely waste ground to the north of the currently built-up area – suggest that it was already a substantial settlement by the ninth century BC (Eck 1983:46); and it was certainly an important religious centre by the time of the Buddha in the sixth century BC. It was during the period between the sixth and thirteenth centuries AD, however, that Banaras was 'established as a stonghold of brahmanical Hinduism' and that 'many of the Puranic traditions about the sacred city were elaborated' (p. 79). The dating of Kashi's greatest *mahatmya* ('eulogy'), the *Kashi khanda*, is uncertain, though it seems probable that it was compiled around the middle of the thirteenth century. But it is also likely that this text represents a working-over and systematisation of traditions which had already been current for some time (p. 81–2, 347–9).

If no visible trace remains of the 'prolific architectural and sculptural achievement' of this golden epoch (p. 79), then both the popular history of Banarasi Hindus and the published sources on the city agree on a single explanation – the five hundred years of Muslim domination which followed: 'for the most part these were hard centuries. The religious life of the city was under almost constant threat' (p. 83). Sacked and looted by Muhammad Ghori at the end of the twelfth century, the city's temples were again destroyed in the fourteenth and fifteenth centuries. By the time we reach the sixteenth century most generalised accounts of the city's history have begun to sound increasingly like a Hindu version of *1066 and all that*. This was the era of the emperor Akbar, who was a good thing, but not perhaps a very good Muslim since he allowed his Rajput allies to rebuild the *ghats* and temples. But Akbar was soon followed by Shah Jahan, who was a bad thing and who knocked them all down again; and by Aurangzeb, who was even worser, with the result that

> Although the city is bestrewn with temples in every direction, in some places very thickly, yet it would be difficult . . . to find twenty temples, in all Benares, of the age of Aurangzeb, or from 1658 to 1707. (Sherring 1868:31–2)

> There is no major religious sanctuary in all Banaras that pre-dates the time of Aurangzeb in the seventeenth century . . . The city of the Puranic *mahatmyas* was no more. (Eck 1983:84)

I have not the competence to assess the objective historical basis for such accounts, nor for the purposes of this book is that necessary. It is perhaps worth noting, however, that although there is certainly evidence that Aurangzeb was religiously more zealous than some of his forebears and did indeed sanction the destruction of the Kashi Vishvanath temple (e.g. Smith 1958:416), there is also evidence that he issued a proclamation forbidding the harassment of the Banaras Brahmans or any interference with their places of worship (Sen 1912:269–73). More generally, Bayly (1981:163) has plausibly argued that the Mughal empire created the conditions for an *expansion* of pilgrimage and funerary cities like Banaras and Gaya. Political unification provided the pilgrim with an unprecedented degree of security on his journey; and the state had a positive interest in promoting this freedom of travel in that it derived substantial revenues from trade and pilgrim taxes. Moreover it was the princely Rajasthani allies of the emperor who initiated the modern phase of building Banaras. But as to the scale and social organisation of the pilgrimage and funerary business during this period, we know little.

For my purposes, however, what is more relevant than the objective historical facts is my informants' firm conviction that the years of Muslim domination were one long story of the desecration and destruction of Kashi's Hindu heritage. Amongst other things, this 'history' provides them with a ready-made explanation for the apparent disjunction between their claim that this or that shrine is 'from time without beginning', and the observable fact that the bricks and mortar are modern. This *is* indeed the very place where Lord Ram worshipped in the *Treta* age, and if the building itself is new, the blame can only lie with Aurangzeb.

For at least a century and a half – and probably longer – pious Banarasi Brahmans and ascetics, like the celebrated Gor Ji (Sherring 1868:105–6), have assiduously 'rediscovered' and restored many shrines and images described in the *Kashi khanda* but lost as a result of the iconoclasm of the city's former rulers and the erosion of time. During my fieldwork, for example, the very spot where the sage Valmiki encountered the demonic *pishach* that was unable to enter the sacred precincts of the city on account of its burden of sin – and where he compassionately instructed it to bathe in the tank of Pishach Mochan in order to be liberated from its demonic state – was 'rediscovered' on a rubble-strewn patch of land by a wealthy *panda* (temple priest) of the neighbourhood. A new shrine was constructed and a Brahman student from the Sanskrit University hired as its *pujari* (priestly officiant). What gave a certain edge to this important archaeological find was that ownership of the land in question was disputed, and that the (re-)construction of this ('ancient') temple on part of the plot – the rest was destined for commercial development – was allegedly intended to provide a prima facie argument for the *panda*'s right to control it.

Whether their predecessors were vandalistically destroyed, were effaced by the architectural ambitions of a new generation of pious patrons, simply fell down of their own accord, or never actually existed, the fact is that today the most ancient and celebrated *ghats* and temples of the city were generally constructed in the period between 1730 and 1810. 'Modern Banares', as Altekar (1947:247) observes, 'is largely a creation of the Marathas.' Like other new Hindu regional regimes manœuvring for position in the wake of the break-up of the Mughal empire, the Marathas invested heavily in the major centres of Brahmanical Hinduism in an attempt to legitimise their Kshatriya pretensions and supra-regional aspirations. Bayly suggests that the number of pilgrims visiting Banaras probably trebled between 1780 and 1820. By the early nineteenth century the city was regularly visited by armed Maratha pilgrimages of up to 200,000. But there were also munificent patrons from other parts of the country. Recently ennobled *zamindars* (landlords), and the socially mobile business and service class which was growing up around the emerging power of the East India Company, for example, began to invest some of their new riches in the spiritual and status rewards associated with pilgrimage and the pilgrimage centre (Bayly 1981; Entwistle 1987:211).

The predominance of Maratha patronage, and the fact that between 1750 and 1790 Banaras became 'the subcontinent's inland commercial capital', are both largely explained by its strategic location on the main trade route which ran from Bengal down into the Maratha territories in the Deccan: 'there can be no doubt that by the 1780s the Banaras region had become the financial and commercial cross-roads for the whole sub-continent' (Bayly 1983:104, 155).

– The pivotal group in this trade were the so-called 'Gosains' – a socially amorphous category of Shaivite ascetics and sectarians variously glossed as 'mendicant soldier traders' (Freitag 1989b:5), as a 'religio-commercial sect, militarised to some degree, and organised according to the *guru-chela* (disciple) principle' (Kolff 1971:213), and as 'Hindu ascetics and mercenaries who emerged as some of the most powerful trading people of the century' (Bayly 1983:29). During its closing decades, Gosains were the largest owners of urban property in Banaras and amongst its most important bankers, money-lenders and merchants. The latter purchased goods in Bengal which they then transacted in major entrepôts like Mirzapur with other Gosains from the Deccan who had come to buy and sell (Cohn 1964).

Their superficially surprising composite role of mercenary-ascetic has to be seen in the light of the fact that by the beginning of the eighteenth century a number of renunciatory sects had already been effectively militarised and organised into *akharas* (the term which is used for the martial arts/wrestling schools mentioned at the end of the last section, and which here has the sense of a militant ascetic order). According to tradition, this militarisation was a response to the need to preserve Hinduism against the proselytisation of Aurangzeb (Kumar 1988:118). In the conditions of the time, when trade needed armed protection, it is also quite understandable that the role of merchant should be added. Not only could the Gosains provide that protection, but they also started with considerable commercial advantages.

Their annual pilgrimage cycle offered a ready-made long-distance trading ⊦ network; as ascetics they were sometimes exempted from full customs rates (Bayly 1983:143), and as a highly mobile armed force it was presumably unwise for anybody either to molest or antagonise them. What is more, the profits from all this commercial activity became the corporate property of the *math* ('monastery') under the stewardship of its *mahant* ('abbot') – the bulk of this property devolving on a *single* successor. This, combined with an inhibition on consumption imposed by a frugal life-style, meant that capital accumulation could be rapid in comparison with other merchant communities (Cohn 1964).

But there was also another way in which pilgrimage played an important part in the commercial expansion of the city during this period. Many pilgrims 'brought with them drafts drawn by their local bankers upon the Banaras *sarrafs* (bankers/money-changers) who would immediately discount and pay them the required cash to finance their stay and other expenses related to the observance of the due rites and ceremonies in the holy city' (Mishra 1975:193). In the 1790s, pilgrims from Nagpur alone carried bills of exchange valued at a yearly average of Rs. 100,000 (p. 94); and in 1815 (the figures would have been higher in the previous century) 'between 5 and 10 per cent of Benares transactions with its best trading partners, the Maratha dominions to the south, was accounted for by the provision of cash for the pilgrims'. The effect was to facilitate trade and the movement of bullion (Bayly 1983:128).

Today the Gosains are no longer of any real commercial significance; nor is Banaras the mercantile and banking centre it then was. But it is tempting to suppose that this legacy has left its imprint on the culture and ethos of a city in which religion, commerce and violence are still continually overlaid, and in which there is for the most part rather little concern to keep them separate.

When the Marathas began to invest heavily in Banaras, the city was still nominally under Muslim overlordship. Though representatives and embodiments of the eternal Lord Shiva, the Banaras dynasty is in fact an eighteenth-century creation. In 1738 a subordinate collector of taxes, a Bhumihar Brahman named Mansa Ram, managed to ease out his former overlord and employer, replacing him as the *zamindar* who collected the revenue for the region on behalf of the Nawab of Awadh. Over the next few years Mansa Ram's successor expanded his area of control at the expense of his rival *zamindars*, was accorded the title of raja by the emperor in Delhi, and consistently endeavoured to establish his autonomy and evade his obligations to the Nawab. Though the latter would periodically send troops to bring his recalcitrant subordinate to heel, by the time they arrived the raja would be out of easy reach. The Nawab would then be confronted with trouble elsewhere, and would be brought to terms by the consideration that some revenue was better than none (Lutgendorf 1989:39–40). In order to resist the Nawab, the raja was dependent on mercenaries recruited from the militarised ascetic orders; and in order to pay him off he was dependent on the city's bankers (Freitag 1989b:7–8).

Theoretically, the Banaras raja and others like him derived their legitimacy from the Nawab; and the Nawab derived his from the emperor in Delhi. But as this imperial heirarchy became increasingly moribund, the local Hindu rajas began to search about for a new language of legitimacy. Lutgendorf (1989:41) persuasively argues that they found this in their patronage of the Ram tradition (most notably in the Banaras case in their patronage of the famous *Ram Lila* held at the raja's capital of Ramnagar). What this tradition provided was 'an explicitly Hindu symbol of royal legitimacy, and thus [a way] to achieve ideological as well as political independence from the Nawabs'. In this way the king who is Shiva became the region's chief impresario for the staging of an epic celebrating an incarnation of Vishnu.

The last vestiges of the Nawab's authority over Banaras were removed when the territory was formally transferred to British overlordship in 1775. Though at first this made little practical difference, the raja soon found himself pressed to pay a very large subvention towards the costs of war with France. When he prevaricated and then rebelled, he was deposed and replaced by a more malleable contender. The state of Banaras retained a degree of minimal autonomy, but the city itself was brought under direct British administration.

During the one and a half centuries of the British *raj*, Banaras continued to attract the patronage both of the rising classes of the imperial order, and of the old established princely houses. The *Pax Britannica* meant that the latter could no longer compete with each other in military adventures; but the effect of this was to provide them with both the opportunity and the resources to spare for pursuing their rivalry through competitive magnamity in pious donations at the pilgrimage centre (Bayly 1981:170; cf. van der Veer 1988:39). Others of the princes were new men of dubious pedigree who had been elevated by the British. 'By acquiring priests of sufficiently high status to perform ceremonies such as *sraddha* [in centres like Banaras], these princes could hope to justify their claim to Kshatriya [Warrior] status which was the pride of the older Hindu ruling houses' (Bayly 1981:162). Seen from the Banaras end, however, my own evidence would suggest that a double legitimation was probably involved. Rajas of doubtful Rajput origin from the tribal-dominated forest areas of, say, Madhya Pradesh would become the patrons of priests of equally dubious Brahmanical status whose rights on the *ghats* were disputed. The priest legitimated the prince as a *bona fide* Kshatriya whose genealogy could be traced back to Ramchandra; while the prince legitimated the priest as a *bona fide tirath-purohit* with royal patrons.

Writing of Banaras in the 1860s, the Rev. M. A. Sherring of the London Missionary Society noted with some dismay the impetus which British rule had given to temple construction and the 'manufacture of idols'. 'Judging by external appearances', he says, 'Hinduism was never so flourishing as it is now'. As his colleague, the Rev. Mullens, summed it up:

All over North India especially, the native merchants and bankers who have prospered by British protection, by contracts with English armies, by the security given by English law to their extensive trade, have filled Banares and other cities with new and costly shrines; and many a Raja, and many a banker, while visiting in state the holy city, has poured into the lap of the attendant priests unheard-of sums, which must have satisfied even their covetous and grasping souls. (quoted in Sherring 1868:39)

Though perhaps largely a product of wishful thinking, there was probably a grain of truth in Sherring's claim that all this investment represented a defensive reaction to 'the new doctrines of European civilization and religion, which they now begin to recognise as formidable opponents'.

What this focus on elite patronage conceals, however, is the extent to which pilgrimage was progressively 'democratised' during the British *raj*. Not only was travel far safer, making the large militarised convoys of pilgrims a thing of the past, but it was also a great deal cheaper, faster and easier. At the end of the eighteenth century, such roads as existed in the Banaras region were in a state of chronic neglect, and even the main commercial centres were connected by mere tracks which became impassable in the rains. By the end of the nineteenth century, an extensive network of roads – many of them metalled – ran throughout the district (Nevill 1909:72–3). Far more important, however, was the coming of the railways. By 1862, trains had begun to arrive at Moghal Sarai – the main rail-head in the Banaras region and an important junction on the line that was to run all the way from Bengal to the Punjab. Very soon Calcutta would be hours away instead of the weeks it might have taken the traveller some twenty years before to come up-stream to Banaras by boat or to be carried by palanquin (cf. Kennedy 1884:9–10). The rail network expanded rapidly, and by the beginning of this century the city had three separate stations – locations which are, as we shall see, quite as important to the *panda* (pilgrimage-priest) as the city's most sacred temples.

Since Independence, patronage from the princely houses has largely dried up, and many of their endowments are in terminal decline. Even by the beginning of this century, the ostentatious river-front mansions of absentee noblemen, used only occasionally by their connections on pilgrimage and left in charge of retainers, were often inadequately maintained and beginning to crumble (Greaves 1909:19). Some substantial buildings intended as *dharam-salas* (pilgrim lodges) have become the more or less private residences of their caretakers and cease to receive pilgrims at all. In 1948, a survey found that aside from the six *ghats* which were under the control of the Municipal Board, thirty-three were still owned by princes from all over India and the remaining thirty-five were 'the achievements of individual philanthropy'. But in neither of these last two cases had any provision been made for repair and rebuilding (R. L. Singh 1955:45). While it is true that the city has attracted new benefactors and philanthropists – rich industrialists, caste-associations of upwardly mobile peasant-cultivators, and well-resourced *gurus* of national and even international reputation for example – it is unlikely that they fully compensate for the patronage that has been lost (though it is striking that nearly all of the *dharamsalas* that are today best patronised were founded within the last fifty years). In any event, some parts of the inner city now have an air of distinctly faded grandeur, others of downright dilapidation.

The pilgrims, however, have continued to arrive in ever increasing numbers, though it is likely that a smaller proportion of them than formerly belong to the highest and most affluent sections of society, and that the 'index-linked' value of the average priestly donation has declined. But this is almost certainly made up for by volume and turn-over. More and more pilgrims come by rail and bus on 'package tours' of a number of sacred centres, and fewer and fewer of them stay in Banaras for more than a couple of days. Perhaps a majority are only there for a few hours.[4] Many are the first member of their family or village to have visited the city, and do not therefore have an hereditary *panda*. Increasing numbers of corpses are also brought to the city for their 'last sacrifice', and more people of rank have aspired to cremate them on the footsteps of Vishnu. This last, as we are about to see, has recently become a source of some conflict.

2.3 On the footsteps of Vishnu

The first firm evidence that death in Kashi was understood as a promise of liberation appears to come from an eighth-century AD inscription which praises the city as a place where people come 'from afar to live, die, and obtain moksha' (Eck 1983:80). In most of the eulogistic *mahatmyas*, however, it is the whole city which has the epithet of 'the great cremation ground', and there is no specific mention of either Manikarnika or Harishchandra as privileged locations for the disposal of the dead. 'Originally', some informants now claim, cremations were conducted anywhere within the sacred area circumscribed by the *Panch-kosi* road. Because of its extraordinary sanctity, Manikarnika is however singled out by several of these texts as a particularly good place *to die*. But only in a chapter of the *Narada Purana*, which is almost certainly later than the twelfth century, is it directly described as a place to be cremated (Eck 1983:249, 348; 1980:93).

Manikarnika was, in 1302, the first *ghat* to be built in stone (Sukul 1974:272). It was rebuilt in 1735 by the (Maratha) Peshwa Bajirao, and again in 1791 by Banaras's most celebrated patron – Rani Ahalyabai of Indore – who funded the construction of one of its most imposing temples and of a (never completed) screened-off area known as Zenana *ghat* where women could bathe in privacy. In oral accounts of its history, however, the key figure of this period was Lala Kashmiri Mal.

By caste a Khatri of Punjabi origin who was granted the title of raja by the Mughal emperor, Kashmiri Mal was not only a dominant force in the north Indian trade in precious stones and a substantial tax-farmer, but also one of the richest and most influential bankers in north India who acted as a receiver of the

Nawab's revenues from the raja of Banaras, and who later became the Banaras treasurer for the East India Company (Bayly 1983:232, 169; Mishra 1975:171). When his mother died – in 1775 according to Sukul (1977:56) – her corpse was carried to Harishchandra *ghat* for cremation. The windfall of such a fabulously wealthy patron with such a reputation for liberality is said to have incited the Dom funeral attendants to demand a 'tax' (*kar*) of quite fabulous proportions. So insistent and unreasonable were their claims that Kashmiri Mal removed the corpse to Manikarnika. Here he purchased a plot of land on which to stage the cremation by covering one whole segment of the *ghat* with gold coins, and appointed a Dom of his own choosing to receive *kar* on the understanding that henceforth Khatris would give only at the unnegotiable flat rate of 5 *paisa* per corpse. Some powerful Khatri families still invoke this agreement today (generously allowing for inflation by substituting an equally token Rs. 5).

It is perhaps significant that the Khatri *chabutra* – the 'platform' on which Kashmiri Mal's mother's body was cremated and which is still reserved for corpses of Punjabi origin – is not immediately adjacent to Charan Paduka (the footsteps of Vishnu). At any rate, the earliest hard evidence of the existence of these footprints appears to be an engraving published by Prinsep in 1831; and it is only sometime later that it begins to be mentioned as the place where the elite of the city are burned. At the beginning of this century, Cape (n.d.:75–6) was told that this was 'a recent invention of the covetous Brahman'. It is probable, then, that cremation at Charan Paduka was a nineteenth-century innovation, and it is tempting to see this as all of a piece with the new forms of royal legitimacy mentioned in the previous section. Just as in life the Hindu rajas of the region were concerned to identify themselves with that paragon of Hindu kingship, Vishnu's *avatar* Lord Ram, so in death they began to emulate Vishnu by submitting themselves to the flames on the very spot where Vishnu had burned with the fire of his austerities to create the cosmos.

During the monsoon rains, the river level is some 40 to 50 feet higher than in the winter. The result is that hardly any space is left for the pyres on the river bank itself. As the number of cremations steadily grew, the problem of how to accommodate so many pyres became acute (and was no doubt exacerbated by the fact that the death-rate peaks at the end of the rains). The most important physical change to Manikarnika in this century has been the construction – completed around 1912 – of a massive concrete platform which stands above the flood level and on which the corpses burn during this season. The funds for this were raised by a public subscription organised by the Chairman of the Municipal Corporation, Raja (Sir) Moti Chand, a banker, *zamindar*, Bengal mill-owner and famous patron of Banaras music and crafts.

Partly no doubt because of the growing numbers of corpses being brought into the city for cremation, the British authorities were at this time becoming increasingly alarmed about the public health hazards of the burning *ghats*. Since the end of the last century it has been consistently proposed that the cremation grounds should be moved away from the crowded city centre; and for at least fifty years local officials have periodically advocated the installation of an electric crematorium. In 1893 this disquiet resulted in the Municipal Board's proclamation that it had the power to close the cremation *ghats*, but this created such a 'great stir' that a second proclamation had to be immediately issued declaring that there was no intention to interfere with either Manikarnika or Harishchandra *ghats*, and 'that it was desired to close only the Assighat which was only occasionally used as a burning ghat and where the burning of the dead was calculated to pollute the water supply' (*Selections from the Vernacular Press*, 1893). The Annual Administration Report for the Benares Municipality for 1925 records that pollution from incompletely incinerated bodies was a major sanitary problem, but concludes with resignation that 'it is impossible to remove the burning ghats from their present location, it is not that the Manikarnika and Harishchandra ghats are there for the city, but that the city is there for the ghats' (quoted in Kumar 1988:68).

To this we might add that if the city is there for the burning *ghats*, the *ghats* are there for the cosmos. But it is not only the proposals of the town-hall bureaucrats to move the cremation ground to the outskirts of the city which threaten to subvert the bond between the place of creation and the place of cremation. That this nexus is a necessary one has – up to a point at least – also been recently contested by some of the sacred specialists themselves.

On a return visit to Banaras in 1981 I learned that in the interim an unlikely coalition of the most powerful pilgrimage-priests (*pandas, tirath-purohits*) in the city had been vigorously campaigning for an end to cremation on the site of Vishnu's footsteps. Representations had been made to the district authorities, the authenticity of the practice had been questioned through a letter campaign to the local press, and demonstrations had been staged on the *ghat* itself during which heavy pressure had been exerted on those mourners who had intended to cremate at Charan Paduka. The son of the *panda* with 'the red seal' of the Raja of Nepal, a close affinal relative of his arch-rival Anjaninandan Mishra (the most powerful pilgrimage-priest in the city), and the present incumbent of what is generally acknowledged to be the 'throne' of Kashi's oldest line of *tirath-purohits*, had been arrested – the latter for lying on top of a newly constructed pyre and insisting that the mourners would have to burn him along with their corpse.

The main instigator of this agitation was Anjaninandan Mishra; and what had brought about the unexpected alliance with his oldest and bitterest competitor was – as everybody else saw it – a matter of simple material interest. As will become clear in the next chapter, the *pandas* have no part in, and derive no profits from, the cremation rituals themselves. But they do derive a substantial income from those who come to the *ghat* to bathe and to make offerings on the banks of the Ganges. These offerings are collected by a *ghatiya*, who sits near the side of the river on a wooden platform (*chauki*) under a leaf umbrella, and who at Manikarnika is generally an employee of one of the big-time *pandas*. The crux of the matter was alleged to be that between them Anjaninandan and Gajanand (the *panda* of Nepal) own the majority of the *chaukis* immediately below the footsteps of Vishnu, and that when a body is burned there, the pilgrims and *ghatiyas* are smoked out. As the number of cremations at Charan Paduka has steadily grown, their income from the *ghat* has declined. Anjaninandan, moreover, had effective control of a grandiose property nearby (a princely endowment) which was being damaged by the heat and smoke from the pyres.

The explanation which most of the *pandas* privately gave for their support of Anjaninandan's campaign was phrased in terms of numbers. The problem was not only the nuisance value of so many cremations so close to the sacred tank to which they conducted so many pilgrims, but also the class of corpse which was now being accorded the privilege of being burned on the footsteps of Vishnu. In the British period this privilege had been restricted to an exclusive elite – to rajas and maharajas, and to the cream of the city's banking and merchant families. All cremations had to be sanctioned by the District Magistrate; and a family which had not previously held the right would only be admitted to the club if their application was endorsed by two other members of it. By now, however, authority to sanction cremation at Charan Paduka had been delegated to the local police station, and permission was being granted to ever-increasing numbers. As the *pandas* saw it, then, all sorts of riff-raff were now being burnt at the feet of Vishnu – social climbers and upstart politicians, even Untouchables like the father of the Dom Raja. It was this sense that the dignity of the place was being compromised by the undignified character of the corpses cremated there which justified the agitation, rather than any sense of the impropriety of past practice.

But in modern India this was not, of course, the way in which they could appropriately put their case across in the press. The main strategy of their letter campaign was rather to deny that cremation at Charan Paduka had any authentic scriptural sanction, and to claim that such a socially divisive practice should therefore be abandoned as entirely out of keeping with the spirit of the times.

These arguments were clearly spelled out in an opening salvo to the correspondence columns of the daily newspaper *Aj* from Anjaninandan Mishra himself.[5] We are dealing, he claimed, with a tradition invented in the early 1860s for 'the self-aggrandisement of sycophants of the British raj'. In any event, the practice could not possibly be ancient since Manikarnika had only become a cremation *ghat* at the time of the death of Kashmiri Mal's mother. Seeing that the Khatris had their own special plot for burning their dead, other elite families felt that their prestige demanded that they too have a place of their own. The site selected belonged to the *tirath-purohit* Mahendar Nath Sukul, and it was agreed that he should receive Rs. 100 for every corpse cremated on it. Originally such cremations were extremely few, and the pyres had all been of (sweet-smelling) sandalwood. But now the numbers were such that the practice had become a serious public nuisance. If, moreover, one starts from the (false) premise that cremation at Charan Paduka does indeed have religious significance, in this 'socialistic epoch' it should surely be available to all. What made this last argument particularly ironic was that Anjaninandan had largely orchestrated his campaign through the Hindu Mahasabha of which he was a state-level Vice-President. As a hyper-conservative Hindu-chauvinist political party, the Mahasabha has not generally been associated with championing the cause of greater religious and social equality.

Most of the subsequent correspondence tirelessly repeated the same arguments,[6] though Anjaninandan's letter also drew an infuriated response from Mahendar Nath Sukul pointing out that it was one of his ancestors, not he, who had granted permission for cremation to take place at Charan Paduka, and that there could be no question of their family ever having accepted a fee at the time of cremation – as though they were Doms.[7] (That this denial was not to be credited was a matter of some scandal on the *ghat*.) Mahendar Nath nevertheless declared himself in favour of Anjaninandan's campaign, as did the *mahant* ('chief priest') of the Vishvanath temple who recalled that many years before, the *tirath-purohit* and celebrated Hindi short-story writer, Shiv Prasad Mishra 'Rudra', had done *dharna* (a kind of coercive self-mortification) at Charan Paduka.[8] Whether his objective was to prevent cremation there is not entirely clear, but the result was that Vishnu's (marble) footsteps had been surrounded by an iron railing, and mourners have subsequently had to make do with building their pyres on the sunken area around the railings, rather than on the very footsteps themselves.

Those who opposed cremation at Charan Paduka did not, however, have it entirely their own way. While the majority of *tirath-purohits* had supported Anjaninandan, the majority of Doms and Mahabrahmans (Funeral-priests) – who *do* have a business interest in cremation – had not. Though 'some people will oppose even Tulsi Das's *Ramayana* for their own interest', the fact – as they saw it – was that cremation at Charan Paduka was undoubtedly *shastrik* (that is, textually sanctioned) and has been practised since the time of Vishnu's austerities.

The most articulate and authoritative champion of this side of the argument was Baikunthnath Upadhyay, who is well known throughout the city for his Hindi translations and commentaries on the *Kashi khanda*, and whose views were given an additional credibility by the fact that he was one of the few parties to the dispute who did not have a direct material interest in its outcome. In a letter printed under the caption 'Charan Paduka's existence from time without beginning',[9] Baikunthnath reaffirmed that the site of Vishnu's cosmogonic austerities had always been a place of cremation. Conceding that 'the great cremation ground' is the sacred area *as a whole*, he attempted to square the circle by arguing that at the time when this 'forest of bliss' (*anandvan*, i.e. Kashi) was a deep and impenetrable jungle, ordinary people must have held their cremations wherever they could. Only rajas and maharajas would have had the means and the manpower to penetrate to its very heart, and they would have unquestionably done so in order to cremate their dead at the world's original *tirath*.[10]

Both sides in the argument, then, invoked a version of the past compatible with their material interests, and both could legitimately claim that matters of important principle were at stake: a practice that had existed from time without beginning should at all costs be perpetuated; a practice that had become debased by interlopers who were unworthy of it should now be abandoned. Though one version of how Manikarnika became a cremation ground may look more like 'real' history than the other, it almost certainly contains elements which are from a historical point of view quite as fictional. While in all probability cremation at Charan Paduka was indeed a nineteenth-century invention of tradition, the clinching argument which 'proved' this beyond doubt – the argument that, prior to Kashmiri Mal, Manikarnika had never been a cremation ground – is unlikely.[11]

Not only should we be wary of accepting either version of events as authentic 'history', but we should also perhaps be cautious about uncritically crediting the stark opposition implied between the 'ideological' discourses in terms of which people justify their actions, and the 'real' material interests which actually explain them. My informants sometimes seem to be quite as culturally prone as the most die-hard of classical economists to attribute to others the most crassly material of motives. It is after all the black age of the *Kali Yuga*. The language of material self-gain is – in a sense – as much a part of the ideology as the language of purity and renunciation. Not that it is a 'value' in the sense of something which is valorised (though in some contexts it is); but it is certainly a pervasive representation of the ways of the world, and also commonly a false one. Whether true or false, the popular conviction that Anjaninandan and his rival were prompted only by pecuniary considerations therefore belongs to the realm of cultural assumptions about human behaviour.

Immediately after the initial agitation, cremation at Charan Paduka was suspended for several months, though no formal prohibition was issued. By the time of my 1981 visit the practice had been resumed – though now under police guard, and on a much reduced scale. By 1992, however, the area surrounding the footsteps had been enshrined under a gazebo-like structure within which cremation is plainly impossible.

So where does all this leave the thesis of the previous chapter – that it is 'symbolically appropriate' that the scene of Vishnu's cosmogonic austerities should also be the pre-eminent place for cremation? Surely the evidence indicates that the connection between them is contested? This is correct, but only within narrow limits. No more than others do Banarasis inhabit a seamless ideological world. Different discourses are available. According to a 'mythological'/'ritual' discourse the relationship between cremation and Vishnu's footsteps is a necessary one; while according to a 'historical' discourse it is merely a contingent product of the 'self-aggrandisement of sycophants of the British raj'. People choose between them according to their ideal and material interests.

The 'narrow limits' referred to are best explained by anticipating another apparent difficulty – the possibility that what the data actually suggest is that the burden of reproducing the cosmos is a royal prerogative. It is not every cremation which re-enacts cosmogony, but only those of the privileged few who are burnt on the footsteps of Vishnu.

While it is admittedly clear that cremation at Charan Paduka stakes a claim to a special identification with Vishnu's creative power, it is I think equally clear that cremation is creation in the general case also. It is, as I have argued, a sacrificial ritual, and as such a repetition of cosmogony. *Both* cremation grounds are associated with a tank which is claimed to be the 'real' site of Vishnu's austerities, and none of those who questioned the propriety of building pyres over the actual footsteps of Vishnu was prepared to countenance a complete rupture which would re-locate the burning *ghat* at an altogether different site.

Moreover, the mythological associations of that part of Manikarnika where the vast majority of corpses are burned, and which is set slightly apart from Charan Paduka, reaffirm the relationship between cremation and cosmic conflagration and renewal. This segment of Manikarnika is known as Jalsayin *ghat*. Jalsayin – 'the sleeper on the waters' – is an epithet of Vishnu (Narayana), and the name evokes yet another well-known account of the world's creation and destruction. During the period of cosmic dissolution Vishnu sleeps on the waters on a serpent couch, the coils of the serpent – Shesha – symbolising the endless cycles of time. Shesha is a form of Vishnu himself. His breath destroys the three worlds at *pralay* (doomsday), the ashes of the cosmos sinking into the primal waters. Only Vishnu/Shesha remains. Indeed Shesha actually means 'remainder', the body of the sleeping Vishnu containing the seeds – as it were – of the dormant cosmos. A lotus grows out of his navel; and Brahma emerges from the lotus to create the world. No less than on the footsteps themselves, here too cremation takes place at a site associated with the creation (and dissolution) of the cosmos. The 'remainder' of the corpse – the *shesh(a)* as it is sometimes explicitly called – is offered into the water at the end of cremation as the seed of future renewal. The dispute over whether Vishnu's footsteps should remain a cremation site for the elite, I conclude, could not seriously compromise the association between cremation and cosmogony. The message is repeated with too much redundancy for that.

2.4 The scale of the business

As we have seen (p. 23), many pious Hindus of advanced years move to Banaras to live out what remains of their lives in the disciplined and abstemious manner befitting those who aspire to the privilege of dying there – a daily round of rising before dawn, a bath in the Ganges, a single meal a day, of temple visits and other religious observances. The total number of these Kashi-*vasis* is difficult to estimate, though it is certainly to be reckoned in four figures.

Many are widows who come – often one suspects with some encouragement from their in-laws – to expiate the bad karma to which the prior death of their husband testifies. On the authority of the *Kashi khanda* (chapter 52), it is sometimes claimed that those who are unable to take up residence in Kashi themselves can gain the merit of Kashi-*vas* by meeting the expenses of another. Though the majority of the widows I encountered did not in fact receive any meaningful material support from their kin, it is possible that those who do are the (somewhat dubious) beneficiaries of this notion, which is what encouraged their family to dispatch them in the first place. More confidently, I can record that several widows told me that they were not the first in their husband's household to become a Kashi-*vasi* – suggesting that some families have a tradition of sending supernumerary widows to the city.

Out of the 440 Kashi-*vasi* widows in the survey on which Saraswati (1985) reports, 33.6 per cent were from Bengal, 16.1 per cent from Nepal and a further 12.3 per cent from the Maithil area of Bihar. The remainder were of very heterogeneous origins. Nearly three quarters of the total sample (72.28 per cent) were Brahmans, and most of the rest belonged to one of the Vaishya merchant castes (22.27 per cent). The majority came from comparatively prosperous rural backgrounds, and over 60 per cent were childless (presumably because those without children have less to keep them in their affinal home, and possibly more to encourage their departure).

Some of these widows (around one quarter in Saraswati's survey) reside with kin in the city; a few in the house where they are employed as a domestic servant, and some in one of the religious refuges (*maths* or *ashrams*) which cater for Kashi-*vasis* (often from one particular linguistic region). But the majority live alone in rented rooms. In the past an affluent widow might make an annuity agreement with a temple or a pilgrimage-priest – handing over her property in return for subsistence until death (cf. Greaves 1909:109; Nevill 1909:91). I personally knew of only one such arrangement however. Most of the widows I encountered had no property to offer, and those with whom I discussed the matter claimed that even if they had, they would be far too wary of the *pandas'* reputation to do so. For their part, the *pandas* expressed themselves equally reluctant, one informant with a very substantial south Indian clientele claiming that he had on several occasions been approached to provide sanctuary to a rich widow on such terms, but that he had always declined to take on such an unpredictably open-ended commitment.

Most Kashi-*vasi* widows have the right to a small pension from the state government (Rs. 40 in 1976); though not all them are able to collect it, and those that can may find that it is subject to free-lance deductions from the clerk or postman. Some support themselves through domestic service; some by cooking for an ascetic or for bereaved families during mourning, while –

according to Saraswati – many derive at least a subsidiary income from begging.

Though Kashi has long been associated both with the penance of widowhood and with the cremation of corpses, it would appear that in the years leading up to its legal suppression, *sati* was not a particularly prevalent practice in the city. Out of the 8,134 widows who are recorded as having immolated themselves on their husbands' funeral pyres in Bengal Presidency between 1815 and 1826, less than 2 per cent are accounted for by the Banaras figures. This represented an average of fourteen cases a year, as compared with thirty for the adjacent district of Ghazipur and twenty-six for Gorakhpur.[12] While *sati* was not specifically, or exclusively, a high-caste phenomenon, in Banaras the overwhelming majority involved upper-caste – and especially Brahman – widows, many with Bengali names (Yang 1987). Though today there are many *sati* shrines in the city, these appear to be treated as repositories of a generalised power, and almost every trace of the individuality of the specific woman whose death is commemorated has been obliterated.

In the past it would seem that a large proportion of those who were brought into the city on their death-beds to reap 'the profit of Kashi' (Kashi-*labh*) were taken direct to the *ghats* where they lay in the open or in a makeshift hut. In the first half of the nineteenth century, Baptist missionaries in Bengal mounted a vigorous campaign against these '*ghat*-murders', alleging that the practice hastened death in a majority of cases, and was consciously intended to promote it in a few (Peggs 1848). Legislation was enacted to prevent such exposures (Bayly 1981:172). But whatever its technical legality, the dying still continue to be brought to the *ghats* – though probably in far smaller numbers than formerly. Others stay with their *panda*, with friends or relatives, in one of the *maths* (monastic refuges) or regular *dharamshalas* (pilgrim lodges), or in the precincts of a temple.

Today, however, the majority – I guess between a half and three-quarters of the total – are taken to one of the hospices specifically intended for the dying. The three principal ones are the Kashi-labh Mukti Bhavan (founded in 1958 by a charitable trust set up by a Marwari family with industrial and business interests all over India), the Ganga-labh Bhavan (founded in the 1930s by a Calcutta business family), and – on a much smaller scale – the Manikarnika Seva Ashram (built a few years later out of funds accumulated through the initiative of a local ascetic, and now run with backing from a pious Bengali trader). Apart from a nominal charge for electricity and cleaning, all of these institutions are free; and one of them provides a number of services including chanted *kirtan* ('devotional songs') and recitations of the *Ramayana* piped day and night through loudspeakers to all rooms.

A total of 558 patients passed through these three institutions during the calendar year 1976.[13] Of these, 257 (46.1 per cent) were male and 301 (53.9 per cent) female. Brahmans accounted for 264 (47.3 per cent) of the total, and Rajputs/Thakurs for 133 (23.8 per cent). The remaining 161 represented 27 different castes and included several untouchables (about 3 per cent). Almost all of the latter, however, appear in the records of one hospice which has a room specifically reserved for untouchables.[14] Though people are notoriously vague about ages, the overwhelming majority were declared as being over 70; the majority were accompanied by three or more relatives, and nearly half died within three days of arrival (and just over 60 per cent within six days).[15]

The areas from which these 558 patients had travelled is summarised on Map 3. Fifty-nine of them came from Banaras district itself; and a further forty-nine from other districts of eastern U.P. Apart from eight from Bengal, two from Madya Pradesh and two from Rajasthan, all the rest (436 or around 80 per cent) were from Bihar.[16] Even more striking is that a single district (Rohtas) provided over half of the total for all areas (293 or 52.5 per cent). The picture is even more pronounced if we look at the old administrative district of Shahabad – which incorporated the present-day districts of Rohtas and Bhojpur. This area accounts for 63.35 per cent of the total. Though something of this bias may be explained by the fact that the (extremely sympathetic) manager of one of the bigger hospices is himself from Rohtas, this is certainly not an adequate explanation. But for want of proper ethnographic information I am at a loss to provide one. This over-representation does, however, offer an interesting contrast with the cremation statistics where Rohtas's contribution to the total is – as we shall see – comparatively modest, and where the Uttar Pradesh district of Jaunpur occupies a similar position of dominance.

Partly on account of the numbers of the elderly and dying, partly because the constant tide of pilgrims, corpses and mourners makes the city a nodal point for the transmission of epidemic disease, Banaras's death rate, though declining, has been consistently higher than all other major cities in the region, and in many years higher than the birth rate (Nevill 1909: table 3; R. L. Singh 1955:54; Bayly 1981:161; Arnold 1989). The highest rates of all are found in the central areas of the city around Manikarnika *ghat* (Singh 1955:79).

At the time of my fieldwork an average of around eighty Hindu corpses a day were being disposed of in Banaras, the vast majority at the two main cremation grounds. Of the latter, nearly three-quarters had been brought into the city from elsewhere. From the nearby villages they are carried; from further away they travel by cycle-rickshaw, taxi, lorry, bus or – very exceptional cases – by air. Several of the nearby towns have bus companies which specialise in the transport of corpses – 'The Last Rites Mail', 'The Heaven Express', and the more prosaically named 'Corpse Waggon' from Jaunpur. Alternatively the 36 mile journey from Jaunpur is made by the corpse and one or two mourners in a cycle-rickshaw (at a cost of around Rs. 40 in 1977) – the other mourners following on by train.

The numbers and provenance of the corpses cremated (or sometimes immersed) at Manikarnika and Harishchandra *ghats* is shown in Table 1 for selected years between 1917–18 and 1989. What is immediately apparent is a pattern of steady growth, from an annual total of nearly 12,000 and a daily

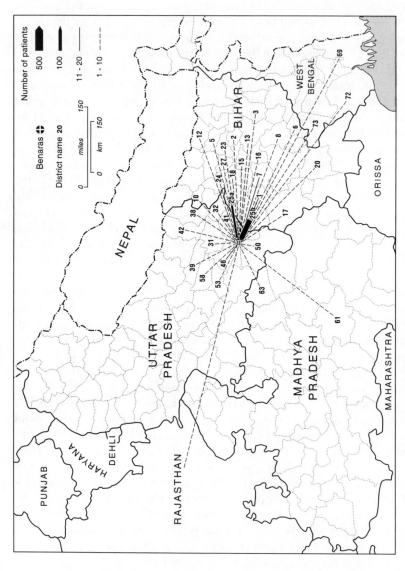

Map 3 Districts of origin of 558 people brought for Kashi-*labh* in 1976

Key to map 3

Map ref.	District	No. of patients
BIHAR		
1	Aurangabad	13
2	Begusarai	1
3	Bhagalpur	6
5	Dharbhanga	1
6	Dhanbad	1
7	Gaya	17
8	Giridih	1
10	Gopalganj	4
12	Madhubani	1
13	Munger	7
15	Nalanda	8
16	Newada	10
17	Palamu	3
18	Patna	5
20	Ranchi	1
23	Sambalpur	2
24	Saran	3
25a	Bhojpur	58
25b	Rohtas	293
27	Vaishali	1
UTTAR PRADESH		
31	Azamgarh	6
32	Ballia	4
34	Banaras	59
38	Deoria	8
39	Faizabad	2
41	Ghazipur	4
42	Gorakhpur	1
46	Jaunpur	12
50	Mirzapur	10
53	Pratapgarh	1
58	Sultanpur	1
MADHYA PRADESH		
61	Mandla	1
63	Rewa	1
BENGAL		
69	Calcutta	1
72	Medinipur	1
73	Puruliya	6
RAJASTHAN		
	District not specified	2
CANNOT IDENTIFY		2

Table 1. *Geographical origins of corpses brought to the two cremation ghats*

	Outside district		District Banaras		City Banaras		Total by *ghat*		Combined total	Daily average
	M. karnika	H. chandra	M. karnika	H. chandra	M. karnika	H. chandra	M. karnika	H. chandra		
1917–18	1,104 (9.3%)		3,995 (33.8%)		6,729 (56.9%)		not available		11,828	32.4
1927–8	1,085		4,018		not obtained				11,472	31.4
1937–8	1,772 (15.5%)	Blank register	3,257 (28.4%)	1,100 (9.6%)	4,236 (36.9%)	1,107 (9.6%)	9,265	2,207		
1943–4	3,061	37	4,395	1,309	not obtained					
1948–9	3,567 (20.8%)	126 (0.7%)	4,269 (24.9%)	1,633 (9.5%)	5,856 (34.1%)	1,704 (9.9%)	13,692 (79.8%)	3,463 (20.2%)	17,155	47.0
1956–7	4,890 (27.9%)	90 (0.5%)	5,520 (31.5%)	1,437 (8.2%)	4,402 (25.1%)	1,170 (6.7%)	14,812 (84.6%)	2,697 (15.4%)	17,509	48.0
1966–7	6,887 (34.4%)	58 (0.3%)	5,503 (27.5%)	1,417 (7.1%)	4,725 (23.6%)	1,437 (7.2%)	17,115 (85.5%)	2,912 (14.5%)	20,027	54.9
1970–1	8,500 (33.9%)	316 (1.3%)	7,191 (28.7%)	2,011 (8.0%)	5,249 (20.9%)	1,797 (7.2%)	20,940 (83.5%)	4,124 (16.5%)	25,064	68.7
1976–7	9,810 (36.7%)	208 (0.8%)	6,957 (26.0%)	2,239 (8.4%)	5,713 (21.4%)	1,777 (6.7%)	22,480 (84.2%)	4,224 (15.8%)	26,704	73.2
1985	12,500 (38.0%)	487 (1.5%)	8,508 (25.9%)	3,433 (10.4%)	5,370 (16.3%)	2,598 (7.9%)	26,378 (80.2%)	6,518 (19.8%)	32,896	90.1
1986	10,813 (39.4%)	455 (1.7%)	6,566 (23.9%)	2,982 (10.9%)	4,383 (16.0%)	2,232 (8.1%)	21,762 (79.3%)	5,669 (20.7%)	27,431	75.2
1987	11,359 (36.9%)	574 (1.9%)	7,773 (25.2%)	3,759 (12.2%)	4,724 (15.3%)	2,608 (8.5%)	23,856 (77.5%)	6,941 (22.5%)	30,797	84.4
1988	10,644 (36.5%)	603 (2.1%)	7,479 (25.7%)	3,763 (12.9%)	4,276 (14.7%)	2,370 (8.1%)	22,399 (76.9%)	6,736 (23.1%)	29,135	79.8
1989	10,224 (34.2%)	2,320 (7.8%)	6,400 (21.4%)	4,179 (14.0%)	3,964 (13.3%)	2,776 (9.3%)	20,588 (68.9%)	9,275 (31.1%)	29,863	81.8

average of around thirty-two in 1917–18, to an annual total of nearly 33,000 and a daily average of over ninety in 1985. The most significant increase has been in the number of corpses brought from outside the city and district of Banaras. Though Banaras's population grew from around 200,000 in 1917 to around 650,000 in 1976, the number of city corpses cremated at Manikarnika and Harishchandra *ghats* has remained remarkably stable. Indeed it is striking that there is hardly any difference between their aggregates in 1917–18 and 1989 – presumably a reflection of the declining death-rate. As a *proportion* of the total number of cremations, however, the city figures show a steady decline – from 56.9 per cent in 1917–18 to 22.6 per cent in 1989. With regard to corpses brought from outside the city, but from within the district of Banaras, the picture is almost the reverse – the absolute numbers grow steadily (from 3,995 in 1917–18 to a high point of 11,941 in 1985); but across all years the proportion of the total varies only within a range of 6 per cent. In the case of the figures for those brought from outside both city and district, the pattern is again different. There is a marked increase both in terms of absolute numbers and in terms of the proportion of the total. In 1917–18, 1,104 outsider corpses arrived at Manikarnika and Harishchandra *ghats* (9.3 per cent of the total); in 1989 the number was 12,544 (42 per cent of the total).

Table 2 focuses on this last category in more detail. Despite a sudden spurt in the popularity of Harishchandra *ghat* in 1989 (on which I will comment shortly), it is clearly Manikarnika *ghat* which has the greater prestige with outsiders. In 1976–7, the vast majority of these outsiders were from various districts in Uttar Pradesh, which contributed 8,350 (83.3 per cent) out of the 10,018 corpses brought into Banaras from outside the district. A further 1,638 (16.4 per cent) came from Bihar, but only four from the neighbouring state of Madhya Pradesh. Ten were from more distant states,[17] and two from outside India.[18]

Map 4 shows the area of origin of the 60,264 corpses brought to the two Banaras burning *ghats* during the eleven years between 1917–18 and 1976–7 for which I have the relevant information. Comparison between Map 5 (the 1917–18 data) and Map 6 (the 1976–7 data) confirms the commonsense expectation that over time the number, distance and diversity of their point of origin has increased. Predictably, too, these maps show that it is overwhelmingly the nearest districts which are most strongly represented in the figures – though less predictably there turns out to be a very considerable variation between them.

This point is made most clearly by Table 3 which shows the numbers of corpses originating from the five districts which share a common border with district Banaras, from nearby Azamgarh (which shows up strongly in the figures), and from Bhojpur (formerly part of the same district as Rohtas, making the two sets of figures difficult to unscramble). In aggregate, this area accounted for 99.1 per cent of the total in 1917–18, and for 93.8 per cent in 1976–7. What is more remarkable, however, is the contrast between district

Table 2. *Corpses brought from outside the city and district of Banaras*

Year	Manikarnika	Harishchandra	Combined total
1917–18	no separate record		1,104
1927–8	ditto		1,085
1930–1	ditto		2,020
1931–2	ditto		1,215
1932–3	ditto		1,034
1933–4	ditto		1,467
1934–5	ditto		1,475
1937–8	1,772	blank register	1,772(?)
1938–9	2,027	13	2,040
1940–1	2,045	20	2,065
1941–2	1,551	25	1,576
1942–3	2,537	15	2,552
1943–4	3,061	37	3,098
1944–5	5,319	29	5,348
1948–9	3,567	126	3,693
1951–2	3,940	34	3,974
1956–7	4,890	90	4,980
1960–1	4,741	not obtained	—
1961–2	7,819	64	7,883
1963–4	6,686	not obtained	—
1964–5	7,101	not obtained	—
1965–6	7,923	79	8,002
1966–7	6,887	58	6,945
1968–9	8,133	95	8,228
1969–70	8,931	108	9,039
1970–1	8,500	316	8,816
1976–7	9,810	208	10,018
1985	12,500	487	12,987
1986	10,813	455	11,268
1987	11,359	574	11,933
1988	10,644	603	11,247
1989	10,224	2,320	12,544

Note to Tables 1 and 2
The 1917–77 figures were collected by myself with the extraordinarily patient help of Om Prakash Sharma. For the 1985–9 figures I am indebted to Sara Ahmed, and I gratefully acknowledge her permission to cite such hard-won data. Both sets of statistics are abstracted from the registers of the municipal clerks on 24-hour duty at the cremation *ghats*, these being held at the office of the Nagar Mahapalika.

A patchy record goes back to 1891, but the first systematic registers date from 1917–18. Before 1937–8 there was no separate record for Harishchandra *ghat*. The clerk at Manikarnika was supposed to enter cremations at both *ghats* – though it seems likely that many of those performed at Harishchandra were never registered. For the purposes of these records the year runs from 1 April to 31 March, and my own figures reflect this convention.

Table 3. *Corpses from adjacent districts*

District	1917/18	1937/8	1938/9	1948/9	1951/2	1956/7	1961/2	1966/7	1969/70	1970/1	1976/7	Total of 11 years	%total of outsiders in these years
Jaunpur	983 (89.0%)	1,467 (82.8%)	1,707 (83.7%)	2,663 (72.1%)	3,112 (78.3%)	3,778 (75.9%)	5,311 (67.4%)	4,514 (65.0%)	5,471 (60.5%)	4,933 (56.0%)	5,692 (56.8%)	39,632	65.8%
Mirzapur	70 (6.3%)	51 (2.8%)	52 (2.5%)	177 (4.8%)	226 (5.7%)	221 (4.4%)	420 (5.3%)	328 (4.7%)	371 (4.1%)	520 (5.9%)	579 (5.8%)	3,015	5.0%
Shahabad (Rohtas and Bhojpur)	9 (0.8%)	48 (2.7%)	37 (1.8%)	204 (5.5%)	193 (4.9%)	346 (6.9%)	700 (8.9%)	725 (10.4%)	1,142 (12.6%)	1,360 (15.4%)	1,413 (14.1%)	6,177	10.25%
Azamgarh	31 (2.8%)	95 (5.4%)	123 (6.0%)	222 (6.0%)	273 (6.9%)	551 (11.1%)	1,060 (13.4%)	1,027 (14.8%)	1,488 (16.5%)	1,456 (16.5%)	1,636 (16.3%)	7,962	13.2%
Ghazipur	1 (0.1%)	2 (0.1%)	3 (0.1%)	3 (0.1%)	8 (0.2%)	5 (0.1%)	36 (0.5%)	22 (0.3%)	64 (0.7%)	53 (0.6%)	68 (0.7%)	265	0.4%
Allahabad	1 (0.1%)	—	1 (0.05%)	3 (0.1%)	1 (0.03%)	—	6 (0.07%)	3 (0.04%)	5 (0.06%)	8 (0.1%)	12 (0.1%)	40	0.1%
Combined % annual total of outsiders	99.1	93.9	94.2	88.5	96.1	98.5	95.5	95.3	94.5	94.4	93.8		

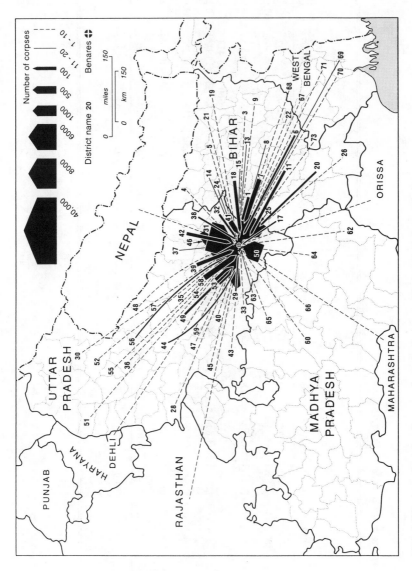

Map 4 Districts of origin of corpses brought for cremation in selected years between 1917–18 and 1976–7

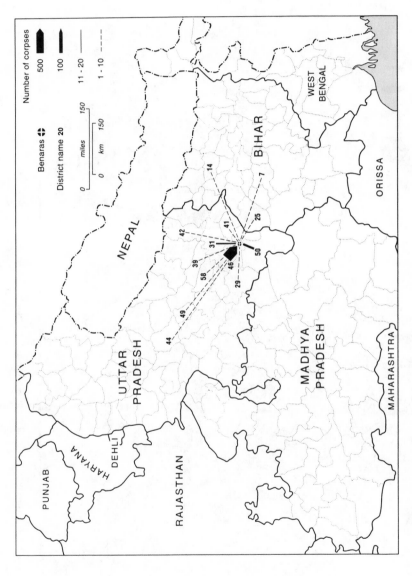

Map 5 Districts of origin of corpses brought for cremation in 1917–18

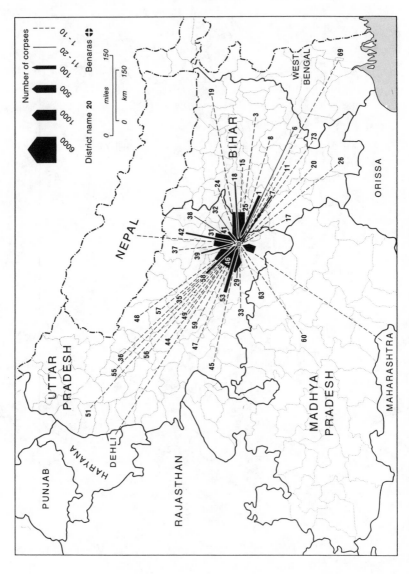

Map 6 Districts of origin of corpses brought for cremation in 1976–7

Key to maps 4, 5 and 6*

Map ref.	District	Aggregate 11 yrs† (Map 4)	1976–7 (Map 6)	1917–18 (Map 5)
BIHAR				
1	Aurangabad	98	98	
3	Bhagalpur	2	1	
4	Champaran (E and W)	3		
5	Darbhanga	2		
6	Dhanbad	59	20	
7	Gaya	234	27	2
8	Giridih	14	10	
9	Godda	3		
11	Hazaribhag	90	7	
13	Munger	11		
14	Muzaffarpur	13		1
15	Nalanda	10	8	
17	Palamu	30	9	
18	Patna	141	31	
19	Purnia	1	1	
20	Ranchi	56	9	
21	Saharsa	1		
22	Santal Pargana	7		
24	Saran	16	3	
25	Shahabad (Rohtas and Bhojpur)	6,177	1,413	9
26	Singhbhum	1	1	
UTTAR PRADESH				
28	Agra	1		
29	Allahabad	40	12	1
30	Almora	1		
31	Azamgarh	7,962	1,636	31
32	Ballia	55	17	
33	Banda	2	1	
34	State Banaras‡	604		
35	Bara Banki	6	2	
36	Bareilly	5	4	
37	Basti	18	9	
38	Deoria	38	14	
39	Faizabad	165	41	1
40	Fatehpur	1		
41	Ghazipur	265	68	1
42	Gorakhpur	132	45	1
43	Hamirpur	1		
44	Hardoi	29	4	1

45	Jalaun	1	1	
46	Jaunpur	39,632	5,692	983
47	Kanpur (both)	7	2	
48	Kheri	6	1	
49	Lucknow	80	10	1
50	Mirzapur	3,015	579	70
51	Muzzafarnagar	5	4	
52	Naini Tal	1		
53	Pratapgarh	740	136	
54	Rae Bareli	6		
55	Rampur	1	1	
56	Shahjahanpur	24	1	
57	Sitapur	8	1	
58	Sultanpur	334	67	2
59	Unnao	3	2	

MADHYA PRADESH

60	Jabalpur	5	1	
62	Raigarh	1		
63	Rewa	11	3	
64	Sarguja	3		
65	Satna	3		
66	Shahdol	1		

BENGAL

67	Bardhaman	4		
68	Birbhum	1		
69	Calcutta	15	1	
70	Haora	1		
71	Hugli	3		
73	Puruliya	3	1	

OTHER STATES:
MYSORE 1
RAJASTHAN 1
DELHI 5 1
TAMILNADU 1
MAHARASHTRA 7 7
ORISSA 1

OUTSIDE INDIA:
NEPAL 1 1
UK 1 1

CANNOT IDENTIFY 38 14

Total 60,264 10,018 1,104

*Districts which are not listed do not appear in the records. Some district boundaries have changed, and some previous districts have been subdivided, but this does not significantly affect the general pattern of distribution. With the exception of Shahabad and State Banaras, all the district names listed were those current in the late 1970s.
†The eleven years covered by map 4 are 1917–18, 1937–8, 1938–9, 1948–9, 1951–2, 1956–7, 1961–2, 1966–7, 1969–70, 1970–1 and 1976–7.
‡State Banaras consisted of two small disjointed enclaves which were incorporated into the rest of the district in 1952. Up to that point, corpses from these areas are counted as 'outsiders'.

Jaunpur and districts Ghazipur and Allahabad. In 1917–18, Jaunpur had provided 89 per cent of the total number of corpses which had come into Banaras from outside. By 1976–7 this proportion had decreased to 56.8 per cent of the total, though the actual number had increased from 984 to 5,692. In comparison, Ghazipur and Allahabad together have never accounted for as much as 1 per cent. Though I do not know what really accounts for this fact, I am confident that it is not simply down to the state of the roads. Nor is it a straightforward function of population size.[19] With regard to Allahabad, it seems likely that the greater proximity of the major pilgrimage centre of Pryag – which has pre-eminence as a place to immerse the ashes of the deceased – detracts from the prestige of cremation in Kashi.

The pattern which has begun to emerge is complex and untidy. The widows who come to Banaras for Kashi-*vas* are most likely to be from Bengal or Nepal; those who are brought for Kashi-*labh* are most likely to come from Bihar (and specifically from Rohtas), while most of the corpses which are brought into the city from outside are from eastern UP (in particular from Jaunpur). Given the number of Rohtas people who come for Kashi-*labh*, it is perhaps surprising that the district's contribution in corpses is comparatively modest. Given its contribution to the cremation statistics, it is perhaps surprising that rather few Jaunpur people come for Kashi-*labh*;[20] and given that in the matter of *sati* it was apparently more 'orthodox' than Banaras itself, the under-representation of Ghazipur in both sets of figures is puzzling. What generates such variation is, in the present state of our ethnographic knowledge of the region, unclear.[21] With regard to the Rohtas/Jaunpur contrast, much presumably depends on the particular practice established over time as prestigious and proper, the example provided by a handful of elite families resulting in a kind of 'chain migration' of either the terminally ill or of their corpses. It is also possible that pragmatic considerations encourage Rohtas people to bring the dying to Kashi and discourage them from bringing bodies. In the event that death occurs in Banaras, Rohtas mourners generally remain in the city to perform the subsequent rites and are thereby able – I was told – to effect a considerable saving. By contrast the transport of corpses to Banaras may be inhibited by the fact that a bus company offering such a service would require a license to operate in two different states, substantially raising the costs.

Though it is true that the number of corpses arriving at the burning *ghats* has grown at a slower rate than the population of the region as a whole, the rate at which they arrive *from outside the district* has grown much more quickly than both the population and the annual aggregate of Hindu deaths. Even in the case of Jaunpur, however, the bodies of only a small fraction of those who die in any one year are brought to Banaras. I calculate that they amounted to less than 2 per cent of Jaunpur Hindu deaths in 1917–18, rising to around 14 per cent of the total in 1976–7.[22] For all other districts, the ratio would of course be very much smaller. Though it is likely that certain villages have a much stronger tradition of bringing their dead to Banaras than others, it must everywhere be a choice from which comparatively few are privileged to benefit.

What then can be said of these privileged few? The first thing is that they are almost as likely to be female as male – the 1976–7 figures of 46.1 per cent as against 53.9 per cent can be taken as representative. Secondly, the vast majority are middle aged or elderly. Just over 90 per cent of them were reported as being more than 40, and just over 80 per cent as being more than 55. That these figures reflect a positive discrimination in favour of the elderly, rather than merely the average age at death, is suggested by the fact that the age profile of this cohort of outsiders is significantly higher than for people brought from within district Banaras. Of the latter only 74.1 per cent were aged over 40 and 63 per cent over 55. With regard to social class, and rural versus urban background, the records are silent – though for what it is worth my impression is that the greater the distance the corpse has travelled, the more likely it is to have come from a relatively affluent urban milieu.

Caste is systematically recorded only for Harishchandra *ghat*.[23] Quite apart from the possibly dubious veracity of some of the information supplied, the identification of caste names is sometimes problematic, and caste status both disputed and variable over space and time. One thing which is certain, however, is that few are tempted to 'pass' as untouchables, and that their proportion of the total number of entries is therefore unlikely to be over-stated. On the basis of the declared caste affiliation of the 589 corpses from outside the city and district of Banaras which were brought to Harishchandra *ghat* during the five years for which I have the relevant information,[24] I think we can conclude with reasonable assurance that while Brahmans (with around 28 per cent of the entries) were somewhat over-represented in relation to their share of the general population of the region, untouchables were not as badly under-represented as might have been predicted. Around 11 per cent of the entries are easily identifiable as people of untouchable caste (as compared with a figure of around 20 per cent for their share of the population of the region as a whole),[25] and it would be surprising if some of the others were not also untouchables who had chosen to obscure their identity.[26]

The general point emerges even more clearly from the figures for corpses brought into the city from *within* district Banaras. Over the five years for which I have information[27] the proportion of entries which are readily identifiable as people of untouchable caste varies between 18 and 22 per cent of the total – which is almost exactly in line with their share of the population. Since the (cremation *ghat*) Doms at Manikarnika refuse to allow Sweeper Doms (a separate sub-caste) to use the *ghat*, it is possible that the number of untouchables who go to Harishchandra is slightly inflated – but it is very unlikely that this makes any significant difference to the overall pattern. Somewhat counter-intuitively, then, my evidence seems to suggest that the disposal of the dead in Banaras has as much significance for untouchables as for other Hindus, and that the two cremation *ghats* attract significant numbers of those untouchables who can afford to bring their corpses there.

One final aspect of this data deserves comment – the apparently enhanced popularity (especially with outsiders) of Harishchandra *ghat* in 1989. I noted earlier that proposals to instal an electric crematorium have been mooted for at least half a century. These have been consistently opposed both by the Doms (whose whole livelihood is at stake), and by much conservative Hindu opinion. In his commentary on the Manikarnika chapter of the *Kashi khanda*, Baikunthnath Upadhyay spoke out strongly against such an innovation, arguing that it would deprive Lord Shiva of the ash with which he bathes his body, would prevent the chief mourner from performing his duty breaking open the deceased's skull with a bamboo stave midway through the cremation (see pp. 178ff), and would detract from the cremation ground as a place which provides an education in detachment (*vairagya*).

Up until the mid-1980s, these various interests ensured that the project was consistently stalled. But with the death of the old Dom Raja in 1985, and the personal intervention of the then Prime Minister,[28] the balance of influence had decisively shifted by 1986 when Rajiv Gandhi inaugurated the Ganga Action Plan to deal with the increasingly serious problem of river pollution. Much of this problem was attributed to the number of whole or partly incinerated corpses immersed in the river. The installation of a modern crematorium, which would provide a cheaper and more efficient alternative method, was seen as an essential part of the anti-pollution programme. In the face of opposition from, amongst others, Anjaninandan Mishra (who had orchestrated the campaign against cremation at Charan Paduka), an 'electric corpse-burning house' (*Vidhut shavdahgrah*) was at last opened at Harishchandra *ghat* in January 1989 – only to be closed again six months later, ostensibly because 'the chimneys were not high enough and residents of the area complained of air pollution' (Ahmed 1990). Re-opened in November, it had by the following February already catered in the first nine months of its operation for no less than 5,700 cremations (Sara Ahmed, personal communication).[29] Whatever the opposition to it, it is clear that others were voting with their feet.

On my brief visit to Banaras in 1992, the Municipal clerks who record disposals at Harishchandra *ghat* were estimating that the figure for corpses originating from outside the district – the category which has shown the most dramatic increase – was now running at about 4,000 per year. As they saw it, the principal reason for the popularity of the new technology is cost. At current prices, a 'traditional' cremation would probably involve an expenditure of at least Rs. 900. The basic fee for using the crematorium had originally been set at Rs. 100, but this had been reduced to Rs. 50 as a result of political pressure on the Municipal Council. In order to cover its costs, it was said, the crematorium would have to charge Rs. 150. Its use is therefore heavily subsidised.[30]

Not all corpses are cremated. Some are weighted down and immersed in the river. These are the bodies of small children, of most kinds of ascetic and of members of various sectarian groups (e.g. the Kabir-*panthis*), of people who have died from certain diseases or in theory from any kind of 'bad death' (pp. 158ff), or sometimes merely of people who cannot afford the costs of cremation. Some of these are brought to one of the two cremation grounds (and are therefore included in the figures I have been discussing). But corpses can be taken out into mid-stream by boat from any *ghat*. Table 4 shows the number of Hindu corpses which are recorded as having been immersed in the river from *ghats* other than Manikarnika and Harishchandra in selected years between 1937–8 and 1975–6. These impressively high figures almost certainly underestimate the real number of immersions – partly because they exclude those which arrive at one of the two burning *ghats*, partly because the way in which the statistics are compiled means that very few corpses brought from outside the city are likely to be included, and partly because a significant number of these immersions go unrecorded anyway.[31] I have no reason to suppose, however, that under-reporting became more prevalent in the period between my earliest and latest statistics. The steady decline recorded in the final column of the table is in all probability largely an artifact of the increasing numbers of corpses brought in from outside (the vast majority of which are taken to Manikarnika and Harishchandra *ghats*). The second column shows a sharp fall after the mid-1960s. This is possibly partly attributable to the decline in neo-natal and infant mortality as a result of the increasing numbers of hospital confinements. It may also owe something to the fact that smallpox victims were invariably immersed, as commonly were those of epidemic diseases like plague and cholera. Smallpox has been eradicated, plague has ceased to be a major killer, and cholera is now susceptible to more effective treatment and control.

The number of corpses immersed in the river almost certainly underwent a further sharp decline in the 1980s as a result of the Swachh Ganga Abhiyan – the 'Pure Ganges Campaign' which was started by the *mahant* (chief priest) of the Sankat Mochan Temple in 1982, and from which the Ganga Action Plan was a spin-off. As a result of pressure from this 'environmentalist' lobby, immersion is now theoretically prohibited – except, I am told, in the case of *bona fide*

Table 4. *Corpses immersed from other* ghats

Year	Number	% of Hindu city deaths*	% of all Hindu disposals†
1937–8	2,032	25.4 (27.6)	15.0
1948–9	2,143	23.2 (22.1)	11.1
1956–7	1,584	23.2 (22.1)	8.3
1966–7	1,628	22.4 (20.9)	7.5
1970–1	974	12.4 (12.1)	3.7
1975–6**	936	13.4 (?)	?

*The first figure is the total number of immersions expressed as a percentage of the total number of Hindu deaths recorded in the registers kept for each ward. The figure in brackets is obtained by taking the number of city deaths as the sum of the number of immersions plus the number of city corpses shown in Table 1. The slight disparity between them is explained by the fact that some deaths go unreported at the ward office.

†I.e. the percentage of the total number of Hindu corpses immersed or cremated in Banaras *including* those brought in from outside.

**The 1976–7 registers were not yet complete when I worked on the records. I therefore made do with 1975–6, though I do not have the cremation-*ghat* statistics for that year.

ascetics (for whom a certificate authenticating their credentials is required from the head of their ascetic order or from the District Magistrate). For the first couple of years the prohibition was reportedly enforced effectively by police and 'home guard' patrols. The latter were however soon disbanded, patrols by the river police became increasingly easy to evade, and in 1992 my informants were claiming that the *de facto* situation was little different from what it had been ten years before. It was possibly a recognition of failure, then, which prompted the Government of UP's plan to release several hundred flesh-eating turtles into a 12 mile stretch of the Ganges around Banaras in 1988. In the longer term, the re-introduction of the Gharial crocodile was being considered (*Time*, 12 October 1987; *The Independent*, 3 October 1987).

Far larger than the number of bodies immersed are the number of ashes scattered in the river. I find it impossible to estimate how many mourners come to Banaras for this purpose, but it would certainly run into thousands over the course of a year. Others send the ashes by parcel post to their hereditary Pilgimage Priest (or even occasionally care of the city's Chief Postmaster). Most ashes are now immersed before the mortuary rituals of the twelfth day, though this would have often been impossible in the past when travel was more difficult, and when ashes were kept for months – or even years – before being brought to the river. I have no systematic information on where they come from, though my strong impression is that the vast majority are of fairly local origin. Mourners from any distance to the west of Banaras are more likely to go to Pryag or Hardwar, which are even more highly extolled for the disposal of ashes.

Some of those outsiders who have cremated their corpse in Banaras stay on to perform the mortuary rituals of the first twelve days; and some who cremated elsewhere come into the city to perform these rites. At certain seasons large numbers of villagers from the surrounding countryside, accompanied by their exorcists, visit the sacred tank of Pisach Mochan to lay the spirits of the malevolent dead to rest (pp. 242ff). During *pitri paksh* – 'the fortnight of the ancestors' – tens of thousands of pilgrims stop off in Kashi to make rice-balls offerings to their ancestors at Pisach Mochan or on the *ghats* before completing their pilgrimage to Gaya, where they will perform rites for their final 'liberation'.

Most pilgrims to the city have not, however, come in direct connection with a family death. Some are there to expiate a heinous sin (like cow-slaughter); some to rid themselves or the world of inauspicious influences (as, for example, at the time of an eclipse when the city is always packed with pilgrims); some come in search of a specific boon (the conception of a child, the cure of an illness, success in a court case) and others for the generalised merit of the pilgimage. In my experience, however, it is not in practice possible to distinguish 'pragmatic' from 'other-worldly' goals (as Bharadwaj's (1973:162, 169) hypothesis requires us to do). A pilgrim performing the *Panch-kosi* circumambulation of the city explains that she is doing it for the next world but also hopes for some relief to an eye condition. Pilgrimages are performed for the remission of sin, and sin is the cause of backache as well as a bad rebirth. Offerings are made for the contentment of the ancestors in the other-world, but contented ancestors are the source of progeny and prosperity in the here and now.

Whatever their motivation, upwards of a million pilgrims visit Banaras in the course of an average year, and – though the circumstances were unusual – there was one month during my fieldwork when it was conservatively estimated that between 3 and 3.5 million pilgrims passed through Banaras.[32] They come from all over the Hindu world, a local agent of Thomas Cook and Sons specialising in pilgrims from Mauritius and Fiji. At different times of the year the city is overflowing with people from different regions – perhaps 80 or 90,000 Nepalis in the winter month of Pus/Paush; tens of thousands from Andhra Pradesh after the March and July harvests; Pujabis during 'the fortnight of the ancestors', Bengalis in the months of *Kuar* and *Kartik*, Tamils at the festival of Shivaratri, and so on. Many are packed into the house of their *panda*; others stay in one of the *dharamsalas* or pilgrim lodges (which often cater to pilgrims from a particular area). But wherever they have come from, and wherever they stay, one of the rituals they are almost sure to perform during their visit is *pinda dan* – the offering of rice- (or flour-) balls to their departed ancestors.

In one way or another, then, death in Banaras is an extremely big business. I turn now to the way in which that business is organised.

Plate 1 A segment of the Manikarnika bathing *ghat*. (Photograph by Margaret Dickinson.)

Plate 2 Part of the Manikarnika cremation ground. The building on the left is surmounted by a now little-visited Shiva temple. The Dom right-holder and his assistants generally occupy the arcaded lower storey of the building, and the Mahabrahman Funeral-priests often watch out for clients from one of the turrets on the upper storey. The concrete platform in the centre of the picture in the middle distance is used for cremation at times of the year when the river level is high. (Author's photograph.)

Plate 3 Pyres at Manikarnika at the beginning of this century. (Photograph by Dr W. L. Hildburgh *c*. 1902 from the photo library of the Royal Anthropological Institute.)

Plate 4 Pyres on one section of the Manikarnika cremation ground in the late 1970s. The two figures in the centre foreground are Dom Funeral-attendants sifting the ashes for gold and silver. Note also the two corpses by the water's edge at the bottom right of the picture. (Author's photograph.)

PART II

Death as a living

3

Shares and chicanery

This chapter describes the division of mortuary labour between various groups of occupational specialists who earn a living on and around the burning *ghats*, a division of labour which is closely constrained by the ideology of caste.[1] One type of caste specialist is for example required to handle the physical remains of the deceased, another to deal with his marginal and malevolent ghost before its incorporation as an ancestor, while a third type of specialist presides over rituals addressed to the essentially benevolent ancestor.

With regard to the way in which rights are allocated to the individual specialist within each occupational category, there are two broad types of system. One of these operates on the *principle* of a long-term hereditary relationship between the specialist and his patrons – a principle familiar enough from the extensive literature on so-called *jajmani* relations in village India. The other variant essentially consists in a rota system such that the specialist has rights, not to a fixed and hereditary clientele, but rather to provide his service on certain days in the year to all who require it. The effect is to maximise the anonymity and transience of the relationship between the specialist and his patrons, and this in turn does little to inhibit his often frankly venal attitude towards those he serves. In one form or another, it is this second system which is most common amongst the various specialist groups who derive a living from the dead – posing the problem of whether its prevalence should be seen as a product of 'practical reason', or of a cultural template which discourages durable ties with those who handle the most polluting and inauspicious aspects of death.

3.1 Turns to be 'ghosts'

At death the soul becomes a disembodied ghost or *pret*, a hungry and malevolent state dangerous to the survivors. On the twelfth day after death a rite is performed which enables the deceased to rejoin his ancestors and become an ancestor (*pitr*) himself. The Mahabrahman Funeral-priest presides over the rituals addressed to the ghost during the first eleven days after death, and accepts on behalf of the ghost the gifts intended for it. A further set of gifts is made in the name of the newly incorporated ancestor on the twelfth day, and these are accepted by the deceased's hereditary household priest (*kul-purohit*) in the case of city people, or by his hereditary pilgrimage-priest (*tirath-purohit*) in the case of outsiders who have stayed in Banaras to perform the mortuary rituals. The Brahman specialist stands in for the soul he serves – the impure Funeral-priest for the ghost, the relatively pure pilgrimage-priest for the ancestor.

Mahabrahman means 'great Brahman'. The caste is alternatively known as Mahapatra: 'great vessels'. An actor is a *patra*, a 'vessel' for the qualities of the character he plays (Kapur 1985:65). In the drama of death the Funeral-priest is a vessel for the rancorous greed of the ghost. Worshipped as the deceased, he is dressed in the dead man's clothes, is made to wear his spectacles or clutch his walking stick, and is fed his favourite foods. If the deceased was a woman, then a female Mahabrahman should (theoretically) be worshipped and presented with a woman's clothing, cosmetics and jewellery. At a rite which marks the end of the period of the most intense pollution the chief mourner, and then the other male mourners, are tonsured by the Barber. But before even the chief mourner, the Mahabrahman should be shaved as if he – as the *pret* itself – were the one most deeply polluted by the death. There is, as Vidyarthi (1961:47) puts it, a 'shamanistic element' to the eleventh-day rituals at which the *kantha* – or 'thorn' as the Mahabrahman is contemptuously known in Bihar – 'is invited to represent the dead, [and] is said to be possessed by the spirit of the dead. The statements that he makes are believed to be coming from the dead.' For Banaras, I would prefer to speak of half-belief, of the Mahabrahman as an icon of the moribund, embodying and giving voice to his ghost. In any event, it is not merely a matter of the Mahabrahman *representing* the deceased. There is some kind of identity between them, and the rituals make them *consubstantial*.

This is most clearly illustrated by the case of Nepali royal and aristocratic mortuary rites at which the Funeral-priest is fed some of the deceased's ground up bone in a preparation of *khir* (boiled rice and milk), and is then laden down with gifts and banished from the kingdom. After the cremation of King Tribhuvan in 1955, the Mahabrahman lived in the palace for thirteen days, 'sleeping in the King's bed, smoking the King's cigarettes, waited upon and taking what he wished of the King's possessions. The royal kitchens prepared what he desired, but the food was deliberately contaminated by a paste made from the bone of the King's forehead'. At the end of this period he received Rs. 10,000 in 'alms' and gifts worth a further Rs. 200,000 including two elephants and a richly caparisoned horse. Mounted on one of the elephants he left for exile in India. 'The people of Kathmandu and Thankot lined the road to stone him and to jeer . . .' (Leuchtag 1958:236).[2]

Writing of the obsequies performed for the Raja of Tanjore in 1801, and for the two of his queens who immolated themselves on his funeral pyre, the Abbé Dubois recorded that some of the bones of the defunct

> were reduced to powder, mixed with some boiled rice, and eaten by twelve Brahmins. This revolting and unnatural act had for its object the expiation of the sins of the deceased – sins which, according to popular opinion, were transmitted to the bodies of the persons who ate the ashes, and were tempted by money to overcome their repugnance for such disgusting food. At the same time, it is believed that the filthy lucre thus earned can never be attended with much advantage to the recipients. (Dubois 1968:336; originally 1816)

Equally clear, though here the consumption is metaphorical rather than literal, is Babb's north Indian evidence that the Mahabrahman is

> presented with a quantity of *khir* . . . spread in the shape of a human figure on a brass platter. This is then eaten by the Mahabrahman, who starts at the feet and ends up at the head. As he eats the *khir* he cries out from time to time that he cannot continue, that the *khir* has changed to blood. At each interruption the family of the deceased must give him some money to induce him to continue . . . It is said that in eating the *khir* the Mahabrahman is removing the last traces of the deceased from the world and is providing him with the substance for a body in the next . . . (Babb 1975:96–7)

All this is paralleled in the Banaras context by the 'gift of milk' (*payas dan*) which is fed to the Mahabrahman shortly before his departure on the eleventh day, and which again consists of *khir*. Though my Funeral-priest informants never explicitly told me that this particular item represents the substance of the deceased, I think this is a legitimate inference not only from the comparative evidence, but also from the fact that they freely acknowledge that they consume the body of the deceased on the eleventh day; and from their endless complaints about the stomach-turning revoltingness of *payas dan*, its devastatingly awful consequences and their determination to avoid eating if at all possible.

Though unequivocally Brahmans, Mahabrahmans are *pret*-Brahmans – ghost-Brahmans – who are in many contexts treated much like Untouchables, and are described as *achhut* ('not to be touched').[3] No fastidious person of clean caste will dine with them. In theory, they should live outside the village and to the south of it – that is, in the direction of death. Writing of the Banaras rural hinterland in the 1940s, Opler and Singh (1950:474) report they may not even enter the village to beg. With regard to such matters as the consumption of meat and alcohol, and the incidence of widow remarriage and breaches of caste endogamy, they could not it is true be described as paragons of Brahmanical orthodoxy. But nor could many of the other Brahman communities who earn a living on the *ghats*. As they themselves represent it, however, the Mahabrahmans' relative degradation is rather a consequence of the fact that they participate in the death pollution (*sutak*) which afflicts their patrons. Since they have many *jajman* they are – as it were – in a permanent state of impurity.

Not only impure (*ashuddh*), the Mahabrahman is also highly inauspicious (*ashubh*, *amangal*). The one does not always entail the other. Although physical contact with a Sweeper woman would be unambiguously polluting, it is auspicious to see her face as one is embarking on some new enterprise. By contrast, it is at any time inauspicious to set eyes on a Mahabrahman; and if you chance to see one first thing in the morning then somebody in your house may die. You should not even utter their name in the morning. Nor may a Mahabrahman come to your door. 'Nobody', as the proverb has it, 'should have the misfortune that a Mahabrahman cross his threshold'.[4] He is somebody to be kept at bay; somebody to whom – in the custom of certain localities – to throw stones as he departs at the end of the mortuary rituals lest he be tempted to return. Salt should not be put in the food he is served, for salt sets up a relationship with the eater and no relationship should be acknowledged with the *pret* (for whom kinship terms are avoided).

The Mahabrahman is regarded with a mixture of fear and contempt. He is regarded with 'a gaze of hate' (*hay drishti*), is known as the 'bitter one' (*katu*), is said to have no 'lustre' (*kanti*) on his face, and the stereotype contrasts his fabulous wealth with the squalor of his demeanour and life-style. He is treated, say Opler and Singh (1950:474), 'with less respect and consideration than the meanest untouchable'. One Mahabrahman friend resentfully recalls his teachers' taunts that he should leave off school to hang up water-pot dwellings for the ghosts; another tells of a Khatri woman throwing away all the chillies drying on her roof when he went to retrieve the kite which had landed on it.

I should note, however, that the discrimination to which the Mahabrahman is presently subjected did not strike me as being as harsh as all this suggests; and that in practice the situation is much more ambivalent. They are after all Brahmans; although undeniably ill-omened ones. Mahabrahman weddings and other life-cycle rituals are presided over by a 'pure' Brahman. One Mahabrahman sells *pan* (the betel-nut which many Banarasis chew addictively) in a quarter of the city where many people must be aware of his caste; while another runs a tea-shop on the main road which passes through his suburban village.

The rites of the first eleven days after death are conducted on the *ghats* or on the bank of some sacred tank. The Mahabrahman who officiates at these rites will only come to the house of his *jajman* (patron) if he is summoned on the day of the cremation to preside over the offering of five rice-balls made between the door of the house and the funeral pyre. On the following day he directs the hanging of the water-pot which serves as the home for the *pret* in the branches of a sacred *pipal* tree; and he subsequently accompanies the *jajman* there on daily expeditions to offer water and a lighted lamp. He also conducts the offering of one rice-ball each day, each of which creates a different part of a new body for the deceased. This body is completed on the tenth day. On the eleventh day it is fed and the *pret* is now ready to become an ancestor. The Mahabrahman's duties are at an end. He is worshipped, fed, given gifts and departs having smashed the water-pot dwelling of the *pret*.

If cremation is carried out in *panchak* – a block of five consecutive lunar mansions (*nakshattras*) during which it is particularly inauspicious to burn a body – the Mahabrahman presides over the rite of 'pacifying the *panchak*' (*panchak shanti*). In cases of 'untimely death' he superintends – on the eleventh day – the additional rite of *Narayani bali* which has the object of preventing the embittered soul from remaining in *pret* form; and he also performs *putla vidhan* – at which an elaborate effigy of the deceased is constructed and then cremated – for those whose corpses were either lost or immersed in the Ganges. 'Bad deaths' generally represent good income for the Funeral-priest.

This inventory constitutes the maximum elaboration of the Mahabrahman's duties. In most cases there is no question of *panchak shanti*, *Narayani bali* or *putla vidhan*. Of the standard repertoire, the Mahabrahman would only expect to perform the full complement for an important *jajman* from whom he expects a munificent offering. For the majority his services are considerably attenuated, and often amount to no more than attending the rituals of the tenth and eleventh days, scrambling them through with much surreptitious editing when the financial pickings look slim, and accepting the gifts with more or less bad grace.

My description requires two further qualifications. The first is that some middle-ranking castes dispense with the rituals of the eleventh day and bid the Mahabrahman farewell on the tenth; while in certain exceptional circumstances the rites are telescoped into a three-day period. The second is that I have spoken of the Mahabrahman 'conducting' or 'presiding over' the rituals when in fact those of the well-to-do are often directed by a *karam-kandi* (a professional ritualist of relatively 'good' Brahmanical status), and the Mahabrahman is merely there to accept the *gifts* (*dan*) and offer his blessings. For his service the *karam-kandi* receives a *fee*, a *dakshina* (see p. 130). The city supports scores of such ritual technicians, but there are twenty-five or so who have a particular name for their expertise in the conduct of mortuary rites. Their services are sought after by those who can afford them, for it is an open secret that most Mahabrahman are not competent to pronounce the Sanskrit in a way acceptable to the gods or to get the complicated ritual sequences right, and that only village hicks and city cynics could be satisfied with their half-hearted endeavours.

The Mahabrahman's presence is, however, essential. He confers salvation, and allows the soul to 'swim across' to the other world. For the successful conclusion of the rites he must be satisfied with the gifts offered. 'His belly must be full', though on such occasions he is seemingly insatiable. Without his blessing the deceased will remain in the limbo of *pret*-hood to plague his family with misfortune and further bereavement; with it their descent line can prosper and increase. His curse is greatly feared, a fact which the Mahabrahman often exploits with veiled threats designed to encourage a tight-fisted *jajman* to loosen his purse-strings.

Before his departure the Mahabrahman accepts the gift of *sajja dan* which consists, or should consist, of a year's supply of grain and other comestibles, cooking utensils, household furniture, bedding, clothes, cosmetics, toilet articles and a lump sum in cash – in fact all the standard requirements of daily life. In practice, a small cash payment is often given in lieu of many of these items. The idea is that the offerings are received by the deceased in the next world. The way in which this transfer is effected was often explained to me by analogy with sending a money order. Just as it is not the actual rupees deposited in Banaras which will be handed across the counter in London, but their sterling equivalent, so it is with *sajja dan*. But clearly what lends the idea of this transfer an additional authority is the theory that the Mahabrahman actually *is* the deceased at the moment the gift is handed over.

The power to bless or curse puts the Mahabrahman in a position of considerable strength when it comes to negotiating the size of the offering. What allows him to exploit this strength to the full is the fact that he owns exclusive rights, not to a fixed clientele, but to a certain number of days in the year when he has a claim to *all* city corpses, or alternatively to all corpses from the surrounding countryside. What this means is that the relationship between specialists and mourners is confined to this one occasion, for the odds are that next time somebody in the family dies a different Funeral-priest will preside. The system thus helps to maintain the anonymity of the specialist which – given their reluctance to sustain any long-term relationship with him – is acceptable enough to the bereaved. But what is less acceptable is that this anonymity tempts the specialist to extract what he can from a patron he is unlikely to encounter again.

At the time when the *sajja dan* is given, the *jajman* finds himself confronted by the right-holder and an echoing chorus of his supporters and servants. In the negotiations which follow they relentlessly press for the entire range of prescribed gifts (which not even the richest patron can reasonably provide). The mourners know the Funeral-priests' reputation for avarice and may start by offering substantially less than they expect to be obliged to give. As a result the Funeral-priests become increasingly insistent and the atmosphere increasingly acrimonious. This or that gift has not been provided; this or that is of poor quality, the cash is too little and do they really imagine that salvation is to be had at such a paltry price? 'What, now you have taken everything else, will you have my penis?' asks the chief mourner beside himself with indignation. The Mahabrahman wryly reminds him that his gift will be received by the *pret*, the chief mourner's own daughter. At such times it is as if the Mahabrahman is taking it out on the bereaved for the contempt in which he is held by society at large.

Roughly fifty Mahabrahman household residents in the city own days on the *ghat*. In addition, about twenty Mahabrahman households from outside Banaras have such rights. In fact most of the city families have migrated in from the surrounding countryside within the last two or three generations; and many of them still have a house, a bit of land and possibly even *jajmani* rights in their area of origin. Some inherited days on the *ghat* from maternal kin; some came as servants of the right-holders and managed to purchase or pirate rights of their own.

In addition to these local Mahabrahmans a handful of funeral-priests from other parts of India have settled in the city and serve their own regional communities. For the Bengalis there is the Agardani Funeral-priest. *Jajman* from Maharashtra, Gujerat and parts of Andhra are served by a Maharashtrian; while two families of Punjabi funerary specialists have successfully claimed the privilege of conducting mortuary rituals for Khatris and Aroras resident in Banaras, though the local Mahabrahmans bitterly resent their reportedly recent appropriation of rights to the latter. These Punjabi priests regard themselves, and are generally admitted to be, of higher status than their Purbiya ('eastener') counterparts since they do not accept gifts in the name of the deceased until the thirteenth day when the ghost has become an ancestor. The rituals performed *within* the city by *clean-caste jajman* from all other areas of north India are presided over by the local Mahabrahmans.

In fact the latter are not wholly averse to officiating for Untouchables if the temptation is sufficient and discretion is assured. Much depends on who is making the money. The right-holders' servants say that they are prepared to do so on a free-lance basis and on their own account, but see no reason to risk the obloquy attendant on discovery when the profits will be pocketed by their employer. But in principle it is the Barber who serves as funeral priest for the lowest castes.

A separate caste – the Mahabappas – are funeral priests to the Funeral-priests. Mahabappa settlements are small and scattered, and each serves the Mahabrahman communities of a considerable area. In Banaras they have to be summoned from outside. One Mahabrahman lineage calls in a Mahabappa from the village of Tara Umri; another from Chaubepur. At its own death rituals, the Tara Umri community makes gifts to 'good' (Upadhyay) Brahmans in the town of Mirzapur; while the latter complete the circle by gifting to regular Mahabrahmans. But other Mahabappa communities reportedly give to Gosains (who in turn patronise Mahabrahmans); while those of Gaya and Patna offer gifts to their sons-in-law (or other wife-taking affines).[5]

No matter on which *ghat* they are cremated (or immersed), the Mahabrahman who has *pari* (his 'turn' in the rota) on the day on which the corpse is brought to the *ghat* has the exclusive right to accept all gifts which will subsequently be made in the name of the ghost – the most valuable of which are generally offered at the rituals of the tenth or eleventh day. The only proviso is that these rituals be performed within the boundaries of the city.

When they are held in one of the hundred or so villages around the city which fall within the traditional jurisdiction of the city Mahabrahmans, the gifts go to the Funeral-priest who owns *pachchh* on the day of cremation. *Pari* rights, then, are to city mourners (and to all offerings made at the *ghat* itself); *pachchh* rights to those from the surrounding countryside – regardless in theory of where the cremation was held.

In practice the city Mahabrahmans are only likely to hear about – or bother with – those who cremate in Banaras, or whose ashes are brought for immersion. The residue represent the least promising donors. In the past, four settlements of village Funeral-priests were appointed by the city Mahabrahmans to watch over their rights, and inform them of any death in the vicinity. Today it is these local representatives who appropriate a large proportion of the offerings made by village *jajman* of the poorer sort. *Jajman* from outside the radius of *pachchh* do not fall within the scope of the Banaras Funeral-priests unless they stay in the city to perform the tenth and eleventh day rituals, in which event they are claimed by the *pari*-holder. But even when this is not the case, he may still derive some income from them by presiding over the offerings made at the *ghat* on the day of cremation. In total, the *pari* owner may acquire ten or twelve *jajman* who will offer him *sajja dan* ten or eleven days later;[6] and earn up to Rs. 150 (about £10)[7] from offerings made at the pyre.

The crucial thing that determines whether a corpse falls into *pari* or *pachchh* or neither is the place where the rituals are held. The physical boundary between *pari* and *pachchh* is clear and unambiguous. But even so there is some scope for competition between the holders of the two different kinds of right, for there are several locations where, for example, one side of the tank beside which the rituals are regularly celebrated falls into *pari* while the other side belongs to *pachchh*. Not surprisingly each of the right-holders tries to ensure that the rituals are held in his territory. Only occasionally does it happen that the same individual owns both kinds of right on the same day.

The Mahabrahmans explain the evolution of the system of *pachchh* and *pari* by reference to a (perhaps mythical) model of five founding ancestors. Four of these were the original right-holders who were continually at each other's throats over claims to *jajman*. The other was an outsider who was called in to arbitrate and who produced a judgement of Solomon from which the present system is derived and by which he himself acquired a one-fifth share.[8] As far as city corpses are concerned, his ruling was that each of the five should take one day in turn. In *pachchh* each took a whole (fifteen-day) fortnight consecutively.[9]

Over time these shares became increasingly fragmented by inheritance, sales and mortgages. In the 'original' *pachchh* cycle, the fifteen-day share of each ancestor would have started again two and a half months after the beginning of his previous turn. At present, not only are all the days in the fortnight likely to belong to different individuals, but some of them will participate only in every third or fourth cycle. As illustrated in Figure 1, the two heirs of a man

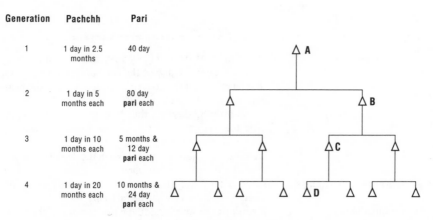

1 Inheritance of *pachchh* and *pari*

with the right to a single day in the two-and-a-half month cycle will each take a turn at five monthly intervals, and each of *their* heirs at ten monthly intervals.

While 'originally' every *pari* came up after six days, today the *pari* with the shortest cycle recurs after every forty days, However, most *paris* recur less frequently – the one with the longest span repeating itself only after eighty-two months. The commonest types of *pari* are those which cycle at intervals of forty days, eighty days, four months and twelve days, eight months, ten months and twenty-four days, sixteen months, twenty months and twenty-one months. All are subdivisions of a basic forty-day unit. This is again illustrated by Figure 1. The forty-day *pari* of the lone individual in generation 1 becomes two eighty-day *paris* in generation 2; four five-month and twelve day *paris* in generation 3, and eight ten-month and twenty-four day *paris* in generation 4.

Though it is extremely rare for a *pari* to be sold outright,[10] its theoretical cost is directly proportional to the number of days in the year on which it yields rights. A ten-month and twenty-four-day *pari*, which comes up once a year and is known as a one *damri pari*, would in 1977 sell for around Rs. 1,250 (about £83). A forty-day *pari*, which generally recurs eight times a year (eight *damris*[11]), would cost in the region of £665. Mortgages are far more common, and in 1978 the going rate was around Rs. 750 (about £50) per *damri*. The creditor must be allowed to enjoy the *pari* at least once before it is redeemed.[12]

The rules for reckoning *pari* are shown in Table 5. The months in the system are lunar months (of approximately thirty days each). The days are week-days. Each formula consists of two rules: a number (of days and/or months) rule and a day of the week rule. In a forty-day *pari*, for example, the number rule states that the *pari* will recur after forty-one days; while the day rule states that it will be on the sixth day of the week after the day of your last *pari*. Now in the case of a forty-day *pari*, the day rule is redundant in that the right number *always* produces the right day. But in other cases there is a discrepancy in that the date given by the number rule does not necessarily fall

Table 5. *Rules for reckoning* pari

1. 40-day *pari*	recurs after 41 days. The day of the week will be the sixth day after the day of the last *pari* (counting from that day) – e.g. if the last *pari* was on a Friday the next will be on a Wednesday.
2. 80-day *pari*	recurs after 82 days on the eleventh day of the week after the day of the last *pari* – e.g. if the last was on Friday the next is on Monday.
3. 4-month *pari*	recurs after 4 months and 1 day, on the day of the week after the day of the last *pari*.
4. 5-months and 12 days	recurs after 5 months and 12 days on the day of the week before the day of the last *pari*.
5. 8-month *pari*	recurs after 8 months and 2 days on the day of the week two days after the day of the last *pari*.
6. 10 months & 24 days	recurs after 10 months and 24 days on the sixth day of the week after the day of the last *pari*.
7. 16 month *pari*	recurs after 16 months and 4 days on the fifth day of the week after the last *pari*.
8. 20 month *pari*	recurs after 20 months and 5 days on the sixth day of the week after the last *pari*.
9. 21 month *pari*	recurs after 21 months and 20 days on the day of the week which falls 11 days after the day of the last *pari*.

on the right day of the week. In this case the day rule always overrides the number rule such that you claim your *pari* on the correct day of the week immediately preceeding the date provided by the number rule. All this may sound rather complicated but the basic principle is really very simple. In effect, the rules merely determine that a given *pari* will recur at exactly the same intervals as a forty day *pari* on every second, third, fourth or nth cycle. To see this, compare Figure 1 with Table 6. The table shows how the forty-day *pari* of individual A in the senior generation of the figure would recur throughout the year if it is first enjoyed on Friday the first day of the first month. But if the *pari* has been subdivided into two eighty day shares, the rules ensure that A's son B will claim precisely the same days as A would have claimed in every *alternate* cycle. By the same token, the five-month and twelve-day *pari* of C in generation 3 will come up in exactly the same way as A's forty-day *pari* would have cycled every fourth time round. Every *pari* thus recurs as if it was a forty-day *pari* which – so to speak – passes on every so many deals; and the consequence of this is that when a *pari* is subdivided it does not throw the whole system out of gear.

By the time we get to the extreme case of a *pari* with an eighty-two-month cycle we have clearly moved a long way from the model of five original ancestors, each taking every sixth day. What, then, is the relevance of this model? At first sight, very little. There is a good deal of vagueness about how

Table 6. *The operation of* pari *rules**

Day	Date	Month	A in Gen 1	B in Gen 2	C in Gen 3	D in Gen 4
Fri	1	1	40 day *pari*	80 day *pari*	5 months 12 days	10 months 24 days
Wed	11	2	40 day *pari*			
Mon	21	3	40 day *pari*	80 day *pari*		
Sat	1	5	40 day *pari*			
Thurs	10	6	40 day *pari*	80 day *pari*	5 months 12 days	
Tues	21	7	40 day *pari*			
Sun	1	9	40 day *pari*	80 day *pari*		
Fri	11	10	40 day *pari*			
Wed	21	11	40 day *pari*	80 day *pari*	5 months 12 days	10 months 24 days

*The fact that I have simplified the situation by assuming that every lunar month corresponds to 30 week-days does not affect the concurrence I am concerned to demonstrate.

the original share-holders were related to each other, and even more about how they relate to present-day kinship groups. The majority are quite indifferent on these matters, but generally suppose that all the original descent lines are now extinct. But despite this apparent lack of concern to fit the present with the past, the five-ancestor model is in fact crucial to the operation of the system in that it acts as a mnemonic device for cross-checking the day on which your *pari* should occur. Every *pari* belongs to the *kunt*, or 'stake', of one of the five named ancestors: and these stakes follow each other in regular sequence, such that if today's *pari* is in the stake of ancestor A, then tomorrow's will be in the stake of B, the next day's of C and so on until we are back with A again on the sixth day. If tomorrow I should have a twenty-one month *pari* in the stake of D, I can confirm my calculation by making sure that today's *pari* is in C, yesterday's in B or the day before's in A.

The mechanics of the system are such that occasionally a *pari*-holder miscalculates, or more likely forgets to show up on the *ghat* on the day of his *pari*[13] (though he will usually have realised his error by the time of the crucial ten or eleventh day rituals). In such an eventuality, Bihari Maharaj – the richest and most powerful *pari*-holder whose servants remain on Manikarnika *ghat* 24 hours a day – takes charge of all *jajman*; and when the rightful owner eventually turns up reimburses him with a proportion of the takings. In the course of the year there are one or two *paris* which remain regularly unclaimed, and for all intents and purposes Bihari has made these his own.

The proof that a Mahabrahman actually owns the *pari* he claims is the record book (*bahi*) he maintains. Each time he enjoys the *pari* he enters the date, the type of *pari*, the name of the ancestor to whose share it originally belonged, and a list of the *jajman* he served. This record is used to calculate his next *pari*, and to prove his right to it, should it be challenged. These documents are kept under great security for should a record book fall into the wrong hands it could be copied and used to usurp the rights of the proper owner. Because there is no general access to record books, and because of the number of shareholders and the sheer complexity of the system, nobody has anything like a complete picture of whose rights come up when, and even those who are on the *ghat* every day do not generally know whose *pari* it is tomorrow.

A single individual is likely to own a combination of different types of *pari*: forty-day, eighty-day and so on. Some of these will be his exclusive possession (*nirali pari*); while others will be held in partnership (*sajhe men*), the cash offerings distributed in proportion to shares, and lots cast for valuable but indivisible gifts (a procedure known as *goti lagana*, 'to take a dip'). *Pari* runs from sunrise on one day to sunrise on the next, and it is the time at which the chief mourner lights the pyre that determines which Mahabrahman has rights. The day itself is never subdivided between shareholders into smaller units of time.

Within the Mahabrahman community *pari* rights are very unevenly distributed. Bihari Maharaj has rights to some seventy-five days a year, while his half-brother and another man between them account for a further fifty-five days.[14] In other words, a third of the year is owned by just three individuals. At the other end of the scale, some households only have rights to a part-share in one or two *damris* (turns) per year, or perhaps to *paris* which recur at less frequent intervals than a year. A more detailed picture of their distribution is provided by Table 7. As a rule of thumb it is said that the distribution of rights to village *jajman* as part of the *pachchh* cycle mirrors the distribution of *pari*, though in fact rights seem to be yet more concentrated in Bihari's hands. One significant difference between *pachchh* and *pari* is that in *pari* the right-holder claims the gift of *sajja dan* offered on behalf of all corpses brought to the *ghats* on the day of his *pari* regardless of whether the offering is made after three, ten or eleven days. But in *pachchh* he takes only the offerings made on the tenth day after he had rights. In other words, what matters to the owner of *pachchh* is not when the corpse was cremated but when the gifts are offered. Any gift made on the tenth day is his, regardless of the timing of the disposal of the corpse.[15]

The fact that he must collect from all his *jajman* on the same day creates a problem for the right-holder. Since *pachchh* covers a wide area and communications are difficult, it is often physically impossible to attend on more than one *jajman* in person. Other members of the family may, of course, be called on if they are available. But even between them they are unlikely to be able to cover the ground. In most cases the only option is to delegate some *jajman* to one or more unsupervised employees. Not without reason, however, most right-holders place little faith in the latter's scrupulousness when it comes to disgorging offerings, the details of which the owner cannot know.

Table 7. *Estimated distribution of Mahabrahman* pari *rights**

Days per annum	No. of household[+]
<5	c. 32
5−9	8
10−20	7
>20	3

*Since there is no general record of rights, exact figures are extremely diffcult to obtain. This information is based on the daily record I myself kept between 1 December 1976 and 30 November 1977. Since I was not on Manikarnika *ghat* every day, I unfortunately missed around 15 per cent of entries. My own observations were cross-checked against informants' estimates, and a record kept for his own purposes by one of the *pari*-holders' servants for the period between 4 January 1972 and 3 January 1973 (from which only 11 per cent of entries are missing). These sources are remarkably consistent, and I am confident that the table represents a reasonable approximation to the actual situation.

[+]These figures exclude the twenty or so Mahabrahman households from outside the city who own *pari* rights. Between them, the outsiders would account for around forty days per year, out of which one Mirzapur household owns ten days.

Furthermore, *pachchh* requires much trudging about the countryside for uncertain rewards. When the right-holder eventually gets there, he may find that some interloper has arrived before him, completed the rituals and disappeared with the offerings. Even if the *sajja dan* gift comes up to expectations, there is the problem of getting it home, and he may find himself forced to sell many items in the village for a fraction of their true value. For all these reasons the owner of *pachchh* will often be glad to sell his rights in specific *jajman* from the more remote villages to a rural Mahabrahman from nearer at hand. Some *pachchh* villages are too far away to bother with in person, and rights over them have been contracted out on a permanent 'share-cropping' basis to a nearby Mahabrahman settlement – 4 annas out of 16 (i.e. 25 per cent) to the city Mahabrahman, 12 to the village Mahabrahman who does the work.

In both *pachchh* and *pari* the right-holder needs the help of several semi-permanent *karinda*-servants in order to be able to attend to all his *jajman*, and to muster a suitably imposing backing at the time of negotiating the offerings. About twenty Mahabrahmans work more or less regularly as *karindas*, most of them for several different employers. On the day of the *pari* one of them will remain throughout the twenty-four hours at Harishchandra *ghat*, and two or three at Manikarnika, where they collect information about prospective *jajman* and preside over offerings at the pyre. On subsequent days they attend, and may direct, the rituals. For all this, they receive a fraction of the total offerings made to the right-holder, plus various minor payments

Table 8. *Remuneration of the* karindas

A. Basic rate:

    i. on *pari*   No share in goods, gold or silver, but 4 annas (about 2 p) per
                      jajman + 6 *paisa* per one old rupee (i.e. 6/64) on all cash offered
                      (except where this is given in lieu of named items). In the
                      offerings of *jajman* from Hardoi and Sitapur districts who
                      perform all the rituals on the day of cremation itself, the *karinda*
                      is entitled to ony 2 *paisa* per Rs. 1 (i.e. 2/64).*

    ii. on *pachchh*   25 per cent share in all offerings except grains (which are
                      generally considered to be the most valuable item given by rural
                      jajman).

These payments are made after the deduction of the Barber's share, and are split
equally between all the *karindas* who worked for the right-holder regardless of which
particular *jajman* they served.

B. Additional perquisites:
    i. 25 per cent share of all cash offered at the pyre.
    ii. Earnest money called *nyautani* or *nimantran* – meaning 'invitation' – paid on
the day of cremation to signify the *jajman's* recognition of the Mahabrahman's
rights. This is generally less than Rs. 1.
    iii. *vedi ki dakshina* – small coins offered onto each rice-ball given in the name of
the deceased.
    iv. *ghant phurai* – money for breaking the water-pot dwelling of the *pret.*
    v. *varni dhoti* – a loin-cloth offered at the time of *sajja dan.*
    vi. food before the Mahabrahman's departure.
    vii. money for breaking the strip of white cloth (*uttri*) worn across the chief
mourner's body by people of certain castes and localities.
These offerings go to those *karindas* who actually performed the service.

Jajman from these areas often come to Banaras to perform *putla vidhan* (the
cremation of any effigy of the deceased), followed on the same day by a minimal version
of the whole sequence of subsequent rituals.

from the particular *jajman* they serve. Details are given in Table 8. Their
earnings, however, are generally derisory and they themselves insist that if
they did not regularly cheat their employers they could not make ends meet.
The greatest scope for chicanery is provided by *jajman* who come into Banaras
from outside in order to perform the tenth or eleventh day rituals – often
because they can ill afford to feed the hordes of people who will attend if they
conduct them at home. The *karindas* pick them up, perform the rituals and
pack them off before the *pari*-holder learns of their existence. What feeds the
karindas' resentment of the situation is that they are regarded as the dregs of
Mahabrahman society, are employed by kinsmen who are inclined to treat
them as servants, and bear the brunt of the tense negotiations and of

impersonating the ghost; while – as we shall see – their employers try to foist them off with the *spiritual* consequences of accepting the offerings while keeping the material substance to themselves. It is significant, for example, that the traditional perquisites of the *karinda* include a loin garment known as the *varni dhoti*. The Mahabrahman who accepts this presentation is held to be responsible for any deficiencies in the ritual.

The Barber also has a claim to share in the proceeds of both *pachchh* and *pari*. In *pari* he gets two annas in the rupee (12.5 per cent) on all cash offerings and in *pachchh* 25 per cent of everything except grains. It is generally through the family Barber that the Mahabrahmans form an estimate of the financial capacity of the mourners,[16] and of their intentions with regard to the offerings, and thus gauge the level at which to pitch their demands. It may also be through him that they come to know of the *jajman* at all. Indeed some Barbers regularly enter into collusion with the *karinda*-servants to defraud the *pari*-owners by witholding information about a death.

The income from *pachchh* and *pari* is quite unpredictable. The profession, people say, is dependent of the sky (*akash-vritti*). Several turns running may yield only the most impoverished *jajman*. But there is always the chance that once in a while the *pari*-holder may enjoy the windfall of a Maharaja, or a Marwari businessman. When he was employed in Bombay, one of the *karindas* with whom I was friendly used to take part in a gambling racket in which bets are laid on the price of cotton on the New York market. *Pari*, he explained, is something similar – you live in hope of a real killing. It is every Mahabrahman's fantasy that sooner or later he will be the one lucky enough to repeat the experience of Bindra Maharaj who received somewhere between £3,000 and £4,000 when the Raja of Sarguja died in his *pari*. Indeed the attitude of the *pari*-holder is that of the next-time-lucky gambler; while the reaction of the one who hits the jack-pot is to 'spend, spend, spend'. The notion that the money is tainted and will be eaten by white ants if you try to put it by, becomes justification for a prodigal expenditure on wine and women. Those who wait for their number to come up may not do so passively. It is at any rate alleged that some Mahabrahmans 'roll the pestle' (*loda ludkana*) to ensure the demise of a man of substance on the day of their *pari* (cf. Opler and Singh 1950:474). A grinding stone is supposedly rolled – to the accompaniment of magical incantations that such and such a person should now die – on a square purified with cow-dung.

Though I provide such figures with diffidence, I calculate that with seventy-five days of *pari* and at least as many days of *pachchh*, Bihari Maharaj probably had an average monthly income of at least Rs. 3,000 in 1976–7. The most industrious and fully employed of the *karindas* would have been making in the region of Rs. 300–400. Rs. 300 would have been roughly equivalent to the salary of a school teacher or clerk with several years service; Rs. 3,000 was at that time positively princely. But no other *karinda* could match these earnings; and few other *pari*-holders had even a tenth of Bihari's rights.

Although it appears to the outsider that the Funeral-priest must be making an extremely opulent living, this impression is largely illusory. After the *karinda*-servants and Barbers have taken their cut, the proceeds from *pari* may be shared between several different partners, none of whom may have rights again for the next two or three months. Despite the most delicate of sensiblities, in such circumstances the Mahabrahman with few *paris* and no other regular income is constrained to bear hard upon his *jajman* if he is to maintain his family at even a modest level. The situation is exacerbated by the fact that the right-holders and their *karindas* have an interest in maximizing different offerings. Each will devote most of his energy to raising the bid on the offerings to which he has an exclusive right, so that as soon as the *jajman* has satisfied one he is confronted by the importunate demands of the other. Since he knows nothing of the way in which shares are apportioned or of the Mahabrahman's domestic economy, he not unnaturally concludes that the community's reputation for venality is in no way exaggerated – a judgement in which, it must be said, many Mahabrahmans themselves concur.

In fact, however, the economy of a significant proportion of Mahabrahman households is not entirely dependent on their *jajmani* rights. Amongst those with other occupations are, for example, a successful coal merchant, a wholesaler of metal buttons, a clerk, a primary school teacher, a driver, a tailor and a betel-nut seller, as well as several with more or less illicit side-lines. One used to be a professional runner of smuggled gold, another a cinema projectionist, while one family – which has now divested itself of it *pari* rights and passes as 'pure' Brahman in another north Indian city – includes a retired Sessions Judge and a senior police officer. For those with a regular income from other sources, *pari is* largely a matter of windfall profits, a lottery largely irrelevant to basic subsistence. Though few have gone so far as to divest themselves of their rights, one or two families with substantial incomes from other sources claim not to accept any of the proceeds of *pari*; and are certainly never to be seen on the *ghats*. The work itself is demeaning; but more importantly the gifts are dangerous (see pp. 122ff).

3.2 Other variants of *pari*

The Untouchable Dom funeral-attendants labour at the pyres under a similarly infamous reputation for rapacity. The cremation ground Doms – who distinguish themselves as Gotakhor ('diver') Doms – insist that they are an entirely separate sub-caste from the Sweeper Doms of Banaras and other north Indian cities, and from the Basket-maker Doms of the rural areas. They number around 670 (Kaushik 1979:1:36), and mainly reside in two neighbourhoods in the vicinity of the two burning *ghats*.

The Dom's job is to lay the pyre and supervise the cremation so that the corpse is properly consumed. But their monopoly over such work is neither uncontested nor complete. Earlier this century, two brothers – described as 'half-breed' (*varan shankar*) Brahmans and employing a team of Chamars (Leather-workers) – are said to have seriously encroached on the Doms' prerogatives at Manikarnika *ghat*. The matter was only resolved when the surviving brother threw in the towel after the other had been murdered. Today a Brahman servant of the Punjabi Funeral-priests builds pyres for the Punjabi trading castes; a Chamar for Bengalis and South Indian Brahmans. The latter is also employed by the Municipal Council to cremate the corpses of indigents at public expense, while a second municipal employee has the task of disposing of the charcoal left over from the pyres so that it cannot be sold or re-used.

What is of far greater symbolic significance than the building of pyres is that the Doms provide the chief mourner with the never-extinguished fire of the cremation ground with which he lights the pyre, and without which – it is sometimes claimed – there is no 'liberation'. But even though some communities do not take fire from the Dom[17], and some do not call on him to construct their pyres, all acknowledge his absolute right to a *kar* – or 'tax' – before the corpse is cremated *or* immersed.[18] On that day, it is said, the Dom is raja. In addition to this tax, the Doms' perquisites include the shroud, the bier and its appurtenances, and five logs from the pyre. More valuable than these, however, is the right to sift and wash the ashes for the gold and silver which was left on the corpse in the form of rings, jewellery or other ornaments. When ashes are immersed in the Ganges by a pilgrim from outside, tax is also demanded in the name of the Dom, though it is a matter of some scandal that in fact this is almost invariably appropriated by the Brahman specialist who presides over the ritual.

The Doms' tax is an extremely lucrative source of income. In 1976–7 it was generally reckoned to net the right-holder at Manikarnika *ghat at least* Rs. 1,000 (c. £66) a day after paying off the fifteen to twenty attendants who service his *pari*.[19] The latter received Rs. 2 per day, a midday meal served on the *ghat*, 4 annas per corpse (shared equally between all those employed on that day), plus whatever they could themselves extract for the labour of building the pyre – in total perhaps Rs. 10–15 from all these sources.

Until his recent death a single individual – Kailash Chowdhury, the so-called Dom raja – owned seventy-four in a cycle of 208 days at Manikarnika *ghat*, or roughly one-third of the year. His father's sister's son occupies a similar position of dominance in the less valuable *pari* cycle at Harishchandra. Kailash lived with his pet alligator and many retainers in a palace overlooking the Ganges, on the balustrades of which are the sculpted figures of two regally rampant lions. His wealth was legendary and supposedly included prime development property in the Cantonment area of the city valued at around Rs. 4 million, as well as land in several areas of Bihar and eastern UP. It is certainly the case that I hardly ever saw him in public except with a brief-case bulging with bank-notes and a bevy of bodyguards. It was Kailash who is often credited with having for many years almost single-handedly stalled the introduction of the electric crematorium discussed in the last chapter.

But whichever Dom has rights on that day is the raja of the cremation ground, and the mourners are never allowed to forget it. During the negotiations over his 'tax', he makes a point of touching the mourners, and treats them with the haughty disdain an Untouchable might normally experience at their hands. Lounging on a bolster, cheeks bulging with betel-juice, a garland round his neck, he addresses the mourners with the disrespectful second person singular pronoun *tu*, while they use the polite *ap* and call him 'elder brother' or 'Chaudhuri (headman) Sahib'. First he elicits their village and caste, which gives him a broad idea of what to expect, and then the pressure mounts.

> Your respected father won't die again and again. You won't perform his last rites time after time. Your father raised you, educated you. Now you must give with an open heart. You have brought him to Kashi to burn. Do the work happily. You will die also. You too will arrive here . . . So how did he die? Did you poison him? It is not enough just to get it written (i.e. the cause of death on the certificate) . . . You say you are poor! You want to teach *me* how to fuck? If you can't give more than that, then go. Take your corpse away, and take your money too. In Pratapgarh you can boast that you gave the Dom raja a thousand rupees.

The sums involved are extremely variable – in my observation from Rs 5 to Rs. 500 – and the Dom will often press village-folk for a promisory note for grains to be collected at harvest-time.

Though I was not sufficiently alert to pursue the matter directly in the field, I suspect that the Dom raja is not merely the king of the cremation-ground, but also a kind of terrestial counterpart to that paradigmatic king, the vengeful Yama, the Lord of Death to whom all souls must eventually pay their debts. In terms of the way their physical appearance is stereotypically described, the way in which they bully and cajole the chief mourner, and prod and poke the corpse – as the *yamdut* (the messengers of death) prod and poke the departed on his journey to the abode of his ancestors – his servants certainly evoke the *yamdut* of Yama. As the Mahabrahman is quite explicitly the ghost, and the household- or pilgrimage-priest is the incorporated ancestor, I think it likely that the Dom raja and his servants are at least fleetingly identified with the Lord and messengers of death, with Yamraj and the *yamdut*.

It must be admitted, however, that the demands of this earthly counterpart are not always acknowledged as irresistable, and that with castes like the Ahir-herdsmen – who have a reputation for violence – the Dom is wise to be circumspect. Nor can the passive acquiescence of others be taken for granted. Several examples come to mind, but the most dramatic and revealing occurred one night early on in my fieldwork at Harishchandra *ghat*. Two village women had brought the body of a female relative who had died in one of the city hospitals. The Dom right-holder agreed to cremate the corpse on a contract basis: for Rs. 86 he would supply all the wood and take his tax – leaving the mourners without their bus fare home. In the event, however, the pyre which the Dom provided was pathetically small – 'hardly big enough to burn a rat', as one bystander indignantly put it – and the wood was wet and would not burn. At this point a party of men from a neighbouring ward of the city, who were accompanying a corpse of their own, decided that things had gone far enough. They caught hold of the Dom, dragged him to the pyre and promised to burn him on it unless he returned the money. Of this they took Rs. 50 to the wood shop where they acquired enough wood for a respectably sized pyre, and returned all but Rs. 5 of the balance to the women for the fare home. They then went in search of the Dom – who had now fled the *ghat* – and when they eventually found him, brought him back, made him provide fire *and* gave him the remaining Rs. 5 as his tax.

In the Dom case each of the two cremation grounds has its own independent *pari* cycle (or rota of rights), and it is rare for a right-holder on one *ghat* to enjoy simultaneous rights on the other. The details are complex and the two systems differ.[20] Here I sketch only the more fragmented variant at Harishchandra. On any one day there are four kinds of rights. The first is *pari* – the right to supply the fire and negotiate the tax, of which the right-holder receives a 6 anna – or three-eighths – share. The various non-cash items which are the traditional perquisite of the Dom – the grains, the shroud, the bier, and the five pieces of wood – go to him alone. A second individual has *tahal* ('watch' or 'guard'), which means that he is responsible for constructing and superintending the pyre. He too receives a three-eighths share of the cash offering, but has no claims on anything else. A third has rights of 'alms' (*bhikh*) for which he has no specific duties but which entitle him to claim the remaining quarter share of the money. Finally, a fourth Dom has rights to *sona* – to sift and wash the ashes for gold. This division is modified for a Bengali corpse (all the gold goes to the owner of *bhikh*) and for South Indian Brahmans (the owner of *bhikh* is excluded, and all the other offerings with the exception of the bier are divided equally between the other three right-holders). Each of these circulates in a manner broadly similar to that I have described for the Mahabrahmans with the result that most right-holders only enjoy them at very irregular intervals.

While a handful of Doms have obtained employment at the new cremator-ium,[21] the value of their traditional rights at Harishchandra *ghat* has sharply declined since its opening. Though I am told that a large proportion of mourners who patronise the crematorium continue to offer tax to the *pari*-holder, the latter's bargaining position has been severely undermined by the fact that the Doms are no longer required to construct the pyres, and that even those who plan a traditional disposal now have a realistic alternative. Business is said to pick up during power-cuts. I was also told, though I have not been able to confirm, that the crematorium auctions (for very substantial sums) the right to dispose of ashes to bidders from the Dom community.

The family Barber has already cropped up in association with the Funeral-priests. He acts as a general factotum throughout the period of mourning; and would normally accompany the funeral procession to the cremation ground where he tonsures the chief mourner, sometimes all sons of the deceased,[22] and sometimes the corpse itself.[23] An experienced Barber will have come to the *ghat* before, may find himself directing many of the proceedings, and is usually expected to negotiate with the wood-seller (who pays him commission of 1 anna in the rupee) and with the shops which sell shrouds and other mortuary goods.

For one reason or another, however, many mourners do not bring their family Barber with them, and will employ one who works permanently on the *ghat*. There are two Barber brothers who have monopolised the cremation-ground part of Manikarnika, who deal almost exclusively with mourners and corpses, and who take alternate twenty-four hour shifts. Fourteen other Barbers have rights at the adjacent bathing *ghat*. A first-time visitor to the *ghat* – a bather, pilgrim or anthropologist – will be served by the Barber who first stakes a verbal claim to his custom. If he ever returns, then the one who originally served him will have the absolute right to do so again. I was myself an occasional client of Rupan, and I could never persuade anybody else to shave me while he was around the *ghat*. Actually Rupan was quite often absent since he – along with two other Manikarnika Barbers – has a profitable side-line buying hair from all over Banaras, and from other pilgrimage centres in the region, and re-selling it (at around ten times the price he pays) to dealers from Bombay and Calcutta for export to Western wig manufacturers.

With regard to certain kinds of customers, however, these fourteen Barbers run a *pari* system. On any given day, one group will have rights to all mourners and corpses that require their services; a second group to all pilgrims from South India; a third to Nepali pilgrims, while a fourth will have no particular rights on that day. Five days later the cycle starts again. Earnings from each of these categories of customer are divided equally by all members of that group who came to the *ghat* on that day, regardless of which of them actually did the work. On Saturdays *pari* is suspended. It is inauspicious to be shaved or tonsured on a Saturday, business is slack and most of these Barbers take the day off. The earnings of those who do attend the *ghat* are pooled. Half the total is distributed equally between them, and the other half goes towards the upkeep of the building which they maintain at Manikarnika. If, as often happens in the winter month of *Pus*, there are too many Nepali pilgrims for the right-holders to cope with themselves, the other Manikarnika Barbers will help out for a three-tenths share of the takings – but no other Barber can work on the *ghat*.

Around 700 small craft are licensed to work the river front. Most are owned and manned by Mallahs, a caste of fishermen and boatmen. Each boat may take passengers only from its own *ghat*, though the right to fish anywhere on the river is unrestricted. An important source of subsidiary earnings on several *ghats* is the right to dredge in the river mud for coins thrown into the Ganges by the pious pilgrims as *gupt dan* – a 'secret' and particularly meritorious gift. At Manikarnika, different parts of the *ghat* are for this purpose assigned to different boatmen. The Mallah stands in the water up to his waist or chest and manipulates an iron sieve with his feet until it is full of mud, which he then sifts for coins. I have seen a skilled operator extract seven or eight rupees in an hour. The big profits, however, are from pilgrims and tourists. Boats are commonly overloaded and undermanned, and every year there are serious accidents in which a number of pilgrims drown. A significant proportion are worked on behalf of their owners by men without sufficient capital for a boat of their own, and for half the takings. Several of the *pandas* who live on the water-front pay the boatmen a *pro rata* commission for every pilgrim delivered to their house; and the boatmen in turn pay commission to the pilgrim-guides who bring them fares.

The way in which passengers are allocated between the various right-holders of a single *ghat* is variable. Dashashvamedh is the most popular bathing *ghat* in the city. The boatmen all sit together on a wooden platform at the bottom of the long flight of stone steps that leads down to the river. As any potential passenger reaches the top of the steps one of the boatmen will stake a claim by calling out 'the one with the spectacles', 'the bell-bottom pant-*wallah*', 'the red monkey Englishman'. Whoever claimed the passenger takes him.[24] If after much haggling about the fare the unsuspecting passenger tries to play the market by negotiating with another boatman, the latter will string him along until an agreement is reached, but he will nevertheless go with the one who originally claimed him.

Because of its proximity to one of the railway stations at which many pilgrims arrive, and to open space where chartered buses can park, the demand for boats at Rajghat is often particularly heavy, and passengers are allocated on the basis of a complex rota system. What is distinctive about this is that any one of the fifty-one shareholders who has nothing better to do can at any time sit in the *pari*-owner's boat and help with the rowing. Two or three pilgrims may thus find themselves accompanied by eight or nine boatmen. The *pari*-owner gets half the fare, and the other half is split equally between the others who went along. But at periods of peak demand there is more likely to be a shortage of boats than a surplus of boatmen. The rules for coping with this eventuality are best explained by supposing that A had yesterday's *pari*, B has today's and C will have tomorrow's. When all B's boats are full, A has the right to take any surplus passengers, but must give B a quarter share of his takings. When all of A's capacity has been used up, B has the right to assign further passengers to any of the other shareholders in exchange for half the fares. When there are no (more) shareholders available, C gets the work without having to remunerate B at all.

On the two cremation *ghats*, and on one of the other *ghats* from which corpses are regularly taken out to be immersed in the river,[25] there is a distinction between live and dead passengers. On each of these *ghats* the boatmen operate a *pari* system for corpses and ashes, but the *boli* system – that is the system of staking a verbal claim – for all other first-time passengers, and a system of theoretically permanent rights in anybody taken before.

At Manikarnika *ghat* there are six established shops which specialise in the sale of what are collectively called 'the goods of the skull-breaking' (*kapal kriya saman*). These consist of shrouds, various offerings to the pyre,[26] and the big water-pot (*gagra*) which the chief mourner throws over his left shoulder at the end of cremation to 'cool' the pyre. These shops also sell stone slabs for weighting down corpses immersed in the river. Forty or fifty years ago a single individual had a monopoly on this business – which he reportedly enforced by smashing pots brought by the mourners from elsewhere. While he was serving a lengthy jail sentence a series of rival enterprises were established by shop-keepers of different caste, who – in order to preclude competition – formed themselves into two separate *pari* cycles (one on the *ghat* itself and the other in the alley leading down to it). On any day, only one shop in the first of these rings can sell mortuary goods, but there is no restriction on other commodities.[27] In the case of the second ring, each of the three shops is only open on the day of its *pari*, and indeed two of them are managed on behalf of their owners by the same individual (who switches shops halfway through his forty-eight hour shift, during which he takes only cat-naps).

By contrast with the *kapal kriya* trade, the wood business at Manikarnika is today a relatively 'free' market. Up until about 1910, however, a single shop – owned and managed by a powerful Rajput family – had a complete monopoly over all wood sold on the *ghat*. This shop still exists and remains the exclusive supplier of wood to the Doms when they negotiate an 'all-in' price which includes the cost of materials. The reason is that the arcaded structure where the Doms sit to negotiate their 'tax', where they eat and store bamboo from the biers, is under this Rajput family's control, and the Doms use it only on their sufferance. The same shop is also the sole supplier of the five maunds of wood which the Municipal Council allows for the cremation of indigent corpses. How its previously complete monopoly on the *ghat* was broken I am unable to say, though one current story has it that – in the tradition of Kashmiri Mal – a powerful coalition of Punjabi Khatris sponsored a new shop in order to undercut the exhorbitant prices which were then being charged.

At any rate, there are today five other woodshops at Manikarnika: four owned by Ahir-herdsmen, and one by a family of merchant caste. Together they employ fifty to sixty hewers and carriers of wood, which is brought in by truck or boat from within the radius of about sixty miles. No formal system regulates competition between them. Prices vary with the quality of the wood (especially its dryness), and from season to season, though not significantly between shops. In the late seventies and early eighties, rates fluctuated between Rs. 8 per maund and Rs. 21.[28] Five maunds[29] is generally reckoned to be the minimum required to cremate a corpse adequately, but those who can afford it will use up to fifteen maunds. It is the Dom's prerogative to supply the straw brand (*sarpat* or *khari*) with which the pyre is lit. During my fieldwork one of the Ahir wood-sellers started to sell this item. Within days he was forced to desist by threats of violence from the Doms, to whom influential high-caste opinion on the *ghat* was in this matter sympathetic.

At Harishchandra *ghat* the new crematorium has had a major impact on the wood-trade. Though I visited the crematorium in 1992, I was unable to see it in operation since it was closed for repairs. New bricks were required for the chimneys, and the coils had been spoilt by the shrunken residue from silk and polyester fabrics. Cremations were suspended for over a month, though it was said that the repairs might have been completed within days had it not been for collusion between the contractors and the wood-sellers. Under the headline 'Half-burnt corpses being immersed in the Ganges', one local newspaper[30] picked up the story and reported that during the crematorium's closure the Harishchandra wood-trade had done Rs. 30,000 worth of business. It also alleged that most bodies were now being burnt on a contract basis for Rs. 300–400, and that those who were overseeing the pyres were extinguishing them before the corpse was fully consumed in order to re-sell the wood. As a result, large numbers of partly incinerated bodies were finding their way into the river, making a complete mockery of the campaign against Ganges pollution.

3.3 *Pandagiri* – the profession of pilgrimage-priest

As we have seen, many mourners bring the ashes of a deceased kinsman to Banaras to immerse in the Ganges, while the vast majority of pilgrims perform offerings to their ancestors during the course of their visit. It is in principle the pilgrimage-priest – the *panda* or *tirath-purohit* – who arranges, and may even preside, over these rituals. In the case of those outsiders who remain in, or come to, the city to perform the post-cremation mortuary rites, it is he who stands in for, embodies and receives gifts in the name of the newly incorporated ancestor at the rituals of the twelfth day.

By contrast with the specialists on whom I have so far focused, the *tirath-purohit* has a theoretically permanent and hereditary relationship with the pilgrims he serves. One, for example, might have rights to those who come from the state of Jodhpur in Rajasthan, another to Punjabi Khatris, a third to Chitpavan Brahmans from Maharashtra. With regard to the ex-princely states, the principle which is still invoked is that 'the one who has the raja has the subjects' (*jis ka raja, us ki praja*) (cf. van der Veer 1988:214).[31] While *tirath-purohit* specifically refers to those who have durable *jajmani* relations of this sort, *panda* is often used by the uninformed laity as a generic term for all the various specialist groups discussed in this section (though the *tirath-purohits* and the temple-priests claim that it only properly applies to them).

The *tirarth-purohit*'s proof of his rights is his record books (*bahis*), in which all previous visits by members of the pilgrim's descent line, village or caste are recorded. These books are his patrimony, and are heritable property that can also in theory be sold or mortgaged – though in practice they are rather more likely to be transferred by theft than sale. The possibility is, however, significant in that it suggests that what is represented to the pilgrim as an immutable relationship has from the priest's point of view a more provisional character.

What the *tirath-purohit* legally owns, and can transfer by gift, sale or will – the principle was established by the British courts in the mid-nineteenth century – is a 'business' and its paraphernalia: the record books, an identifying flag, the right to set up wooden platforms (*chaukis*) on the banks of some sacred river or tank, and so forth. The books and *chaukis* can be divided between a man's heirs, but in juridical theory rights over specific castes or localities cannot. Nor does the *tirath-purohit* have a claim to any pilgrim's offerings which can be legally enforced against 'poachers' (unless the latter have infringed his 'property interests' by using his record books or operating under the banner of his 'business'). What is given is a 'pure' gift; and a 'pure' gift – the British jurists assumed – must be one which is 'free' and unconstrained.[32] Since no pilgrim could be forced to accept the services of, or make donations to, a particular *panda*, the latter could not be said to have property rights in his offerings. 'It is impossible', as one judge phrased it, 'to hold that a beggar's right to receive alms is a right to property in any way.'[33] In order to enforce their claims against interlopers, the *tirath-purohits* have consequently had to fall back on less formal sanctions – of which the threat of violence has over the past two centuries been undoubtedly the most important.

The *panda* puts the pilgrims up in his own house or in one of the numerous pilgrim hostels, arranges their visits to the shops, temples and other sacred sites and for the rituals they perform, and accepts the gifts associated with them. He is, he says, 'a contractor of religion' (*dharam ka thekedar*) – a phrase which nicely captures his role as a general purpose 'fixer' for both the this- and other-worldly comforts of his clients. Most of my *panda* informants claimed that even in the time of their fathers and grandfathers they had little objection to accomodating pilgrims of low caste, or to presiding over their offerings to the ancestors or their bath in the tank at Manikarnika – though before 1956 Untouchables could not openly enter the Vishvanath temple. This relative lack of concern with the caste of their clientele is justified on both ideological and pragmatic grounds: according to *shastrik* precept the rules of caste are suspended on pilgrimage (cf. Turner 1974), and it is anyway often impossible to tell the difference.

There are several hundred such priests in Banaras, but of these I estimated that only thirty-five to forty would themselves accomodate more than a few hundred pilgrims in the course of a year. One of the top ten who has rights to a really valuable catchment area might have upwards of 70,000 pilgrims visiting him each year, often concentrated in very short periods. In the winter month of *Pus*, well over 50,000 Nepalis descend on Gajanand, who reckons to be able to shelter up to 5,000 pilgrims a night in his own house and out-buildings just behind Manikarnika *ghat*. The income from this scale of business is extremely difficult to gauge, but the estimate of an annual turn-over of *at least* half a million rupees in the late 1970s is not implausible. During 'the fortnight of the ancestors' (*pitri paksh*) I watched one of the less wealthy *pandas* collect Rs. 1,750 in small donations from rural pilgrims in the course of twenty-five minutes (though it is true that half this sum would probably have been disbursed again as commission to his agents). A pilgrimage-priest of substance is also likely to have other business interests, perhaps a saree emporium, a hotel or a cinema. At one point, Anjaninandan Mishra had a major stake in a coal-mine, and in a travelling circus in Bengal.

Though many are accused of blemished descent, a proper pilgrimage-priest must be a Brahman – though the kind of Brahman varies. The picture is complicated, and the boundaries between groups rather permeable. The most prestigious and exclusive are the *Nau kul sardar* (literally 'the nine chiefly descent lines'), otherwise known as *Gangaputras* ('Sons of the Ganges'). They identify themselves as Kanya-Kubj Brahmans, and claim to be the genuinely 'enthroned' (*gaddi nashin*) *panda* families of the city with the most ancient and extensive rights. In the past they were associated with an eccentrically courtly style of life – one indulging a fancy for caged birds, another spending hours on end playing a yo-yo out of an upstairs window as he gazed vacantly down on the throngs of pilgrims being shepherded in and out of his house by his servants. But by now their former glory is distinctly faded, only four of the nine 'thrones' are left,[34] and the incumbents of three of them have fallen on hard times – in no small measure owing to the depradations of the fourth, the city's most powerful pilgrimage-priest.

The title 'Sons of the Ganges' is also claimed by a group of Sarjupari Brahman pilgrimage-priests, less contentiously known as 'The thousand brothers' (*Hazar bhai*). In the past they are said to have worked for the *Nau kul sardar* as *jurnihar* – those who 'joined' the pilgrims to their priest by going to conduct them from other pilgrimage places or from their own towns and villages.[35] By taking pilgrims who were *apurv* – literally, 'that which has never happened before' – they managed to acquire legitimate rights of their own; and by encroaching on the clientele of their employers they acquired illegitimate ones as well.

Not surprisingly, the *Hazar bhai* themselves often invoke a more august account of their origins, according to which their rights go back as far as it is possible to go – to Lord Vishnu's creation of the world at Manikarnika *kund*. When Siva came upon Vishnu burning with the fire of his asceticism beside the tank which he had dug with his discus, he desired to take a purifying bath in those sacred waters, and required a worthy recipient to accept the gifts which would complete the ritual. As Vishnu himself adamantly refused to perform this service, Shiva created 'The thousand brothers' out of the palm of his hand. Since that time they have been extending their palms to receive the gifts of pilgrims who bathe in the tank, beside which is a big stone platform known as 'the throne of the thousand' (*takht hazara*) on which they sit.

While the *Nau kul sardar* are closely intermarried, the claim that they constituted a strictly endogamous unit until comparatively recently is implausible in the light of genealogical evidence. Though they are said to be Kanya-Kubj Brahmans, one of Anjaninandan's father's wives was the daughter of a leading *Hazar bhai* family (who are said to be Sarjuparis). Today both groups have many affinal connections with non-priestly Brahman families of the region,[36] as well as with pilgimage-priests in other major centres – in particular with Pryag and Ayodhya (though not with Gaya where the *panda* community remains largely endogamous (Vidyarthi 1961:56)). While even affines from non-priestly households may get sucked into the business empire of a big-time pilgrimage-priest, and are commonly drafted onto the *ghats* at periods of peak activity, affinal relations with *panda* communities elsewhere are likely to have even greater pragmatic significance, as is suggested by the case of the Ayodhya *panda* to whom van der Veer (1988) gives the pseudonym Gangaram.[37]

Born into a Banaras *tirath-purohit* family (Figure 2), Gangaram married the daughter of Ayodhya's Lal Mohriya *panda* – the pilgrimage-priest with the 'red seal' of the raja of Nepal. As part of his dowry he received *jajmani* rights in Ayodhya, where he took up residence in the house of his father-in-law, to whose 'throne' (*gaddi*) he eventually succeeded (after allegedly poisoning his brother-in-law). From this base, and with a house strategically located on the main road, Gangaram embarked on a policy of predatory expansion from which he emerged as the 'godfather' who now controls the lion's share of Ayodhya's pilgrimage business (van der Veer 1988:252ff).

In Banaras his two brothers at Rajghat succeeded to the opulent 'throne' of their grandfather, Dhunman Panda, and claim rights to pilgrims from Gonda, Basti and Faizabad districts in UP, and from Hazaribagh district in Bihar. The locations are significant. Rajghat is situated at the edge of the city close to the railway station at which Gaya pilgrims arrive and depart, and on the main road between Gaya to the southeast and Ayodhya to the northwest. Ayodhya is more or less at the centre of the three UP districts in Dhunman Panda's *jajmani*, while Hazaribagh is adjacent to Gaya. The family, in short, occupies a series of pivotal 'nodes' on one of north India's most popular pilgrimage routes. Gangaram lives at the heart of the area in which supplies his Banaras family with the majority of their *jajman*, has managed to capture a major slice of the Ayodhya pilgrimage market for himself, and is consequently well placed to put a great deal of business the way of his brothers. For their part, the latter feed him with pilgrims travelling west from Banaras and Gaya, where they have numerous agents drumming up business not only amongst their Hazaribagh *jajman* but also amongst the passing trade.

But not all Gangaram's pilgrims travelling east to Banaras and Gaya can be dispatched to his brothers at Rajghat. While in Ayodhya it is Gangaram who is the *Lal Mohriya panda* of Nepal, in Banaras it is Gajanand – not Dhunman – who has the 'red seal'. But Gajanand is both factionally allied and affinally

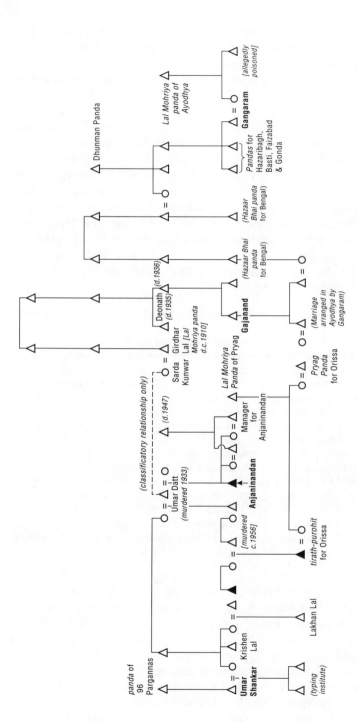

▲ Current incumbent of one of **Nau Kul Gaddis**

2 Genealogical details relating to *panda* case histories

related to Dhunman's family, who at busy times accommodate his surplus pilgrims in their *dharamshala* (lodge). Moreover, one of Gajanand's sons is married to the (brotherless) daughter of an Ayodhya *panda* (from whom he is expected to inherit) – a match which is said to have been arranged by Gangaram. The two *Lal Mohriya pandas* have clearly developed a viable working relationship.[38]

'The nine chiefly descent lines' (*Nau kul sardar*) and 'The thousand brothers' (*Hazar bhai*) distinguish their function as *tirath-purohits* ('pilgrim-age-priests') from that of the Panch Dravids (or Kashikars) who are merely *Kshetra-purohits* ('area-priests'). The latter are Brahmans of Deccani or South Indian origin whom the Panch Gaur (the northern *pandas*) claim to have originally employed to deal with southern pilgrims. Their independent right to accomodate and preside over the rituals performed by their southern *jajman* has, however, long been acknowledged. But what is disputed is their authority to receive offerings made on the banks of the Ganges (and other sacred waters), and it is their alleged incapacity to do so which provides the basis for the *tirath/kshetra purohit* distinction.

> The claim was first contested, as far as can be ascertained, in 1717, when the Panch Dravids, Maratha priests who migrated centuries ago to Benares to minister to the wants of pilgrims from south and west India, claimed the offerings made by certain pilgrims of this description who had bathed at the Manikarnika Kund [tank] under their guidance. The case was decided by the Qazi of Muhammudabad, then the official name of Benares, and the claim of the Panch Dravids was admitted, after consulting not only certain *farmans* of Akbar and Shah Alam, who had remitted the poll-tax on pilgrims, but also a copper-plate of the days of Anangpal. Two years later, however, the matter was compromised, and it was agreed that the Gangaputras alone should get the offerings, and that the breach of this agreement should be punished by fine or imprisonment. The East India Company at first ordered all offerings to be paid into the treasury, but in 1803 expressly recognised the claims of the Gangaputras with regard to offerings made by pilgrims on the banks of the Ganges. In 1813, and again in 1820, the Gangaputras successfully established their rights against the Panch Dravids in the civil court . . . In 1829 [they] . . . successfully resisted an attempt on the part of the Panch Dravids to get hold of Pisach Mochan and other tanks, as the Commissioner held that the ruling of the High Court applied to these as well as to the bathing places on the river . . . (Nevill 1909:69–70)

Their right to perform all the other functions of the north Indian *panda* was however continually upheld by the courts, and today at any rate the distinction between 'pilgrimage-' and 'area-priest' is largely rhetorical. The Panch Dravids do, however, constitute a linguistically, culturally and residentially distinctive priestly community.[39] There are perhaps twenty Panch Dravids with recognised claims to certain areas of South India. But many southern pilgrims acknowledge a north Indian *panda* – one of the richest of whom has an exclusively South Indian clientele.

In the past, a distinctive group – the Jatrawals – served as specialist pilgrim-guides (especially for Bengalis), and also established themselves as *tirath-purohits* for a few limited areas. Also derisively known as *Busiya* ('chaff of grain'), they claimed the exclusive right to patrol a 60 yard segment of the alley which passes in front of the main entrance of the Vishvanath temple, and to conduct the pilgrims they met there in their *darshan* (their 'worshipful viewing') of the deity. Of the latter's offerings they would receive half (as well as a substantial share of the price paid to the flower-sellers for the garlands offered). Today there is a mere handful of Jatrawal who still pursue their 'traditional' calling, and it is another group – the Joshi-Bhandars – who provide the vast majority of the city's pilgrim-guides.

Though each acknowledges the others' claim to be *bona fide pandas*, the pilgrimage-priests and temple-priests distinguish themselves as *pindiya* and *lingiya pandas* – those with the right to preside over rice-ball offerings to the ancestors (*pinds*), and those with the right to preside over offerings to the phallic emblem of Siva (*ling*). The division of labour is clear-cut,[40] and – by comparison with relations within each of these categories – what is striking is the lack of any serious conflict between them.

No *panda* of substance can possibly serve all his pilgrims himself. Most of the rituals they perform take place on the banks of the Ganges and are presided over by a *ghatiya*. The *ghatiya* sits beside the river on a wooden platform, known as a *chauki*, shaded by a leaf umbrella. Much of his time is spent watching over the clothes and valuables of the bathers, to whom he provides comb and mirror, a *tilak* (an auspicious mark on the forehead made with vermillion or sandalwood paste), and the opportunity to start the day by offering a few coins to the image of the deity he keeps on his platform. In the case of city bathers he will often have a long-term relationship. For his *nemi*, his 'regulars', his platform is a place to meet, exchange gossip, pontificate about politics and religion, or merely relax in congenial company.

In the context of this book, however, the *ghatiyas*' most important function is that they conduct many of the ancestral offerings of the pilgrims (in a ritual known as *tirath-shraddh*), and they generally preside over the immersion of the ashes. The theory (upheld by the courts since 1821) is that *ghatiya* has no right to the associated gifts of *dan*, but only to the much smaller *dakshina* which is a fee or payment for his ritual services.[41] In fact, however, the *panda* also pays him a commission of 2 annas in the (16 anna) rupee on all gifts offered at his platform.

Some *ghatiyas* have proprietary rights on the *ghat*; some have taken their platforms on fixed-rent leases and some are the employees who work for half the takings. The proprietor's right is to a specific site, or rather series of sites to which his platform is moved as the water-level rises and falls. On the whole length of the river-front there are 187 platforms which are regularly manned. At Manikarnika there are currently twenty-two regular *ghatiyas*, of whom about fifteen are the tenants of one of the major pilgrimage-priests. Twenty or thirty years ago there would have been nearer to fifty. Most, but not all, are

Brahmans – though the pilgrim assumes that they are. Five or six out of nearly 200 are women; and on the less profitable *ghats* some are part-timers.

Most crucial to the pilgrimage-priest, however, are his agents – his *dalals* and *gumashtas*. The former are his local representatives in the area to which he claims rights, or in other nearby places of pilgrimage. They receive a half share in all the gifts made by the pilgrims they deliver (plus travel expenses). In the past the *panda* would often himself visit the home areas of his *jajman* in order to drum up business, collect previously promised gifts, or escort parties of pilgrims back to the city (cf. Vidyarthi 1961:77; van der Veer 1988:242). Today such visits continue only on a reduced scale: those most in tune with the spirit of the times find mass mailings and telephone calls to their agents a more efficient use of resources.

The *gumashtas* are the *tirath-purohit*'s agents who are based within the city. An important pilgrimage-priest will have up to twenty-five to thirty permanent *gumashtas*, and will double or even treble this number at periods of peak demand. Their job is to collect their master's pilgrims from Pryag, Gaya and Ayodhya or meet them at the railway and bus stations, take them to visit the temples and deliver them to the *ghats* for the rituals, which at busy times they may even conduct themselves (though they are not necessarily Brahmans[42]). For this they receive a 25 per cent share in the gifts, and they also collect a 25–50 per cent commission from the shop-keepers and boatmen for any business they put their way. The *pandas* and *gumashtas* have an elaborate code language in which such shares can be negotiated in front of the pilgrims, an argot which apparently derives from that of the river-thugs of the early nineteenth century (Mehrotra 1977:36, 85), and which is so impenetrable to the average pilgrim that even Mehrotra – a trained linguist and a native of Banaras brought up in a merchant community with its own code language – reports listening to a thirty-minute exchange of which he could follow nothing (p. 46–7).

The stations are in many ways the key to a *panda*'s business, and a successful one needs rather more accurate knowledge of the railway time-table than of the Sanskrit *mantras*. Access to the platforms has been a major source of violent competition throughout this century, and although the 'Sons of the Ganges' have now lost control of the Cantonment station (their 'customary rights' to which were reaffirmed by an order of the District Magistrate in 1903),[43] Anjaninandan Mishra has managed to retain a monopoly on the suburban station just up the line, which means that his own men can approach the pilgrims before they arrive. It is here above all that a *panda* needs tough and resourceful *gumashtas*: 'to steal the *jajman* of others and to break the hands and feet of those who steal ours'; to drive the pilgrims off the platform where many of them sleep at night by taking a broom and water and pretending to be a sweeper.

'Brahmans and dogs', people say, 'are two castes that cannot live together [in peace].' A *panda*'s chances of a violent death are strikingly high; and in the past several of the most prominent served as patrons for one of the city's numerous wrestling schools. This not only reflects a cultural preoccupation with the perfection of the body (see pp. 167ff),[44] but also a need for strong-arm men to protect their interests. That this patronage has declined over recent decades is often put down to a more sophisticated technology of violence (guns and sulphuric acid), and to a greater reliance on less heroic means of defending one's rights (the courts and helpful contacts with the police). It is also probably part of a more general withdrawal of elite patronage from Banarasi popular culture (Kumar 1988).

Much of the conflict has surrounded the determination of Anjaninandan Mishra – the most powerful representative of the *Nau kul sardar* and the self-styled raja of the *pandas* – to exact a *chaharam*, a levy of 4 annas in every rupee gifted as *dan* along almost the entire river frontage. We can pick up the story (with the help of Figure 2) in the 1880s when the family of Umar Shankar, who claimed to be the *Chaudhuris* ('headmen') of the *Hazar bhai*, asserted their right to a quarter share of all offerings made in the vicinity of Manikarnika *ghat* by pilgrims from the ninety-six Pargannas during the intercalary month (*adhik mas*) that is added to the Hindu calendar in every third year. The ninety-six Pargannas were the domain of the Maharaja of Banaras. Umar Shankar's family claimed the Maharaja as their *jajman*, and on this basis the right to levy a 4 anna share in all offerings made by his subjects as 'the kingdom's portion' (*raj ansh*). The intercalary month is the most popular time for performing the *Panch-kosi* pilgrimage which circumambu-lates the city, and which begins and ends with gifts to Brahmans at Manikarnika *ghat*. The pilgrims come in tens of thousands, and nearly all of them are of local origin.

By the early years of this century Umar Datt – the father of Anjaninandan Mishra – was upstaging Umar Shankar by asserting the right to collect at all times a quarter share of the gifts made by any pilgrim between Gay *ghat* and Assi. The basis for this claim is obscure, some informants representing it as the assertion of an independent and ancient right; some as a usurpation (and considerable extension) of the rights exercised by the *Chaudhuri* of the *Hazar bhai*; most as a purely opportunistic demand made 'on the strength of the stave'. In any event, it provoked countless skirmishes on the *ghats*; and Umar Shankar and Umar Datt – who were already at loggerheads over claims to Gujerati pilgrims – now disputed the other's right to exact a quarter share during the intercalary month. Caught without cover by Umar Datt's men, Umar Shankar was hospitalised for weeks, and his son (who has now abandoned *pandagiri* for the calmer waters of a typing institute) recalls never going to school without two or three bodyguards. Uma Datt was murdered in 1933; Umar Shankar was tried and acquitted, but died shortly afterwards.

Since his father's death, Anjaninandan has continued to insist on his share – though his demands have been continuously resisted by those with the power to do so. One of these is Gajanand, in whose *jajmani* rights Anjaninandan had

taken an early interest. Until his death in 1910 (or thereabouts), Girdhar Lal
Pathak had been the *Lal Mohriya panda* of Nepal, and had also held a 6/16
share in the hill areas of Almora, Kumoan and Naini Tal. His widow, Sarda
Kunwar, then appointed Deonath (her husband's father's father's brother's
son's son) to manage the business. When he died in 1935, Gajanand acquired
the red seal and pilgrim registers. In 1937, however, Sarda Kunwar began legal
proceedings for their recovery at the instigation of her classificatory brother's
son, Anjaninandan Mishra, and on the understanding that he would
henceforth manage these rights on her behalf. The pattern recurs: a
well-heeled widow needs an experienced *gumashta* (who is probably a
kinsman of some sort) to manage the business; her rights are progressively
eroded and she is then prevailed upon to accept the help of a powerful *panda*
who recovers them largely for himself. Though the rules of litigation preclude
champerty, they are easy enough to evade. In this particular case, however, the
strategy was only partly successful. The appeal court accepted Gajanand's
claim that the Maharaja of Nepal had appointed Deonath to succeed to
Girdhar Lal, and therefore ruled that Sarda Kunwar had no legitimate
interest in the 'red seal' of the kingdom. She was however entitled to the return
of the pilgrim registers for Almora, Kumoan and Naini Tal, though nobody
could prevent Gajanand from entertaining pilgrims from these areas who
came to him of their own accord.[45] Anjaninandan published fly-sheets
informing these hill pilgrims that he was now their proper *panda*, but the court
receiver experienced great difficulty recovering the record books from
Gajanand (who was sentenced for contempt).

During and immediately after these protracted legal proceedings, Anjaninandan devoted considerable energy to persuading Gajanand to acknowledge his right to the quarter share. A number of violent incidents occurred,
culminating in the death of one of Gajanand's men at Manikarnika in
December 1947. Feelings at the time were running particularly high because of
the recent intercalary month, when armed police had been posted at the *ghat*
to prevent any trouble with Krishen Lal and Lakhan Lal who were now
collecting Umar Shankar's *raj ansh* – the share that the latter had claimed as
'the kingdom's portion'. It was alleged that the police intervention was not
entirely even-handed. Some of Anjanandan's *gumashtas* had apparently been
taken into custody as a preventative measure, and others intimidated from
going about their legitimate business. In the trial which followed the death of
Gajanand's servant, the defence was to insinuate that Krishen Lal and
Lakhan Lal had inspired the malicious attempt to implicate (the absent)
Anjaninandan.

The prosecution case was that he had been attending the tenth day
mortuary rites of his father-in-law at Manikarnika *ghat*, along with the two
sons of the deceased (both Anjaninandan's employees) and a group of armed
gumashtas. When Gajanand and several retainers came to the *ghat* in
attendance on a Nepali pilgrim, Anjaninandan had decided that the size of his

party provided a persuasive argument why his rival should now submit to his claims. Twelve of his followers were subsequently arrested and charged with murder, though the court records describe Anjaninandan himself as 'absconding'. It was said at the time (and is endlessly repeated today) that he was hiding out with his travelling circus in Bengal.[46]

The aftermath of this incident explains much about the contemporary position of the Joshi Brahmans (otherwise known as Bhandars or Bhanreriyas), as freelance pilgrim-guides who meet the trains and buses, pick up parties of pilgrims in – say – Pryag and Ayodhya, or deliver them on to Gaya. The *tirath-purohits* describe them as 'chemical' or 'road-brand' (*sarakchhap*) *pandas*; as *dakotiya* Brahmans who take the highly dangerous and inauspicious gifts which rid the donor of the afflictions of the planet Saturn,[47] or as not really Brahmans at all. Since the Joshis have no long-term relations with the pilgrims, they say, they exploit them without let. 'They want to take all the golden eggs even if it means killing the chicken.' There are roughly four hundred Joshis working as pilgrim-guides in the city.

Before the events I have just described, the Joshis were delivering most of their pilgrims to the *tirath-purohits* for a 25 per cent share of the gifts of those from established areas, and a 50 per cent share in the gifts of pilgrims without an established *panda*. Anjaninandan was apparently the chief beneficiary of this arrangement; but during the course of their dispute Gajanand declared himself willing to offer them a 75 per cent stake, and to recognise their right to take pilgrims wherever they chose. Within weeks he reportedly had over a hundred Joshis bringing pilgrims to his riverside platforms, and a group of disaffected *ghatiyas* had begun to serve others they brought. By cutting out the *panda*, the Joshi triples his share, and the *ghatiya* doubles his. By 1983, however, relations between the Joshi caste association (the Joshi Brahman Sangh) and the association of independent *ghatiyas* had turned sour, the latter trying to establish a rule which would compel the Joshis to bring pilgrims *only* to the platforms of their members.

Since the Joshis have every interest in encroaching on their rights, and now have a much improved chance of getting away with it,[48] the less powerful *tirath-purohits* find it ever more difficult to retain an effective monopoly on their 'traditional' clientele; and today the Joshis have succeeded in cornering much of the market in the poorer rapid-turn-over pilgrims. They have also consistently sought to legitimise their position by supporting the administration's repeated proposals to require that the profession of pilgrimage-priest should be licensed[49] – a measure which would, they believe, establish beyond doubt their credentials as *bona fide* card-carrying *pandas*. It is partly for this reason that the *tirath-purohits* have systematically blocked the proposal, which would also limit their freedom to take on extra *gumashta*-servants at busy times of the year, and would give the police *carte blanche* to deny licences to anybody with a criminal record (which is to say, a great many).

The in-roads which the Joshis have made on the Banaras pilgrimage business since the beginning of this century have parallels in Gaya and Ayodhya. It would I think be a mistake, however, to speak of a complete transformation of the pilgrimage system, or to over-emphasise the discontinuities with the past. With reference to Gaya, Vidyarthi (1961:96ff) reports a general decline in the volume of pilgrims and value of gifts in the post-Independence period. Partition deprived the Gayawal *pandas* of some of their most valuable catchment areas; land reform legislation and the abolition of the princely states placed many of their most magnanimous donors in much reduced circumstances. The secular spirit of the times has reduced not only the numbers of pilgrims but also their generosity, while the intense factionalism which has infected the Gayawal community has encouraged a host of unscrupulous interlopers. Once 'famous for their holiness and piety', the cynical materialism with which they have now come to be associated provokes only 'contempt and ridicule' (p. 109).

These conclusions are broadly endorsed by van der Veer's Ayodhya study. 'The mafia-like activities' and 'growing internal competition' of the contemporary *panda* community are the consequence of an almost complete breakdown of the old configuration. Durable long-term relations between priests and their patrons have been replaced by 'the emergence of a totally impersonal religious market' (1988:188), a controlled trickle of elite donors by a torrent of hoi polloi pilgrims, and the relationship between *panda* and pilgrim has been replaced by that between *panda* and agent as the pivot of the system. *Pandagiri* is a less profitable business than it was; and it is this – combined with its commercialisation and impersonality – which explains the low esteem in which *pandas* are now generally held, their present sense of degradation, and their desire that their sons should enter some other occupation. 'The reputation of the *pandas* has exceedingly declined' (1985:320) from a past in which theirs was 'an honourable profession, in which the brahman did a service to the lords of the land and people in North India and was honoured for that service' (1985:310).

What these authors offer, then, is one further proof of a fact well known to most Hindus: though the Kali Age has been in process for centuries, time is degenerating at an ever accelerating pace. That there have been important changes in the scale and nature of pilgrimage to Banaras, and in the kind of patronage which the city attracts, is not in doubt (see pp. 38ff). That these changes represent a complete 'transformation of the old configuration', that the past was quite so golden as the *pandas* themselves portray it, or that the present is to be understood as 'a totally impersonal religious market' is rather less clear.

For Banaras at least it is likely that pilgrim numbers have continued to grow in the post-Independence period;[50] and that the aggregate – as opposed to average – value of their offerings has not significantly declined. Nor thirty years on from Vidyarthi's study does it seem entirely safe to assume that a spirit of secularism poses such a serious threat to the *panda*'s livelihood. I have, more importantly, found it impossible to identify a historical base-line at which a solidary and harmonious community Banaras pilgrimage-priests were famed for their 'holiness and piety', at which the 'business-like' behaviour which van der Veer sees as the hallmark of the contemporary situation was absent, or at which the *panda*'s relationship with the majority of his *jajman* can have been anything other than transitory and impersonal. Though the Joshi Brahmans have only mounted a serious challenge to the *tirath-purohits*' monopoly in the course of this century, they are simply the latest in a long line of interlopers who have sought to establish themselves 'on the strength of the stave'. Though peshwas and princes would have doubtless enjoyed the personal attentions of their *panda* (as the politician and industrialist does today), how many members of the 200,000-strong armed Maratha convoys arriving in Banaras at the beginning of the nineteenth century can really have experienced a comfortable intimacy with their *tirath-purohit*? *Pandagiri* (the profession) has had a very poor press for a very long time, and the Dharmashastra literature roundly condemns the fallen Brahman perverted enough to accept gifts on the banks of the Ganges. Though it is obviously true that a niche in this profession is valued in proportion to its profitability, it is equally obvious that financial incentive is not the same as status-honour; and it is altogether too simple to assume a straightforward congruence between the esteem in which *pandagiri* is held and the wealth it confers.

3.4 The values of purity

Hindu society is often represented as caste society. In Dumont's (1970a) influential model, caste society is defined by a strict hierarchical disjunction between (religious) status and (politico-economic) power. Status is based on purity, and purity is the 'encompassing' value in terms of which everything else is as far as possible expressed. The Brahman is the acme of purity; the priest is the paradigmatic Brahman and hence a paragon of purity. A specialisation of tasks between castes is required if those of superior status are to maintain their purity; and this division of labour reveals an orientation towards the whole which 'sharply distinguishes the Indian form of the social division of labour from the modern economic form, which is oriented towards individual profit and in which, in theory, the market is left to regulate the whole' (p. 92).

In the light of Dumont's model, a striking aspect of my data is the pervasiveness, not of the language of status, but of the language of power. *Supposedly* the pre-eminent representative of the values of purity, the priest is So-and-so *Maharaj* who sits on the '*throne*' of this or that forebear (as does the merchant in his shop). The *Nau kul sardar* (*sardar*, a 'chief' or 'commander') claim to be the city's only genuinely 'enthroned' pilgrimage-priests, and take pride in a glorious past in which they lived like *princes* – in youth devoting themselves to martial arts and to defending their family honour in hand-to-hand combat; in sedate maturity indulging a taste for rare orchids, Urdu poetry, fine music and dancing girls. Not only the priest but the 'contra-priest' is a 'king'. Towering over the river-front with its regally rampant lions is the palace of the Dom raja. Even the generally impoverished Barber is honorifically known as the *Nau thakur* ('the Barber lord'). While Hocart's (1950) model of caste would lead us to suppose that it is the *jajman* who replicates the royal function at the local level, here it often seems to be the specialist who borrows the raja's robes. While Dumont's model would lead us to suppose that dominance is as far as possible expressed in the language of status, here – at the heart of the Hindu world – status is as likely to express itself in the language of dominance. It is in this context perhaps worth recalling that the Maharaja of Banaras is himself a Brahman.

My experience of matters of purity began before I had even stepped off the Kashi–Vishvanath Express at Varanasi Cant station on a steaming monsoon day in 1976. As the train juddered to a halt, a burly *dhoti*-clad figure, red-check *gamchha*[51] over one shoulder, swung open the door and clambered over my mountain of suitcases, barking '*hat jao, hat jao*' ('out of the way, out of the way') and brusquely gesturing for me to stand well back lest I inadvertently contaminate the immaculately laundered elderly gentleman he was accompanying. I knew enough already to recognise a *panda*'s agent and important pilgrim; but not enough to allay an immediate sense of panic. How was I – a *mlechha* (a polluted foreigner) – to gain any kind of access to this hyper-orthodox world?

This vignette is indeed revealing – but only of one part of the reality I encountered. As I later learnt, the incident was – as likely as not – an almost self-conscious enactment of a public rhetoric from which private practice is often remarkably deviant. For my priestly informants, orthopraxy is part of a professional persona. Even in its absence, a show of fastidiousness must be made for *jajman* one is particularly anxious to impress. Sita and Ram Maharaj are two brothers who work at Manikarnika *ghat* as *karam-kandis* (as specialists in Brahmanical ritual). Despite coming into continual physical contact with the mourners they serve, neither would generally bother to bathe until the end of their working day. Nor in most contexts would either of them acknowledge any ritual imperative to do so. But I vividly recall Sita Maharaj roundly berating his brother for neglecting to take – or rather to be seen to take – a purifying bath in the Ganges at the end of a mortuary sequence performed by a wealthy local magnate of whom he had great expectations. Some of my informants were indeed rigidly orthoprax, and I do not wish to imply that considerations of caste and purity are not strongly internalised values. But many are not; and in general the Banarasi Brahman is no more 'a slave to a custom' than Malinowski's (1926) Trobriander.

As my Brahman informants represent it, caste affiliation is predominantly patrilineal. A child, it is true, is the product of the bodily substance of both its parents. Its flesh is formed from the uterine blood of its mother; its bones from the semen of its father. Since these are the more enduring contribution, the semen – they say – 'is pre-eminent'.[52] Pure descent is idiomatically expressed as having 'clean bones', on which an inferiority in the mother may produce a 'blemish' (*khot, dag*), though this does not disqualify her children from membership in their father's caste. Indeed I was several times told that if a girl is married before the menarche she automatically acquires the caste of her husband, and that it is only if she marries afterwards that the children are to be regarded as 'half-breeds' (*varan shankar*). Though it may not be safe to explain the behaviour (breaches of caste endogamy) by the ideology (the notion that the status of the mother does not fundamentally determine that of the child), the fact is that in all the priestly communities I have discussed a significant proportion of 'conjugal' unions are across caste boundaries, and/or involve a woman who has been separated or widowed.[53]

Even those who live openly with a mistress or 'kept woman'[54] of uncertain caste origins may be extremely pernickety in matters of diet or about other sources of pollution – prohibiting onions and garlic (let alone meat and eggs) in the house, and decontaminating the freshly laundered clothes returned by the Washerman by sprinkling them with Ganges water. Impurity, and especially an impure diet, is often cited as a source of misfortune, illness and even death. Not only is one's bodily substance created out of food, but so is one's moral disposition (Marriott 1976). 'From eating the grains of a Shudra the intellect is overturned. As the grains you eat, so will be the mind.'[55]

Between different priestly communities, and even between individuals of the same community, there is however considerable variation. Many Mahabrahmans and Joshis make no pretence to be vegetarian or teetotal; and though *pandas* and *karam-kandis* generally do, a few at least are notorious tipplers. One brother would sit down to eat with me in public and even accept food from our kitchen without any obvious qualms; another would plainly find the very idea repugnant and refuse water from my hand. Food prepared in such-and-such a way can only be eaten from such-and-such people; but having stated the rule my informants would often complacently observe that *prem ki bat aur hai* – that 'affection is a different matter'.

Though the anthropological literature (e.g. Douglas 1966:130) often asserts that pollution rules are clear and unequivocal – the only question being whether the forbidden contact has in fact occurred – I found a degree of indeterminacy. Such is its sacred power that Ganges water is often said to provide a complete prophylactic against pollution. But does its protection last for eighteen hours after bathing (as one informant claimed), or merely as long as it takes for the water to evaporate from the skin (as his friend was arguing)? My wife was invited to act as official photographer at the annual festival of the goddess of the Manikarnika tank by the *Nau kul panda* who was organising the event. In order to get pictures of the most solemn part of the proceedings, she needed to go down the steps to the water's edge; but to this several of the assembled Brahmans strongly objected. Our host was livid. Though our taken-for-granted impurity was not at issue in the argument which followed, opinion *was* divided over whether this could possibly pollute a sacred space and an image of such extraordinary power.[56]

As we have seen, nobody normally objects to Untouchables bathing in Manikarnika *kund*; many *pandas* are prepared to accommodate them,[57] and provided discretion is assured some Mahabrahmans are happy enough to accept their gifts. But whether interpreted as evidence of an easy-going pragmatism, or of the ideological suspension of the rules of caste during pilgrimage, these selected facts convey a picture which is as much an over-simplification as would be one of rigid caste orthodoxy. Even today the burning *ghat* Doms prevent Sweeper Doms from cremating their dead at Manikarnika, where the temple dedicated to Shiva as the Lord of the Cremation Ground was still displaying in the early 1980s a large notice warning Untouchables against entry.

What can be said without equivocation, however, is that purity is only one measure of hierarchical status, and that the priest is certainly not the epitome of Brahmanical superiority. The best Brahman is a scholar and a teacher, preferably of independent means. Though some it is true are better than others, no priest is entirely respectable, and the Funeral-priest is often regarded as little better than an outcaste. What is more, at least as much about his degraded status is explained by his inauspiciousness as by his impurity, and – as we will see in the chapter which follows (pp. 122ff) – the relative status of different priestly specialisms is widely represented in terms of the relative inauspiciousness of the gifts they receive. It is therefore misleading to imply – as does Raheja (1988:46) – that ideas about inauspiciousness are a quite separate dimension from the values of hierarchy (cf. Toffin 1990); and equally misleading to imply (as does Dumont) that status is simply a matter of purity, or that the priestly Brahman is the supreme embodiment of either.

3.5 'The law of the fishes'

Dumont is, however, clearly right to claim that the division of labour between castes is 'oriented towards the whole' rather than towards the quest for individual profit institutionalised by the modern market. One might even go as far as to say that the system reveals 'an anti-market mentality'. It is of course true that there are endless instances of the members of one group encroaching on the rights of another – of *ghatiyas* who pocket the 'tax' demanded in the name of the Dom at the time of the immersion of the ashes; of *pandas* who masquerade as Mahabrahmans to receive the gifts of the ghost; of Joshis who warn an arriving pilgrim that his hereditary pilgrimage-priest will demand a fortune while he would be far more economical. But there is no question of the specialist having a legitimate right to respond to demand by switching 'lines', or of the run of 'buyers' being indifferent between alternative 'sellers'. Nor is competition *within* the specialist group seen as either right or proper, however pervasive it is in fact. Indeed the *pari* rota system is quite explicitly represented as a device to eliminate conflict and competition between members of the same occupational group. Even the Joshi who maintains the theoretical principle of *manvritti* – of the pilgrim's entitlement to go with whomsoever he chooses – acknowledges that he should never approach one who has already been propositioned by another Joshi, and would certainly claim rights over any he had served before. While there is in practice no shortage of maximising men on the *ghats*, and while the haggling between the specialist and his patrons is often interminable, bargaining does not imply competition and maximising does not make a market. The business of death is clearly not run on the principles of business economics.

But there is also plainly a difference between collective goals and those of the individual actor; and between the way in which people ought to act in an ideal world and the behaviour expected of them in the real one. By definition, 'an anti-market mentality' can only exist in an ideological universe which has also conceived of its opposite. As I have previously argued (p. 49), my informants' understanding of human motivation is often robustly cynical, and they are quite as prone as the most hard-nosed utilitarian to interpret the actions of others in terms of a single-minded quest for material self-gain – hence, I believe, their preoccupation with elaborating an institutional framework which curbs it, and their endless concern with the precise specification of shares. It is as if regulation must be imposed if chaos is to be kept at bay. The alternative is 'the law of the fishes'. At least in part, the legitimacy of the order I have described depends on a vision of the world that would otherwise be: a world in which big fishes gobble up little ones without any restraint.

What goes for the over-arching order applies also, I believe, to the person. According to Marriott (1976) and his Chicago colleagues (e.g. Inden and Nicholas 1977), in the Indian world-view bio-genetic substance and moral code are two aspects of the same thing. Substance determines conduct; conduct modifies substance. A person's moral qualities, that is, 'are thought to be altered by changes in the person's body that result from eating certain foods, engaging in certain kinds of sexual intercourse, undergoing certain ceremonies, or falling under certain other kinds of influences' (Marriott and Inden 1977:228). To a greater or lesser extent, almost any transaction involves an exchange of bio-moral qualities, and consequently transforms the sub-stance-code of the parties to it. Transactors, says Marriott (1976:111), 'give out from themselves particles of their own coded substances . . . that may then produce in others something of the nature of the persons in whom they originated'. The corollary is that Indian thought is not only 'emphatically monistic and dynamic' but also 'highly particularistic'. By contrast with the Western concept of the individual as an autonomous, indivisible, bounded unit with an immutable bio-genetic make-up, South Asians represent the person as 'divisible' and – as it were – constitutionally volatile 'since circulations and combinations of particles of substance-code are continually occurring'. Not only is 'each actor and action unique', but the 'unique essence' of each is *constantly* changing (Marriott 1976:112; cf. Daniel 1984:72).

Though there is much in this picture that I find persuasive and immediately recognisable, I suspect that it is also somewhat overdrawn. It is, no doubt, difficult for us to think ourselves into a world in which persons conceive of themselves as quite such protean entities ready to be shaped anew by every chance encounter, or to imagine a social world in which my intimate associate of today may be a *substantially* different person tomorrow. But certainly such a conception does not altogether accord with the quite robust and stable sense of self which many of my Indian friends seem to project. Nor – to put the problem slightly differently – is it altogether clear how this construct of the person as composed of highly fluid substance squares with Marriott's earlier writings on caste ranking, which were premised on the assumption of an equivalence between all members of the same caste such that each caste could be assigned to a single cell in the matrix of food transactions (e.g. Marriott 1968). How, one wonders, could such equivalence be sustained in a world in which *each* actor's substance-code is endlessly modified and transformed by the myriad exchanges in which he is *uniquely* involved? How indeed can anybody ever decide with whom, and on what terms, to interact?

Yet there is surely something in both these – on the face of it mutually inconsistent – formulations which rings true to the ethnographer's experience. At least for certain purposes, castes *are* regarded as units of equivalence composed of people of the same general kind; and persons *are* seen as having a transformable bio-moral substance which is continually modified by the transactions in which they engage. How can this be? Unlike either Dumont or Marriott, I am prepared to entertain the possibility of a contradiction here, for I am not persuaded that either Hindus, or others, really think quite so systematically as these authors imply. What I want to suggest, however, is that there is a sense in which these two strands in the ideology fit together, and that the protean representation of the person sustains and reinforces the static ideology of caste.

In a great many contexts Hindus often appear to see themselves as engaged in an endless battle against impending chaos and disintegration, of which the ever-present danger of a disintegration and degeneration of the actor's own person is the most immediate and apprehensible manifestation. Constant vigilance is required to hold the balance of the body (see pp. 178ff); decay and death result from involvement in disequilibriating transactions. The impact of this menacing vision can surely only be a message of strict obedience to the rigid order of caste. What, in other words, the ideology of fluid substance implies is nothing less than the disintegration of the self results from stepping off the tried and tested tracks of the established pattern of caste interactions. Since, moreover, one's bio-moral substance extends into other persons – both through one's transactions with them and through the body particles shared with kin – any irregular exchange in which one engages also represents a direct threat to these other selves. In such a world nobody can be allowed to act as an autonomous individual, and all with whom one associates have a directly *personal* interest in monitoring one's conduct. I therefore believe that the protean construct of the person, which Marriott and his colleagues rightly identify as at least one important aspect of the Hindu world-view, acts as an 'ideology' in the classic Marxian sense. As with 'the law of the fishes', it is the symbolic elaboration of louring disorder which creates and sustains the world of order and regulation.

Society and person: at both levels regulation is so important because chaos is so close. And with time of course it gets closer still, for we live in the Kali Age, and the velocity of our descent into disorder is increasing. Though all our endeavours may ultimately be as futile as those of King Canute, the tide can be temporarily stemmed by shoring up the dykes – by tightening the rules which impose some semblance of control. It is therefore no accident that many practices (hypergamous unions between members of different *varnas* for example) which were acceptable in former epochs have now been declared *Kali-varjas* – acts prohibited in the Kali Age.[58]

3.6 *Pari* – practical reason or symbolic determination?

But if a strict division of labour between castes and a meticulous specification of shares within them is required to inhibit a ruthless pursuit of egoistic advantage in which the big fishes swallow the little, we still have to explain why some kinds of rights are allocated on the principle of a long-term hereditary relationship between the specialist and his patrons, while others are assigned on the basis of turns in a rota (*pari*).

Not only opposed in principle to market competition, the whole orientation of the *pari* system is also at odds with what J. C. Scott (1976) identifies as the fundamental premise of 'the moral economy of the peasant'. According to Scott, secure subsistence is the peasant's 'primordial goal'; his over-riding objective is to minimise risks rather than maximise returns. Somewhat similarly, Epstein (1967) had earlier argued that the so-called '*jajmani* system' is a system of fixed rewards geared to reproducing the minimum subsistence requirements of the specialist castes irrespective of the size of the harvest.[59] *Pari* by contrast is seen as institutionalising risk. In spirit it is closer to the casino than to the cautious ethic of the peasant. Not like a market, not like 'the moral economy of the peasant', in crucial respects the *pari* system is also not like our received wisdom about the nature of *jajmani* relations in rural India. It plainly precludes the stable long-term ties between patrons and specialists of the sort which Wiser (1936) described, and which have often been taken as the hallmark of the division of labour in the 'traditional' village.

It is at first sight tempting to see this absence of enduring *jajmani* relationships as all of a piece with the inevitable anonymity and transience of relationships between the vast number of pilgrims and mourners who flood into the city and the sacred specialists who serve them. Similarly, the amount of overt antagonism and the covert threat of violence which surrounds many of the interactions I have described might be simply put down to the opportunities this situation provides and to the amount of money at stake, while the tolerance of risk might be explained by the nature of an urban economy in which other sources of income are available, and few live on the 'subsistence precipice' on which the peasant supposedly teeters.

Without ruling such considerations out of court, it would I think be a mistake to put too much emphasis on them, or on the discontinuities with rural India. That local conditions preclude the development of enduring *jajmani* relationships is patently false. The *pandas* manage their business on precisely that footing; and many city people sustain long-term hereditary ties with a Barber, Washerman and household priest. That they do not do so with the Dom or the Mahabrahman cannot therefore be explained by the inevitably 'impersonal, superficial, transitory and segmented' nature of the social relationships which Wirth (1975:35) identifies as typically urban. Moreover, Sharma's (1978) picture of the latent violence of social relations in a village in the immediate rural hinterland of Banaras, and of the insistent haggling which surrounds the customary rewards of the service castes, would argue that the situation I have described is rather more continuous with the rural one than much of the literature might suggest. Nor are *pari* systems an exclusively urban phenomenon. Orenstein (1965a:311), Randeria (1989) and Parry (1979:65) have all reported their occurrence in widely separated parts of rural India, though as we are about to see it is arguably significant that in the last of these cases it is *only* the funeral priests who allocate rights on this basis.

Although a curious inversion of the bluff pragmatism on which he insists when explaining the relative inferiority of the Brahman priest by reference to the contemporary politico-economic conditions of the pilgrimage centre, van der Veer (1988:207) hints at a straightforwardly idealist solution to our problem in which practical reason gives place to symbolic determination. Mahabrahmans cannot set up long-term ties with those they serve because they embody the ghosts with whom nobody is willing to establish an enduring relationship. Following this line of thought, we might perhaps argue that there is an 'elective affinity' between *pari* systems and the most polluting and inauspicious aspects of death. While the *panda* deals with – and stands in for – the generally benevolent ancestor with whom a lasting bond is desired, the Dom and the Mahabrahman is associated with what must at all costs be got rid of, the corpse and the ghost. Since their patrons are unprepared to acknowledge a relationship with them, they must by default allocate rights on a different basis. It is at any rate striking that an association between death and *pari* runs throughout much of the ethnography I have reviewed: in one of the cartels which have been formed by the *kapal-kriya* shop-keepers at Manikarnika *ghat*, *pari* operates for *mortuary* goods but not for other commodities; the

Manikarnika Barbers have *pari* for corpses and mourners but are concerned to establish long-term relationships with most other kinds of customers; the boatmen consistently allocate corpses and ashes, but generally not other kinds of passengers, on such a basis.

But while the most polluting and inauspicious aspects of death are consistently handled on the basis of *pari*, not all *pari* systems are associated with death. The Barbers at Manikarnika also allocate the right to serve Nepali and South India pilgrims on such a basis; and the Rajghat boatmen have *pari* for ordinary passengers. The most obvious example, however, is that in many major temples in Banaras and elsewhere priestly rights to perform public worship 'for the well-being of the world' are allocated on a rota basis[60] – and it is indeed difficult to imagine how responsibility for these complex rituals could be otherwise assigned.

If in this last example pragmatic consideration appear to be pre-eminent, is it not possible that the *cultural* logic I have just outlined is rather less significant than I have implied? Take the case of the Mahabrahman. I have estimated that there are likely to be an average of ten to twelve *jajman* who will offer him *sajja dan* ten or eleven days after the day of his *pari*. But if, instead of allocating days, the Mahabrahmans allocated areas of the city, each of the right-holders would have to attend the *ghat* daily in order to make contact with his *jajman*. Given the large number of shareholders, and the relatively small number of *jajman*, the result would be a great deal of waiting around for rather scant rewards. For the significant proportion of Mahabrahmans whose domestic economies are dependent on other sources of income which require their presence elsewhere, such a system would obviously be unacceptable.

This hypothetical scenario does not of course exhaust the theoretical possibilities. Instead of hanging about on the *ghat*, in a different ideological world the Mahabrahman might rely on the *jajman* over whom he had established rights to send him word whenever his services were required. But since the latter are unwilling to acknowledge a relationship with him, they clearly cannot be expected to do so. I therefore conclude that – for the Mahabrahmans at least – a *pari* system is in fact the most pragmatically efficient way of organising their business, but that one of the crucial reasons why this should be so is set in the realm of symbolic values. 'Practical reason' is constrained (but not determined) by cultural ideas, and by itself neither offers an adequate explanatory framework.

Plate 5 A *ghatiya* on his platform. (Author's photograph.)

Plate 6 Body-builders on the *ghats*. (Photograph by Margaret Dickinson.)

4

Giving, receiving and bargaining over gifts

This chapter is concerned with the ideology which surrounds the gifts which the pilgrims and mourners make to the priests who serve them. In the first section I focus on the donors' perspective, in the second on the spiritual consequences for the priestly recipient of gifts which are held to embody the sins of the donor, while in the third I try to explore the logic which underlies this set of ideas about the poison in the gift. The fourth section discusses some of the implications of my data for other South Asianist writings, and the chapter concludes with an account of the insistent bargaining which accompanies the gift.

4.1 Sweating it out on the *ghats*

> Where, then, in the complex large-scale societies and historical religions are we to look for the topography of the inclusive, disinterested, and altruistic domain? The short answer is in their system of pilgrim centres. (Turner 1974:186)

My initial problem can be simply stated. Death and pilgrimage are big business; competition for control of the more lucrative aspects of this business can reach murderous proportions, and – in the judgement of both parties – the specialists' dealings with their *jajman* is on occasion chillingly unscrupulous. Given that many of the latter come with a shrewd (or sometimes even exaggerated) idea of what to expect, the religiously 'unmusical' outsider may perhaps be forgiven for wondering why they come at all. A number of answers to this question – worldly prestige, the expiation of sin, the acquisition of merit, the quest for salvation – are of course possible, most such answers suggesting that they come *in spite of* the notorious political in-fighting of the priests and the venality of their demands. What I want to suggest here, however, is that it may also be partly *because* of these exactions that the pilgrimage and death rituals yield their fruit.

With regard to the in-fighting, I have – like van der Veer (1988:266) – often been struck by the apparent paradox that the most ruthlessly predatory of *pandas* may be rated amongst the 'best' and most orthodox Brahmans. But unlike van der Veer (pp. 187–8), I am reluctant to speak of a 'contradiction' between the priest's capacity to absolve his pilgrims from the most heinous sins and 'his own maffia-like activities', or to attribute this 'contradiction' to the 'complete breakdown' of the pilgrimage system and to the development of 'a totally impersonal religious market'. On the 'complete breakdown' and 'total impersonality' I have already commented (pp. 108–9). As to the 'contradiction', it is perhaps largely illusory. The priest is *par excellence* a ritual technician, and from this point of view his political skulduggery with regard to the allocation of rights is not strictly relevant. The most damning criticism to be made of him is not that he is immoral, but that he is incompetent or ignorant in matters of ritual. In short, the chicanery to which his competitors are victim can be ignored (or even condoned) as beside the main point.

With regard to his transactions with the pilgrims and mourners, there is I believe a sense in which the antagonism by which they are often accompanied is fed by the ideology itself. According to this ideology, the gift (*dan*) which is offered to the priest must be a pure gift which is given up to the limit of one's capacity (*yatha shakti*). True *dan* is a voluntary and disinterested donation made without ostentation or expectation of *any* kind of *this*-worldly return. Even the desire for *other*-worldly rewards is regarded with equivocation, so that paradoxically the full quotient of merit is held to rebound only to the donor who gives without thought for his spiritual harvest. The merit acquired, in spite as it were of the ideal donor's disinterest in it, is proportionate to his or her means – the widow's mite being in theory the equal of the jewel-encrusted treasures of the prince. It is also proportionate to the worth of the recipient, which is – as we shall see – defined largely in terms of his reluctance to accept gifts.

In practice, however, the pilgrim is probably all too aware of the priests' reputation for rapacity. He knows that they are not nearly as disinterested as they should be, and that once the gift of an umbrella has been fulfilled, the gift of a cow will be demanded. Mindful that tomorrow he leaves for Gaya where there are other – and, who knows, perhaps more worshipful – priestly bellies to fill, he prudently keeps something in reserve. But the *panda* knows that the pilgrim holds back, and feels justified – by the ideology of the magnanimous and disinterested donor who gives without counting cost – in pressing him harder. 'It is not by buying the train ticket, brother, that you obtain salvation; it is by offering gifts.' The acerbity of the encounter is – in part at least – an almost inevitable consequence of the unrealisable ideal which the ideology sets for it.

But there is also, I believe, a sense in which the predatoriness of the priests is positively promoted by what many of the pilgrims and mourners consider most salient about their visit to the city. Though my fieldwork focused on the former, and my contact with the latter was generally transient, the clues I picked up are consistent with Gold's (1988) more solidly grounded findings. Most of the Rajasthani pilgrims with whom she travelled 'expressed real skepticism concerning the soteriological pretensions of pilgrimage' (1988:63);

few had much faith in the cleansing power of bathing at a place of pilgrimage, and many were dubious about the value of the largely incomprehensible rituals they performed there. What they emphasised rather was the import-⨍ance of giving away, and using up surplus money. Spending 'both for the sake of these experiences (the initial fare) and during them (the constant drain of rupees and paisa into the outstretched hands of *pandas* and beggars) is good for the soul. The effect is one of lightening: the returning pilgrim should be ✝ thinner and poorer' (p. 263).

To this I would add that what is also emphasised – by both pilgrims and *pandas* – is that while on pilgrimage one must never accept gifts or food from others. The ideal is to remain an entirely unilateral donor. It is moreover only that which is superfluous to family subsistence, and over which the donor has complete proprietary rights, that should be offered in *dan* (cf. Nath 1987:16, 155). In the Banaras region the pilgrim to Gaya must at the time of his departure circumambulate the village or neighbourhood in a procession lead by a drummer (and known as *dhindhora pitna*, 'to proclaim abroad'). It is thus that a man proclaims abroad that all the debts of the family have been discharged, and that he is therefore at liberty to take his ancestors on this final journey which will release them from the cycle of rebirths.

Yet if gifting one's surplus is widely regarded as the real aim of pilgrimage, it is not – as Gold observes – an easy matter

> for peasants to spend money, especially for selfless reasons. But on pilgrimage they constantly encounter *pandas* and beggars who forcefully persuade them to loosen their purse strings, although they may struggle against it. However unpleasant the process may be, there is a residual satisfaction in knowing that the money has gone for *dharma*. (ibid p. 291)

Seen from this angle it seems clear that the priest who sweats their money out of them is a crucial, even necessary, part of the experience. It is for this reason that I claim that there is a sense in which it is because – and not in spite – of the predatory *panda* that the pilgrims continue to come. His apparently unprincipled exactions are to be endured and tolerated. It is all for one's own good. The pilgrim is (quite explicitly) a temporary renouncer; his pilgimage an act of *tapasya* (an ascetic austerity). Priestly rapacity is (implicitly) part of his bed of nails; and the more painful the renunciation, the greater its spiritual 'fruit'.

But why come to Banaras to make gifts when it is of course perfectly possible to do so at home? An important part of the answer is that, not only are their fruits more abundant, but that the ideal *dan* is a hidden and anonymous donation made in a spirit of complete disregard for any worldly return, either material or immaterial. In fact the best *dan* of all is *gupt dan* or 'secret' *dan* which has no earthly recipient. The money is (surreptitiously) thrown into the Ganges. By contrast, any gift which is made in the village is considered to be inevitably tainted by calculation and interest, or by a desire for renown.

First appearances notwithstanding, the motto from Turner with which I
prefaced this section is not therefore quite so wide of the mark as all the
✗ chicanery might suggest: the pilgrimage centre does represent a domain of
altruism. Its continued importance and vitality is in significant measure
dependent on the importance and vitality of the ideal of the disinterested
donation. The altruistic *ethic* of the gift and the cynically instrumental egoism
of the *panda* are two sides of the same coin. That the second feeds off the first is
obvious enough. But what is perhaps less obvious is that the voracious
appetite of the priest enhances the pilgrim's sense of offering, up to the very
'limit of his capacity', gifts for which he has no expectation of any this-worldly
return.

4.2 The accumulation of sin

According to *priestly* theory, however, even the most well-intentioned donor
has little cause for complacency. Though only the more doctrinally sophisticated of the pilgrims and mourners would be aware of the risks they incur,
there are very real dangers in the gift which is injudiciously offered. *Dan* must
be given to a Brahman of unimpeachable character for 'by worshipping the
unworshipful famine results'.[1] The recipient must be a 'worthy vessel'
(*supatra*); and if the *jajman* is unwise enough to bestow his charity on an
'unworthy vessel' (*kupatra*) he becomes responsible for the latter's sins. If, for
example, the Brahman spends the cash you give him on womanising or liquor,
the sin is yours as well as his. This is so even though you are quite ignorant of
his true character. According to the *Garuda Purana*, one who donates a cow to
the undeserving goes to hell; while the recipient not only condemns himself but
also 101 generations of his forebears to such a fate. 'A Brahmana', warns
Manu (4:190), 'who neither performs austerities nor studies the Veda, yet
delights in accepting gifts, sinks *with the* [*donor* into hell] . . .' It is as if from a
moral point of view the donor and recipient are metamorphosed by the gift
into Siamese twins. Clearly the *jajman* – if he did but know it – is in an
impossible position. On the one hand it is highly meritorious to give *dan* in a
place of pilgrimage, but on the other hand he cannot possibly know whether
the recipient is worthy or just a rogue. The real catch, however, is that if he is
prepared to accept your gifts he is almost certainly not worthy to receive them.

This ties in with the ideal of the ascetic Brahman who shuns the material
world; lives by gleaning the fields after the untouchable women; refuses grain
in *dan* if he has sufficient for the day; solicits provisions from a maximum of
three houses and before eating immerses them in the Ganges to render them
tasteless.[2] He is said to be like the black bee who gathers pollen from the flower
without leaving any trace that he has been there. Though I have never met
such a paragon the ideal is not without its influence on daily life. Its most
striking result is that even the most prosperous of priests may be tempted to
cultivate an image of frugal simplicity. Having noticed that my friend Sita

Maharaj never wore a wrist-watch, I decided to bring him one from England. He added my gift to a biscuit-tin containing eight or nine others, explaining that he does not usually wear a watch lest his *jajman* should see no reason to give one.

The problem with *dan*, however, is not just that it subverts the ascetic independence of the ideal Brahman, but more importantly that it is held to contain and transmit the sins[3] of the donor to the priestly recipient, who is likened to a 'sewer' or 'drain' (*nali, nala*) through which the moral filth of his patrons is passed. In a perfect world he would be able to 'digest' the *dan* and evacuate the sin by dint of an extraordinary ritual fastidiousness involving the daily repetition of *mantras* and the performance of elaborate rituals of expiation – an essential qualification for which is that he should wear the sacred thread and be married. One who takes *dan* before undergoing these ceremonies will go mad as a result. But it is above all by giving away *with increment* to a number of other Brahmans the *dan* which he has received that the priest rids himself of the sins which he accepts from his *jajman*. He should split it up as small as possible, add to it, and get rid of it as fast as possible.

In the real world, however, all this is regarded as an impossible ideal. Few priests actually do the immensely time-consuming daily rituals they are supposed to; and most of them frankly admit that they are ignorant of the proper Sanskrit formulae and correct ritual procedures, and claim that even if they were not they would have neither the time nor the resources to perform them. Inexorable economic necessity means moreover that the professional priest can ill afford to give away much of what he receives if he is to live. While the 'worthy vessel' is the Brahman who approximates his behaviour to that of the ascetic, the paradox is that the ideology also requires him to embrace the opposed role of householder – for the acceptance of *dan* will drive him demented unless he is married. The fact that he must feed a family, combined with the fact that this is also a culture which places high value on material acquisition, plainly puts the ideal well beyond reach of the majority. The result is that they see themselves as perpetually accumulating sin, and that many of them live in what I can only describe as a perpetual state of moral crisis. While the perfect Brahman is likened to the philosopher's stone (*paras*) which turns base metals into gold, they themselves have become a kind of sink for the sins of the Hindu world. The *dan* is 'not digested' (*nehin pachta hai*); the sewer (their idiom) becomes a cess-pit (mine).

Those with a large financial stake on the *ghats* often try to evade the problem by shifting responsibility elsewhere. At the time when the *dan* is handed over, the donor offers water, *kusha* grass and sesame seed (when the offering is for the departed) or barley (when the offering is for the gods) from his right hand into the right hand of the recipient. This is known as *sankalp* and announces, in the witness of the gods, the binding resolution to make such and such gift to such and such a Brahman at this particular time and place for this particular purpose.[4] What the *panda* or Mahabrahman of substance claims is that by directing the *jajman* to offer the *sankalp* into the hand of his servant, it is the latter who assumes the sins while he can appropriate the now decontaminated gifts. Alternatively, the priest may insist that the *sankalp* is offered onto a piece of *kusha* grass, the fictional recipient. Most people, however, see such stratagems as sheer sophistry, claiming that it is the intention which counts and that 'the sin is in the money'.

The result of accepting *dan* that is only imperfectly 'digested' is that the priest's intellect is enfeebled, his body gets blacker and blacker and his countenance loses its 'lustre' with every gift received. He is liable to contract leprosy and rot; to die a premature and painful death vomiting excrement, and to suffer the most terrible torments thereafter. Thus the horrible fate of the fearful demon encountered by the sage Valmiki at the Pishach Mochan tank was the result of his former incarnation as a Brahman who accepted *dan* in a place of pilgrimage. Once the Funeral-priest has served a thousand *jajman*, it is said, he cannot survive. His children inherit the sins, and with them an evil disposition; and his descent line dies out in two or three generations.[5] Some kinds of *dan* are said to be particularly 'hard', 'heavy' or 'indigestible' and may lead to an immediate end. But no *dan* is good *dan* and the best Brahman is one who steers well clear of the priestly calling.

A story which is frequently told on Manikarnika *ghat* relates how a wealthy *jajman* once proposed to donate a golden effigy on the banks of the Ganges. But no Brahman could be induced to accept the gift, for every time a potential recipient approached, the effigy raised one finger in warning. Eventually some paragon was found who, when the effigy raised its finger, responded by raising three of his own – thus signifying that he unfailingly performed all three of the daily *sandhya* rituals required of a Brahman. At this, the effigy's protests ceased and the donation was made. But no sooner done than the Brahman's whole body turned black. When he then broke the effigy into pieces, and gave it away to other Brahmans, half his body was restored to its normal colour. The other half was only restored after lengthy expiatory rituals and the distribution of his entire property. But even after all this the thumb of his right hand remained ineradicably black. The moral seems clear that even the Brahman who conscientiously strives after the ideal can never entirely rid himself of the taint of *dan*.

No great sociological subtlety is, I think, necessary to see why many Brahmans are prepared to accept *dan* despite the perils involved: they need (and want) the money, and the temptations are sufficient to overcome their scruples. There is moreover the paradox that one of the principal ways in which they vindicate their own spiritual worth is by their capacity to attract the gifts of the pious. Munificent offerings demonstrate the excellence of the 'vessel', while simultaneously the acceptance of them puts that excellence in question. In priestly rhetoric, however, a different kind of explanation is generally offered: *dan* is taken as a matter of *noblesse oblige*. As a father willingly accepts punishment on behalf of his miscreant son, so the priest accepts responsibility for the sins of his *jajman*. By so doing he not only saves souls, but preserves the cosmos. Without *dan* there is no ritual, and without ritual the world would come to an end. It is for this reason that the highest scriptural authorities make the acceptance of *dan* one of the six sacred duties of the Brahman and many myths recount how the gods created the Brahmans because they needed appropriate recipients for their offerings.

It is not only the recipients of *dan* who are an endangered species; as we have seen, it is the donors as well. Indeed it is hard to imagine that they could sleep soundly at night if they really knew what every priest claims to know, that the donor not only shares responsibility for any misuse of his gift, but that it is almost in the nature of such money that it is misused. I have often heard it said – in tones which suggest that it could hardly be otherwise – that all the money taken in *dan* by the big Banares *pandas* is soon disbursed in fees to lawyers, doctors or prostitutes. To the priest such money can never be of lasting benefit. Were the ideal theory actually followed it would remain forever in high velocity circulation resting nowhere long enough to represent investment capital. But even though this ideal is totally subverted, the money cannot be put to productive use. 'There is no abundance in it (*barkat nehin hoti*)', they say. 'It does not bear fruit (*phalta nehin*)'; 'it is never fructified (*phalibhut*)'. Nor can it be hoarded, for when it is put by it is eaten by white ants. It comes and goes, flowing through the priest's hands like some foul liquid. One day he is so poor he eats his food off stones; the next he receives a munificent *dan* and lights his hearth with new cloth. 'The money is like that' they say – speaking as though it squandered itself.

It is true that in reality a few priestly families have managed to use the offerings made by their pilgrims to establish successful *commercial* enterprises.[6] But for every new business that succeeds, scores fail – thus 'proving' the theory that the money itself is barren. There is, however, an important asymmetry here. While the profits from *dana* cannot be productively utilised in commerce, commercial profit can be transmuted into *dan and thereby increased*. People often talk as though the business ventures of a magnanimous merchant who unstintingly gives to worthy Brahmans are rewarded with success on account of the merit he accrues.

'Money', said the Emperor Vespasian apropos his tax on public latrines, 'has no smell' – even though it is 'made from urine'. Banaras people, by contrast, often talk as though the money transacted in *dan is* tainted. Does it, then, retain this taint once it has been exchanged for commodities, and can it be utilised by others for productive investment if it is passed on to them in a different transactional mode?

Some of my evidence would suggest that such money does indeed retain the odour of sin when it enters into a different transactional sphere, as it certainly keeps its character when it is passed on to others as *dan*. I have, for example, heard it said that the businesses of those who have taken an interest-free loan from a priestly friend or kinsman never prosper until the money is repaid; and that a clerk who accepts 'the money of expiation' from a priest as a sweetener for some bureaucratic favour courts misfortune and illness. But this is not to say that the shop-keeper from whom the priest buys provisions is likely to give a second thought to the origins of his profit. Looked at from the priest's point of view, though, the provisions which he has purchased with such money are certainly contaminated. It is as if the sin which inheres in the gift is transferred to the commodity for which it is exchanged. As I interpret the evidence, then, the basic notion is that it is only when the exchange is a unilateral one without proper reciprocation that the money of *dan* transmits its taint if transacted in a different mode. But when a balance is struck, as in the case of the shop-keeper, the sin can safely be assumed to remain with the priest.

What I hope to have conveyed so far is some sense of the moral peril which the priests experience in relation to the offerings on which their livelihood depends. Such a livelihood is continually denigrated by the priests themselves as dependent on a combination of callous extortion and obsequious sycophancy (*ji hazuri*); and – in opposition to money earned by the honest sweat of one's brow (*khare pasina ki kamai*) – as constituting an unearned income. Though in fact the amount of effort devoted to eliciting *dan* may be quite considerable, in ideological terms *dan* is a *gift* and *not* a remuneration for priestly services, which are rewarded, as we shall see, by a separate emolument known as *dakshina*. However hard the actual work by which *dana* is obtained, the money of *dan* is not 'the money of hard work'.

It is not therefore surprising that those who can afford to often renounce their hereditary calling and repeatedly cite the demeaning nature of *dan* as their reason for doing so. But the interesting thing is that such individuals appear to have few misgivings about going into trade. It is not money or the material world that they renounce – few become ascetics. It is the proceeds of *dan*. On his death-bed the medieval merchant of Cologne instanced by Tawney (1972:49–50) directs his sons to pursue a less spiritually perilous occupation than trade, and one can well imagine him recommending the priesthood. In similar circumstances the Banaras priest cautions his sons against the priesthood, and one can well imagine him recommending trade.

'Look', said my friend Pahalvan Pande (a corpulent ex-champion wrestler and now a prosperous wholesaler of coal),

> look at my boy Bhima. See how healthy and strong he is, for he has eaten grains which are pure and bought with the money of hard work (*mehnat*). My elder brother [a priest] was once just as good-looking and even stronger than I. But now that ill-begotten money has turned his face black as the coal I sell, and you see how thin he is. Yet every day he is performing *rudrabhishek* and *gayatri jap* [in expiation]. What of those who do not [do even that]?

The only gloss that it is necessary to add is that the priestly elder brother is generally regarded as the most knowledgeable and ritually fastidious member of their community, and that from the point of view of its commercial ethics the coal trade is as notoriously grubby as its product. Yet hardly anybody I think – least of all his elder brother – would radically dissent from the contrast Pahalvan was drawing between the spiritual dangers of their two occupations.

I say 'spiritual dangers', but more accurately they are both physical and spiritual. The sin emerges as excrement evacuated at death; it causes the body to rot with leprosy, seeps into the hair (which is why it is necessary to be tonsured on many ritual occasions), and makes the corpse particularly incombustible. When the corpse of the Chief Minister of Bihar was brought to Manikarnika *ghat* in March 1983, it burnt only with the greatest difficulty despite the size of the pyre and the liberality of the *ghee* and resin applied to it – all on account, said my friends, of the enormous burden of sin accumulated with his corrupt earnings. Sin, then, is a bio-moral phenomenon which manifests itself in quite tangible and material ways. It is something which can be transferred from one person to another. It is 'in the money' offered in *dan*. You can give it and take it. The real difficulty is in eliminating it, this giving rise to what Shulman (1985) has neatly characterised as the 'hot potato' view of Indian social dynamics. The most obvious thing to do is to pass it on.

Dan is often given in monetary form, though nearly every cash payment is an explicit surrogate for goods of one kind or another – a cow, a bed, or a set of clothes for example. Generally such a payment represents only a fraction of the purchase price of the object for which it stands: Rs. 5 for 'the gift of a cow' when a real cow would cost many times that amount. Specially affluent and fastidious pilgrims and mourners tend, however, to regard it as more seemly and appropriate to donate the specified items rather than their cash equivalent. These are either bought in the shops or supplied out of the priest's own stocks, that is, he will 'sell' his cow (or whatever) to the pilgrim and then receive it back in *dan*. Though the fact that the same cow may have been gifted to the same priest several hundred times over is commonly the occasion for caustic comment on the spirit of the times, the priests themselves welcome this arrangement; and in general *they* prefer cash to kind since the goods they receive are generally surplus to requirements, of poor quality and difficult to dispose of at a reasonable price. Indeed the homes of some of the larger *pandas* have the musty air of delapidated warehouses for substandard beds, cooking utensils, umbrellas and other household paraphernalia. The essential point here, however, is that whether the gift is in cash or kind has no bearing on the risk which the recipient runs.

But as we have seen some kinds of *dan* are worse than others. Especially virulent are gifts given in the name of the malevolent ghost, or to rid oneself of evil planetary influences (amongst which the influence of Saturn is the most 'cruel'). Those who specialise in the receipt of such gifts (the Mahabrahman and the Joshi) are therefore rated as the most degraded of Brahmans. Certain specific items – gold, an elephant, horse, water-buffalo, emeralds and sesame seeds (the list is somewhat variable) – are also said to be particularly dangerous.[7] But speaking generally, 'there is no such thing as good *dan*', my informants would tell me. 'It is all vile (*nikrist*); whoever takes it burns his hand.'

I must immediately concede, however, that this picture is occasionally qualified by informants who are prepared to distinguish between 'bad *dan*' (*kudan*) which is given 'with desire' (*sakam*) in order to atone for a sin, counteract a malign planetary influence or win a boon from a deity, and which is likened to a bribe (*ghus*); and 'good *dan*' (*sudan*) which is given to a 'worthy vessel' (*supatra*) 'without desire' (*nishkam*) for any specific reciprocation. In spite of such statements, however, I persist in claiming that *all dan* is perceived as a danger. In order to see why, we need to distinguish between the ideal theory and people's perceptions of practice. If 'good *dan*' is given without desire to a perfect donee, then in the degenerate conditions of our age there is no such thing, for there are no wholly disinterested donors and (more importantly) no really worthy recipients. The latter would be the accomplished Brahman ritualist who is learned in the Veda and who gives away more than he receives, or, failing that, the one who resolutely refuses to take *dan* at all. The reality, then, is that the only 'vessels' who are actually available to accept *dan* are by definition more or less unworthy to receive it. Ergo all *dan* is more or less bad.

In most contexts the appropriate recipient is a Brahman. But in north India wife-taking affines – *par excellence* the husbands of one's daughter and sister – are also the regular recipients of *dan*, which is consistent with the fact that in this hypergamous milieu they too are persons of superior status. Along with her dowry a girl is transferred in marriage as *kanya dan* ('the gift of a virgin'), and throughout the marriage this asymmetry persists with the *dan* flowing unilaterally from wife-givers to wife-receivers.

That which is taken in *dan* must, as we have seen, be given away in *dan*, thus implying the generalised exchange of sin within the priesthood. But this injurious circulation cannot remain confined within purely priestly circles, for the wife-taking affines of priestly families are the most important recipients of their donations and are not always priests themselves. Even the affinal prestations of non-priestly families are somewhat problematic, for although such gifts have not been subject to the same snow-ball effect they too are imbued with the sins of the immediate donors. 'In "the gift of a virgin" there is also sin and expiation' my informants would say when I asked whether the axiom that all *dan* is dangerous applies even to marriage. Gifts to priests and gifts to affines are again equated in the general complaint that nowadays the groom's people tend to be quite as ruthless and importunate in their dowry demands on the bride's family as priests are in their dealings with pilgrims. This intrinsically equivocal nature of the marriage gift re-emerges, I suggest, in the ideas of the lower castes about spirit possession.

Bhut-pret are the spirits of people who have died a 'bad death' (the result of bad *karma*), or whose mortuary rites have been inadequately performed. Either way, they are the product of sin. Such spirits cause a whole range of misfortunes; but amongst the several symptoms which are likely to be listed in any given case, one of those most persistently cited is that although the family earns well, the money – like the money of *dan* – just seems to melt invisibly away. *Bhut-pret* are most likely to molest members of their own family and lineage, but are also said to travel between affinally related households in the same direction as women and gifts (cf. Planalp 1956:643). That is, they go from wife-givers to wife-receivers. By contrast, ghosts never *spontaneously* go 'against the grain' by transferring themselves to wife-giving affines. In a number of the cases I recorded, the spirits had moved across more than one link in the chain of affinity. That is, they had originally belonged, not to the afflicted household's immediate wife-givers, but to *their* wife-givers – to the affines of affines. As women and gifts flow asymmetrically from lineage A to lineage B to lineage C, so the *bhut-pret* follow the same path, possessing as they go not only the girl with whom they came but also any other vulnerable member of her husband's household. But why should this be? My informants say that the ghosts 'follow the money'. They 'remain attached to it' and therefore 'come on top of it'.

What I am suggesting, then, is that such predominantly low-caste notions about the likely behaviour of malevolent ghosts reveal an underlying fear that the gifts given in marriage entail very much the same kinds of consequences as the gifts made to the priest. Both rate as *dan*, both should be purely unilateral transactions, and both are saturated with the evil consequences of the donor's conduct, or of the conduct of those closest to him. The sin is 'in the money' donated to the priest; and the unsatisfied spirits whose sad fate is a consequence of their sins 'follow the money' donated in marriage. For both kinds of recipient the result is suffering and misfortune, though both can hope to pass the problem on down the line to their own recipients. Consistent with all this, the belief that the money donated to the priest is barren and cannot be used for productive purposes is paralleled by the idea that the money given in marriage may be accompanied by a ghost, who ensures that that money will never yield sufficiency and that the family fortunes of its recipient will never prosper. I conclude therefore that whether we have to do with prestations to priests or prestations to affines, the oriented gift of *dan* is seen as highly problematic and as containing evil and dangerous mystical influences.[8]

But not everything which we would call a 'gift' rates as *dan*; and those which do not are not seen as a comparable moral peril. Unlike *dan*, most are governed by an explicit ethic of reciprocity. *Neg* prestations, for example, are given in return for the ritual services performed at a life-cycle ceremony by a specified relative or by some functionary of the household, like the Barber and Washerman. If, alternatively, I go to somebody's house taking fruit or sweets for the children, or if I give a wrist-watch to Sita Maharaj in token of our friendship, then that is *bhent* not *dan* and is part of the regular 'give and take' that exists between us. The *bhiksha* (or *bhikh*) given in alms to an ascetic (or beggar), and the *chanda* donated towards the upkeep of a monastery, represent exceptions to this rule of reciprocity; but neither of them is said to contain the sins of the donor or place him in jeopardy if the recipient of his charity misuses his gift for sinful purposes.

This clear-cut contrast between the poisonous nature of *dan* and the essentially benign character of other gifts is blurred only by the somewhat ambiguous category of *dakshina*. Sometimes *dakshina* is described as a supplement to *dan*, a gift added to the *dan* to make up for any deficiencies in it. So, for example, if I donate a cow to a Brahman, then I must add a small sum of money to my gift to top it off. This *dakshina* 'consecrates' (*pratishta karna*) the *dan*, which without it 'bears no fruit'. At other times, however, informants use the term to refer to a fee paid to a Brahman priest for his ritual services.[9] When, for example, a well-to-do patron employs a specialist ritual technician – a *karam-kandi* – to perform a particular ritual which his hereditary household- or pilgrimage-priest is incompetent to conduct, the *karam-kandi* receives *dakshina* as a fee for performing the ritual; but the *dan* (which is significantly greater in value) is given to the hereditary priest who sat idly by throughout the ritual. What complicates the matter, however, is that in such a case the *dan* which goes to the latter is also accompanied by a (nominal) *dakshina*; and it would clearly be possible to interpret this either as a gift which supplements *dan*, or as a 'fee' for the ritual labour involved in accepting it. This essentially ambiguous nature of *dakshina*[10] – as 'gift' or 'fee' – is reflected in my informants' equivocation over whether or not it embodies the dangers of *dan*. Many stories suggest that it does, though equally often this is denied.

Leaving the difficult case of *dakshina* aside, it is clear that it is in *dan*, and not in other kinds of gift, that a dire moral peril resides. The question is, why?

4.3 The source of the peril

At first sight it might seem that the problem thus posed is misconceived. The reason is simple: *any* kind of profit derived from death is almost equally dangerous, regardless of whether it has its origins in the acceptance of gifts or the sale of commodities. Because of such money, one wood-seller's family was decimated within a generation, while their wife-taking affines fell to murdering each other over the dowry provided out of the commercial profits from the sale of wood from the pyres. Similar stories are told of the takings of the shop-keeper who specialises in shrouds and other mortuary paraphernalia, the fees of the burning-ground barber and of the exorcist who deals with the spirits of the malevolent dead. 'The money of the cremation ground', people say, 'will never allow anybody to prosper.'

As I have tried to suggest at various points in the discussion so far, and as I have argued more fully elsewhere (Parry 1989), neither in the Banaras of my informants, nor in the tradition at large, is the normal run of commercial profit seen as a particular ethical problem. Certainly nothing I have ever heard would suggest that trade is regarded as *intrinsically* bad, or that traders see themselves as confronted by the kind of moral peril which is so strongly internalised by the priests. Nor is a sense of such peril conveyed by the literature on Indian traders; and I can think of no ethnographic or historical evidence for a conception of trade remotely comparable to that of the philosopher-theologians of medieval Europe whose attitude to commerce was, as Tawney (1972:47) put it, 'that of one who holds a wolf by the ears'. It is not business in general, but the business of death, which is morally loaded.

The point was brought home to me by the case of a young man I knew well, whose family owns one of the shops which specialises in the sale of the 'goods of the skull-breaking'. Most of the time he himself works as one of Banaras's numerous commission agents (*dalals*) or 'guides', showing foreign tourists around the city and taking a cut on any purchase they can be persuaded to make. These sometimes include narcotics, and one day I met Bhola in jubilant mood after he had made a very considerable sum on a sale of morphine. Despite the fact that he had many times told of the terrible misfortunes his family have suffered as a result of selling the goods required for cremation, he denies any qualms about transactions such as these.

Given that commercial profits derived from the cremation ground are also highly problematic, it might on the face of it seem sensible to suppose that it is death not *dan* that lies at the root of the difficulty. The obvious answer to this is that it is *all dan* – and not just that which is given during the mortuary rites – which is evil. As Fuller (1984:67ff) has pointed out, however, the fact remains that in the major north Indian pilgrimage cities like Banaras it is death which dominates the religious field (in a way that it does not in the temple towns of the south). It might therefore be argued that, in the particular context I describe, the prototypical *dan* is the *dan* of death, which – by a kind of halo effect – contaminates all other *dan* and renders it perilous. Though there is perhaps a sense (to be specified shortly) in which *all dan*, regardless of context, is ideologically implicated in death, the difficulty with Fuller's formulation is that he himself cites a number of sources which clearly show that even in the south similar ideas about the perilous nature of *dan* in general are by no means absent; while, as Raheja (1988) clearly demonstrates, such notions exist in a highly elaborated form in certain *rural* areas of the north. They cannot therefore be adequately explained by reference to the particularities of the north Indian sacred centre – to its association with death or to the uneasy consciences of those most heavily implicated in the chicanery and profiteering of the pilgrimage business. I therefore believe that I have formulated the question correctly: why is *dan* such a problem?

One possible answer will, I hope, be already apparent. The ideal Brahman should as nearly as possible approximate his life-style and behaviour to that of the world-renouncer, but the problem with *dan* is that the priest's acceptance of it irretrievably compromises this ideal of ascetic autonomy and inextricably enmeshes him in the material and social order. It is (following Heesterman 1971) the Brahman's ascetic transcendence of the world which qualifies him as a 'worthy vessel' for the gifts of the pious; but the paradox is that his receipt of such gifts inevitably endangers this very transcendence. But if for no other reason than that its focus on the perspective of the priesthood fails to account for the similarly problematic nature of the *dan* offered to affines, it seems clear that this is not the whole story.

The notion that the gift transmits, and is therefore capable of removing, sin not only tends to subvert its own ethic of disinterested generosity, but also presupposes that ritual – and indeed financial – reparation can be made for moral transgressions. Such attempts to dispose of ethical burdens by ritualistic means are a central preoccupation of Hindu religiosity; though the idea that this can be done does not go unchallenged in the tradition at large. Certainly the ethic of intention completely repudiates any notion that atonement for sin can be simply purchased. It might, then, be possible to interpret these beliefs about the mystical dangers of *dan* as part of the inevitable backlash against offering ritual solutions to moral problems, and as expressing a deep unease that this is an ultimately futile and fraudulent endeavour. When the gift is transformed into a purchase price for salvation – as it inevitably is – this endeavour becomes all the more problematic. Danger lies in the moral deception in which both of the parties to the exchange collude, and it is this which explains what is in a comparative perspective the most striking feature of the ideology: that here the gift is liable to demean the donor as well as the recipient.

It might further be argued that what gives this problem a special poignancy in the Banaras context is that the sanctity of the city largely derives from the belief that all who die – according to some, all who are cremated – within its precincts are automatically liberated from the cycle of rebirths. As I pointed out at an earlier stage (pp. 27–8), the priesthood clearly has a considerable interest in upholding this dogma on which the religious pre-eminence of the city, and hence their own livelihood, is founded. But equally clearly this same notion places the significance of their sacerdotal function in question, for the rituals at which the Brahman officiates become an irrelevance to the salvation prospects of many of their patrons. Moreover, the ideology of *bhakti* – which has exercised a profound influence on modern Hinduism and according to which devotion to a personal god is sufficient for salvation – reduces the Brahman to a similar irrelevance. Thus, in the all-important matter of one's ultimate destiny, the mediating function of the priest is subverted from two different directions at once, and by ideas to which the priests themselves will more or less readily assent. It is not altogether surprising, then, that they should have a somewhat uneasy conscience about their earnings from an occupation which a part of their own belief system declares redundant.

Much of the ideology of *dan* is foreshadowed by that of Vedic sacrifice. Indeed my informants explicitly say, on impeccable textual authority (cf. Manu 1:86; Biardeau 1976:27), that the gift is a surrogate for sacrifice appropriate to our degenerate age. As Heesterman again shows, the sacrifier is reborn and triumphs over death by transferring the burden of death and impurity to the priest through his gifts. These gifts represent parts of the *jajman*'s body, 'so that partaking of the offerings, as the priest is required to do, and accepting [the donations] amounts to man-eating or partaking of a corpse . . .' (Heesterman 1962:25). At the outset, the sacrifier is loaded with death and impurity which, through the medium of his gifts, he off-loads onto the priest whose qualities he appropriates. He is reborn and proclaimed Brahman. According to this theory, then, there can be no mystery about how the Funeral-priest becomes the ghost: cremation is a sacrificial ritual in which the deceased offers himself on the pyre; and during the course of the sacrifice, the sacrifier and priest change places. It also becomes clear that there is a sense in which all gifts are mortuary gifts, and in which it is not just the Mahabrahmans but all priestly Brahmans who take upon themselves the onus of death.

Consistent with its ideological roots in sacrifice is the fact that *dan* embodies something of the bio-moral substance of the donor – something nasty at that – in a way and to an extent that other forms of gift do not. The identification between the sacrifier and the victim – which in the classical theory is explicitly a substitute for his own person – is carried over into the theory of *dan* as an identification between the donor and his gift. It stands, moreover for what he must extirpate: the sins and impurities which are the cause of his own mortality. An extreme case of this identification is *tula dan*, where the donor is weighed against some valuable commodity which is thus equated with his 'gross body' (and is consequently said to contain his blood, marrow and excrement), and which is then gifted in *dan*. But whether the gift contains the blood and excrement of the donor, or merely his 'sins', its acceptance entails incorporating into the self the inferior essences of others. In an hierarchical world, such a transfer is bound to be problematic and even subversive of the heirarchy itself. If people of different strata are beings of different species, the gift becomes a kind of miscegenation. It is hardly surprising, then, that it assumes the form of a moral peril.

If the gift is a surrogate sacrifice, the purpose of this 'sacrificial gift' is clearly, in Hubert and Mauss's (1964) terms, one of 'de-sacralisation'. It is when, as they argue (p. 55), the objective of the sacrifice is to eliminate '*bad* sacredness' that the identification between sacrifier and victim is closest *before* the immolation, and their subsequent separation is as final as possible. Consistent with this, the identification of the donor with his gift is often highly elaborated before the transfer (as for example in *tula dan*), and his separation from it afterwards is absolute.

As Mauss (1966:10) perceived

> one gives away what is in reality part of one's own nature and substance, while to receive something is to receive a part of someone's spiritual essence. To keep the thing is dangerous . . . it retains a magical and religious hold over the recipient. The thing given is not inert.

But the conclusion which Mauss drew from this – that the gift is therefore a kind of loan or pledge which must eventually be returned to its *foyer d'origine* – does not apply. What is given is alienated in an absolute way, and the very definition of the gift is that it involves the complete extinction of the donor's *proprietary* rights in favour of the recipient (Aiyar 1941:77; Law 1926:1). The gift threatens to cement the two together in a dangerous interdependence; but every attempt is made to sever their bond[11] by insisting on the complete alienation of the thing. Under no circumstances, and on pain of terrible supernatural penalties, is the gift resumed. Its evil 'spirit' must *not* come back. While Mauss originally introduced this notion of 'spirit' to explain the inalienability of the object and the necessity of making a return, what it in fact explains in this context is why the gift *must* be alienated, should *never* return, and should endlessly be handed on. A pure asymmetry must therefore obtain, and the obligation to make a return is *not* encoded in the *danadharma* ('the law of the gift'). With prestations other than *dan*, by contrast, the rule of reciprocity does generally apply; but there is little indication that the gift contains the donor – except in the loose sense that it may be interpreted as an objective manifestation of his subjective dispositions (or perhaps as material testimony to the skills with which his caste is innately endowed). Where the gift is most heavily imbued with the 'spirit' of the donor, reciprocity is denied; where there is reciprocity there is not much evidence of the 'spirit'. The two aspects of Mauss's model do not hang together.

I emphasise this denial of reciprocity because it seems to me to represent *the* most fundamental source of the peril. Certainly the priests themselves commonly attribute their degradation and relative inferiority to other Brahmans to their (exaggerated) view of themselves as purely unilateral receivers of gifts. Amongst the six conventionally ennumerated duties of the Brahman is to receive *and give dan*. Direct reciprocity (even as we have seen in the form of the *quid pro quo* of priestly services) is, of course, entirely contrary to the whole spirit of *dan*. But so too is the notion that the immediate recipient is the final terminus of the gift – which must at all costs be passed on with increment to another worthy recipient. The root of the problem, however, is that this is impossible for the professional priest, and the greater the disproportion between his receipts and disbursements the greater the burden of sin he accumulates. It is the money and goods which are siphoned out of the flow of exchange by being retained which are really barren, and which infect the family fortunes with their evil sterility. 'When you give seventeen annas having taken sixteen, then that is auspicious (*shubh*). From this no shortage will result. But if you do not give [in this way], then there will always be a continual decline (*hamesha ghatta rahega*).'

Now it is true that it might be argued that the gift is in fact reciprocated by the liberation from sin which the donor receives *in direct exchange* for his material prestations. But on the one hand the ideology denies that the gift made out of such interested motives is a 'true' gift at all; while at the same time it is widely held that the Brahmans of today – or at least the ones who are prepared to soil their hands with *dan* – are so fallen and unworthy that, far from releasing the donor from sin, he is more probably dragged down into hell by the bonds which the gift creates between them. In short, the profligate priesthood cannot deliver on its side of the bargain and the gift *is* therefore unreciprocated. In any event, the mechanism of the return is the entirely impersonal mechanism of *karma*, and the recipient is merely a 'drain' for the elimination of sin, or a conduit for the flow of merit which he does not himself dispense. In no way constrained by the gift, it is not for him to reciprocate.

It is also true that the *bhiksha* offered in alms to an ascetic is an unreciprocated gift, but does not appear to entail the kind of moral difficulties associated with *dan*. The crucial point here, I suggest, is that such prestations are given to the *renouncer*, with whom no relationship is possible since he is outside the social world. What is threatening about *dan* is that it is donated to people who have at least one foot within a social order founded on reciprocity, but from whom no return is received. The man-in-the-world belongs within a conceptual order in which all are both givers and receivers, all castes perform their allotted function on behalf of the collectivity and nobody gets anything for nothing. The mystical dangers of *dan* express the uncomfortable recognition that there are some who do.

But of course the whole theory insists that *dan* must be given *without* expectation of any immediate return, or any form of *quid pro quo* from the recipient. It is, as Trautmann (1981:279) puts it, a 'soteriology, not a sociology of reciprocity . . .' Yet the social world in which men actually live is inescapably founded on what Gouldner (1960) calls the 'moral norm of reciprocity'. There is therefore an inherent tension, even a contradiction, between a soteriology which denies reciprocity and a social order which is premised on it. This tension, I suggest, finds eloquent expression in the moral ambiguity of the gift, the soteriological orientation of which repudiates the ethical basis of society.

4.4 Some comparative considerations

There are, as the specialist reader will be aware, many parallels between the data I have presented and Raheja's (1988) invaluable discussion of gifts in the western UP village of Pahansu. The two analyses, however, go in different directions. According to Raheja's account, *dan* is a poison because, *tout court*, it embodies the 'inauspiciousness' which afflicts the donor. When Lévi-Strauss (1973:xlvi) criticised Mauss for allowing himself to be mystified by the native in explaining a general structural principle (exchange) by a culturally specific rationalisation for it (the Maori *hau*), he was not I think entirely fair (Parry 1986). In my view, however, Raheja leaves herself open to just such a charge. Her analysis ends, that is, at the point at which it should arguably begin – when she has provided an account of what people say and think about *dan*. To me it seems that an adequate sociological account must ask why they should say and think these particular things. 'Poison', I have proposed, is at bottom a cultural idiom in terms of which our informants talk about a more general and fundamental problem common to all human societies: the problem of reciprocity.[12]

As to how they employ that idiom, there are several significant differences of emphasis. In Banaras, the poison in the gift is predominantly seen as a matter of sin. In Pahansu, by contrast, the problem is 'inauspiciousness', a concept which Raheja sharply distinguishes from that of 'impurity'. As she represents it, the notion of 'inauspiciousness' subsumes the ideas of sin (*pap*), fault (*dosh*), distress (*kasht*), danger (*sankat*), illness (*rog*), terror (*dar*) and ghostly affliction (*pret-badha*) – these terms being used 'for the most part interchangeably', and in association with verb forms which imply that the affliction derives from a source external to the afflicted person. Inauspiciousness is given away with the gift, and thus removed. Impurity can be 'spread' (*phailna*) by being transmitted to others, but is not thereby off-loaded elsewhere. The polluted person remains polluted. Gifting has to do with the removal of inauspiciousness and not with the removal of impurity. The contrast is clearly signalled in language. While 'inauspiciousness' is said 'to become attached to' (*lagna*) or 'to come on top of' (*uske upar a jana*) the one who suffers it, and has to be 'made far' (*dur karna*) or 'caused to go away' (*hatana*), impurity simply 'is' (*hona*). It is something one 'observes' (*manna*) until it 'ends' (*khatam hona*) or 'dissipates' (*likarna*) through the passage of time. Sickness, death or other forms of misfortune are never attributed to impurity, but are always 'discussed primarily in terms of the *nasubh* (inauspiciousness) which must have brought them about'. The two dimensions involve an entirely 'different reckoning' (p. 43–5).

With regard to the linguistic usages recorded for Pahansu, I can report that in the Hindi of my Banaras informants the various terms which Raheja includes under the general category of inauspiciousness are *not* used 'for the most part interchangeably'. *Pret-badha* (which specifically refers to a ghostly affliction) has a far narrower semantic range than a term like *kasht* ('trouble' in a very general sense); and though either *may* be a *product* of 'sin' (*pap*), neither is a synonym for it. Nor, I believe, could any of these concepts be properly described as a sub-species of 'inauspiciousness' (*ashubh, amangal*). I can also report that the verb forms which Raheja associates with the discourse of inauspiciousness are regularly used in connection with impurity (e.g. *sutak lagta hai* – 'death pollution is *attached*'), and that those she associates with impurity commonly occur in conjunction with concepts she assimilates to 'inauspiciousness' (e.g. *mujhe dosh hai* – 'to me sin/fault *is*').

Linguistic quibbles aside, my own evidence overwhelmingly suggests that notions of 'sin' and 'pollution' commonly shade seamlessly into each other, and that both are a source of misfortune. Illness – and even death – are often attributed to an impure diet, and spirit affliction is commonly blamed on the filth and pollution of its victims (pp. 229ff). In the well-known story, a quarter share of the *sin* of Indra's brahmanicide was passed on to women, from whom it emerges in the form of menstrual *pollution*. Like brahmanicide, cow-slaughter is a source of *both* sin and impurity, requiring elaborate rituals of expiation involving bathing in the Ganges and donations to the Brahmans. Although it is perfectly true that in the Banarasi idiom the gift embodies 'sin', it would not only be straining the evidence to claim that priestly donations deal with the (spiritual) sin while bathing in the river is merely a matter of (bodily) pollution, but also an odd line of argument for one trained in the tradition of Chicago ethnosociology, given that *jati*'s insistence on the essential monism of South Asian thought (e.g. Marriott 1976). Sin and impurity are difficult to disentangle since the one often entails the other, and I believe that it would be misleading to claim that it is only the first which the gift embodies. Rather than previous writers having conflated a clear conceptual dichotomy (as Raheja alleges), it is to my mind rather more likely that the clarity of the Pahansu dichotomy is – in a comparative perspective – somewhat atypical, and even perhaps partly an artifact of the requirements of an anti-Dumontian polemic (cf. Parry 1991).

Consistent with her rejection of Dumont's preoccupation with hierarchy, Raheja emphasises that Pahansu people often give *dan* to various non-Brahman specialists (like the Barber and Sweeper) who are inferior in status to the donor. From this it follows that the poison in the gift cannot be explained in terms of the structural position of the Brahman in relation to the ascetic, or attributed to the dangers inherent in accepting gifts from *inferiors*. *Dan* is not a hierarchical prestation.

The fact that low-caste specialists receive such gifts is certainly telling, though the fact that within the caste they are invariably given to (superior) wife-*taking* affines is I think glossed over too lightly. But however this may be, in the Banaras context *dan is*, I believe, conceptualised as a pre-eminently hierarchical prestation (hence my informants' repeated emphasis on the general rule that *dan* should properly only go to the worthiest vessels). I also believe that the inferiority of the donor does represent one of the dangers (why else should the Brahman be enjoined to refuse the gifts of the lowest castes?).

The circumstances in which low-caste specialists receive *dan* on the *ghats* are limited. The Barbers claim a share in the gifts made on the eleventh day after death (p. 89); but this is a *payment* from the Mahabrahman in consideration of the services they render him, and not *dan* from the *jajman*. In the mortuary rites of the Untouchables, however, the Barbers are unquestionably the recipients of *dan* – but from inferiors. Nearly all my informants deny that the 'tax' of the Dom is a kind of *dan*; though I have heard it described as *dan* of a 'low' or 'mean degree' (*niman koti ka dan*). All are however agreed that on his day the Dom is the raja of the cremation ground, and that on such an occasion he is one's superior. *Dan* is certainly given to the Doms (and Sweepers) at the time of an eclipse. Eclipses are caused by the demon Rahu (or Khetu) casting his polluting shadow on the sun (or moon) as he tries to swallow it. By giving *dan* to the Dom the sun's afflictions are relieved, the gift being represented as a 'bribe' to Rahu, made over to his earthly representatives, in order to induce him to desist. At this time it is as if the whole order of the universe is in danger of being turned upside down, for 'during an eclipse the Dom is everybody's raja'. In each of these cases, in short, the recipient has (or is said to have in this specific context) a status superior to that of the donor.

If *dan* really involved considerations of an entirely different order from those of hierarchy (as Raheja claims), it would clearly make little sense to explain the relative inferiority of the Brahman priest by reference to the nastiness it contains, or the relative rank of different priestly occupations by the degrees of nastiness involved. Yet this is precisely the idiom in which Banarasi Brahmans consistently discuss such matters.

It is, of course, perfectly obvious that, on one dimension at least, the priesthood is valued in proportion to its profitability; and that the less money there is to be made out of it, the more likely it is that the priest will follow the promptings of his conscience and abandon the profession. But van der Veer's (1985) radical reduction of the problem of priestly status to considerations of this order is, I think, unconvincing. Whatever his 'real' motives, the priest who aspires for his sons to follow some other occupation will almost invariably represent his misgivings in terms of the evils of *dan*. Neither these evils themselves, nor the degradation in which they result, can possibly be construed as epiphenomena of the specific conditions of the modern pilgrimage centre, and there is no warrant for supposing that they only have any ideological salience in that context. The inferiority of the priest is not adequately explained by his poverty, but has much to do with the dangers of the gifts he receives in the course of his duties.

But if the language of hierarchy is rather more pervasive than Raheja's discussion would suggest, and if rather less is explained by hard-nosed materialism than van der Veer imagines, an unreconstructed Dumontian model is equally hard to sustain. According to Dumont (1970b:42), 'the Brahmans, *as priests* superior to all other men, are settled in the world comfortably enough' (emphasis added). My data cast doubt on both propositions contained in this statement. 'Sacerdotal purity' is certainly not 'the essential feature of Brahmanic preeminence' (Dumont 1970b:16);[13] the remarkable feature is rather that the Brahmans are pre-eminent despite their association with the hazardous and highly equivocal profession of priesthood (cf. Marriott 1969:1171). Nor can the Brahman be straightforwardly opposed to the ascetic as the man-in-the-world to the world-renouncer. The complacent domesticity of the Brahman householder is disturbed by the uncomfortable expectation that he should participate in the renouncer's ideal of an independence from the material and social order. It is as the this-worldly representative of the transcendent other-worldly values of asceticism that the Brahman derives his authority. The paradox, however, is that while it is chiefly by virtue of representing these transcendent values that the Brahman is necessary to his *jajman*, the latter's offerings put that transcendence in jeopardy, leaving only – as Heesterman puts it (1985:155) – 'an empty husk'. It is easier for a camel to pass through the eye of a needle than for a priest to be a perfect Brahman.

4.5 Bargaining for salvation

That it is an ascetic withdrawal from the world which sets the standards of perfection for the man-in-the-world, and that this is a culture which simultaneously puts great store by the things of the world, is no doubt paradoxical – but it is also perfectly understandable. Renunciation of the world can by definition only exist in reaction to it, and is only likely to have much ideological force in a culture which values it highly. A propensity to pursue one's material self-gain is taken, as I have observed, for granted; and it is recognised that such motives cannot be confined to some notionally separate sphere of the 'market' from which the sacred and ritual sphere is entirely insulated. It is, of course, true that some good Catholics also take a robustly cynical view of priestly acquisitiveness, and of the Church's propensity to store up treasures on earth as well as in heaven. But – notwithstanding the ideology of the 'worthy vessel' – I believe that 'traditional Hindus' characteristically display a far greater degree of indulgent tolerance towards the priesthood's pursuit of egoistic this-worldly advantage. That *artha* (politico-economic interest), or more precisely *swartha* (*self*-interest), penetrates the moral order of *dharma* is not only acknowledged as inevitable, but is also seen as a necessary (if regrettable) condition for the maintenance of *dharma* in the imperfect world in which we live. This inevitability is most strikingly acknowledged through a sometimes grudging acquiescence in the idea that one will be forced to *bargain* with the priest over the price of salvation. So pervasive is the practice that one wonders whether there is not perhaps some sense in which bargaining is an almost essential part of the ritual, a possibility I explore in what follows.

Echoing Malinowski's (1922) continuum of Trobriand exchanges with the 'pure gift' at one pole and 'real barter' at the other, the assumption which continues to inform the anthropological literature on bargaining is that it is opposed to unbargained exchange as commodities are opposed to gifts. Bargaining, in other words, is held to be associated with 'trade' and the 'market', and is seen as 'a technique geared to the realisation of strict equivalence' (van Baal 1975:40); while gift exchange – in which too nice an attention to strict equivalence is liable to dissolve the relationship – is held to *preclude* bargaining, which would reduce the gift to a species of barter (Khuri 1968:699). It is further assumed that bargaining exists where social relations do not; where people – as Khuri puts it – 'confront each other not only as opposed interests in the market, but also as social equals interacting on free unbounded bases, free from social obligations' (1968:700–1). Though *economically* integrative (because it results in exchange ratios acceptable to both parties), it is for Polanyi (1957) *socially* 'disintegrative' (because it involves antagonistic, competitive and mistrustful relationships). Similarly, Sahlins (1972) sees bargaining as a procedure akin to chicanery and characteristic of the unsociable extreme of 'negative reciprocity' where each party to the exchange endeavours to maximise his own utility at the expense of the other. Though Khuri (1968), Davis (1973) and Geertz (1978) somewhat soften the picture, they nevertheless continue to associate bargaining with essentially *impersonal market* transactions.

More precisely, it is held to be characteristic of an *imperfect* market in which information is at a premium. It allows the fisherman who is selling, but who has been at sea since before dawn, to get an inkling of the going price; and the fish-trader who is buying to form an estimate of fishing conditions and the likely volume of supply. Both parties can, as it were, test the water (Firth 1966:195). For Geertz (1978), the essence of bargaining is this search for information; the search for information is the essence of the Moroccan *suq*, and the Moroccan *suq* is the type case of a whole species of economic organisation. Bargaining is at the basis of the 'bazaar economy'. It exists, as many writers stress (Khuri 1968; Dewey 1962:73ff; Davis 1973:161ff; Stirrat 1988:73ff), in the context of uncertainties over quantity, quality or supply. When uncertainty is reduced – as for example when products are standardised – so too is the propensity to haggle (Davis 1973:161; Geertz 1978:162; Fanselow 1990). One further premise which is taken for granted in much of the literature is that each party enters the transaction with a previously determined price limit, and that bargaining is a means of negotiating an agreement in the region between them (cf. Alexander and Alexander 1987). In other words, the eventual price represents a compromise between the maximum the buyer is prepared to pay and the minimum which the seller is prepared to accept. The wider the overlap between the two, the easier it will be to reach an agreement. If there is no overlap, there is no deal.

The crucial assumption in the whole model – that bargaining only makes sense in the context of trade and the market – has been uncritically assimilated into the literature on the so-called Hindu '*jajmani* system'. This 'system' was supposedly founded on principles entirely opposed to those of the market, and it was therefore often simply *assumed* that bargaining was absent. Drawing on Bennett's Gonda Settlement Report of 1878, Neale (1957:228) for example declared that 'neither inter-family nor inter-caste bargaining was practised'; while, as Kolenda (1967:294) has noted, the implication of Wiser's (1936) classic study is that we are dealing with '"traditionally" standarised rates'. But in fact, as Kolenda and Harper (1959) also note, we know next to nothing about the way in which rates are *actually* determined.

This did not inhibit Harper from proceeding as if we did, and making bargaining into one of the key features which distinguishes the system of economic relations he encountered in Malnad from a 'proper' *jajmani* system. The local Malnad economy is tied into regional, national and world markets; production is largely for *exchange*, and remuneration for a large proportion of services is paid in *cash* at *bargained* rates. The '*jajmani* system', by contrast, is associated with the 'closed self-sufficient village', where production is largley for *use*, and where relations between patrons and specialists take the form of 'enduring, even inherited, *jajman-kamin* relationships . . . [with] "little bargaining over wages and prices"', which are generally paid at *fixed* rates in *grains*. Bargaining is absent in the second case, but present in the first, not only because there is no point in bargaining where relationships are immutably fixed and there are no substitutes from whom one might obtain the same goods and services, but also because grain payments remain constant in relation to human needs, whereas payments in cash do not, with the result that they have to be constantly re-negotiated (p. 775). Not only is bargaining again associated with the market, but it has now become an explicit corollary of *monetary* exchange. Both are therefore held to be absent from the world of *jajmani* relations. On both counts, however, Harper was wrong.

With regard to money, Fuller (1989) has recently concluded from a review of the historical evidence that the notion of some pristine pre-British *jajmani* system from which monetary exchange was excluded is largely a figment of the anthropological imagination. With regard to bargaining, there has not – to my knowledge – been any systematic attempt to collate such data as exists. But that not everything is as the model supposes is suggested by Sharma's (1978:106) report of 'fierce haggling' over customary payments at the time of marriage and birth in a village in the vicinity of Banaras. 'There were huge fireworks on each occasion', she writes, 'resplendent with curses on both sides, but there seemed to be no hard feelings after an agreement was finally reached. Indeed, this is the expected sort of behaviour.' Similarly, Gaborieau (1977:38) reports that in Hindu Nepal the musicians, the *purohit* (family priest) and the sister of the groom have the right to bar the way to marriage and extort money as *neg*, while Raheja (1988:216) quotes the Pahansu adage that 'everybody fights for their own *neg*'. Most reminiscent of my own data, however, is the tenacious haggling of the trans-sexual *hijras* who in north India come to the house to sing and dance in celebration of the birth of a son. The *hijras* cash in quite brazenly on their power to curse and to expose the impotent, threatening to lift up their skirts and expose *themselves* if their escalatingly extortionate demands remain unmet (Nanda 1989:6, 49ff). Though bargaining is certainly prevalent in secular contexts, I am struck by how much of that mentioned in the anthropological literature occurs within a ritual frame, and particularly at the time of rites of passage. If bargaining is a mechanism for negotiating uncertainty, its association with points of fluidity and transition in the social structure might perhaps be seen as symbolically appropriate.

Certainly everything in the context of the Banaras mortuary rites is subject to haggling – from the price of wood for the pyre, to the tax of the Dom, to the gift of *dan* which is given to the Mahabrahman in the name of the *pret*-ghost, and to the *panda* in the name of the ancestors. But the important point is not so much its pervasiveness as the fact that much of this bargaining takes place over *gifts*. Though the ideology requires that donors should give without counting the cost, and recipients should reluctantly accept whatever is offered, in practice there is considerable licence to bargain – a licence of which full advantage is taken. Khuri's apparently self-evident proposition that 'a bargained gift exchange becomes a barter' is far from self-evident after all. *Dan* is *dan* despite the fact that it is extracted by methods that stop scarcely short of the third degree.

Of all people, anthropologists should surely know better, for is not the assumption that gifts preclude bargaining a product of *our own* cultural categories which postulate a peculiarly sharp opposition between the morality of the gift and the morality of commodity exchange (cf. Parry 1986)? Since the gift is supposedly free and spontaneous, one which is bargained becomes a barter; since it is both personal and supposedly disinterested, haggling over its value makes it akin to a normatively interested and anonymous market exchange. In many other cultures, however, what is ideologically fore-grounded is the notion that the ability to make material demands on others is an index of the closeness of the relationship – an assertion of the interdependence and mutual obligation. An insistence on receiving one's due may thus be a measure of social proximity rather than signifying the distance or absence of the relationship. That the *panda* and Mahabrahman endlessly press their claims cannot therefore be taken as *prima facie* evidence that the gift has been perverted into an impersonal market transaction.

The fact that bargaining on the *ghats* is mainly over gifts makes it very different from the kind of bargaining described in the literature in another important respect. The Mahabrahman stands in for the *pret*-ghost; the *panda* for the ancestral *pitr*. The gifts they receive are gifts both to, and for, the deceased: food that he might eat, a lamp that he might see, clothes in which to dress. The whole ideology is one of unstinting liberality; the *jajman* must give *yatha shakti* – to the very limit of his capacity. So while the expected objective of the buyer in the bazaar is that he should obtain the goods and services of the seller at the least possible cost, here the ideal is that he should pay at the highest possible price. He gives as much as he can afford, not as little as he can get away with. The proper objective of bargaining is not to obtain 'a bargain', but to ensure – for the sake of the soul of the departed – that the limits of the donor's capacity have really been reached.

Similarly, the economistic assumption that the 'buyer' begins with a fixed ceiling on what he will pay, and the seller with a floor to what he will accept, is unrealistic. Though the village pilgrim or mourner may intend to set a limit at the cash in his pocket, he not uncommonly finds himself cajoled into promising grains or money which will be collected after the harvest by a roving agent of the *panda* or Dom. More importantly, none of the priests appear to operate with a rock-bottom asking price below which they will under no circumstances budge. They demand the sky, and – since it is better than nothing – settle for whatever they can get. After all, the salvation and merit they confer are at no cost to them, and a blessing today does not mean that there will be nothing left to offer tomorrow. As a result, I have only once seen a Mahabrahman refuse eventually to pocket his money, though as often as not he stomps off with bitter recriminations about how little that was.

The disparity between opening bids is often a chasm, the Dom demanding an ambitious Rs. 5,001 for supplying the cremation fire, and the chief mourner suggesting a paltry Rs. 5.25. Since the Dom and the Mahabrahman have a theoretically complete monopoly on all mourners who come to the *ghat* on the day of their *pari*, and the *panda* a monopoly on all pilgrims who come from certain areas, there are no legitimate substitutes for the services they supply, and no competition between rival 'sellers'. By contrast with its effect on market transactions, bargaining does not therefore establish anything like a 'going rate', and different *jajman* pay wildly differing amounts for the same ritual service.

In several other respects, however, the economic anthropology model does appear to bear a fairly close relationship to the situation I observed. As it predicts, bargaining occurs in the context of considerable uncertainty. Given the uncertainty of the transition between this world and the next, and between ghost and ancestor, I have already suggested that its association with death might be seen as symbolically fitting. But the uncertainty of the situation has several other sources, of which two are particularly striking. According to Fanselow (1990), what above all characterises the bazaar, and explains much of the sharp practice associated with it, is a marked information asymmetry between buyers and sellers. The buyer parts with something of relatively certain value (namely, money) in exchange for something relatively uncertain (namely, unstandardised commodities which are subject to adulteration, short-measure and other forms of chicanery). On the *ghats* this asymmetry is clearly compounded to the nth degree. The priest gets something certain; his patron something which is even more unknowable than the quality of the ghee he buys at Ram Ji Yadav's shop – for without 'the divine sight of the yogi' who can be quite sure of salvation?

In another, and perhaps more important, sense *both* parties to the transaction are generally scrabbling around in the dark. The pilgrims and mourners are, for the most part, strangers to the priest. *They* don't know exactly what they should give, and the priest has little idea of what he might be able to extract. Bargaining allows both to explore the possibilities and arrive at a 'price' in the absence of proper information. Moreover, if offerings were made on a fixed scale – Rs. X for ritual Y, take it or leave it – the poorer pilgrims would be inhibited from approaching the *panda* at all, and the richer would be giving far less than they could actually afford. The priest would be at a financial loss; and many of his *jajman* would be at a spiritual one since some would not have donated at all, while others would have given below 'the limit of their capacity'. Seen from the patrons' perspective then, bargaining is a procedure which permits everybody to gift whatever they can – and sometimes rather more. Seen from the priest's perspective, however, it is necessary not so much because it is in some sense part of the ritual, but rather because it is the most rational way of conducting his business (and, in the case of the big-time *pandas*, the one best suited to keep the tax-man guessing).

Certainly the language in which the *pandas* and Mahabrahmans themselves describe the process of bargaining is commonly more redolent of the street-trader than of some reverend ancient *rishi*. 'Blowing our conch-shells, we Brahmans throw dust in people's eyes.' A Mahabrahman who is too soft-hearted may be derided by his colleagues as *dila* ('loose' or 'slack'); one who is made of sterner stuff will 'squeeze them hard' or 'wring their necks'. If they did not 'demand', they complain, they could never make a living;[14] though they hope to be able to 'force' their *jajman* 'with love'. With or without love, a pilgrim is, in the *pandas*' argot, 'one who is destined to die' (*marti*). Linguistic code-switching goes on at a bewildering pace. In the space of a couple of minutes, the *panda* instructs his assistant in argot on how much to ask; calls across the *ghat* to a friend in local Bhojpuri dialect, instructs the pilgrim in Gujerati, answers the tiresome anthropologist in standard Hindi, and gabbles a *mantra* in Sanskrit – or at least what passes for Sanskrit since none of the rest of us know the difference (cf. Mehrotra 1977:29).

Certainly also the strategies employed would do credit to any Lebanese trader raised in a West African market. The *panda* has one of his *gumashtas* hand over some totally inflated sum which has *supposedly* been offered by another pilgrim at the conclusion of the very same ritual he is now performing. One Mahabrahman takes on the role of 'hard man', while another plays the 'nice guy' who establishes the rock-bottom price to which the other only acquiesces with the greatest show of reluctance. Both kinds of priest regularly adopt the gambit of multiplying the number of gifts they demand of a *jajman* from whom they suspect there is more to be had. If the 'gift of a cow', 'the gift of gold', and 'the gift of grains' have already been fulfilled, then there is always 'the gift of land', 'the gift of an umbrella', of shoes or sugar or sesame which can be added to the list of those which are absolutely *de rigeur* at this particular ritual. The risk of under-pricing is not therefore great. I particularly recall one *sajja dana* that was so unexpectedly munificent that the Mahabrahmans were momentarily stunned into silence, only recovering themselves when one of them noticed the lantern. 'But where', he cried, 'is the oil? Grandfather needs oil for a year.' At this the chief mourner's brother guffawed derisively, and even the Mahabrahmans could not help smiling. They knew they had done well, and the atmosphere was uncharacteristically relaxed.

But things sometimes turn nasty, as the following paraphrase from my notebooks suggests:

Seven Mahabrahmans are present at an eleventh day ritual at Lalita *ghat* which is in the *pari* of Kali Prasad, who will therefore receive the lion share of the gifts. The chief mourner – a middle-aged man who loudly professes advanced social views – belongs to a well-known, well-heeled and politically well-connected Goldsmith family. He is accompanied by his uncle, young nephew and the family Barber.

The chief mourner wants to pay the Mahabrahmans a lump sum in cash at the end; but throughout the ritual the Mahabrahmans try to insist on individual gifts. Sunil, one of Kali Prasad's *karinda*-servants, demands a *dhoti* (a loin-cloth which is a perquisite of the *pari*-holder's helpers). 'I want it to wear, not to sell', he explains. 'It should be like the one I am wearing now.' After a great deal of wrangling a cash payment is agreed in lieu. Somewhat encouraged, Manni Lal asks for a *dopatta* – a kind of shawl – but this is rejected out of hand. 'No, no, I don't mean a [top quality] Jaipuri one. A Madrassi *dopatta* will do.' When even this modest request is declined, the Mahabrahmans start to moan about how things have come to a pretty pass when a family which had been so generous in the past is now so mean. 'You people are wealthy merchants (*seths*)', protests Bachchha. 'No, no, we plough the fields. We are just simple farmers.' The chief mourner mutters darkly about writing to the newspapers to expose these parasitic Funeral-priests, and complaining to Kamla Patti Triparthi (the local MP and then a minister in Mrs Gandhi's Cabinet). But the Mahabrahmans treat this with contemptuous mirth. 'We have seen many like you', they say, 'but when it comes to the point you Congress-*wallahs* spend lavishly.'

'Come on, let's get on with it.' Manni Lal instructs the chief mourner to take water and *kusha* grass in his hand for the *sankalap* (ritual dedication) of the gift of a *dhoti*, though for good measure he adds in the disputed shawl as well. 'Repeat after me, "Hey Father, I am obtaining one loin-garment and one Madrassi shawl that you may accept in heaven"'. The chief mourner stops himself just in time.

An argument now breaks out over the utensils that should be part of any *sajja dan*, but for which the mourners are proposing to substitute cash. 'Alright', says Kali Prasad, 'just listen to me. In the old days you people gave gold drinking cups, gold and silver rings and much else besides. It does not matter that you have not brought these now; but you should certainly give me a gold chain. It is my daughter's wedding. I am not asking for myself. I tell you the truth.' The uncle advises them to forget the past and what they got then. The chief mourner begins a lecture on the evils of dowry.

The ritual proceeds. Various ritual dedications are to be repeated after Sunil; but Manni Lal keeps butting in to criticise the chief mourner's pronunciation of the Sanskrit. The seven Mahabrahmans are pressing in closer round the three mourners, and the atmosphere is increasingly tense. 'Offer it with the *right* hand', barks Manni Lal. 'Don't you know anything?' 'This is the *mantra* for sweets and sugar and there isn't even any molasses here.' The *sankalp* for the gift of a cow is recited. 'Where is the cow?' 'Enough', says the chief mourner scrambling to his feet, 'finished. I am not going on.' He storms off down to the river and stares into space. 'So now what?' asks the uncle in a conciliatory tone. 'I'll tell you what', shouts Manni Lal. But he doesn't get a chance as complete pandemonium has broken out with both sides angrily berating each other.

Twenty minutes later the mourners have put down Rs. 51 as an offering in lieu of *sajja dan* – which in theory should consist of a bed and bedding, clothes, utensils, grain, an umbrella, everything in short which the deceased might need to tide him over the coming year. 'Rs. 51', protests Kali Prasad, 'that won't fill my belly.' The

Mahabrahmans insist that they will not take less than Rs. 101. 'You can forget about the extra loin-garment. If you take that away we are only demanding another Rs. 20 or so.' It is the time of the Emergency, and the chief mourner remarks that these days the Government is arresting beggars. After more wrangling he jumps to his feet and announces that he is going to chuck the *pind* rice-ball offerings in the river and give the money to the first passer-by. But the Mahabrahmans are unimpressed, and start insisting that they should be given a quarter *tola* gold ring. 'Put down the money and let's go', says the chief mourner to his uncle. 'No, no', say the Funeral-priests, 'the work is not finished.' More recriminations and invidious comparisons with the past. The chief mourner complains that they are offending his religious sentiments, and then – with heavy irony – begins to sing at the top of his voice, *ai malik tere bande ham* . . . ('Oh god, we are your devotees. Our deeds should be such that when we die, we die laughing').

'Listen', shouts Manni Lal. 'My daughter's wedding is coming', shouts Kali Prasad. 'Please give something more . . . some gold. Rs. 51 does not fill the belly.' A long pause follows during which we all sit in a stubborn silence, eventually broken by the uncle saying that they will certainly be lodging a complaint with the District Magistrate.

'Come on, get it over quickly', says the family Barber. 'Can't you see the boy is upset.' The mourners put down another Rs. 21, making the offer up to Rs. 72. Manni Lal pushes for another Rs. 10, but quickly gives up and instructs the chief mourner to fold his hands and repeat the *sankalp*: 'Oh father, after intimidating the Mahabrahmans I have given . . .' The *jajman* intones: 'Oh father, after the greedy demands of the Mahabrahmans I have given . . .' 'Now', says Sunil, 'we must all be fed.' 'No.' 'What about the money for breaking the water-pot dwelling (*ganth*) of the ghost?' 'No.' The Mahabrahmans now fall to quarrelling with the family Barber about his share of the takings, and as they finally leave, Sunil and Bachchha call back over their shoulders, 'quickly the *paratha* (a kind of flat bread) will turn over' (meaning, I was told, that somebody else in the house would die very soon).

With regard to the amount of antagonism generated, this case could be matched by a dozen others I recorded – several of which I personally found far more disturbing. An old man whose only son – an eighteen-year-old boy – has died in appallingly tragic circumstances is ruthlessly harried over Rs. 5. 'My son died. I am burning. You did not feed Nandu. It was I who fed him in my lap. My son is dead and . . .' 'Your son is dead, so what can I do?' Sometimes, as in this last example, the chief mourner does indeed throw away the rice-ball offerings. But always, as again in this example, he is eventually prevailed upon to begin the ritual all over, during which he will be subjected to renewed demands. Only once did I see a rite which was not – after some fashion or other – completed.

What *is* perhaps unusual about the Goldsmith case just cited was that it involved a relatively rich and powerful family, for my experience suggests that, as a rule of thumb, the richer and more powerful the *jajman*, the less importunate the demands of the Dom and the priest. It is possible, however, that my own experience is misleading, for many stories tell of even rajas and maharajas being subjected to systematic harassment. On the day of his *pari*, the Dom and the Mahabrahman is himself a king who bows to none, and who – as a king – has the *right* to demand. 'See here grandfather', says the Mahabrahman to the old man whose eighteen-year-old son has just died, 'today ours is considered to be the rank of raja, and we are not asking much . . . The whole world respects us on this day.'

But the Funeral-priest also, of course, impersonates another and altogether more sinister figure. At the time of the eleventh day rituals he stands in for – and even embodies – the marginal and malevolent ghost. His insatiable rapacity is entirely in character. The hungry greed of the *pret*-ghost who can never get enough to eat is acted out in the hungry greed of the *pret*-Brahman who represents him. Through his voracious and importunate demands the latter reveals his 'true' nature; and since he cannot escape his reputation, he is not unnaturally tempted to exploit it for all it is worth, thus 'proving' that he is what he is supposed to be, a virulent and venomous ghost. By the same token, at the rituals of the twelfth day, when the *pret*-ghost has become an ancestral-*pitr*, the *panda* stands in for – and even embodies – the ancestor. His demands are somewhat less strident than those of the Funeral-priest, but then ancestors are an altogether better class of being than ghosts. As the Mahabrahman betrays through his bargaining the predatory predelictions of the *pret*, so the *panda* might be said to give voice to the legitimate demands of the *pitr*. As for the Doms, I have earlier suggested that they are to be seen as worldly representatives of the *yamdut*, 'the messengers of death' who mercilessly harry the deceased to the other world.

Seen from this perspective, of course, bargaining *is* a part of the ritual. Through it, their terrestial counterparts enact the roles, and assert the claims, of the celestial protagonists who are its principal focus. Moreover, there is – as I started this chapter by arguing – an important sense in which the spiritual goals of the pilgrims and mourners are positively promoted by the material acquisitiveness of the priest. It is by sweating gifts out of them that the priests purify the souls of those they serve; and it is partly for this reason that their licence to do so is at first sight puzzlingly permissive. The proposition that bargaining might be an integral aspect of the rituals themselves is also suggested by the fact that in the context of village rituals certain kinds of people are plainly expected to assert the right to demand or even extort their customary dues.

It is surely clear, however, that some of the bargaining I have described goes far beyond the exercise of a legitimate privilege, and that when Manni Lal intones 'Oh father, after intimidating the Mahabrahman I have given . . .' he is deviating from the standard manuals of ritual practice. Nor is my impression that the rich and powerful are largely immune from the most importunate forms of harassment entirely consistent with the notion that such behaviour is a crucial part of the ritual sequence. If it were, one would surely expect them to get more of it rather than less. Though I have tried to show that some aspects of the economic anthropologists' model of bargaining are badly flawed – in particular the pervasive assumption that it is incompatible with gift exchange – I have also suggested that much about the situation I describe is entirely predictable on purely economic grounds. As the model supposes, bargaining on the *ghats* exists in the context of chronic uncertainty, and this uncertainty makes it the most pragmatically sensible way for a priest to organise his business.

In line with the conclusion that I reached at the end of the last chapter about the prevalence of *pari*, I therefore believe that the bargaining I have described cannot be adequately understood as *either* an aspect of ritual *or* as a simple matter of economics. It is in a sense over-determined – both by 'culture' and 'practical reason', and the challenge for an anthropological analysis is to understand the complexity of their interaction.

PART III

Death into birth

5

The last sacrifice

5.1 Introduction

While the two previous chapters have been primarily concerned with the livelihoods made from death, the next two focus on the death rituals themselves. The present chapter is concerned with the proper way to die, with the disposal of the corpse and with the sacrificial idiom which pervades both processes. Chapter 6 follows the sequence of post-cremation mortuary rituals which convert the marginal and malevolent ghost into an incorporated ancestor, and which create a new body – or rather, a series of new bodies – for the deceased. Reborn through the sacrificial fires of the cremation pyre, he is now reborn all over again in the subsequent rites. Though death is *dehant* – 'the end of the body' – it is not normally the end of the soul's embodiment.

As we have seen (pp. 110–11), it is the father's semen which is said to be the 'pre-eminent' determinant of a person's social being. According to my priestly informants, his only real justification in spending that semen is to produce *a* son to perform his obsequies and to perpetuate the ancestral offerings he has made. Subsequent progeny are merely the product of desire (cf. Malamoud 1983:32). The performance of such rites is the most solemn of filial duties, and one of the three inescapable debts which a man must discharge in the course of his life (the other two being to the gods and his *guru*).[1] Without a son there is no prospect of attaining heaven; and before the Kali Age no son would have been so unfilial as to predecease his father.

Thus the father repays his debt to the ancestors by siring a son; the son repays his debt to his father by giving him birth on a new and higher plane, and this newly created ancestor in turn confers fertility and material prosperity on his descendants. If the mortuary rites are neglected or inadequately performed, the cycle is disrupted and the result is barrenness, miscarriages, the death of infants and a decline in the family fortunes (chapter 7). Not only is the son responsible for the rebirth of his father, but there is also perhaps a sense in which he is himself reborn *as his father* – or at least as the bearer of his father's worldly status and responsibilities. He is described as the 'rebirth' (*punar-janam*) of his father, and as his 'replica' (*pratimurti*).[2]

It is in any event through *ritual* that ancestors are made, and the initial creative force through which these rituals work is unleashed by an act of sacrificial destruction. Life is created out of death. As Shulman (1980:90) puts it:

> The Hindu universe is a closed circuit: nothing new can be produced except by destroying or transforming something else. To attain more life – such as a son, or the 'rebirth' of the sacrificial patron himself – the life of the victim must be extinguished. Life and death are two facets of a single never-ending cycle . . .

By itself, however, the sacrificial act is seemingly insufficient. The formless and chaotic power it engenders must be structured by subsequent ritual acts (Smith 1989). As a result of the prototypical self-sacrifice from which creation proceeded, Prajapati had 'fallen to pieces' and had to be reconstituted through the ritual performances of the gods. At their birth, his human counterparts are similarly formless and inchoate, and must be given form and completeness by the sacremental life-cycle rituals (*sanskars*) by which their lives are punctuated. The sacrificial destruction of their bodies at death is a creative act analogous to *biological* birth: a 'birth' which produces only a 'flawed creation' – a disarticulated and formless ghost – which must be transformed and perfected as an ancestor by subsequent ritual action (pp. 82–101). Ritual completes an originally incomplete incubation; as Smith's sources suggest, it repairs and perfects an originally botched creation.

5.2 The expression of grief

At death it is *men* who give birth. In nearly all communities, women are regarded as too faint hearted to accompany the corpse to the burning *ghat*, and it is exclusively men who assist at cremation. Even in the absence of a son it is almost invariably a man who serves as the *dagiya* ('the one who gives fire'), and who performs the subsequent rites. What then is the role of women? The short answer is, to grieve.

The Khatiks are butchers and vegetable sellers. They are a low caste and most of my informants regard them as Untouchables. Kamla Khatik presides over a large joint family which occupies a compound at the back of the house in which I was living at the time when his ancient, and somewhat cantankerous, mother died. She had been ill for some weeks and her death was not unexpected. It occurred at night, and from the moment of death until the funeral procession left for the cremation ground, her corpse – which had been laid out under a canopy in the courtyard with the feet pointing south – was continually surrounded by weeping, lamenting women.

By early next morning friends and relatives were beginning to arrive from all over the city. Many of them came by cycle-rickshaw, but they all walked the last hundred yards or so, the women (but not the men) removing their shoes. The men came into the courtyard silently; the women broke into loud sing-song wails as they entered, to which the group round the corpse responded with renewed laments of their own, the theme of which was that now they were bereft and deserted children. 'Oh! mother, mother, where have you gone? Why have you left us?' 'Mother, mother, who now will feed mangoes to Papu?' Some beat their breasts; others allowed their hair to become loosened and dishevelled. Mourners of both sexes went straight to the corpse, the face of which was immediately uncovered so that they might have *darshan* ('auspicious sight') of it. The women and children then joined the huddle round the body; the men drifted off into little knots on the periphery of the compound, and chatted quietly amongst themselves. Kamla himself sat to one side – immobile, silent and apparently stunned. Many of the mourners had brought shrouds, of which a daughter's husband took charge, showing each perfunctorily to Kamla, and then to the group of women round the corpse, by whom they were examined more critically.

By late morning the courtyard had become a hive of activity. Kamla and the women remained where they were; but more distant male kin and affines were organising an imposing wooden bed which had been purchased to serve as a bier. A new cotton carpet (*dari*) was spread out over it, and the headboard and foot of the bed were copiously decorated with red pennants, fruit, garlands, paper streamers and balloons. Two separate bands, which had been hired to lead the funeral procession, started to play just outside the compound walls. As the women wailed inside, the younger men – those without responsibility for the practical arrangements – drifted out into the street and started to dance, vying with each other in the suggestiveness of their movements and smearing each others' faces with *abir* (an auspicious red powder).

The corpse was now meticulously washed by the women, wrapped in a white shroud and laid out on the bed with thirty-seven other brightly coloured shrouds draped over it. When it was moved to one side for its bath, and when it was lifted onto the bed, the women burst out into a chorus of wails and had to be cajoled by the men to relinquish it. But when each stage was completed, they gathered about it and posed for my wife to take photos. More garlands and balloons were added to the bier; a golden sari was tied to a long bamboo pole, a red sari to another. These were to serve as standards which would lead the funeral procession. *Abir* was rubbed on the face of the corpse. It was time to move; but the women who surrounded the bed were reluctant to make way for the pall-bearers and had to be coaxed aside. As they shouldered it, the women cried out in anguish, the two bands were playing different tunes, the young boys were dancing frenziedly, and most of the men raised a triumphant cry of *Har, har, Mahadev* (a greeting appropriate to Lord Shiva) – though Kamla himself remained solemn and silent.

The women were allowed to accompany the procession only a short way. At the first cross-roads they broke a pitcher filled with water, an action later repeated by the men at the cremation ground to signify a break in the relationship between the survivors and the departed. It was not, however, until the second cross-roads at the border of our *mohalla* (neighbourhood) that the women yielded – with a show of reluctance – to the increasingly preremptory commands of the men that they should now turn back. Straggling home, they sat outside the compound walls for some minutes before going in. While the children played happily with the surplus balloons left over from the bier, the adults cleaned up the courtyard, and then went off to bathe in a nearby tank, after which they were served sweets and water. By mid-afternoon the female visitors had begun to leave.

Though at a brisk walk the cremation ground is no more than twenty minutes away, it must have taken the men an hour and half to reach it, for the procession was endlessly halted for dancing and virtuoso performances by the bandsmen. Holding it only by his teeth, the one on the big base drum balanced it on his chest and thumped it vigorously, then put it down on the ground, arched his back over it like a gymnast, and beat it with arms across his body. People came out of the shops and houses to watch; rice and coins were thrown over the bier. When we had arrived at the burning *ghat*, each of the mourners – there must have been around eighty – offered five cupped handfuls of water onto the old lady's face. A heated argument broke out with the Doms over whether the bed, the *dari* and the thirty-seven sarees were to be burnt with the corpse or go to them; and as Kamla was about to light the pyre, the so-called 'English band' struck up with the tune of what sounded to me like a somewhat discordant version of *Auld Lang Syne*. By early evening the cremation pyre had more or less burnt itself out. The mourners went off to bathe in the river at the adjacent *ghat*, and after consuming black pepper and a plateful of sweets made their way home.

Over the next nine days, Kamla sat largely immobile and impassive on an old sack in the middle of his courtyard, facing north and with a *lota* of water beside him. A stream of visitors came on condolence calls, each new arrival being greeted by the weeping and wailing of the women of the household. Female visitors and those to whom they were offering their condolences sat in the courtyard with their heads on each others' shoulders wailing together for some minutes, and then exchanged news until the next person arrived. The men conversed calmly with Kamla.

In common with other low castes, the Khatiks terminate the period of mourning with a feast which follows the rituals of the tenth day. The serious work now done, the atmosphere was one of revelry. Perhaps 150 guests were fed; the courtyard had been decorated with fairy lights; popular songs blared out over a loud-speaker system; and one of my wife's photographs of the old lady's corpse, which had been framed and garlanded, was placed on a chair by the entrance behind a toy speed-boat driven round and round a basin of water by the infant Lord Krishna. By the next day, only the debris of the previous night, and a few of the family's closest relatives, remained. The men spent it in a state of happy drunkenness; the women cleared up.

The point I hope will be obvious: the legitimate expression of grief is structured by gender (Das 1986; Bloch and Parry 1982). Women weep. They refuse to bow to the inevitable separation of death. Like the *pret*-ghost itself, they try to hang on to the corpse. But however deep their personal anguish, the close male mourners are enjoined to show restraint, to accept what is inevitable, and to get on with the serious business of begetting an ancestor. According to the *Garuda Purana* (Parts 10 and 11), regarded in Banaras as the ultimate textual authority on mortuary matters, the only point at which the chief mourner may give vent to his feelings is at *kapal kriya*, when – mid-way through the cremation – he cracks open the deceased's skull with a bamboo stave. Should he cry at other times the ghost will have to drink his tears. As for more distant male mourners, they are free from the outset to express the joyous triumph of a 'good death'. While the women wail, the young men dance in a burlesque of female sexuality – gyrating hips, upturned thumbs held in front of the chest to suggest breasts, and sometimes a woman's shawl draped over the head and with mock allurement half across the face.

With certain qualifications the pattern is typical. In some castes – for example amongst the Gotakhor (cremation ground) Doms and certain Punjabi communities resident in the city – women do attend the cremation. Even then, however, they do not join the funeral procession but make their own way to the *ghat*. There they sit apart from the men and away from the pyre, weeping and playing no part in the practical arrangements or ritual proceedings. The gender division remains strongly marked. Other details apply only to the lower castes – the termination of mourning on the tenth day, the consumption of alcohol and the fair-ground atmosphere of the final feast. Though in the case of a 'good death' still a joyful occasion, no Brahman would regard a loud-speaker system and fairy lights as in keeping with its dignity. Nor, however venerable her age, would a high-caste *widow's* funeral be celebrated in so triumphant a fashion, such a send-off being reserved for elderly patriarchs or grandmothers with living husbands.

In all castes, of course, this joyous celebration of death – the bands, the erotic dancing, the elaborately festooned and decorated bier – is characteristic only of the funeral procession of an old person who has lived a full and complete life and who has died a 'good death'. The funerals of those whose lives have been cut short at an early age, by accident, violence or by certain diseases, are solemn and mournful occasions; and in such instances the sharp gender division in the expression of grief is likely to be somewhat muted. The revelry of the young men would be quite out of place, and stoical self-restraint may prove beyond the father whose only son has died in tragic circumstances and in the flower of youth. When the death is an 'untimely' one, the expression of personal grief is liable to overspill the limits which the culture tries to impose on it. Notwithstanding popular Western stereotypes, it is not my

experience that Hindus confront death with greater equanimity and resignation than people in contemporary Western societies, or that their distress on
bereavement is any less intense. Private emotions are one thing; their public
expression another. Whatever the former, violent displays of grief are
expected of women, its suppression of men – and this gender division is most
† strikingly realised when the death is considered a 'good' one.

While the problem of the modern West is sometimes alleged to be a cultural
effacement of death, its 'privatisation' and inadequate ritualisation (e.g. Gorer
1965),[3] it is by no means obvious that the ideological and ritual elaboration
surrounding it, and the high degree of public participation, make it any the
easier for the bereaved Hindu to come to terms with his sorrow. I shall have
more to say about the ideas of 'good' and 'bad' death in the next section, and
here I want only to note that the two ideas clearly reinforce each other. The
joyous celebration of a 'good' death draws its meaning and emotional force
from the terrifying possibility of a 'bad' one. To me it often seemed that the
cultural explicitness and ritual elaboration surrounding the latter was actually
exacerbating the emotional turmoil of the bereaved and their difficulty in
coming to terms with their loss. Not only must they contend with that loss
itself, and with the tragic circumstances which led to it, but – as we shall see –
they must also cope with the endlessly reiterated message that responsibility
for this evil must ultimately lie with the sinful nature of the deceased himself,
and that despite their best endeavours he is liable to get stuck as a wandering
and malevolent ghost on a long-term basis.

Veena Das (1986), from whom my discussion takes its lead, has recorded
case material which reveals a very similar gender patterning in the behaviour
of Punjabi mourners.[4] This she interprets in the light of what she sees as a more
or less universal need to mediate between two opposite, but equally
unacceptable, reactions to death – 'between a fatal fascination to follow the
fate of the dead man and the terrible temptation to deny his very existence' (p.
197). The behaviour expected of women exemplifies the first possibility; that
expected of the men of the household the second. The role of affinal kin is to
encourage the women to distance themselves from the dead, and the men to
abandon their distance. The work of mourning is thus to establish a kind of
dialogue between these extremes, a dialogue in which 'the binary distinction of
gender is used to articulate this opposition between complete conjunction and
complete disjunction between life and death' (p. 203).

With this interpretation I am only in partial agreement. Das is, I think, right
to see the women's behaviour as an object lesson in the futility of an excessive
identification with the deceased; but wrong to see the detachment of men as a
problem to be overcome. Given that the chief mourner must cremate the
corpse and perform the elaborate sequence of subsequent rituals, it is not clear
that his behaviour can be said to represent a 'complete disjunction between life
and death'. He is, as we shall see (p. 183), in many ways identified with the
departed, for whom he serves as a 'vehicle' and who 'rides upon his skull'.

Indeed it is tempting to suggest that the chief mourner's stoicism should be seen in the light of the fact that he is a kind of living counterpart of the deceased. In order to die well, the attitude of the dying man himself should be one of calm resignation (pp. 158ff). We might in other words argue that self-restraint is expected of the chief mourner, not because there is a complete *dis*junction between him and the departed, but rather because the *con*junction between them is so strikingly asserted. It is in any event *enjoined* by normative texts like the *Garuda Purana*, and stands, I believe, for the ideal. Not that he is expected to be indifferent; but he should master his emotions, bow to the inevitability of death and acknowledge the transient nature of human relationships. The fact that men prove able to do so is 'proof' in turn of their superiority.

The funeral of an old person is often described as their 'second wedding' and their funeral procession as a *barat* – as a marriage party which accompanies a groom to the house of his bride. Traditionally women do not go with *barat*, just as they do not accompany a corpse to the cremation ground. Instead they remain at home where they stage a raucously obscene mimicry of the wedding and its consummation. Expected at death to show immoderate grief, at marriage they display an immoderately licentious concern with the carnality of conjugal relationships. On both occasions they remain inordinately preoccupied with the 'gross' physical body; and at death their exaggerated grief reveals an inability to recognise its ephemeral nature. Like the ghost itself, they have to be persuaded to relinquish the corpse. Less spiritually developed than men, they are more bound up in the world of relationships and less able to reconcile themselves to their transience.

The general lesson – reiterated in slightly different forms in a large number of other contexts – appears to be this: inferiors are to a greater extent enmeshed in the world of physicality, more deeply sunk in a mire of social dependency, than their superiors. A person of lower status is in consequence liable, as we shall find, to be more severely polluted by the death of a superior connection than the latter is by his demise (pp. 218ff). As I will also argue (pp. 245ff), his ritual world is represented as dependent on that of his superiors, while theirs can exist without his. Forever bound in a relationship to a husband who is already dead, socially the high-caste widow is herself half dead. But the converse does not apply. The social persona of a man is, in general,[5] scarcely touched by the death of his wife. Indeed, it is in large measure the relative autonomy from his inferiors to which the superior lays claim that forms the basis of his superiority. Through their stoicism at death, men assert their ability to distance themselves from the world of relationships; through their ostentatious grief women reveal their inability to do so.

Rather than interpreting the different roles they play as a commentary on two universally problematic reactions to death, what I am therefore tempted to emphasise is the way in which these roles become part of a process by which hierarchical relations between the sexes are reasserted and their legitimacy

'proved'. I do, however, recognise that the two interpretations may not be
entirely incompatible. The problem with Das's hypothesis, as I see it, lies with
her claim that the apparent detachment of the close male mourners can be
read as a denial of the deceased's existence and expresses their 'complete
disjunction' from him. Reformulated as a contrast between women's reluctance to relinquish the departed and men's acknowledgement of the necessity
of doing so, her proposition would not only apply to the case at hand but also
conform to a far more general pattern. My point, then, would be that in Hindu
culture (as no doubt in others), these contrasting reactions to death are
hierarchised, such that their association with the two sexes reinforces an
ideology of gender hierarchy.

5.3 'Good' and 'bad' death

As I have already suggested (pp. 30ff above), death, and more especially
cremation, are symbolically constructed as a sacrificial offering of the self to
the gods. Sacrifice is a pre-eminently creative act which not only results in the
rebirth of the sacrifier, but also renews the cosmos. In order to serve as a
means to such momentous ends, not only must the offering itself – the
sacrifier's own person – be worthy, but his renunciation of it must be complete,
for the essence of sacrifice is the sacrifier's *tyag*, his act of renunciation or
abandonment (Biardeau 1976:19).

Death must therefore be a *voluntary* relinquishment of life, a *controlled*
evacuation of the body. In the paradigmatically 'good' death (*sumaran*[6]), the
dying man – like the sacrifier before the sacrifice (Kaelber 1978) – forgoes all
food for some days before death, and consumes only Ganges water and the
mixture in which an image of a deity has been bathed (*charan-amrit*,
charanodak), in order to weaken his body so that the vital breath may leave it
more easily; and in order to make himself a worthy sacrificial object free of
foul faecal matter.[7] He should die to the sound of the chanting of the names of
God, for his thoughts at that moment may determine his subsequent fate; and
he should be empty of all desire for the things of this world, for those who
remain in bondage to it are condemned to wander in misery for a thousand
years as a malevolent ghost. Moreover, those who obstinately cling to life
when their time has come imperil others. If an old person refuses to heed its
summons, death will carry off a younger member of the family as a surrogate.
A 'good death' occurs after a full and complete life having lived to see the
marriages of one's son's sons, when one is still in full command of one's
faculties, and in the presence of all one's close family. Having previously
predicted the time of his going, the dying man gathers his sons about him and –
by an effort of concentrated will – abandons life. He is not said to die, but to
relinquish his body.

For a (high-caste) woman to die well she must predecease her husband; for
both sexes it is essential to have a son to perform one's obsequies. Though

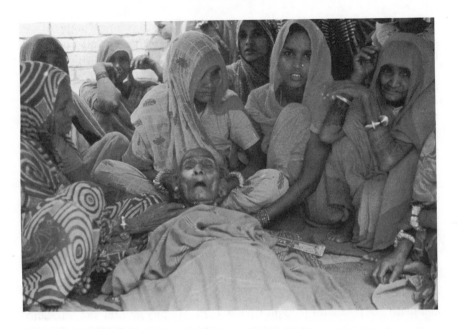

Plate 7 The women of the family surrounding the corpse of the old Khatik lady after its final bath. (Photograph by Margaret Dickinson.)

Plate 8 Part of the Khatik lady's funeral procession with the bier decorated with balloons, streamers and garlands. (Photograph by Margaret Dickinson.)

another may give fire to the cremation pyre and construct a new body for the
pret-ghost, it is said that only a son can effect the merger of this body with
those of the ancestors at the ritual of *sapindikaran*,[8] by which the deceased is
transformed into an ancestor himself. Those without sons are consequently
liable to get stuck in the limbo of *pret*-hood.

A 'good' death occurs at the right time and at the right place – ideally in
Banaras on the banks of the Ganges with the lower limbs in the water. Failing
Banaras or some other place of pilgrimage, one should die at home on purified
ground and in the open air, and not on a bed or under a roof. Even in Banaras,
there are good and bad times to go. Death in *uttarayan* – the six months of the
year that begin with the winter solstice (*makar sankranti*) – is propitious, for
this is the day-time of the gods. During *dakshinayan* (the other six months)
they spend much of their time asleep and do not therefore take much notice of
human affairs. But the ancestors are now wide awake, so *dakshinayan* is
auspicious for the performance of the *shraddh* rituals addressed to them, and it
is during this period that *pitri paksh* – the 'fortnight of the ancestors' – is
celebrated. *Pitri paksh* is itself a good time to die because 'the doors of heaven
are open' and anybody can just walk in. 'Nobody at all will even ask about sin
and merit.' The bright fortnight (*shukul paksh*) of any month, and especially
its eleventh day (*ekadashi*) – when heaven's 'storehouse' is open – is again
auspicious. The worst time is during *panchak*, a term which refers to a
grouping of five consecutive *nakshattras*, or lunar mansions, in a cycle of
twenty-seven (each of which lasts for approximately one day). More precisely,
the general priestly view is that the *dosh* – the 'sin' or 'fault' – consists in
burning the corpse during *panchak*, and that no special rituals of expiation are
required for one who dies within this period but is cremated outside it. If
cremation cannot be delayed, as it normally cannot, four or five effigies (even
the manuals of ritual practice are inconsistent) should be burnt along with the
corpse lest the deceased lure four or five other members of the family after him.
The *panchak* is ritually 'pacified' on the eleventh day after death (*panchak
shanti*).

The inconvenience of having to do so is, however, unlikely to affect the
paragon, whose spiritual force gives him a degree of mastery over the time of
his own death. The paradigmatic example comes from the *Mahabharata*:
Bhisma lay on his death-bed riddled with arrows refusing to die until the
uttarayan began – enough time for a disquisition many thousand verses long
on the difficult problems surrounding the gift of *dan*.

The soul's route of exit from the body through one of its seven orifices is a
measure both of its spiritual state, and of the quality of death. The 'vital
breath' (*pran*) of a just and pious man emerges through the suture at the top of
the skull (*brahmand*), which – in the case of a man of great spiritual force –
happens by a kind of spontaneous combustion at the time of cremation. That
of an abject sinner who dies a 'bad' death emerges through his anus as
excrement, through his mouth as vomit, or through one of his other orifices.

Such an evacuation is a sure sign of damnation to come – a notion which is perhaps not unconnected with the idea that it is best to die on an empty stomach.

Consider, for example, the exemplary case of an old householder, whose extraordinary spiritual development had gained him a circle of devoted disciples, and whose subsequent mortuary rituals I attended. For the last nine months of his life he had left off eating grains; for the last two months he would only drink water from the Ganges, and for the last twelve days he refused to sleep on a bed. When a doctor examined him towards the end, he was amazed to discover that the patient's heart had already stopped beating, though there he was instructing his disciples. A few days before he finally departed, he announced that he would be relieved of his illness on the following Friday and would take a walk the very next day. It was only later that the family understood his real meaning: his death and journey to the cremation ground (and in the event it turned out that his funeral procession left home that Saturday at precisely the hour at which he had been accustomed to set out for his daily walk). When the time had come for him to abandon his body, he was sitting up straight as a ram-rod listening to a reading from the *Bhagavad-Gita*, and surrounded by his sons, grandsons and great-grandson – though in order to spare their distress he had sent the women away on some pretext or other. This copybook death was consummated on his funeral pyre when his burning corpse successively manifested itself to a privileged few in the forms of the celebrated religious teachers Sai Baba, Mehar Baba and Rama Krishna Paramhansa, as the terrifying god Bhairava (Lord Shiva's *kotval* or 'police-chief' in Banaras) and finally as Shiva himself. A rounded protuberance was seen to move up the spine of the corpse, burst through the skull, soar into the air and split into three parts. One fell in Banaras, another went north to the abode of Shiva in the Himalayas and nobody knows what happened to the third.

As all of this suggests, a good death is the product of a good life (cf. Madan 1987:122),[9] and promises a good state after death (*sadgati*). It further promises well of pious and worthy descendants. It is hardly surprising, then, that – in the recounting – the actual death of a loved one is rather rapidly mythologised and sanitised. Conversely, there is a marked tendency to dwell on the agonising end of an enemy: a body wracked by pain and rotted by leprosy, bowels over which all control has been lost. A group of Funeral-priests who, with some rancour, were regaling me with the story of the seizure of their hereditary rights by one of their rich and powerful colleagues, clinched their evidence of his iniquity with the gleeful recollection that he had died vomiting excrement. As for his son, their present employer, 'he will reap . . . leprosy is coming out on him. He will rot as no one in our caste has rotted before.'

Nor is it merely the manner of death and the demeanour of the deceased which tend to be mythologised, but also the last services which the living rendered him. In cases of fraternal strife, somewhat selective recollections of these ministrations are liable to be resurrected in the propoganda war of family feuding. Who was really present at the death; which brother had served the dying parent in the final illness, what that parent had said about those who had proved less filial, all become subject to completely contradictory claims.

Not only does the quality of life determine the quality of death, but it also determines that life's duration. Generally speaking, those whom the gods detest die young, an early death being the fruit of the sins of this and previous existences. The commonest expression for what I have called 'bad death' is *akal mrityu*, literally 'untimely death'.[10] Strictly speaking, it is not the age of the victim but the manner of dying that is diagnostic of an *akal mrityu*, and the death of an old person may be 'untimely' if it was caused by leprosy, violence or sudden accident. The expression *alp mrityu* (meaning 'death in youth') is however often used as a virtual synonym for *akal mrityu* – such a death being almost *ipso facto* bad. The good death occurs at the end of a properly completed life, the life-span appropriate to our degenerate age being one hundred and twenty five, and this a mere fraction of that of former epochs. The fact that few attain even this modest target is a consequence of the sins of this and former lives; and the greater the burden of sin, the greater the shortfall. Those who die before the age of forty are certainly 'heading for hell' (*narak-gami*), while the stillborn infant is probably some reprobate expiating his crimes by a succession of seven such births.

There is also, however, the notion that the sins of the father may be visited on the son, and that the attenuation of this life may be a consequence of the wickedness of one's forebears. The relationship between the living and dead is a symbiotic one, and the actions of the former may continue to affect the posthumous fate of the latter. If the son turns out a sinner, the ancestors may be even evicted from heaven – a fate for which they will certainly exact retribution. 'Yamraj will say "*Ja sale*, go you bastards (literally 'wife's brothers'). Such have been raised in your descent line." Then those ancestors will curse'.

By contrast with the controlled and voluntary release of life which is the ideal, a bad death is an uncontrolled and involuntary evacuation of the body. Sometimes known as *akasmik mrityu* – 'sudden', 'abrupt' or 'accidental death' – bad death is conventionally glossed as death by violence, by being burned in fire or drowned in water, by falling from a tree or being bitten by a snake, though the category also includes the victims of traffic and train accidents, women who die in childbirth, indeed anybody whose time has been cut unexpectedly short. Such a person 'did not die his own death', the underlying notion being that the victim was forced to relinquish life prematurely, with the result that his embittered ghost is liable to return to afflict the survivors unless the appropriate propitiatory rituals are perfectly performed – a matter of notorious difficulty. Ghosts have insatiable passions and desires. They remain bound to a world they have only half left, and it is this which makes them so vindictive (and, by a principle we have already encountered, such an inferior class of beings). As a consequence of their malevolence, bad death in the family tends to be cumulative, the victim of one causing another. There is a sense, then, in which the deceased perpetuates in others his own experience of death. Indeed that experience is also likely to be repeated in his own future existence – witness the cautionary tale of a priestly Brahman who accepted the *dan* of Nepali Untouchables. The penalty he paid was to be murdered by thugs and reborn as a chicken. It is, as my informant explained, a statistical probability that a chicken will suffer a similarly violent end.

Though as a rule death by violence is always bad, over a soldier's death in battle there is some uncertainty. Most of my informants unhesitatingly rate it as an *akal mrityu*; but most would also claim that the spirits of those who have laid down their lives in a just cause do not join the ranks of ordinary ghosts, but become *birs* or 'hero ghosts'. Punitive and perhaps capricious, though never entirely malevolent, *birs* are more powerful than most other *pret* and can be used to control them. For this reason they often become territorial guardians, and – along with *satis* and certain ascetics – are one of the very few kinds of dead who are memorialised in permanent shrines.[11]

To come to Banaras with the intention of dying there is of course the most laudable of objectives; and, as we have seen (pp. 22–3), religious suicide is sanctioned by certain texts. In general, however, suicide is rated as an unequivocally bad death. But why should this be when it appears to conform to the ideal of an end which is willingly chosen? Some of my informants differentiated between *atam-hatya* ('self-murder') and *atam-dah* ('self-immolation' or perhaps 'the burning up of the self'), between 'ordinary' suicide and a willed renunciation of life in the sacred centre, a death which the victim himself may have actively hastened. The idea behind this linguistic distinction is, I think, general. Those who die a bad death are still ensnared by desire. Suicide is a surrender to the disappointed desires of this life and thus evinces an acute involvement with it. Abandoning one's body in Banaras (*atam dah*) is, by contrast, testimony to an absence of worldly desire and a calm indifference to mundane existence.

A bad death is one, then, in which the deceased has revealed no intention of sacrificing his body (e.g. the victim of violence or accident), or of renouncing its desires (e.g. the suicide). Alternatively it is that of a person whose body does not constitute a fit sacrificial object – the extreme case here being the leper, though this also applies to the one-eyed and paralysed, the goitrous, hunch-backed and lame. A flawless body is an index of a flawless soul, and a prerequisite for a flawless death: in theory at least, imperfect bodies such as these must not be cremated but rather immersed in the Ganges.[12] Indeed it is almost as if the fire itself would reject an offering so unworthy. Hence the peculiarly incombustible nature of the corpses of sinners, that for example of the corrupt Chief Minister instanced in the previous chapter (p. 127). Conversely, the cremation pyre of the 'true wife' (the *sati*) who voluntarily joins her husband in death is commonly represented as igniting spontaneously.

Apart from leprosy (*kusht rog*), those who die from various other illnesses are also said to die badly. The list is somewhat variable, but epidemic diseases like cholera (*haija*) and plague (*pleg*) are generally cited (presumably because they result in sudden death).[13] Some claim that jaundice (*pandu rog*), tuberculosis (*kshay*) and cancer (*kainsar*) should be included, though in most such cases the corpse is in fact cremated, and it is unlikely that the propiatory rituals which normally accompany an untimely death will be performed unless and until some further family misfortune gives rise to the suspicion that the deceased has remained a *pret*.

Asked how death can be considered 'untimely' when it occurs at a time and under circumstances precisely determined by the individual's karmic balance, my informants would generally concede that it is so only by linguistic convention. The moment of one's death is provisionally fixed at one's birth, but is brought forward by sin or put off by meritorious actions and devotion to the gods. As everybody knows, Markandey was destined to die at the age of twelve. His days, however, were spent in single-minded devotion to Shiva, so that when the messengers of death (*yamdut*) came to claim him, their noose fell on Shiva's *ling* and the great god himself appeared. Though the *yamdut* properly insisted that what is written must be, for Shiva there is always a way round such bureaucratic inflexibility. Twelve years was right, but twelve years of Shiva – which left billions and billions to go.[14]

If ready to settle for less than Markandey, many Banarasi people also take ritual steps to increase their life-span and avert an impending death, the repetition (*jap*) of the Amriteshvar *mantra*[15] at the temple of Mahamritunja Mahadev for example. Though the temple is dedicated to Lord Shiva as the Conqueror of Death, *jap* of this sort can have many objectives: to neutralise malign planetary influences, to ensure the birth of sons, the winning of kingdoms or success in litigation, or to bring cholera epidemics – and even wayward daughters – under proper control (the greater the project the larger the number of repetitions required). Of these, however, the avoidance of untimely death is certainly the most celebrated.

While *jap* at Mahamritunja may be used to deflect an immediate danger, long-term immunity to bad death is also afforded to those who bathe along with their married sister in the Jamuna river from Yamraj *ghat* in Mathura on the second day of the bright fortnight of the month of *Kartik*, and then offer a lighted lamp at the Goverdhan 'mountain'. The 'mountain' is associated with Krishna's protection of his devotees and their cattle from the 'bad deaths' which Lord Indra jealously threatened to inflict on them.[16] The river is the twin sister of Yamraj (the lord of death). When a sister ties a protective thread (a *rakhi*) on the wrist of her brother, she has the right to demand something of him. On one such occasion Jamuna demanded that all who came to bathe in her waters should not be summoned to her brother's court – should not, in other words, die. Yamraj complained that if he granted this request he would have nothing to do and get terribly bored;[17] and it was therefore agreed that the boon should be restricted to those who fulfil the conditions just specified. The prophylaxis is completed when the brother takes food – *phara*, a mixture of rice and horse-bean lentils (*urad*) is prescribed – in his sister's house and receives from her a *tilak* (an auspicious forehead mark) of turmeric and lime powder (*roli*).

Though many of my informants know that these precautionary measures are possible, as far as I am aware none had visited Mathura in order to take advantage of them. The notion that a married sister can and should provide her brothers with protection against bad death is, however, both a persistent theme in popular thought and one which is ritually acted on.[18] When, for example, I returned to Banaras in the summer of 1981 the streets and *ghats* were packed with processions of women taking yellow saris to offer in the Ganges, a phenomenon I had never encountered before. This sudden craze had apparently started in Mirzapur only two or three months earlier, and had spread throughout the towns and villages of the surrounding districts. It began, it was said, with a woman who had learned in a dream that in order to save her two brothers from imminent death she should ask them to give her a yellow sari which she should then offer to the Ganges on their behalf. When informed of the danger, however, her brothers had scoffed and refused to provide the offering. Both were dead within days. As the funeral procession of the younger brother was departing, an unknown old woman approached the sister and told her to take the shroud off the corpse, offer it to the Ganges and then put it on. She did so immediately, and her brother was miraculously restored to life. News of this event spread far and fast and was soon picked up by the local press, with the result that by the beginning of August the streets of Banaras were thronged with women heading towards the river carrying baskets containing yellow saris and other offerings paid for by their brothers, or heading homewards wearing the offering that had just been made. The rush was particularly great because by now it was being said that these offerings would only be fully effective if they were made before the approaching festival of Nag Panchami, and that those who made them subsequently would be required to carry a grinding stone (*sila*) and pestle (*lodha*) to the Ganges on their heads. By the time I next returned to the city (March 1983) the craze appeared to have petered out completely.[19]

While in its strictest recension the doctrine of karma suggests those who die a bad death can have only themselves to blame, the harshness of this judgement may in practice be rejected by those most closely touched by the event. On rare occasions karma doctrine itself is called into question, as, for example, by one chief mourner at the *Narayani bali* ritual he was performing for his wife whose recent suicide was the culmination of an appalling sequence of family misfortunes. Launching into a bitter tirade against the credibility of karma theory and its unfathomable justice, he protested: 'I do not know – and cannot know – what I did in my last life; and in this life I have seen so many wicked people enjoying themselves. If God wants me to believe in the fruits of karma, he should let me see the immediate results of my good and bad deeds.'

More importantly, however, an ostensibly bad death can be seen in an altogether more positive light without compromising karma theory at all. Jamuna Prasad Shastri's granddaughter was left severely retarded by meningitis contracted at the age of two. Six years later she died after a prolonged and distressing illness through which the family had nursed her devotedly, and which had placed a considerable strain on their financial and emotional resources. What, Jamuna rhetorically asked when he gave me the news, could she have possibly done by the age of eight to deserve such suffering? It could only have been the fruits of her former existences. Yet to have been born, and to have died, in Banaras she must have been some *sant-mahatma* (saint) in her previous life; and it could therefore be presumed that her sufferings in this one were an anticipatory *Bhairavi yatna* – a pre-emption of the intense punishment which Bhairav inflicts on those who die in Banaras in order to purify their souls in preparation for Shiva's gift of salvation (see p. 29). It was in other words a pre-mortem purification of her soul – a 'direct harvesting' (*pratyeksh bhog*) of karma which had burned up the residue *before* her death and had qualified her for 'immediate liberation' (*sakshat mukti*). Rather than a symptom of her sinful nature, it was rather a mark of spiritual privilege. An apparently bad death was really a particularly good one. A similar construction was put on the agonies of one of Banaras's most celebrated and saintly traditional scholars who had lain dying in hospital with numerous tubes running in and out of his body. In distress my informant had reportedly asked him: '*Prabhu* (Master), how is it that I see *you* in such a state at the end?' and was told that it was only the deservingly fortunate who might thus forestall far worse to come.

There is often, as all this suggests, a degree of indeterminacy about whether a particular death should be rated as good or bad, and the application of these constructs to real situations is far from mechanical. Take, for example, the case of a middle-aged Aggarwal woman whose cremation I attended. Shortly before her death her husband had had a bad fall and broken an arm. In her haste to help him, the wife had gashed her foot badly on a rusty nail. She had died from tetanus. A sudden and unexpected death, the result of a random accident, many might regard it as a bad one – all the more so since her corpse was cremated during the inauspicious period of *panchak*. What the family chose to emphasise, however, was that she had not only died before her husband, but also in the performance of her most sacred duty: his service. Her death was therefore an auspicious one. The same facts are thus open to different interpretations, and in the last resort it may be only subsequent events which enable the bereaved to judge between them. Further misfortunes suggest the possibility of a dissatisfied ghost who has died an untimely death; a period of tranquil good fortune the blessings of benevolent ancestors.

5.4 The body and its refinement

We have seen then that the good death is represented as a willing renunciation of the body, which must be a fit sacrificial offering to the gods. But how can this be, given that the body and its processes are widely represented as a dangerous source of pollution? In addressing this paradox I begin at the beginning – with conception and birth, the symbolism of which we shall find constantly recurring throughout the rituals of death.

In the very beginning, according to the male Brahman informants who were my principal source on the matters discussed here, was *Brahman*, in which all opposites are unified, and which is without shape, name, colour or any physical attribute (pp. 13-14). The world is created out of this unitary primeval protoplasm by a process of progressive differentiation which is triggered by a disruption of the precarious equilibrium which exists within each material entity.

Differentiation implies degradation: movement away from the original ineffable wholeness of *Brahman*. The universe is steadily running down towards cosmic dissolution, and we now live in the basest and most degenerate of the four epochs of the world cycle. The human body is equally subject to this law of time. In the golden age of the *Satya Yug*, man's vital breath (*pran*) resided in his bones; he subsisted on air alone, enjoyed a life-span of 100,000 years and reproduced asexually. In *Treta* the vital breath was situated in his bone marrow and he lived for 10,000 years; in *Dvarpar* it was in the blood and life expectancy was reduced to a thousand years. But now in the *Kali Yug* the vital breath resides in the grains we eat, and we live to a maximum age of 125. The objective of much indigenous medical practice (cf. Egnor 1983), and of many of the rules and practices to which the ordinary householder subjects himself (cf. Daniel 1984), is to arrest this disequilibriating flow within his own body; or even to swim against the stream and refine it, the project of the ascetic being to get all the way back to source and realise his identity with *Brahman* (chapter 8).

There are conventionally said to be 840,000 kinds of life form (*yoni*) arranged in an elaborate hierarchy with crawling and slithering creatures at the bottom, and men at the top. Every soul (*atma*) moves up this ladder (passing through each one of the 840,000 life forms) until it is incarnated in a human body. Some say that such a body is envied even by the gods, for only human beings are capable of pursuing the path of 'liberation' from the endless cycle of rebirths – though few will actually attain this goal. While the most heinous sinners fall right back to the bottom of the ladder from where they must begin their ascent all over again, most people are expected to return as a human being in a station and with a fate appropriate to their karmic balance.

The body they assume begins to take shape when the father's semen is 'caught' by the menstrual blood (*raj, masik dharam*) of the mother. Such 'bad blood' is then retained throughout the period of gestation to form the flesh of the embryo. The hard parts of the child's body, especially the bones, are the product of the father's semen; and are, as we have seen (pp. 110–11), the more significant and enduring contribution. With the mixing of semen and menstrual blood a *pind* is formed, a term which can denote any rounded mass, which here signifies an embryo, but which most commonly refers to a rice-ball offered to the ancestors. The *pind* is matured – I am tempted to say 'cooked' – in the woman's stomach by her 'digestive fire' (*jatharagni*). By the end of the first month the head has been formed; and by the end of the fifth month the body is complete. Up to this point it appears to be regarded as pure matter, as body without soul. The soul or 'vital breath' (*pran*) – my informants do not discriminate[20] – which will now enter it has meanwhile been wandering in the atmosphere (*vayumandal*) in search of a new 'house', having left its previous one five months before. But it is only at this point that its quest can succeed. Entry is gained through the suture at the top of the foetus's skull.

The material body is now quickened by consciousness (*chetna*), and spends its last five months in the womb in a state of acute mental and physical torment. While we tend vaguely to picture the foetus as luxuriously floating in the secure and balmy bliss of its own custom-built swimming pool, my informants see things differently. Bound in excrutiatingly constricting confinement, suspended in filth and pollution where every minute is as a year, it serves its time contemplating the sins of its previous life – the knowledge of which it looses at parturition. When I asked people why liberation from the cycle of rebirths should have any appeal, they would often explain that having attained it you no longer 'have to bear the pain of the womb'.

At the end of the ten-lunar-month period of gestation, the baby negotiates a river of blood, mucus, excrement and other foul substances to emerge from this 'hell' (*narak*) head-first. Its first act is to yell from the pangs of hunger. All human beings are born through the same vagina (*bhag*), all emerge from 'the place of urination', and consequently all are equally Shudras by birth. Brahmans are not born, but made by the life-cycle rituals through which they pass. Only the product of Brahman seed has the capacity for such transformation, however. Only one whose father and father's father were Brahmans can learn to pronounce Sanskrit with the inflection necessary to please the gods and ancestors.

A person's disposition, however, is almost as likely to be explained by what his mother happened to eat before, or see immediately after, conception as it is by genetic inheritance. 'Having eaten what did your mother give birth to you?' one might reprovingly ask. The raja's son behaves like a Washerman, the Washerman's son like a raja, because these were the first persons their mother happened to see after intercourse. Even more important is the time at which conception takes place and the parents' thoughts at that moment. 'If you think, 'Oh god, this is good', then the child will be like that. He will say, 'While you two were enjoying yourselves I just happened to drop by in the middle.'' Intercourse for a man is a dangerous squandering of vital fluids; its only proper justification is the conception of a dutiful son, and this requires scrupulous scheduling. Conceived at the wrong moment a Brahman child will be like a demon (*rakshas*); while even an obliviously improvident Shudra who by chance ejaculates at the right one will sire a paragon. Intercourse should therefore be regulated by the almanac: certain days (e.g. *puranmasi*, fast days), certain parts of the night (the first) and certain times in a woman's monthly cycle (the first seven nights after the onset of menstruation) should be avoided; odd nights for a girl, even for a boy; the most dutiful son conceived on the fourteenth night, and so on. Family planning is a precise and ancient art; and was a subject on which I received much unsolicited advice.

Not only is the Brahman a Shudra by birth and his flesh formed out of the 'bad blood' of a woman's menses, but this blood is the precipitate of sin. 'A woman's pollution', my informants say, 'is the pollution of murder (*hatya*).' What is invoked here is the well-known story of the god Indra's brahmanicide, the sin of which could only be eliminated by dividing it up and passing it on to others. From women – who received a quarter share – it emerges in the form of menstrual blood. In passing I note that each year, the *men* perform the ritual of *Shravani* at which they purify themselves of the sins of the previous twelve months, and that what my informants endlessly emphasise is the expiation of sins connected with the improper circulation of gifts. The female equivalent is *Rishi Panchami*, but in their case the pre-eminent stress is explicitly on sins concerned with the improper circulation of food during their periods. This is emphasised by the story (*katha*) to which they must listen on that day, and by the fact that girls only start to participate when they are about to attain puberty, while women who have reached the menopause terminate their observance with a closing ceremony (*uddyapan*). The main point that I want to stress here, however, is that the body is not only made out of polluting substance but that substance is the product of the most horrific of crimes. The claim that any equivalent of the notion of original sin is entirely absent from the Hindu universe is therefore exaggerated.

Sudhir Kakar (1982:236–7) draws a sharp contrast between 'the legacy of rejection of the body in the West [which] persists in the unconscious fantasy of the body as a dirt-producing factory', and the positive attitude to the body which is characteristic of Indian culture. It is certainly the case that my informants are unashamedly explicit about their bodily functions, and are in general unconcerned to eliminate waste-products under the conditions of Fort Knox-like security on which Westerners are apt to insist – as if truly depositing gold. Banarasi Brahmans are, however, nonetheless liable to represent the body as a sack of impurities. A consistent preoccupation is with the idea of food lying rotting in the stomach, and with the need to evacuate it speedily (pp. 211ff). The body, moreover, is both the cause and agent of lust (*kam*), anger (*krodh*), greed (*lobh*) and infatuation (*moh*). Each of the five elements of which it is composed is associated with one of the senses (earth with smell, water with taste, wind with touch, fire with sight, and sky with sound) – any of which is sufficient for damnation, in combination inexorably lethal.

The body's equilibrium is subject to constant disturbance, the strategy of Ayurveda, 'the science of long life', being to correct such imbalances between, above all, its three humours (phlegm (*kaph*), bile (*pitta*) and wind (*vayu*)). But good health depends on a thermal as well as humoural equilibrium. Colloquially, one whose 'blood had frozen' or who has 'become cold' (*thanda hogaya*) is a corpse; while a woman whose periods are long-delayed, or whose sexual desire is deprived of all outlet, becomes dangerously over-heated and is likely to go mad. Again medicines – the thermal properties of which depend on climate and season – are prescribed to restore the balance.

In order to preserve it, a stringent self-discipline involving a strict regimen of the body is required. We have already encountered the dangers of sex, but what is even more elaborated are the dangers of irregular dietary practices. The wrong kinds of food, prepared and served by the wrong person, eaten at the wrong time or place corrupt the body, rot the brain and spoil the character. Not only sex and food, but sleeping – even breathing – seem to represent a health hazard. Great stress is placed on the importance of early rising. Sleep (Nidra Devi) is the younger sister of Death (Mrityu); the scriptures are said to recommend a maximum of three hours per night and it is widely held that the less you sleep the longer you live. The explanation for this is that each of us is granted a finite number of breaths, and that in the waking state one breathes predominantly through one nostril only which uses up a smaller proportion of one's quota. By the control of breath (*pranayam*) the adept yogi can enormously prolong his life – by up to a thousand years according to one confident estimate.

At bottom, it is sin and pollution which are the really life-threatening conditions. Bodily pollution is not only the ultimate cause of much organic illness, but it lays one open to ghostly affliction and cuts one off from the protection of the gods. 'Man dies from sin' which manifests itself in emaciation, illness and decay. It grows out of our bodies in the hair (which must therefore be shaved off at the time of important rituals of expiation). Consistent with all this, the term *dosh* refers both to 'a moral fault' and to 'a disorder of the humours of the body'. The state of the body thus provides an index of the state of the soul. No less than in many of the cultures of Highland New Guinea, the external body reveals the inner self; the moral condition of the person shows on the skin (O'Hanlon 1983; Strathern 1979). The sinner rots with leprosy; the face of the priest who accepts the gifts of the pilgrims and mourners rapidly loses its 'lustre'.

So far I have stressed the dark side of the picture; but to leave it at that would be to distort a far more complex and paradoxical reality.[21] We have already seen that even the gods may envy the human body, and that Hindu thought regularly postulates a homology between body and cosmos (pp. 30ff). The *Garuda Purana* (part 15) describes the 'transcendental body' (*parmarthik sharir*) as containing the fourteen 'worlds' (*bhuvan*), the seven island-continents (*duip*), the nine planets (*grah*), all the gods and so on. The temple too is constructed on the plan of a human body (Beck 1976), and the sacred space of Banaras itself is represented as a body. It is by an absolute mastery of his own body that the ascetic attains salvation. 'The wealth of the yogi is his body. Than this there is nothing more precious.'

What this already suggests is the body's capacity for transformation, refinement and even perfection. Many myths suggest that even gender is not immutable. The pre-eminent agent of all such transformation is heat, which matures the embryo, which distils semen out of blood, and which can be generated by an ascetic austerity that burns up the sins of the body. Both symbolically and in terms of the etymology of the word itself (*tapasya*), such austerities are a process of heating the body; and it will be recalled that it was through the heat of the austerities he performed at Manikarnika *ghat* that Vishnu created the world at the beginning of time (pp. 11ff). Austerities, like pilgrimage, undertaken by the householder are not only directed at saving the soul but also at salving the body. There are sixteen *sanskars*, or 'sacraments', through which the twice-born should theoretically pass between conception and death – of which the most important are birth, initiation, marriage and death itself. The term *sanskar* has the connotation of 'purification', 'refinement' or even 'rendering perfect' (Inden and Nicholas 1977:37). Those who fulfil them are 'rendered perfect'.

A whole and perfect body is both a sign of one's moral state, and a prerequisite for making sacrificial offerings to the gods and ancestors. A one-eyed man or hunch-back has no right to perform 'the work of the gods'. A Brahman who has black teeth, bad nails or is excessively corpulent should be excluded from the feast for Brahmans held on the thirteenth day after death; and nobody with an open wound should act as chief mourner. In animal sacrifice the victim's body should be without blemish; and it is a sin to worship an image of a deity which is broken or cracked. Consistent with this premium on physical perfection, perhaps, is a certain prediliction for forms of violence aimed at disfiguring one's enemies – in the internecine competition between powerful *pandas*, the throwing of sulphuric acid.

This quest for bodily perfection brings me back to the wrestlers and body-builders who are such a conspicious part of life on the *ghats* (pp. 37–8). It is perfectly true that the violent competition to which I have just alluded partly explains their ubiquity and earnestness, and that those who regularly exercise often attribute their devotion to a desire that people should know that 'someone is coming' when they walk down the street. But what I would like to emphasise is that such activity is also given a religious cast, and is to be conducted in a state of purity having *first* bathed and evacuated the bowels (Kumar 1988:113). A wrestling school is an *akhara*, a term which also refers to an ascetic community – recalling that the English word 'asceticism' derives from the Greek for 'gymnastic practice'. Many are held to have been founded by religious leaders, some are attached to a temple and most contain a shrine to the god Hanuman who is famed for his prodigious strength. This is closely associated with his celibacy, as is any real prowess as a wrestler. Wrestling, then, is a pastime particularly appropriate to the first of the four stages of life: the stage of *brahmacarya* before one becomes a householder. Its object, however, is a more enduring refinement of the body. But not only the body, for by developing the body one also refines the soul. Not just a mirror of the soul, the body is its material counterpart and a transformation of one brings about a transformation of the other. Body-building builds body *and soul*, and this I believe is its ultimate justification: it not only sets one up for life but more importantly it also sets one up for death as a worthy sacrificial offering. The apparently incongruous juxtaposition of the corpse and the body-builder which is one of my dominant visual memories of the *ghats* is perhaps not quite so incongruous after all.

The project of bodily refinement continues, as we shall see, beyond death. The soul acquires a succession of more and more etherealised bodily envelopes, until finally a real 'end of the body' is achieved and the soul merges back into *Brahman*.

5.5 The end of the ('gross') body

The 'gross' outer body is said to have three possible fates: it is eaten as carrion and turns to excrement; it is buried and turns to maggots; or it is burnt and turns to ash. The rotting or putrescence of the body is viewed with particular repugnance, and the last of these is consequently the least unpalatable and is seen as the swiftest way of recycling the five elements (*panch tattva, panch bhut*) from which the body (and cosmos) is constituted.

There is, as this suggests, at least a sense in which nothing is totally lost at death: the five elements return to the common pool for re-use; the soul is immortal and is reborn, the body particles a person shares with his kinsmen endure in their bodies.[22] The person is never entirely new when born; never entirely gone when dead. Both his body and soul extend into past and future persons, and to a significant degree his biological substance is shared in the present with kin who have the same body particles.

Various omens tell of an impending death (dogs howling in the neighbour-hood at night; dreams of a naked woman, a bride in all her finery[23] or of a tooth falling out); and various physical symptoms signal its approach (the inability to smell the smell of a newly extinguished lamp, to see one's reflection in the sacred well of Siddeshvari, or to feel pain when hair is plucked from the scalp). When death is near, the patient should ideally be placed on ground which has been scattered with mustard (*sarson*) and sesame seed (*til*), freshly plastered with cow-dung, on which the name of the Lord Ram has been written and on which a *kusha*-grass mat has been spread. Death should occur in the open air because a roof would impede the soul's passage upwards. It is bad to die on a *charpai* (the string-cot on which most people sleep), on a roof or in the upper storey of a house 'because this is considered equivalent to dying in mid-space (*antariksh*)'. There is, however, no impropriety in dying on a *chauki* (a raised wooden platform often used as a bed). The explanation I was offered for the difference is that the soul of one who expires on a cot will be caught in its string webbing and remain enmeshed in the world. This obliquely alludes, I infer, to the rule that an ascetic may sleep on a *chauki* (or on the ground) but not on an ordinary bed. At death even the householder must be a renouncer.

One who is about to expire should be oriented with feet pointing south – a position in which people are careful to avoid sleeping, for south is the direction of Yamraj's kingdom. A Brahman should be summoned to receive his last donation, the gift of a cow which will help his soul across the terrifying Vaiturni river which he will have to negotiate on his subsequent journey.[24] Gold, *tulsi* (basil, which is sacred to Vishnu) or Ganges water are placed in his mouth to destroy his sins, and to protect his corpse from being seized and reanimated by one of the evil spirits which hover about it. A Salig Ram – a black ammonite fossil which represents Lord Vishnu – or some other image of a deity should be placed in the patient's line of vision, and he should die with the name of God in his ears. Just as a person's disposition may be determined by what his parents happened to see or think at the moment of his conception, so his posthumous fate may depend on his thoughts or visual impressions at the moment of death. Should he happen to see a goat or pigeon, he is liable to be re-born in that form. A lamp is lit near the patient, and is kept alight until his corpse is taken out of the house. Its flame is a sign to the soul that it should go straight up, and also affords protection against the evil spirits which threaten to invade the corpse (and which are also kept at bay by the women who continually surround and touch it). Immediately after death, the domestic hearth is extinguished and is not re-lit that day.

My priestly informants are clear that as soon as the soul leaves the body, the *yamdut* (messengers of death) take it straight off to the court of their master with a noose around its neck. There they show it the torments of the various hells which await it before returning to earth. It is 86,000 *yojans* (about 688,000 miles) to *yamlok* (the kingdom of the dead), and it will subsequently take the deceased a complete year to reach it. On this occasion, however, the round trip is accomplished at extraordinary speed – in 48 minutes (2 *dand*) I was several times told. The structural logic which requires a *double* journey to the kingdom of Yamraj – one now, and one in the year to come – is unclear. My informants' rationalisation is that bureaucracy is never quite perfect, that cases of mistaken identity sometimes occur, and that the *yamdut* must therefore present the deceased to higher authority before the corpse is cremated and any error becomes impossible to rectify (cf. Stevenson 1920:180). Finding himself back home, the deceased tries to re-enter the body he has recently vacated, but is held back by the *yamdut*'s halter. For the next ten days the disembodied soul hovers miserably about the scene of its death searching for a 'house' to inhabit.

For its journey to the cremation ground, the corpse is washed and dressed by immediate family members of its own sex (perhaps with some help from the Barber or his wife). In theory seven pieces of gold, alternatively basil leaves, should be used to seal its seven bodily orifices, though in practice most people make do with putting one of these substances in the mouth. The shroud which covers the corpse of a man or a widow is generally white, though a yellow silken cloth known as *pitambar* is used for an elderly man who has died a good death. The corpses of high-caste women who have pre-deceased their husbands are the most elaborately adorned. Dressed in bridal red, or in an auspicious *chunri* sari (with yellow speckles on a red ground), her feet are decorated like a bride's with henna, she is decked in ornaments, made up with cosmetics and presented with comb and mirror. Her corpse is garlanded, a *laddu* (a kind of sweet) is placed in each hand, and her husband smears vermillion (the symbol of her married state) into the parting of her hair. This last detail is significant in that it suggests that her body remains in a state of comparative purity. A woman is prohibited from applying vermillion when she is menstruating, polluted by birth or death, or of course widowed (cf. Das and Uberoi 1971:36).

A widow has the vermillion rubbed out of her parting before her husband's corpse leaves for the *ghat*, one of the fingers of his lifeless hand being used to erase it. The bangles on her wrist are removed by being smashed against the side of his bier. She is in some sense responsible for his death, and a high-caste widow must expiate the misfortune she has brought him for the rest of her days. While a wife is her husband's 'half-body' (*adhangani*), one can almost say that on his death she becomes half-corpse. She must henceforth dress in a white shroud-like sari and is excluded from any significant ritual role on auspicious occasions like marriage.

Of one whose husband is still alive (a *suhargin*) it is said that 'she came full [of auspiciousness], and she goes full'; and, in the custom of certain regional communities, she is carried to the cremation ground with her face uncovered. But if she has died in childbirth, needles may be stuck in her feet to prevent her coming back to molest her surviving children – though my priestly informants disparage the practice as unsanctioned by textual authority. What it reveals, however, is an unstated assumption which they too share: that what is done to the corpse is also experienced by the ethereal 'microscopic body' (*suksham sharir*) of the ghost.

The bier (*arthi, tikhti*), generally a ladder-like structure made of bamboo, is prepared by the men while the last of the mourners arrive. This often takes some time not only because they may come from far, but also because they may bolt some food before setting out. They know that they will not be able to eat again for several hours. As the funeral procession is about to set out for the *ghat*, the most closely related mourners take formal leave of the departed by circumambulating the corpse and touching its feet. In the Punjabi community, for example, all males directly descended from the deceased (including the sons of daughters), and all their wives (but not the daughters and sisters of the family) circumambulate the corpse with coconuts which are offered at its feet. These are then taken to the cremation ground and burnt on the pyre.

The bandsmen who lead the procession of an old person are generally Muslims or Untouchables. The same people (and indeed many of the same tunes) are used at weddings. Though difficult to generalise, the corpse of an elderly person of some distinction may be followed by 120 mourners; that of a young child by just two or three. In the case of an adult, the obligation to show solidarity with the bereaved at such a time is keenly felt. Ideally the mourners would follow the bier bare-foot; and it is important that each of the sons of the deceased should shoulder it for at least a few paces.

The priests say that the corpse should be taken to the *ghat* head-first because that is the way in which a baby is born. Repeated play is made on the phonetic similarity between Shiva and *shav* (a corpse); and along its route, it is periodically greeted as Shiva with cries of *Har, Har Mahadev*. But the continual chant which is kept up all the way to the cremation ground is '*Ram nam satya hai*' – 'the name of Ram is the [only] truth'.[25] This is said to keep malevolent spirits at bay, and to enjoin the deceased to reconcile himself to the destruction of his body and to concentrate only on God.

As the funeral procession proceeds, the mourners throw small coins, puffed paddy (*lava*) and mustard seeds over the bier. The coins may subsequently be hung around the neck of a child as protection against *sukhandi rog* (a wasting disease to which children are prone), or *upari hava* (spirit affliction; literally 'wind from above'). When paddy is parched it expands and becomes shining white. It is also thrown at marriage, and on both occasions the message is said to be that the family should expand and shine like *lava*. Mustard seed attracts ghosts and ancestors. After cremation the disembodied *pret* will try to find its way back home; but in retracing its steps it is greedily distracted by the seeds and will hopefully never arrive.

Up until the ritual of *sapindikaran* on the twelfth day after death, at which the deceased is transformed into an ancestor, his ghost represents a positive danger to those who survive him. Unable to reconcile itself to the separation of death, it beckons others to follow. The bus which carries the corpse and the mourners to Kashi has a crash; the pressure lantern which lights the funeral procession's way in the dark explodes; a funeral attendant is pulled into the pyre by a sexually predatory female ghost and is badly burnt about the groin. The living must therefore put a safe distance between themselves and the departed, and as we shall find their disjunction is ritually marked at various points in the subsequent sequence. At no point should any relationship with the ghost be acknowledged – by, for example, using a kinship term or caste title to refer to it.

On the day of cremation, six *pind* (rice-ball) offerings – the so-called *Khat pind* – are made:[26] at the place of death, at the door of the house as the corpse leaves it for the cremation ground, at a cross-roads on the way and at a place where the bier is laid down to rest, on the corpse's belly as it lies on the pyre, and finally at the time when the cremated bones are collected for immersion in the Ganges. Though informants are precise about the proper time and place for these offerings,[27] and about the correct way of making them,[28] they are invariably vague about their purpose and even about who receives them (and the ritual manuals are no more illuminating). The commonest view is that they are sacrifices (*bali*) which buy off the malevolent ghosts who hover round the corpse and threaten to reanimate it.

On arrival at the cremation ground, the funeral procession halts at the office of the *murda munshi* – the 'corpse clerk' employed by the City Council – to whom the chief mourner hands over the death certificate (often simply a slip signed by the chairman of his village panchayat) and a small gratuity. The *murda munshi* enters the details in his register and gives the mourners a token for the Doms without which they cannot proceed with the cremation. The corpse is then taken down to the river where it is bathed and put with its lower limbs resting in the water. Known as *adh-jal kriya* ('the rite of half-water'), this is the ideal position in which to die. At this point the mourners offer cupped handfuls of water (*anjali*) onto its face. 'The one who gives fire' will then be tonsured by the Barber,[29] and will bathe in the river to purify himself in preparation for the great sacrifice he is about to perform.

Though the pyres are built by the Doms, many high-caste mourners go to great lengths to ensure that they do not touch the corpse itself, which is generally laid on the pyre face upwards with its feet towards the south – the 'correct' orientation according to the standard manuals of mortuary practice, though many pyres are in fact 'wrongly' positioned. It is however significant that the furnaces of the new electric crematorium on Harishchandra *ghat* are oriented on a north–south axis. Practice notwithstanding, my priestly informants insist that in theory only the corpse of a man should be cremated face up, while that of a woman should be burnt face down, for that is the way in which the two sexes enter the world. Only the city's Bengali community follow this rule. If, by chance, a husband and wife both die at the same time, they should be cremated together, the husband being placed face down on his wife in what is explicitly represented as the position of copulation.

For reasons of auspiciousness the wood which is purchased for the pyre should weigh an odd number of maunds. Odd numbers suggest incompletion. They leave, as it were, some 'remainder' which is seed of future growth, regeneration or multiplication – which is why *dan* always consist of an 'incomplete' amount: Rs. 1.25, 11, 51 or 101 for example (Daniel 1984:134). The kind of wood which is used for the pyre depends on availability. It is, however, important to include at least some fragments of sandalwood (*chandan*), mango (*am*) or wood-apple (*bel*) because these are 'sacred' (*pavitra*), though far too expensive to use on their own. *Tulsi* (basil is also put on the pyre to purify the wood; and – funds permitting – ghee and resin (*ral*) are liberally sprinkled over it to make it burn well and to render it pure. Wearing his sacred thread over the left shoulder so that it hangs down over the right side of the body, the so-called *savya* position appropriate for offerings to the gods, the chief mourner makes five clockwise circumambulations of the pyre,[30] touching the fire-brand – held in his right hand – to the mouth of the corpse (*mukh-agni*) on each revolution. The position of the sacred thread, the right hand, the number five and the clockwise circumambulations are all said to be auspicious.

After the pyre has been lit, *dashang* – a fragrant compound of ten substances used in fire sacrifice – is thrown into the flames. Mid-way through the cremation, the chief mourner performs *kapal kriya*, 'the rite of the skull', by cracking open the cranium of the deceased with a bamboo pole from the torn apart bier. Often *kapal kriya* in fact consists in a general breaking up of the partly incinerated corpse, and a stoking of the fire so that it is more completely consumed. Nowadays many sons do not have the stomach to deal the deceased a more than symbolic blow, and some refuse to go through with the rite at all. Ghee and basil should now be offered onto the skull.

Towards the end of cremation a fragment of the remaining carcase may – as an act of merit – be unceremoniously poled into the river 'to feed the fishes'. When the pyre has more or less burnt itself out, the chief mourner writes the figure 94 with a stick in the ashes. The Devanagiri symbols for 9 and 4 are said to resemble the shapes of Vishnu's conch and discus. The chief mourner then heaves a large earthenware pot of Ganges water onto his left shoulder, stands with his back to the pyre, and lets the pot fall behind him so that it smashes onto the burning embers. Without looking back he must now leave the *ghat*. By this means he is said to 'cool' the pyre and inform the deceased that their 'attachment' (*mumta*) is finished. As the saying goes, 'pot broken, relationship finished' (*gagri phute, nata tute*). Though I have never been explicitly told as much, it may not be too far-fetched to see the pot as a symbolic skull, the breaking of which would therefore be a recapitulation (or surrogate) for the rite of *kapal kriya*. This interpretation is borrowed from Evison (1989:56), who notes that in Sanskrit the pot is *kapala*, a 'skull'. Consistent with this, my informants invariably list a pot as one of the absolutely essential items in the so-called 'goods of the skull breaking' (p. 96); while I am told that mourners who patronise the new crematorium at Harishchandra *ghat* (and for whom the real thing is of course impossible) now often describe the pot-breaking as *kapal kriya*.[31]

The place of cremation is sluiced down by the Doms (or sometimes by two or three mourners who have stayed behind). In the process, the ash and remaining fragments of bone are flushed into the river. The soil of Kashi is gold and can only be taken outside the city on pain of having to repay an equivalent in one's next life. The ashes of those who have been cremated there should consequently not be taken elsewhere for immersion, and there is no formalized procedure of collecting the bones.

Leaving the cremation ground, the mourners move to one of the adjacent *ghats* where – chief mourner first – they bathe in the Ganges, and offer the departed cupped handfuls of water in which sesame seeds are sprinkled. Both actions are again said to cool him down after his ordeal in the pyre (cf. Dubois 1968:487). All are then given margosa leaves (*nim ki patti*), black pepper or a red chilli to chew. They spit this out with the complaint that it is 'hot' (*tita*) or 'bitter' (*karva*) and are then offered sweets made out of cooling milk products. Hot and bitter is replaced by cool and sweet, for the deceased has become hot and bitter and must be cooled and sweetened.[32]

On returning home, various prophylactic measures are necessary before the mourners may re-enter the house. Maithils, for example, touch fire, water, iron and stone – repeating the sequence three times. Villagers from the Banaras region put a pot of water containing *akshat* (unhusked rice), a margosa branch, a stone, a mustard oil cake, a dish of barley and a piece of burning cowdung cake outside the house. In order to restore the wholeness of their bodies, the mourners dip the branch in the water and sprinkle it over their feet, touch each of the other objects and extend their hands over the fire (Planalp 1956:608).

5.6 Birth, sex and sacrificial violence

Cremation is known as *dah sanskar* (the 'sacrament of fire') or, more revealingly perhaps, as *antyeshti* (the 'last sacrifice'). 'Very closely connected with sacrifice . . . the dead man [is] an offering to the gods' (Shastri 1963:ii). The typical Brahmanic sacrifice is a fire sacrifice (*hom*), and the sacrifier's 'last oblation' (*antyahuti*) to the fire is his own body (Aiyangar 1913:14). The *Shraddh Parijat* – one of the standard manuals of mortuary practice – equates cremation with fire sacrifice; and the *Satapatha Brahmana* represents the sacrificial fire altar ritual as a symbolic reenactment of Prajapati's sacrificial dismemberment of his own body, and then goes on to lay down precisely the same rules for handling the corpse of a deceased sacrifier as for treating the sacrificial altar which represents the body of the god (Levin 1930).

The parallels between cremation and the sacrificial procedure are, as Das (1982:122–3) points out, almost precise.

> Thus the site of cremation is prepared in exactly the same way as in fire-sacrifice, i.e. the prescriptive use of ritually pure wood, the purification of the site, its consecration with holy water, and the establishment of Agni [the god of fire] with the proper use of *mantras* . . . The dead body is prepared in the same manner as the victim of a sacrifice and is attributed with divinity. Just as the victim of a sacrifice is exhorted not to take any revenge for the pains which the sacrifice has inflicted on him (Hubert and Mauss, 1964) so the mourners pray to the *preta* to spare them from his anger at the burns he has suffered in the pyre (*Garuda Purana*).

The corpse is given water to drink, is lustrated, anointed with ghee and enclosed in sacred space by being circumambulated with fire – which is precisely what Hubert and Mauss (1964:31) describe as happening to the sacrificial victim. Like the sacrificial victim, the corpse is itself treated as a being of great sacredness, even as a deity. It must be guarded against pollution, is circumambulated in the auspicious direction, and the funeral pyre is ignited by the chief mourner only after he has passed through an elaborate series of purifications and with his sacred thread worn in the manner appropriate for offerings to the gods (as opposed to that appropriate for offerings to a ghost or ancestor). Further, the same set of ten substances (the *dashang*) which are offered in the pyre are also used for the fire sacrifice (*havan*); while according to the *Pret Manjari* (p. 4) – regarded as the most authoritative of the mortuary manuals – the wood used for the pyre should be that which 'pertains to a sacrifice' (*yagyik*).

Given that the good death is a sacrifice and sacrifice is an act of regeneration through which both sacrifier and cosmos are recreated, it is only to be expected that the beliefs and practices associated with cremation are pervaded by the symbolism of birth and parturition. According to one well-known text which deals with sacrifice (the *Satapatha Brahmana* again), there are three kinds of birth: that which is had from one's parents, from sacrifice, and from cremation (Lévi 1898:106–7; Levin 1930). Indeed the ritual techniques involved in both of the latter might be described as a branch of obstetrics. Having dispersed his own body in the sacrifice, the sacrifier reverts to an embryonic state and is then reborn (cf. Heesterman 1959; Kaelber 1978); while, as we have seen, the manner in which the dead body should be carried to the cremation ground, and the position in which it should be laid on the pyre, supposedly mimic the birth of a child. During the fifth month of pregnancy the vital breath enters the embryo through the suture at the top of the skull and it is from here that it is released during cremation by the rite of *kapal kriya*. Throughout the pregnancy the baby is sustained by the digestive fire which resides in its mother's belly, and at death it returns to the fire from which it came and is thus reborn (cf. Knipe 1975:1). 'We came from fire', I was told, 'and we go to fire.' At both parturitions an Untouchable specialist acts the indispensable role of midwife, cutting the umbilical cord at birth and providing the sacred fire and superintending the pyre at death.

At other points the symbolism of the maternity ward is replaced by that of the bridal chamber, reinforcing the idea that death should be lovingly embraced (Das 1986:199). As we have seen, the funeral procession of an old person is described as a second marriage party and is accompanied by erotic dancing; while a husband and wife who die within a few hours of each other are supposedly placed on a single pyre in a position evoking the sexual act. We might also recall that the loins of Kashi are at Manikarnika *ghat* (p. 17). In some texts the corpse is described as rising as smoke from the pyre, turning into clouds, rain and then vegetables, which when eaten are transformed into

semen (O'Flaherty 1973:41–2; 1976:28). The destruction of the corpse is thus
converted into the source of future life – a message repeated in my informants'
notion that properly recycled ancestors confer progeny and prosperity on
their descendants.

But if death regenerates life, there is much in both textual and popular
traditions to suggest that the regeneration of life causes death. In myth, for
example, death enters the world as a result of sexual increase (O'Flaherty
1976:28, 212). In folk dream-analysis a naked woman or a bride is a
presentiment of impending death; and in ethno-medicine the loss of semen
results in disease, old age and death, while its retention confers vitality and
even immortality (cf. Briggs 1938:324; Carstairs 1957:84–5, 195–6; Eliade
1969:248–9).

This line of interpretation gives rise to an obvious difficulty. There would on
the face of it seem to be a flat contradiction between our received wisdom that
the corpse is pre-eminently polluting and dangerous, and the notion that it is a
fit sacrificial offering to the gods. The situation is complex and the data
somewhat contradictory. Much of it certainly supports the view that the
corpse is contaminating. But this is far from the whole story, for as I have
shown it is in certain respects treated as an object of great sacredness which
must be carefully protected from pollution. Consistent with this, the corpse of
a woman who has died in childbirth or during her monthly course must – in
the custom of certain regional communities represented in Banaras – undergo
special purificatory rites before she is fit for the pyre, as if only those in a state
of purity are appropriate offerings (cf. Stevenson 1920:151; Kane 1973:4:231;
Pandey 1969:270–1).[33]

One possible angle on the problem might be to start from the classical
Hindu theory of sacrifice, according to which the sacrifier has acquired,
through the initiatory rite of *diksha*, a sacrificial body sufficiently august to be
offered to the gods. During the sacrifice his profane body remains behind in
the safe-keeping of the presiding priests (Malamoud 1976:161, 193). The
problem with cremation, however, is that it is hard to suppress the fact that it
is not only this sacred entity which is dispatched by the fire, but also the
sacrifier's profane and mortal being. It might therefore be possible to see the
ambiguity over the condition of the deceased as a reflection of the difficulty of
drawing, in this instance, a clear conceptual distinction between the two
bodies of the sacrifier. As representative of his sacrificial body, the victim is
pure: but as his patently profane and corruptible corpse it is also impure.

I believe, however, that a more revealing place to begin is with the definition
of death as the instant at which the *pran*, or 'vital breath' leaves the body.
According to the theological dogma expounded by many of my informants,
this occurs, not at the cessation of physiological functioning, but at the rite of
kapal kriya, at which the chief mourner delivers the *coup de grace* by cracking
open the deceased's skull in order to release the 'vital breath' from his charred
corpse on the pyre. Some say that it is the heat of the pyre which 'causes the

"vital breath" to climb into the *brahmand* at the top of the skull (its point of exit in the case of a good death), thus implying that it is cremation itself which ensures a proper evacuation of the body. A few non-priestly informants put the emphasis elsewhere – on the chief mourner's calculated act of aggression towards the departed. As they represent it, the principal purpose of the rite is to make him understand that he is definitively banished from the world of the living. In either case, however, it would seem that life or consciousness remains in the corpse, which is consistently spoken of as though it were a sentient being. 'If you burn your finger', I was invited to reflect, 'think how much you suffer. What then of the whole body?'

Though the conventional formula is that it is the 'vital breath' (*pran*) which remains trapped in the skull, hardly any of my informants were prepared to distinguish this entity from the 'soul' (*atma*). In general, however, they invariably speak of the latter as singular – one 'person' (*vyakti*), one 'soul' – whereas they often refer to *pran* in the plural. The best informed priests know that the textual authorities postulate five, or even ten, types of 'breath' (*pran*) or 'wind' (*vayu*), which are located in different parts of the body and perform different functions associated with the circulation of blood, the digestion of food and the elimination of waste-products. One of these, the *dhananjay vayu*, pervades the whole body and it is this, they say, which remains in the corpse to be liberated by *kapal kriya*. Even so, it was only a single informant – a man of formidable learning and considerable scholarly reputation – who insisted on a fundamental distinction between *pran* and *atma*. The *pran*, he explained, are multiple; are located in specific parts of the body and may cause pain in their vicinity when they do not function properly, and are forms of 'air' (*vayu*) which will merge with the air at death. As opposed to the *pran* which are located and 'active' (*kriya-van*), the *atma* is 'all-pervasive' (*sarv-vyapi*) and passive. But whichever theory one follows, all agree that some crucial aspect of the person's life-force remains imprisoned in the body when normal physiological functions (pulse, heartbeat, breathing) have ceased. Consistent with this, it is held to be completely inappropriate to refer to the deceased as a disembodied *pret* until after the rite of *kapal kriya*.

The corollary of this notion that life is finally extinguished on the pyre is that it is only at the moment of breaking the skull that death pollution begins. Nor – certain texts tell us – is it until after her husband's cremation that his wife becomes a 'widow' (Leslie 1991:189). The first of these points is best illustrated by the case of corpses which are immersed in the Ganges rather than burnt. In such an instance, it is often claimed, no death pollution is incurred until after the *putla vidhan* ritual at which the deceased's body is re-created in the form of an effigy, into which his soul is invoked, and which is then cremated. Since this rite may be delayed until several months after the disposal of the actual body, and since there is no impurity in the interval, it is clear that death pollution springs from the act of cremation rather than from the corpse or its physiological demise. It is, in the Banaras idiom, a consequence of 'the sin of burning the body hairs of the deceased'. Hence as Pullu Maharaj explained, the chief mourner remains in a state of great purity before igniting the pyre, 'because he is performing a *mahayagya* – a great sacrifice. It is we who pollute him by our touch and not he us.' After cremation, however, he is defiled 'for he has burnt the flesh'. Of a piece with all this is the fact that Vedic *mantras* should be recited at the time of lighting the pyre (cf. Pandey 1969:23), but my priestly informants insist – on the authority of the *Garuda Purana* (Pt 10) – that their subsequent use is prohibited until after the rituals of the tenth day which terminate the period of maximum pollution (cf. Stevenson 1920:160).[34]

What all this implies, then, is that before the cremation the corpse is not a corpse but an animate oblation to the fire. As one informant spontaneously put it, the departed 'does not die but is killed. He dies on the pyre.' Cremation, he went on, is violence (*hatya*) and death pollution (*sutak*) the consequence of that violence. On this theory cremation becomes a sacrifice in the real sense of the term: it is ritual slaughter that makes of the chief mourner a homicide, parricide or even slayer of the gods. According to Planalp's (1956:608) informants from a village in the rural hinterland of Banaras, he assumes one-fifth of the responsibility for the death – one-fifth because the *dhananjay* is one of five *prans*. In view of all this it is hardly surprising that his subsequent isolation and purification are – like that of any sacrifier (Hubert and Mauss 1964:33) – an act of atonement resembling the expiation of a criminal. It should not be thought, however, that the victim is a reluctant one, for, as we have seen, a crucial aspect of the 'good' death is that it is a voluntary offering of the self to the gods. The corpse is thus not only alive but also a willing victim, and hence a being of extraordinary sacredness.

I hasten to emphasise that all this refers to a somewhat esoteric level of theological discourse, and that at another level it is of course universally acknowledged that a man is dead once the physical manifestations of life are extinguished. Reasoning from this starting point, other informants held that death pollution begins at the moment of physiological arrest, and that the corpse itself is a source of severe impurity. Those best versed in the texts, however, tended to steer a middle course between these two theories by distinguishing the case of the Agnihotri (by whom sacrificial fires are continuously maintained) from that of the ordinary householder. While for the former there is no death pollution before cremation, for the latter it begins when respiration ceases (cf. Abbott 1932:177, 192, 505; Pandey 1969:269). What is acknowledged by all, then, is that death pollution starts at the point of death. The disparity arises over what that is. On the view that it occurs during cremation, the deceased's body represents a pure oblation to the gods; while on the view that life is extinguished at the time of physiological arrest, the corpse is merely an impure carcass.

This ambiguity over the point at which death 'really' occurs gives rise to a further ambiguity over the timing of the subsequent rites. In the event that the cremation is delayed for a day or two after the physiological demise, some say that the tenth day rituals be scheduled by counting from the one, and some from the other. A similar difficulty arises in the event of *panchak dosh* – the 'fault' or 'sin' of the five lunar asterisms (see p. 160). One view is that the problem stems from dying in *panchak*, though most of the priests claim that the 'fault' only arises from cremating a corpse during this period.

These ambiguities over the point of death and the ritual state of the corpse are by no means the only ones. On the one hand death is clearly thought of as an inauspicious event. It not only gives rise to an impure and incipiently putrescent corpse, but the mourners must also contend with a resentfully malevolent ghost which is bent on causing them harm. It is hardly surprising, then, that the symbolism of separation recurs throughout the sequence we have reviewed. No relationship should be acknowledged with the ghost, which must be prevented from reanimating the abandoned body, discouraged from returning home from the cremation ground, and violently taught that it now belongs to a world apart from the living. But on the other hand, much of the symbolism of cremation signals its auspiciousness, and throughout the mortuary sequence the chief mourner and his 'victim' remain closely identified. Symbols that mark their disjunction (the smashing of the pot, and – as some represent it – the smashing of the skull) coexist with those which emphatically affirm their conjunction.

Immediately after the death, the family Barber is sent to purchase a single length of white muslin (*malmal*). One part of this length is torn off to serve as a winding sheet for the corpse, and the remainder is used to make two *dhotis* (loin-cloths) and an *angauchha* (a kind of towel) for their chief mourner to wear at the time of cremation and throughout the period of mourning. These must remain unstitched, for it is said that by stitching the chief mourner's garments one would stitch up the mouth of the ghost and prevent it from drinking (cf. Stevenson 1920:166). 'The one who gives fire' becomes the 'vehicle of the *pret*' (*pret ki svari*). 'Because he has burnt him, the deceased is always behind him. Because he has cracked open the dead man's skull, the latter rides on *his* skull.' Throughout the next ten days he mixes the food on his plate with the food of the *pret*, for whom he is said to eat. As the ghost has become isolated from all human relationships, so the chief mourner is placed in a kind of quarantine and should never be formally greeted.

In principle, 'the one who gives fire' is the deceased's eldest son. Some people say that if the latter is not for some reason available, then the duty devolves on the next in age; others that in his absence the youngest son should officiate. In my experience, however, there is a good deal of flexibility about which son is actually chosen, and much depends on who can take time off work, the relative fortitude with which they bear their bereavement, or other contingent factors. In the absence of sons or grandsons, a brother or brother's son may assume the role, or occasionally even a wife, daughter or daughter's son. Indeed I have known several cases in which one of the latter insisted on their right to do so, for in the cases of disputed inheritance the courts are said to favour the claimant who performed the mortuary rituals. What all my priestly informants adamantly rejected, however, was the possibility that a son-in-law (*damad*) should serve as chief mourner.[35] 'We do not even allow his shadow to fall on this work', I was told. 'He is the "tenth planet" (to be compared, that is, with the burden of a malign planetary influence). His water will not be accepted by his father-in-law.' In the dominant ideology of north Indian kinship, gifts should flow *unilaterally* from wife-givers to wife-receivers (pre-eminently to the husbands of one's daughters). How then could the departed accept offerings from his son-in-law's hand?

The symbols of disjunction clearly make sense in the context of a desire to distance oneself from a polluting corpse and a dangerous ghost. But how are we to explain the close – and even more emphatically stated – *conjunction* between the deceased and the *dagiya*? The answer lies, I believe, in the logic of sacrifice. According to this logic, the victim stands in for the person of the sacrifier who is reborn through the death of a surrogate. An identity must therefore be established between them.

But this provides us with another problem. Both 'the rite of the skull breaking', and the notion that death pollution results from 'the sin of burning the body hairs', would seem to suggest that it is the chief mourner who serves as the sacrifier and who takes upon himself the onus of sacrificial death. The concept of the 'good death', however, suggests that it is the deceased who offers *himself*. Who then is the sacrifier? The dying person, or the one who lights the pyre? The answer I believe is both. The two are equated, and *both* are reborn through the sacrifice – the father on a new and higher plane, and the son as his father's replacement in the world which the latter just left. But if the chief mourner is homologised with the departed, the departed is identified with Shiva himself. This series of identifications between sacrifier, victim and god is characteristic not only of Indian sacrifice (as illustrated by Coomaraswamy 1941, Kaelber 1978 and Herrenschmidt 1979), but also of sacrifice in many other societies (for example, Leach 1976:88ff; Turner 1977; Sahlins 1978), and is of course precisely what Hubert and Mauss's (1964) celebrated discussion of its logic would lead us to expect.

5.7 The immersion of bodies and ashes

Certain categories of corpses are not cremated, but sunk in the river. Before immersion, however, the body is circumambulated with fire, which is touched to its mouth on each revolution.[36] The corpse is then weighted down and ferried out into mid-stream by boat. In the case of a renouncer, the skull should be smashed with a coconut by one of the disciples.

The ascetic, who has performed his own mortuary rites at the time of initiation, is already dead to the social world and is said to remain on earth as a wandering ghost. His corpse is either immersed or buried. Householders of various sects built up around the message of the renouncer also abjure cremation. A somewhat similar case is that of a childless person who while living performs his (or her) own obsequies – typically at the shrine of Badrinath in the Himalayas. This is known as *jivit-shraddh* (*jivit*, 'living'); and involves cremating one's own effigy, offering a rice-ball known as *kapal pind* ('the ball of the skull'), celebrating the rite of *Narayani bali* (generally reserved for those who have died a 'bad death'), and feeding and gifting the Brahmans. Those who have performed *jivit-shraddh* are also described as ghosts, and in theory none should accept their food. When they physically quit this world their corpses should not be cremated.

It is also improper to burn the very young. The commonest formula is that a child is ineligible for cremation before it has teeth with which to masticate (cf. Kane 1973:4:227) – recalling the textual injunction that an animal is unfit for sacrifice until it has cut its teeth (Malamoud 1982:446). Alternatively, it is often said that a boy is qualified for cremation by the sacred thread ceremony, and a girl by marriage. I was repeatedly told that when a pregnant woman dies, the foetus should be surgically removed for immersion or burial, but I know of no case in which this rule was actually followed.

The ban on cremating lepers is most commonly explained by the idea that an infectious 'gas' would escape from the body. Hygienic considerations too are held to justify the (contested) view that victims of plague and cholera should also be immersed. Smallpox is a different matter. The deceased is said to have been possessed by the goddess Sitala. 'God is without birth (*anjana*). Why', I was rhetorically asked in a formula again invoking the notion that cremation is creation, 'should we burn one who is neither born nor dies?' To do so is likely to mean that another member of the family will succumb to the disease. There is also the idea that the body of a smallpox victim has already become dangerously over-heated, and that immersion is necessary to cool it down.

The idea of over-heating is also present in the case of those who die from snake-bite. Here the prescribed method of disposal – which I have never witnessed myself – is unique. Rather than being weighted down, the corpse should be placed on a raft made from banana leaves and stems. The reason given is that there remains a chance that the poison will be 'cooled' by the water, that the victim may revive, and that the raft may then enable him to escape from drowning.

Not only victims of snake-bite, as a rule of thumb it is commonly claimed that all who have died a 'bad' death should be immersed rather than burnt, a notion for which there is solid textual authority (e.g. Pandey 1969:273). But although certain Dharmashastra texts prohibit the cremation of a suicide – on whose death no impurity is incurred by the surviving kinsmen (Kane 1973:4:223) – in my experience such corpses are in fact generally cremated. Nor in practice have I ever encountered any serious objection to the cremation of a victim of violence or sudden accident. While on my most recent visit to

Banaras the priests with whom I discussed the matter were, to a man, critical of the ritual conduct of Rajiv Gandhi's last rites – which they had avidly watched on the now ubiquitous television – none questioned the propriety of cremating his remains.

While piecemeal explanations of each individual category of the sort I have cited are often provided, the most striking thing about this inventory of those regarded as ineligible for cremation is that – as Das (1982:123) has observed – it constitutes a single set organised around the idea of sacrifice. It consists, that is, of those who are not fit sacrificial objects (paradigmatically the leper), those who have already been offered to the gods (the renouncer, the person who has performed *jivit-shraddh*) or possessed by them (the victim of smallpox), and those whose death cannot be represented as an act of self-sacrifice (young children and, in theory, those who have died various other kinds of 'untimely' death).

Given that cremation results in rebirth, how we may ask are those whose bodies are unworthy of the cremation pyre to be reborn? The answer is by making them a worthy one through 'the method of the effigy' (*putla vidhan*). The corpse itself is immersed in the river, and the Mahabrahman (or the Barber in the case of a low-caste death) constructs an elaborate and anatomically detailed effigy of the deceased out of fifty-six ingredients: red beads for nipples, white wool for the hair of an old person and black for that of a young one, aubergine for the penis, honey for blood, *khas* grass for veins, potash for lungs, coconut fibres for pubic hair and so on. The deceased's spirit is then invoked into the effigy (*pran ka avahan karna*) by lighting camphor in the navel. While it burns the mourners are instructed to chant the names of God, and when it is extinguished the person is said to have expired. The effigy is then covered with a shroud and cremated in *exactly* the same way, and with all the same rituals, as an ordinary corpse. The unworthy body of the deceased is replaced by a worthy offering to the fire; a 'bad' death is re-run as a properly controlled release of life.

That 'bad' death can thus be converted into 'good' may perhaps help to resolve the disparity between the Shastric theory that *no* death pollution is incurred for one whose death is 'untimely' (pp. 219–20), and my informants' notion that pollution begins at the point at which the deceased's effigy is cremated. The apparent contradiction disappears if we assume that in cases of 'bad' death no pollution *is* incurred; but that as soon as a 'bad' death is re-staged as a good one the mourners become liable to impurity. This idea that death pollution only commences with the incineration of the effigy is of course also consistent with the theory that this form of impurity is a consequence of 'the sin of burning the body hairs of the deceased' – that it results from the violence of cremation.

Though the rituals of the effigy are often performed immediately after immersing the corpse, they are sometimes delayed for some days, even months, after death. *Pitri paksh* ('the fortnight of the ancestors' corresponding to the dark fortnight of the month *Ashvin* in late September/early October), the dark fortnight of *Chaitra* and the month of *Pus* (both the latter being known as *khar mas*, the 'hot' or 'cruel month') are held to be particularly propitious periods for performing *putla vidan* and other rites addressed to ghosts and ancestors (and particularly unpropitious times for auspicious life-affirming rituals like marriage). But however long it is delayed, *putla vidan* is indispensable for all who have not been cremated. Without it the deceased will remain indefinitely stuck in the limbo of *pret*-hood. The only partial exceptions admitted are for the renouncer and the one who has performed his own obsequies while still alive (*jivit-shraddh*). They have already cremated their own effigies during their life-times. A *putla vidhan* should be staged in cases in which the corpse is never recovered, or when a person has been missing for some years and is presumed dead.

In some guise or other, then, all are offered to the fire. Corpses which are to be immersed are first circumambulated and singed with fire, and a substitute offering is subsequently cremated. Equally all are immersed in water. In Banaras a fragment of the charred corpse is shovelled into the river 'to feed the fishes'; and the ashes of those who have been burnt elsewhere are brought to the Ganges for immersion. It would therefore be misleading to imply that cremation and immersion are simple alternatives. Both procedures are properly present in every case.[37]

Though in general terms the pattern clearly conforms to the widespread phenomenon of double obsequies, there is not the neat congruence which Hertz's (1960) model supposes between on the one hand the secondary disposal of the deceased's remains, and on the other the final purification of the mourners and the incorporation of the wandering ghost into the world of the ancestors. When the corpse has not been cremated on the banks of the Ganges, its ashes will be stored outside the house until such a time as they can be brought to the river. On the authority of the *Garuda Purana* (Part 10), I was often told that the journey should be made before the rituals of the tenth day, and – thanks to modern transport – this is now common practice. In the past, however, those who lived far away might have had to wait years before they could join a party with whom they could safely travel (cf. Gold 1988:85).

When ashes are brought after the mortuary rites have been completed, and when there is no pressure to return home in a hurry, those with sufficient means may immerse some of them in Hardwar, some in Pryag and the rest in Banaras. They are generally carried in a small earthenware pot, or in a cotton bag strung around the neck. The ritual of immersion (*asthi-visarjan*) is comparatively simple. The chief mourner takes a purificatory bath in the Ganges, is tonsured by the Barber, invites the deceased to reside in Banaras as a deity and to look after the welfare of his family, and informs him of the gifts he is making in his name. Some then take a boat out into mid-stream; others merely enter the water up to their waists and scatter the ashes close to the bank. The *ghatiyas* allege that these days some mourners have become so fly and cynical that they neglect all proper formalities, hiding the ashes under their loin-cloth and releasing them surreptitiously while bathing.

It is, I think, obvious that to immerse something in the Ganges is to sacralise it – before cremation, the corpse and the chief mourner for example. But what is also clear is that the Ganges can equally serve as an agent of de-sacralisation, returning both persons and things charged with sacredness to a more ritually neutral state. Thus the temporary festival image of a deity is immersed in the Ganges when it has served its purpose, as are sacred books which have begun to disintegrate and the superseded pilgrim registers of a *panda*. In the villages of the area, one is deemed to be guilty of cow-slaughter if the animal was merely tethered, or yoked to a plough, at the time of its death. The sinner is required to bring the rope or halter to Banaras to dispose of in the river, thereby deactivating the evil it embodies. By the same token we can, I suggest, see 'the immersion of the bones' as a method of de-sacralisation – as a partial withdrawal from the dangerous power unleashed by the sacrifice and a 'detoxification' of its remains.

In the Sanskritised Hindi of my informants, the ashes are the *avshesh* – the 'remainder' or 'relics' – of the departed. The term itself evokes the 'remainder' of the sacrifice, which is the seed of future fertility (Malamoud 1972). Consistent with this, Gold (1988:201) reports that Rajasthani pilgrims to Hardwar make a point of taking Ganges water from the very spot at which they immerse the ashes they bring. The water is then carried home, where it is drunk by the bereaved group which thereby 'reincorporates the life-substance of the dead'. In colloquial Hindi, the ashes are most commonly known as 'flowers' (*phul*), a term which Gold's informants also revealingly use for a 'boy-child' (p. 79).[38]

I have referred to 'ashes', but my informants almost invariably speak of 'bones' (*asthi*). Bones, as we have seen, are the product of the father's semen; flesh is the product of the mother's milk and menstrual blood, and hair is the repository of sin. What cremation completely eradicates are the flesh and the 'body hairs' of the deceased – causing 'sin and expiation (*prayashchitt*) to fly about in the smoke' at Manikarnika *ghat*. The implicit logic seems to be that cremation destroys what has to be got rid of – sin and female flesh. By so doing it distils out a pure (masculine) residue of bone, which is not only the product of semen but which serves like semen as a source of future fertility when delivered into the (female) Ganges.

5.8 The language of sacrifice and renunciation

The idea of death as a source of fecundity has run throughout this chapter, and I have tried to show how this recurrent theme is intimately associated with the idea of sacrifice as the paradigmatically creative act. Sacrifice, I have argued, provides a model for the cremation ritual itself and a template which structures some of the most central ideas about death. Not only does it underlie Hindu thinking about 'good' and 'bad' death, but it also makes economical sense of the rules which require that certain categories of corpses should not be cremated.

But to what extent is this master concept part of conscious thinking and explicit ritual exegesis? That cremation is known as 'the last sacrifice', that the texts liken it to fire sacrifice, describe the corpse as the sacrifier's 'last oblation' and prescribe the use of 'sacrificial wood' – that all this does not merely conjure a dead metaphor without any real resonance for my priestly informants is I hope clear from the verbatim statements I have quoted. It is true that I have given the sacrificial logic underlying their ideas and ritual practice a more systematic and explicit form than they would ever have reason to provide, but I believe that that logic is clearly discernible in the data, and never far from the surface of consciousness. Whether an illiterate villager or Western-educated middle-class urbanite unversed in the Sanskritic tradition is able clearly to articulate it may be open to doubt. But this, I suggest, is as irrelevant as whether the man on the Clapham omnibus recognises that the values of individualism inform his ideas about romantic love, or whether the speakers of a language are conscious of its grammatical rules. Whether they know it or not, the model of sacrifice structures not only the rituals they perform but also much of their thinking about death (and in particular about what constitutes a good one).

It is, however, not only the language of sacrifice but also the language of renunciation that pervades the mortuary sequence (cf. pp. 217–18). Death should be willed renunciation of life. The ascetic should not sleep on a cot, and at death the householder should become like an ascetic and refrain from dying on one. Cremation, it is sometimes said, should be seen as a kind of ascetic austerity (*tapas*), and certain of the texts clearly represent it as such (Knipe 1975:132; cf. Kaelber 1976). Just as the renouncer must abandon the fire of his domestic hearth at the time of his initiation, so at death the domestic hearth is extinguished so that the deceased can be consumed by the fire of cremation (represented as the fire of ascetic austerity). In other words, both the renouncer and the deceased leave the fire of their domestic hearth behind them in order to offer themselves up into the fire of their asceticism.

There is yet another sense in which it is tempting to see in the radical obliteration of the 'gross' body effected by cremation the influence of the renouncer's message. The Brahmanic theory of the four stages of life supposes that in his declining years a man will abandon the world to become a wandering and homeless ascetic. In fact, of course, this ideal is hardly ever realised in practice. But it is here, perhaps, that cremation fits in as a kind of surrogate for the ascetic's abrogation of the world. It is a kind of catching-up on the renunciation of carnal existence which should ideally be the conclusion of every (male) life. Cremation must therefore be represented as a *voluntary* act of self-sacrifice. The conventional observation that renunciation is a kind of death may thus be reversed: death takes the form of a kind of last-ditch renunciation.

That the symbolism of sacrifice and the symbolism of renunciation should be mixed up together is in some ways entirely predictable. In Hindu theory the two institutions are intimately associated. *Tyag* ('abandonment') is the essence of both. Asceticism was prescribed as a surrogate for sacrifice in an epoch which had passed beyond the Age of Truth (as gifting *dan* is a surrogate for both in the Kali Age). But there is of course another way in which the two sets of symbols are discordant. Sacrifice has to do with the regeneration of life and the world; renunciation is directed at escaping from it. The tension between these objectives, continually played out in Hindu mythology (cf. O'Flaherty 1973; Shulman 1980), recurs through the rituals and representations surrounding death.

Though sacrifice is the pre-eminently creative act, it produces only – as we saw at the start of this chapter – a flawed creation. After sacrificing himself, Prajapati must be put together again by the ritual actions of the gods. His human counterpart who offers himself on the cremation pyre becomes a formless and disarticulated ghost, and must be re-constituted as an ancestor by subsequent ritual performances. The way in which this is accomplished is the subject of the next chapter.

6

Ghosts into ancestors

6.1 The structure of the rites

The objective of the post-cremation mortuary rites described in this chapter is to convert the marginal *pret*-ghost into an ancestral-*pitr*, and to facilitate the arduous journey of the deceased to 'the abode of the ancestors' (*pitr-lok*) where he arrives on the anniversary of his death. Rites addressed to the ghost are presided over by the Mahabrahman Funeral-priest; those addressed to the ancestors by the deceased's hereditary household- or pilgrimage-priest (pp. 75ff).

In Banaras both sets of rituals are collectively known as *shraddh*.[1] Etymologically *shraddh* is closely related to *shraddha*, or 'faith', *shraddh* being popularly defined as that which is offered to the ancestors 'with faith'. The offerings are of two kinds. The first is *pinda-dan*, 'the gift of *pinds*' – balls of rice, barley flour or *khoa* (a thick paste made by boiling milk).[2] The second kind of offering is mediated by the Brahmans who are fed and offered gifts. This makes merit for the deceased and mitigates his sufferings. But more importantly, the Brahmans represent the deceased, 'the idea being that whatever nourishes and benefits the Brahmans, nourishes and benefits the Pitris' (Monier-Williams 1883:304).

In many ways the whole idiom is explicitly transactional. The performance of *shraddh* is said to discharge a man's debt to his ancestors (*pitr rin*). The parent who nurtured the child is now nurtured by that child, who liberates the deceased from his ghostly condition and ensures that he attains a 'good state' (*sadgati*) after death. According to both schools of Hindu law the right to inherit entails the concomitant duty to perform the deceased's obsequies. In the Dayabhaga code, inheritance is actually *contingent* on the conduct of the mortuary rituals in that the one who confers the greatest spiritual benefit on the deceased has the greatest claim on his property. But even in the Mitakshara code (where the rights of the heirs are established from the moment of their conception), 'whoever took the wealth of the deceased was bound . . . to offer *sraddha* and *pindas* to him' (Kane 1973:4:510). Not only property, but also the ancestors' blessings in the form of progeny and a bounteous supply of food is the reward of those who fastidiously fulfil these duties. Sustenance is given and sustenance received.

The whole sequence of post-cremation mortuary rites is conventionally said to involve the offering of three sets of sixteen *pinds*. The number sixteen denotes totality or completeness (Malamoud 1981). There are 16 annas in the rupee, and 100 per cent of anything is expressed as 16 annas. Prajapati was sixteenfold and so therefore is his creation (Knipe 1977). It is (theoretically) sixteen *sanskars*, or 'sacraments', which complete and perfect the twice-born, and which culminate in their 'last sacrifice'.

The 'gross' (outer) body (*sthul sharir*) of the person envelops an ethereal microscopic body (*suksham sharir*) the size of the thumb (*angusthmattra*). Cremation destroys the first, liberating the second into the air around. The first set of sixteen *pinds* constructs for this 'airy' being a new outer casing, which measures the distance between the elbow and the tips of the fingers (*hastmattra*). A second set of sixteen *pinds* follows. The deceased then sets out on his journey to 'the abode of the ancestors', sustained by a third set of sixteen offerings. On his arrival he sloughs off his body the size of a forearm, but retains his microscopic thumb-like body through which he suffers the consequences of his past actions. The rituals, however, represent this outer casing as being dissected and merged with the bodies of his three immediate lineal ascendants in a rite which is at least suggestive of sacrifice – and thus of the fate of this earthly body on the cremation pyre. Just as the latter has been perfected as a worthy sacrificial offering by the sixteen sacramental life-cycle rituals, so the first set of sixteen *pinds* culminates in the completion, and the third set in the destruction, of the temporary bodily form inhabited by the deceased.

The gods (with Vishnu in the leading role) are introduced into these rituals after the construction of the *pret's* arm-length body during the first sequence, and play a key part in its transformation into an ancestor. While the characteristics of ghosts and ancestors are in many ways contrasted (pp. 229ff), in the symbolism of *shraddh* they are treated as a single category in opposition to the gods. In addressing the gods, for example, the *jajman* faces east and wears his sacred thread over his left shoulder (*savya*); in addressing the undifferentiated dead he faces south and wears his sacred thread over the right shoulder (*apsavya*). For the ritual dedication (*sankalp*) of some offering, sesame is required for the departed and barley for the gods. When sandalwood paste (*chandan*) is offered to the dead it is given with the index finger (*tarjani anguli*); when offered to the gods it is given with the ring finger. The gods are said to be particularly influenced by the devotional feelings (*bhavana*) of the worshipper, the ancestors by the correct pronunciation of the Sanskrit *mantras*.

The complete sequence of three sets of sixteen *pind* offerings is in fact rarely completed. As we will see, most mourners miss out all but one of the *pinds* of the middle sixteen. The low castes generally end their observance on the tenth day, by which stage only the first set of sixteen *pinds* will have been presented.[3] But though the sequence is considerably truncated, the way in which even untouchables perform *pinda-dan* conforms rather closely to its Brahmanic prototype (though the ritual dedications are made in the vernacular rather than Sanskrit). This is not surprising since the Barber who presides will probably have assisted at scores of high-caste *shraddh* rituals.

With regard to both ritual and belief, my informants draw a sharp distinction between those elements which they believe to be *shastrik* (or scriptural) and hence of unquestionable authenticity, and those which they believe to be *laukik* (or 'popular') and hence of dubious validity. All of the highly formalised ritual sequences I describe are held to belong to the first category, but many of the somewhat variable penumbra of observances which frame them are held to belong to the second.

Unless he knows it by heart, the priest more or less follows a printed manual (*paddhati*) when he presides at a *shraddh* ritual. But this does not mean that their performance is completely standardised. One reason for this is that different regional communities have their own distinctive styles of *shraddh* encoded in different manuals. In the case of local Banarasis, the priests generally follow a *paddhati* known as the *Pret Manjari*. But printed editions of this text vary considerably in length – the most extensive containing many details omitted from the shortest.

An even more important source of variation, however, is that the priests generally find it necessary surreptitiously to edit the extremely lengthy and complex ritual sequences – the extent of this editing being largely dependent on the anticipated size of the offerings. Most of them, moreover, do not properly understand the logic of at least some of the sequences they direct, and are therefore apt to garble them. Indeed the priesthood itself has a whole repertoire of engagingly self-deprecating – and often obviously apochryphal – stories to illustrate their own incomprehension: the story, for example, of the manual which contained the misprint *muttra* (urine) for *suttra* (thread), and of the priest who directed the offering accordingly. Or again, there is the famous case of the young man who had picked up his knowledge of the rituals by slavishly memorising the performances over which he had seen his father preside. On one occasion a kitten had started to frolic with the offerings, and the father had thrown a wicker basket over it to keep it out of the way. When the son came to perform this particular ritual, he would always demand that a cat and a basket be present.

Occasionally the ritual sequences prescribed by the manuals are creatively elaborated rather than telescoped. I have previously referred (p. 180), for example, to the fact that in some regional communities the corpse of a woman who dies in childbirth should be purified by 108 baths before cremation. Intrigued by this information, I asked a large number of the local priests what they would do in such circumstances, and was consistently assured that no special rituals were required. One of these was my friend Sita Maharaj, with whom I discussed the matter at length, and to whom I told what I had heard from my original informant. Visiting the cremation ground some weeks later I was surprised to find Sita Maharaj presiding over the 108 baths of a female corpse. He had eventually tracked it down in an old book, he explained, and had decided that it was an authentically *Shastrik* practice. But given the conservatism of the clientele, Sita's brother Ram was critical of such innovations – however impeccable their textual sanction. 'I do what they want. In my whole life I have only performed two or three *shraddhs* according to the *Shastras*. I emphasise *lokachar* [the popular tradition]. What the women of the family say, that's the truth. Blowing our conch shells, we Brahmans throw dust in people's eyes.'

The variations in ritual performances remain, however, within fairly narrow limits. But their exegesis is often much more widely discrepant. The manuals tell the priest what to do and say; not what it means. More specifically, these texts consist of a Hindi commentary detailing the actions prescribed; and a set of ritual dedications in Sanskrit which accompany each offering, and which say what it is and who it is intended for. Finally, there are the Vedic verses which are recited at critical junctures in the ritual and which empower the action. These have often been stitched together from a number of different texts, and commonly bear a fairly transparent relationship to the action. On offering water, for example, the accompanying verse might invite the celestial and terrestial waters, those which are gold-coloured and apt for sacrifice, to be kind and bring luck to the offerer. The minority of priests who are competent in classical Sanskrit and can understand the dedication are quite unable to comprehend the archaic language of the Veda. Even amongst the traditional scholarly community of Banaras, and despite persistent enquiry, I experienced enormous difficulty in finding a pandit who could confidently render any of these Vedic verses into Hindi.

My description of the rituals which follow cremation focuses on those performed by indigenous high-caste Banarasis. In citing local understandings of the 'meaning' of specific ritual elements, I have, unless otherwise stated, limited myself to those on which there is considerable measure of expert consensus.

6.2 'The impure sixteen'

With these preliminaries in mind we can begin to look at the sequence in more detail. Death signals the beginning of the first set of sixteen *pind* offerings – the *malin shodashi* or 'impure sixteen' – which will be completed on the tenth day. This set is subdivided into two: the *khat pind* (the 'six *pinds*') and the *dasgattr* (literally, 'ten body') *pinds*. The 'six *pinds*' we have encountered already (pp. 175–6). The first five (in Banaras all six) are offered on the day of cremation itself and are vaguely held to buy off the malevolent ghosts who hover around the corpse and threaten to reanimate it. Outside Banaras the last is given on the following morning at the rite of *asthisanchay*, 'the accumlation of bones', when milk, rice and a *pind* made of horse-bean lentils (*urad*) are offered onto the remains of the pyre 'in order to cool it' (cf. Aiyangar 1913:22).

Milk, rice and horse-bean lentils are precisely what the mourners themselves eat on that day. This meal is known as *dudh-bhat* (literally, 'milk-rice'), is the first to be cooked in the bereaved household since the death, and is attended by their closest agnates,[4] whose commensality on this occasion delimits the group which participates in the full rigours of mourning. In other dialect forms, the meal is alternatively described as 'bitter' or 'useless rice' (*karva* or *nikamma bhat*) and its unappetising nature must be loudly proclaimed. It is, people say, 'the food of sorrow' (*gam ka khana*). The rice is boiled without salt, and garnished with horse-bean lentils and a *little* milk (my informants insist on its meagreness). The diners sit in a row facing south, the direction of death. A leaf-plate is placed for the *pret*-ghost at the head of the line above the chief mourner who mixes the food served for the *pret* with his own, and puts the equivalent of five mouthfuls back on the *pret*'s plate – to which all the other participants add a single mouthful.

The symbolism of rebirth is present once more. *Dudh-bhat* is described as the deceased's first *ann-prashan*, the name of the life-cycle ritual at which a child is fed its first solid food. This too consists of milk and rice, just as *dudh-bhat* is 'milk-rice'. The other obligatory ingredient of the meal – the horse-bean lentils – also deserves comment. In other ritual contexts, these lentils are described as a surrogate for meat or flesh. It was this which led one of my informants to wonder whether the mourners were not really consuming the flesh of the dead man. Since I have never heard anybody else say as much I would be tempted to discount this remark were it not for the fact that, as we shall see, the symbolism of consuming the body of the deceased is quite transparent at various other points in the ritual sequence.

Of the 'impure sixteen', the remaining ten *pinds* are offered between the time of cremation and the rituals of the tenth day. Ideally one should be given each day,[5] though in practice all ten are commonly offered on the tenth day. These impure offerings must be made away from the house, on the river bank or by some sacred tank. The chief mourner faces south to offer the *pind* on top of a piece of *kusha* grass – which both stands for a Brahman and, like the Brahman, is a transmitter or conductor of offerings. The *pind* itself is then presented with various offerings: flowers, fragrance, incense, woollen threads, resin (*ral*), betel-nut, a medicinal leaf called *bhringraj* (or *bhanraiya*), and leaf-cupfuls of water containing sesame seed – one for that of the first day, two for the second, and so on up to ten. The *pind* and other offerings are finally deposited in the river (or tank), though the *kusha* on which a *pind* has been placed must always be burnt since it is said to turn into a snake if immersed in water. Alternatively the *pind* may be fed to a crow, which is a temporary embodiment of the *pret*, who signals his acceptance of the offering by eating it. Since, as we are about to see, the *pind* is the bodily substance of the departed, there would seem to be some sense in which the deceased eats himself.

The ten *pinds* must all be made out of the same kind of grain. They must be round, 'like a womb'. 'When the father's semen (*virya*) and the mother's uterine blood (*raj*) mix', my informants say, 'they form a ball like an egg or a lychee. Therefore the *pind* should be round.' As we have seen (p. 168), one meaning of *pind* is an 'embryo', or more generally a 'body'. But there is yet another sense of the term – one resonant of the idea that a man discharges his debt to the ancestors by making them offerings. In colloquial Hindi the expression *pind chorna* ('to relinquish the *pind*) has the sense of release from a claim; while *pind parna* (*parna*, to fall) has the sense of a burden descending on one. Here, then, the word has connotations of 'debt' and 'obligation'.

All three senses come together in the 'ten-body' *pinds* which are not only offerings to the departed and, as it were, debt-repayment installments, but which also construct a new body for the deceased. They are offered over ten days paralleling the ten (lunar) month period of gestation; and each *pind* constitutes a different part of this new body. Thus according to the *Pret Manjari* (which furnishes the most cited scheme), the head is made on the first day (as the head of a foetus is formed in the womb by the end of the first month). The eyes, nose and ears are formed on the second day; the neck, arms and chest on the third; the navel, sexual organs and anus on the fourth; the thighs, legs and feet on the fifth; the vital organs on the sixth; veins on the seventh; nails teeth and body hair on the eighth; semen on the ninth, and hunger and thirst on the tenth. Other sources provide a slightly different scheme, and my informants would sometimes express it as a matter of creating a different sense organ (*indriya*) on each day. All variants agreed, however, that what completes the body on the tenth day is the creation of hunger and thirst – or, as some people put it, the creation of the digestive system.

More precisely, the ten *pinds* are both nourishment for the *pret* and the substance of its new body. Taking their cue from the *Garuda Purana*, the ritual experts sometimes explain that each *pind* is divided into four parts. One is purloined by 'the messengers of death', one is food for the *pret* and the other two parts are absorbed into the five elements from which the deceased's new body is created (cf. Stevenson 1920:160). By the same token, the priests often speak as though some of the items which are presented to the *pind* are both gifts to the *pret* and the constituents of its new body. *Bhringraj* leaves give it blood, the wool gives it hair and resin makes its vital breath.

In the normal course of events, the body-*pind* offerings are completed on the tenth day. When the deceased is a young child, however, or when an effigy is cremated some time after the death, the sequence is generally telescoped so that it ends on *triratri* – after 'three nights'. Another exception is when the day preceding the new or full moon (*amavasya* or *purnima*) occurs before the ten days are up. In that event it is common to offer however many *pinds* remain on that day; and I have been told that this is particularly important when the death is that of a relatively junior member of the lineage. The principle, as Sita Maharaj explained, is that the construction of the *pret*'s body should not span two different fortnights. Incompletion promises future increase (p. 176) – an outcome clearly to be avoided in the case of ghosts, particularly when they are the resentful ones of those whose lives have been cut unexpectedly short. Closure and termination are therefore symbolically stressed.

Until its new body is ready the ghost exists in a 'microscopic' form which is represented as being a precise miniature replica of the 'gross' body it has left behind. Its mouth is the size of the point of a needle. Ingestion is consequently a problem and it is always hungry and thirsty. Because of its parching experience on the cremation pyre, it is thirst which is the worst of these agonies. After cremation, a water-pot (*ghant*, or *ghat-kumbh* meaning 'body-pot') is hung in the branches of a *pipal* tree. *Pipals* are described as 'the residence of ghosts', and the pot as 'the house of the *pret*' (as the body is 'the house of the soul'). Morning and evening the chief mourner offers water into this pot with a verse which proclaims that he is cooling the *pret* down because he was burnt in the fire. The pot has a small hole drilled in the bottom so that the water drips slowly out. The *pret* waits on the ground below. Each drop shatters into atoms and some of these fall into its microscopic mouth. In the evening a lamp (*chirag*) is placed near the pot 'to light the way' for the ghost. When he goes to tend it, the chief mourner would normally be accompanied by his Barber, though the Mahabrahman might assist a *jajman* of real substance.

The *pind* of the tenth day completes the first set of sixteen offerings and marks the end of the period of the most intense pollution. Death has cut the bereaved household off from both the gods and the ancestors. After the tenth day rituals they become eligible to perform 'the work of the ancestors' (*pitr karya*), though it is not until after *sapindikaran* on the twelfth day that they can resume 'the work of the gods' (*dev-karya*). Facing south, the chief mourner – and then the other male mourners – are tonsured, shaved and have their nails pared by the Barber. 'Out of respect', however, those with living fathers should not have their moustaches shaved off. Even before the chief mourner, the Mahabrahman as the embodiment of the ghost itself should be tonsured, though in practice he is only likely to consent to this if he is expecting a princely donation on the following day. Mustard oil, or a 'burning' and 'bitter' mustard cake, is then applied to the chief mourner's head, the residue being taken away and buried in the name of the *pret*. After this, he bathes, dons a new sacred thread and is fed with a sweet. As at the end of cremation (p. 178), the sweet replaces the hot and bitter which are taken away to be buried and washed away with a bath.

On the tenth day the chief mourner writes the figures 9 and 4 – standing for Vishnu's conch and discus – on the sand altar (*vedi*) on which the offerings have been made before he destroys it. This is also what he scratches in the ash of the cremation pyre before leaving the *ghat* (p. 177), and we are perhaps justified in interpreting it as a symbol of termination. In the custom of certain castes, he will make his way home from the *ghat* by a different route from the one by which he had come. With him he carries a pot of curd which he will feed to a dog (an attendant to Yamraj). The change of route is explicitly said to signify his separation from the inauspiciousness with which he has been in contact, while the curd is a sign of auspicious beginnings. On arrival home he distributes *pharuhi/bahuri* (rice which has been husked, soaked and then parched) to his assembled kinsfolk. In the meantime the house has been purified and freshly plastered with cow-dung by the women, whose nails have been cut by the Barber's wife and who have washed their clothes and hair. All the mourners are then fed, the chief mourner eating first and all the diners putting a little aside on their plates for the *pret*.

When the practice is followed (and it suggests a considerable short-circuiting of the sequence of intermediate bodily forms which the Brahmanical rituals postulate), it is on the tenth (or alternatively twelfth) night that the deceased's household smooth over the ashes of their domestic hearth in the hope of finding clues to his posthumous fate when they inspect them next morning. The idea is that they will be able to discern, say, a footprint of the animal form into which he has taken rebirth. When they find nothing, they are entitled to conclude that he has been liberated from the cycle of rebirths.

On each of the first ten days after death – in some cases for the first thirteen – the *Garuda Purana* is read in the house of the deceased by the household-priest or by a specialist *karam-kandi*. This should ideally take place at the very spot on which the death occurred, and is said to be for the 'peace' of the departed soul. But since much of the text consists of spine-chilling accounts of the torments awaiting the sinner, it seems more directed at the edification of the survivors.

During the period of mourning, the bereaved household take only one 'proper' meal a day – that is, a meal which includes grains. This must be eaten before sunset, for that which is eaten after becomes 'the food of demons' (*rakshas bhojan*) and completely obviates the rituals. *Phalahar*, the food of fasting and the food *par excellence* of the ascetic, may however be taken after dark.[6] Only one kind of grain (echoing the rule that the ten *pinds* which create the *pret*'s body should all be made from a single variety of grain), and only cooling *sattvik* food conducive to a tranquil *sattvik* disposition, should be eaten, since the senses must be kept under strict control. Salt,[7] fried food and turmeric (associated with auspicious occasions like marriage) must all be avoided. The bereaved household should not make use of the services of a Washerman, and its members should abstain from sex. No jewellery should be worn, nor new or brightly coloured clothes.

The restrictions to which the chief mourner is subject are a good deal more stringent (as are those expected of a widow who must follow a very similar regime). He cannot sleep on a bed, should use separate bedding and should engage in no profane activity. At all times he must keep a knife (or some other iron implement) by his side as a protection against evil spirits. Though he should bathe everyday in the river or one of the sacred tanks, he must not cut his nails, shave, use soap or groom his hair; and he should wear neither shoes nor stitched clothes[8] – all of which suggests a suspension of the normal concern with the boundaries of the body (Das 1982:127). He must cook for himself on a separate hearth (located if possible outside the house) and eat from separate utensils as he sits facing south. As we have seen (p. 183), he is in numerous ways identified with the deceased. One of the most striking aspects of this identification is that he is said to 'eat for the *pret*, who receives the food he digests. In the dialect of the Maithil community of Banaras the term for chief mourner is, in fact, *mukhya pachak* – 'chief digester'. Consistent with all this, one of my informants told me that if you were to weigh him at the time of cremation, and then stuff him with sweets throughout the period of mourning, his weight at the end would not be an ounce more than it was at the beginning.

'Untouchability is finished' on the tenth day, it is said, when the chief mourner's knife, utensils, bedding and clothes are given to the Barber. But none will yet eat with the bereaved household, who will not visit the temples, or perform domestic worship or *jap* (the repetition of *mantras* or the names of a deity). There is, however, an ambiguity here. Though it is said that they only become fit for 'the work of the gods' when they have completed the twelfth day rites, the priests point out that the ritual sequence requires them to invoke various deities and to recite Sanskrit *mantras* during the eleventh day rituals, and that their ineligibility must therefore have been removed on the tenth.

6.3 'The middle sixteen'

With a significant addition, the identification between the chief mourner, the Funeral-priest and the *pret*-ghost is strikingly reiterated by the now rarely performed ritual of *Vrishotsarg* (literally, 'bull sacrifice') which is supposed to be celebrated on the eleventh day. A bull is married to two or more heifers (I have seen four) under a wedding canopy which has been set up on the *ghat*. It is then branded – on the left flank with the trident of Shiva and on the right with Vishnu's discus – and set free to wander at will for the rest of its days.[9] The calves are gifted in *dan*. The ritual is elaborate, expensive and prolonged, but the core of the preceding sequence consists in establishing a set of five 'shrines' in the form of pots: in the west a pot for Vishnu covered with a yellow cloth; in the east for Brahma with a white cloth; in the north for Rudra (a fierce form of Shiva) with a red cloth, and in the south for Yamraj with a black cloth. In the middle is a pot for the *pret*. The deities are worshipped and given offerings, and a fire sacrifice (*havan*) is performed in order that the ghost might be liberated from its ghostly condition. This seems to be effected by homologising – or at least identifying – the *pret* with Lord Vishnu as represented by the miniature golden image (known as 'the golden man', *kanchan purush*) which is placed on his pot.

This 'divinisation' of the ghost emerges clearly towards the end of the ritual in what is for my purposes its most instructive phase. What it evokes is the deceased's journey to 'the abode of the ancestors'. Half-way along his road, the departed – driven forward with unremitting cruelty by the messengers of death – must cross the terrifying Vaitarni river, which is described as flowing with pus and blood, has banks of unscalable bone, mud of flesh and gore, and entrances congested by hair. One of the heifers given at *Vrishotsarg* helps the soul across, and this scene is acted out in the course of the ritual. A trench has been dug to represent the Vaitarni (which flows south I was told – making this river of pollution an inversion of the paradigmatically pure Ganges which in Banaras flows north). The trench is filled with water on which red powder is scattered to signify blood. A miniature boat is constructed out of sugar-cane; the boat is put on the river, and 'the golden man' is put in the boat. The Mahabrahman now prays to the heifer (in standard Hindi in the example I quote): 'Oh cow mother, spread flowers and sweet-smelling things on the way instead of thorns. Help the departed cross the Vaitarni without difficulty. Let him not experience fear of Yampuri [the city of Yamraj] and let him arrive there with jubilation.' The chief mourner puts the boat containing the miniature image of Vishnu under one arm and holds onto the Mahabrahman, who holds on to the tail of the calf. Together all four of them cross the river. That the chief mourner and Funeral-priest should play the part of the *pret* crossing over into the other world should already be predictable enough. What is new is that the ghost is now also equated with 'the golden man'.

At first sight this scene might seem out of sequence, for what follows will clearly suggest that the deceased's journey to 'the abode of the ancestors' is yet to begin. Its appositeness here, however, becomes plain when we remember that on the eleventh day the deceased is born into a new body that has been prepared over the preceding days, the crossing of the Vaitarni river being a clear metaphor for the birth passage of a child (which is also represented as a matter of negotiating a river of blood and gore (p. 168)). Moreover, the only one of the next set of sixteen *pinds* which is held to be absolutely indispensible is now offered, and this is food. As a baby yells from the pangs of hunger as soon as it is born, so the newly created body of the deceased must first be comforted with food.

When there is need for it, *Narayani bali* is also performed on the eleventh day. Narayan is one of the names of Vishnu, and *bali* is a 'sacrifice' – as I would gloss it, a sacrifice of 'de-sacralisation'.[10] The purpose of the rite is to eradicate the *pret*-hood of the *pret*, and in Banaras it is normally performed only in cases of 'bad death'. It is, however, held to be exceptionally difficult to get right, and is often deemed to have failed – in which case the supplementary ritual of *tripindi shraddh* will eventually become necessary. (p. 242).

In barest outline the rite consists of an opening sequence in which the sixteenfold worship (*shodashopchar*) of Vishnu in the form of a Saligram (a black stone containing fossil ammonite) is performed. An eight-petalled lotus is then drawn on a white cloth which has been spread over a purified area. A pot into which Vishnu is invoked is established in the middle of this design, and eight of his consorts are seated in the petals. These deities are worshipped and prayers for the ghost's liberation are addressed to them. This first phase of the ritual, then, consists of the invocation and worship of eleven supernatural beings – two forms of Vishnu, his eight consorts and the ghost.

The second phase repeats a sequence we have encountered before. Five 'shrine'-pots are established in five directions for five supernatural beings. Each rests on grain of a different type, has cloth of a different colour put over it, and is surmounted by a miniscule image made of a different metal. Thus:

Brahma	– east	– wheat	– white cloth	– silver image
Vishnu	– west	– rice	– yellow cloth	– golden image
Rudra	– north	– *mung* (pulse)	– red cloth	– copper image
Yamraj	– south	– *urad* (pulse)	– black cloth	– iron image
Pret	– middle	– sesame seeds	– green cloth	– lead image

Having invoked, worshipped and given offerings to these 'guests', a fire sacrifice is performed to remove the sins of the *pret*, during the course of which the chief mourner is instructed to contemplate the departed in the form of Vishnu. Once more it would seem that the objective is to identify the ghost with the creator of the cosmos (cf. Shastri 1063:272).

The rite for 'pacifying' the *panchak*, the five lunar asterisms during which it is particularly inauspicious to die (p. 160), again has a strikingly similar fivefold form, and this too is normally held on the eleventh day. At the end of this ritual, however, a sequence is added in which the chief mourner looks at his reflection in a bowl of oil which is then donated to the Barber. This procedure is said to remove his inauspiciousness, and is also performed on other ritual occasions designed to neutralise malign planetary influences (e.g. Parry 1991).

The second set of sixteen *pinds* – 'the middle sixteen' (*madhyam shodashi*) – is also scheduled for the eleventh day. It is an at first sight puzzling fact, however, that in practice all but one of them is generally omitted by even the most fastidious. The reason, I suspect, is that the prescribed form of these offerings merely reproduces the structure laid down for *Narayani bali*. There is first of all a set of eleven offerings to a *mélange* of supernatural beings (which is admittedly different from those worshipped during the first phase of *Narayani bali*, but which also includes Vishnu and the ghost). This is followed by a set of five offerings (to Brahma, Vishnu, Shiva, Yamraj and the *pret*) which precisely replicates its second phase. The logic seems to be that if *Narayani bali* was performed these offerings have already been taken care of; and if there was no need to perform it (because the death was a 'good' one) they are superfluous. In any event, only one of these *pinds* is invariably offered. This is food for the *pret* whose new body is now experiencing hunger.[11] It seems to me significant, however, that this offering is described as 'Vishnu's *shraddh*' and the *pind* as 'Vishnu's *pind*'. It is also significant that at the end of the rite, the chief mourner picks up this *pind* and smells it. From a number of contexts it is clear that to smell something is to consume it,[12] while in this context it is explicitly a surrogate for eating it. Once more, then, the chief mourner 'eats' the food of the *pret*.

Not only the chief mourner, however, but also the Mahabrahman Funeral-priest. At the end of the eleventh day rituals the Mahabrahman is fed on the favourite foods of the deceased 'for the satisfaction of his ghost'. In Bihar these specialists are said to eat the eleventh day *pind* itself. But more than merely the food of the deceased, the evidence already presented (pp. 75ff) would suggest that they also eat his bodily substance. They do so literally in the Nepali and Travancore instances I have cited – in the former being fed some of the deceased's ground-up bone in a preparation of *khir* (boiled rice and milk). In north India they do so only in a symbolic sense, the substance of the deceased being represented by a *khir* effigy of his body in the case reported by Babb (1975:96–7), and in Banaras by the *payas dan* which should be fed to the Mahabrahman shortly before his departure, and which again consists of *khir*.

Payas means 'milk', but in the Sanskrit texts the term often refers to semen (O'Flaherty 1980a:18, 43). Though my informants did not directly equate *payas dan* and semen, this is nevertheless suggested by the notion that a man should ideally drink milk after sexual intercourse in order to replace what he has just discharged; and also by their version of at least one well-known mythological incident. Raja Dasrath was childless. In order to remedy this situation his *guru* performed a sacrifice, the *khir* from which was fed to his three queens, who then conceived. Here *khir* clearly doubles for semen; and this would seem to suggest that what the Funeral-priest consumes is the semen of the departed as a metonym for his body. For want of more direct evidence this interpretation must remain speculative, but I suggest it as a possibility since it bears directly on my later argument that what the Brahman recuperates through his digestive powers is the distilled productive essence of the departed.

Both the symbolism of eating the deceased (or at least some aspect of him) and the symbolism of eating on his behalf are also clearly present in the ideology surrounding the gifts which the Mahabrahman receives. At his departure he accepts the gift of *sajja dan* which should ideally include a year's supply of grains (p. 80). Throughout the year to come the Mahabrahman will eat for the deceased, the idea being that whatever the Mahabrahman consumes in the name of the departed will be received by him in the next world. As we have seen (pp. 80 and 139ff), the size of this gift is characteristically the subject of bitter wrangling between the mourners and the Mahabrahmans, who powerfully express their dissatisfaction in terms of their rumbling stomachs. 'Oh, Babu ji', they darkly grouse, 'that won't fill my belly.' Moreover, the gifts which a Brahman accepts represent – according to the classical theory of *dan* – the bio-moral substance of those who donate them. Consuming such offerings therefore amounts to a kind of symbolic cannibalism or necrophagy (Heesterman 1962:25). The problem, as we have seen (pp. 122ff), is to 'digest' such dangerous sustenance. The model, however, is clearly one in which the priest has to ingest and digest some crucial aspect of the physical-cum-spiritual essence of those he serves.

Before his departure on the eleventh day, the Mahabrahman is required to smash the 'body-pot' dwelling of the *pret*, and to hand some turmeric to the chief mourner as a sign that he is now returning to a state of auspiciousness. On taking his leave he should confer his blessing: that the chief mourner's descent line should flourish, contain many generous donors with faith in the Vedas, experience no shortage of milk and curd, and should always be able to offer hospitality.

In these rituals of the eleventh day – as indeed throughout the post-cremation mortuary sequence – the pre-eminent deity is clearly Vishnu. At the beginning and end of each crucial phase in the offerings, the chief mourner turns towards the east and invokes his power; and as we have just seen he endeavours to equate the departed with the deity. Moreover, cremation, I have argued (pp. 30ff and 45ff), is a kind of re-enactment of Vishnu's cosmogonic austerities, and it is on his footsteps that the elite have aspired to be burned. *Pitr rupi Janardana*, 'the form of the ancestors is Janardana' (Vishnu as the 'giver of rewards'), as my informants endlessly quoted. But it is, of course, also the case that the *shav* (corpse) is said to be Shiv(a) and is greeted as the 'Great God' (Mahadev), whose boon to all who die in his city is a final liberation from the cycle of rebirths. Why this double identification?

The answer, I think, lies in Shiva's persona as the ascetic *par excellence*, and Vishnu's persona as cosmogonic sacrifier. When the deceased is equated with Shiva what is foregrounded is his voluntary renunciation of life, and his ultimate quest for salvation and the extinction of individual existence. When he is identified with Vishnu the focus is on the regeneration of life, both collective and individual. But there is also possibly another aspect to this second association which has to do with the opposition between Vishnu's heaven (which is enjoyed by those of great virtue) and the terrifying realm over which Yamraj presides (for which the sinner is destined). By identifying the deceased with the heavenly Lord of *Vaikunth* the rituals endeavour to determine his destination.

6.4 'The highest sixteen'

The final set of sixteen *pinds* – 'the highest sixteen' (*uttam shodashi*) – is for the sustenance of the deceased on his year-long journey to 'the abode of the ancestors', one for each of the way-stations through which he passes. In theory a *pind* should be offered each month, with separate ones for each fortnight in certain months. In fact the whole lot are generally offered on the eleventh day as a postscript to the *pret's* first-feeding, or on the twelfth day as a preliminary to the rite of *sapindikaran*. Sometimes 360 diminutive *pinds* are also offered, one for each day of the year.[13]

Sapindikaran should theoretically be performed on the anniversary of the death; though in these degenerate times – when few can devote so much time and energy to the rites and restrictions of mourning, and some might die in the interim – it is almost invariably celebrated after twelve days rather than twelve months. The ritual itself represents the deceased's arrival at his destination and his union with his ancestors. The *pret*-ghost becomes an ancestral *pitr*. *Sapindikaran* is the first of the post-cremation rituals which may be conducted inside the precincts of the house, and the first at which a 'pure' Brahman presides. By comparison with the tense and shell-shocked atmosphere which characteristically pervades the proceedings of the previous days, I was often struck by the comparatively relaxed feeling of the occasion – often one of almost joyful relief.

Literally, *sapindikaran* might be rendered as 'making one flesh'. Consistent with the meaning of *pind* as 'body', the *sapinda* relatives of the legal treatises are those with whom one shares body particles. Inheritance, the prohibited degrees of kinship for the purposes of marriage, and the contagion of death pollution are all defined by these texts in terms of the *sapinda* group – though the way in which this group is specified varies from one context to another (Dumont 1983). At *sapindikaran* it consists of a purely agnatic unit.

The ritual begins with the feeding of five Brahmans who embody the *pret*,[14] his three lineal ascendants and the Vishvadevas. The latter represent the remote ancestors of the deceased (Knipe 1977), though my informants are generally vague about their identity. I was often told that they are representatives of Vishnu. Dumont (1983) characterises them as 'ancestor-gods', and the rituals certainly accord them a quasi-divine status. In making them offerings the chief mourner faces north and wears his sacred thread over his left shoulder (whereas he faces south and wears the sacred thread over the right shoulder for the ghost and his more immediate ancestors). In fact the Brahmans are there in a notional rather than a physical sense. Representing different categories of supernatural being, they are themselves represented by strands of *kusha* grass.

In the second phase of the ritual an elongated *pind*, which stands for the body of the *pret*, is offered onto the first of two altars; and three round *pinds* representing the deceased's father, father's father, and *his* father are placed on the second.[15] These three ancestors are identified with a different category of supernatural being located in a different cosmic layer: the father with the Vasus on earth, the father's father with the Rudras in mid-space (*antariksh*), and the great-grandfather with the Adityas in heaven (cf. Knipe 1977:117ff). Inhaling from the north and exhaling onto the *pinds* to the south, the chief mourner breathes life into them. Each of these *pind*-bodies has been formed out of grains which were left over from feeding the 'Brahman' representatives of the ghost and the ancestors in the first phase of the ritual, and whatever now remains after making the *pinds* is offered to them as food. They are made out of food, and the food which made them must then be given to sustain them.

The really crucial part of the rite – *pitr miloni* ('the mixing with the ancestors') – now follows. The chief mourner cuts the *pret*'s *pind* into three equal parts with a piece of *kusha* grass, or a gold wire (which will subsequently become a perquisite of the Barber). One part is merged with the *pind*-bodies of each of the three ancestors. Some people say that the lower part of the *pret's* body is joined with the body of his father, the torso with that of his grandfather and the head with that of his great-grandfather (cf. Stevenson 1920:185–6).

If a son should predecease his father, his *pind* will be merged only with two other *pinds* – that of his grandfather and great-grandfather. If the deceased was a married woman whose husband is still alive, she is merged with her husband's mother, his father's mother and father's father's mother. Over the case of a widow there is some dispute. Some say that she can only be mixed with ascendants of her own sex, while others claim that she is joined to her husband, his father and grandfather. No *sapindikaran* is held for an unmarried girl who has no 'descent line' (*gotra*) and whose spirit 'disappears into the air'.

My informants insist that the *pinds* which are merged at *sapindikaran* are the actual bodies of the ghost and his ancestors. They were, however, uncomfortable and evasive when I suggested that this made of the ritual an act of butchery. But elsewhere this implication is unflinchingly drawn.

> So strongly do they feel that the 'body' of the *pret* itself is cut, that they will not do the cutting themselves, but call in a man of a special caste (Katiliya) and pay him two or three rupees for performing this dire office; but once it is performed, they dismiss him, and . . . the chief mourner will not even look at him, either then or ever. (Stevenson 1920:185–6)

Here, then, is my justification for suggesting that *sapindikaran* might be seen as a kind of sacrifice replicating the earlier sacrifice of cremation.[16]

At the end of the ritual the three ancestral *pinds* may be made into one. Whether this happens or not, the chief mourner smells at least one *pind* and thereby symbolically consumes it. So while on the eleventh day he had symbolically eaten the *food* of the *pret*, he now eats the bodily substance of his ancestors. Stevenson (1920:187) reports that by smelling the *pind* of the father's father the chief mourner will be blessed with a son; while I have often been told that if he feeds it to his wife she will conceive a boy (cf. Shastri 1963:100; Kane 1973:4:346–7, 480). This *pind* thus has the quality of semen and may beget a new *pind*-embryo (cf. O'Flaherty 1980b). Though the notion is clearly inconsistent with karma theory, the idea is that the great-grandfather will come back as his own great-grandson.

Even amongst those who would deride such procedures as entirely without efficacy I have often encountered the same idea. In an earlier context (p. 161), for example, I referred to the exemplary death of a venerable Brahman preceptor. At that time, his great-grandson was aged about eight. Not only was this boy spoken of as the 'replica' of his great-grandfather, and said to have the very same tastes and personal qualities, but he was also credited with having completely mastered Sanskrit at a truly miraculous rate (as though he had merely begun where the old man left off), and was treated by the assembled disciples with all the deference due to their deceased *guru*.

As soon as the *sapindikaran* ritual has been completed, the chief mourner marks his renewed eligibility to perform 'the work of the gods' by worshipping Lord Ganesh, who is represented by a pot placed in the courtyard. Ganesh is the guardian of temporal and spatial thresholds, and should always receive the worshipper's first homage (p. 15).

A second gift of *sajja dan* – offered to the household- or pilgrimage-priest – now follows. This should include the same range of goods as is given to the Mahabrahman (though now they are generally of better quality). In theory he too should be given a year's supply of grains so that he may eat for the deceased. Dressed in the deceased's clothes, he is sat on a bed to be circumambulated, worshipped and to have his calves and feet massaged as if he had just completed a gruelling journey. His juniors stoop to touch his feet and receive his blessing. It is an emotional moment. At the end of his travels, the deceased has tangibly – if fleetingly – come home in the person of the priest.

After *sajja dan* a turban is tied on the chief mourner in formal recognition of his succession as household head. While his younger brothers are presented with new caps, and also have an auspicious mark applied to their foreheads by the family priest, it is only the chief mourner who is given a turban. It and the caps come from the household of their mother's brother, or from their respective fathers-in-law; but I find in my notes that the turban is almost always wound round the head by the priest who accepted the *sajja dan*. I failed to enquire whether this represents a deliberate choice, but it seems to have an obvious appropriateness. It is as if the newly incorporated ancestor is himself presiding at the succession of his worldly replacement. After the turban-tying, other affinal relatives formally present the chief mourner with gifts (known as *karni* or *neota*), which consist of cash, a quantity of grains and pulse, and perhaps a coloured *dhoti*. A careful account is kept of these offerings which will be repaid in the fullness of time when there is a death in the donor's family.

The essential part of the whole sequence ends with a feast (*Brahman bhojan*) held for the Brahmans on the twelfth or thirteenth day, when the favourite foods of the deceased should be served. In the case of an affluent family, the numbers may be large and the provision lavish. In 1977, for example, I was present when 150 Brahmans were fed. Each was given a *dakshina* of Rs. 2; twelve of them received a set of utensils, some clothing and a straw mat; and five Brahman women were each given a set of jewellery in the name of the deceased (an elderly Marwari matriarch).

Many Brahmans claim, however, that they will not accept such an invitation 'because at that time we eat the dead man'. One or two of my informants specified that it is his sins that they consume. For most, however, it is a question of eating his body, the fried cakes of horse-bean lentils (*uradi ka bara*) which are served being explicitly identified with the flesh. Employing an imagery I have several times encountered, one of my informants put it thus: 'On the thirteenth day the messengers of death bring the body and soul of the dead man and scatter it about. They cause his *shredded intestines* to fall on the plates of all who eat. In this way they eat the flesh of death pollution.' The Brahman who digests for the deceased must now digest his organs of digestion. Similar notions are clearly articulated in the Dharmashastra literature where it is held that 'by dining at a *sraddha* in the first year one eats the bones and marrow of the deceased, in the second year his flesh, [and] in the third year his blood . . .' (Kane 1973:4:548). When I asked Anant Maharaj why in these circumstances any Brahman would consent to attend at all, his reply was characteristically caustic. '"The mosque is destroyed for the sake of the rubble"', he quoted. 'The world's a buffoon.' From another point of view it is perhaps as well that it is. Feeding the Brahmans on such occasions is a prerequisite for the peace of the deceased's soul, and their non-appearance may occasion a state of near panic (Dumont 1983).

Once they have eaten, the relatives, neighbours and caste-mates of the bereaved are fed. This rite of commensality signifies the reincorporation of the bereaved household into the normal social order from which they have been set apart during mourning. These feasts are often lavish affairs attended by scores of unbidden guests, and avoiding their expense is one of the main reasons why many outsiders remain in Banaras to perform the post-cremation mortuary rites. Nirad Chaudhuri (1970:48) talks of people walking fifty miles in pre-railway days to eat at the mortuary feast of a Calcutta grandee, and recounts how the family of a wealthy relative of his had to resort to rubber-stamping the 'common people' to prevent them from eating twice.

6.5 Remembering and effacing the dead

Since the *pinds* offered to sustain the deceased on his journey to Yamraj's kingdom have probably been given on the twelfth day, any offerings made over the next twelve months are essentially commemorative. In some communities it is customary to feed a Brahman each month on the date on which the death occurred, and to feed twelve at the end of the year. Those who perform *pinda-dan* during this period will probably only do so at *chhamahi*, which is notionally the ritual of the sixth month, though it is often celebrated on the fifteenth day. *Barsi* – the anniversary of the death – is generally marked by *shraddh* and the feeding and gifting of Brahmans. But again it is often brought forward, generally because no family wedding can take place before it. Festivals like *Holi* and *Divali* are not celebrated that year.

In subsequent years, *pinda-dan* is again performed, and the Brahmans fed, on the anniversary of the death and during *pitri paksh* – 'the fortnight of the ancestors'. In *pitri paksh shraddh* should be offered to each individual ancestor – to one's parents at least – on the day of the fortnight which corresponds to the day on which he or she died. It is also performed for the ancestors collectively on the day of *amavasya* (the day before a new moon) which brings the fortnight to a close. In principle, *tarpan* – libations to the gods and ancestors – should be offered daily at the time of taking one's bath in the Ganges. Many people who are unable to keep this up throughout the year make a particular point of performing *tarpan* during *pitri paksh*. For its duration those who are offering *shraddh* should observe a regime of mourning: remaining celibate, consuming only a *sattvik* diet, eating only one proper meal in the day, not shaving[17] or having a hair cut, not using soap or oil, or the services of a Washerman.[18] No auspicious life-cycle rituals can be held in *pitri paksh*. Kanya-Kubj Brahmans will not even visit their *manya* – their worshipful wife-taking affines. *Pitri paksh* is not observed in a year during which a member of the family has died, a child has been born or a marriage celebrated.

The ritual specialists draw a distinction between *shraddh* which is offered to a single recipient (*ekoddist shraddh*) and *shraddh* which is offered to a collectivity (*parvan shraddh*). In most contexts the core of this collectivity is constituted by six ancestors in the paternal line (the father and mother, father's father and mother, and father's father's father and mother), and a further six in the maternal line (the mother's father, *his* father and paternal grandfather, and their wives). It is these ancestors, for example, who receive offerings and are invited to provide blessings at the *Nandimukh shraddh* performed on auspicious occasions like marriage and initiation. No longer tinged with the inauspiciousness of death, in *Nandimukh shraddh* (uniquely) these proximate ancestors are approached as if they were gods. In making them offerings, the *jajman* faces east (rather than south), wears his sacred thread over his left shoulder (rather than right), and performs the ritual dedications with barley (rather than sesame seeds).

The *tirath shraddh*, performed by most pilgrims to Banaras, conventionally consists of a set of seventeen *pind* offerings. The first twelve again consist of offerings dedicated to the six paternal and six maternal ancestors to whom I have just referred. The list of those who receive the next four is subject to improvisation. It might, for example, include a paternal uncle and his wife, a brother or his son, one's own wife or son, the father- and mother-in-law, and one's *guru*. The final *pind* – 'the *pind* of religious duty' (*dharam pind*) – is given to those who died a 'bad death', who died in the womb and whose existence is forgotten, or who were blind, crippled or deformed.

The ancestors can hope eventually to be liberated from the 'airy' bodies they inhabit by some pious descendant performing the pilgimage to Gaya. This may be done only once in two or three generations, and the deceased cannot be taken within the first year of his death. Many pilgrims wear the ochre-coloured clothes of the renouncer; many invite the ancestors to be seated on cloves which are inserted into a coconut which is tied onto the end of a stick and which serves as their vehicle. At Gaya, *pinda-dan* is performed at a series of different sites, and through these performances the ancestors are said 'to swim across'. A real 'end of the body' is at last achieved and their souls merge back into *Brahman* (p. 13). As a result there is no further need to offer them *shraddh*.

The eschatological picture is confusing, even contradictory. A theory of rebirth coexists with apparently incompatible ideas about the dead residing in a separate ancestral realm, enjoying the blessings of Vishnu's heaven or suffering the torments of hell. It is an over-simplification to speak of *a theory* of rebirth. The ashes of the domestic hearth may be inspected on the morning of the eleventh (or thirteenth) day for some sign of the form in which the deceased has taken rebirth – suggesting that he is reincarnated after the completion (or destruction) of his *pret*-body. But the soul is also said to wander in the atmosphere for five months before it can find a new 'house' to inhabit (p. 168). In yet other contexts people speak of a much longer interval. Less than a fully articulated theory, there is only a fluid series of more or less *ad hoc* representations. Nor are these always consistent with *karma*. Regardless of ethical behaviour, the father's father returns as his own great-grandson.

Though this last idea crops up in the context of notions about the consumption of the grandfather's *pind* at *sapindikaran*, other strands in the symbolism of this ritual suggest a different kind of fate for the soul (though a similar disregard for karmic consequences). Ghosts become ancestors, and ancestors eventually fade away into the oblivion of social extinction. Each of the three ascending generations is associated with a different and increasingly remote cosmic layer. Each is steadily progressing towards a more etherealised state of being, and with the death of a direct lineal descendant, the one who stood on the highest rung of the ladder is – as it were – promoted off the edge into the unknown world beyond. Entitled only to the wipings of the chief mourner's hand, the father of the great-grandfather has passed beyond meaningful social recognition. This admittedly relates only to a rather esoteric level of ritual discourse. But the general idea is very much part of popular consciousness. Sooner or later the ancestors should be taken to Gaya where their individual existence is finally extinguished, rendering any further commemoration of them otiose. Perfected by a good life in preparation for a good death, it is as if the soul then passes through a sequence of increasingly refined states of embodiment, until ultimately the body is transcended altogether and the soul is absorbed back into its source 'as water mixes with water'.

The lack of consistency between these eschatological theories does not seem to bother my informants, who make little attempt to reconcile them – probably in part because they tend to invoke the theory of rebirth to explain the present, and the theory of heaven, hell and salvation to visualise the future. Perhaps, as Pocock (1973:38) suggests, their *own* future – rebirth being

> primarily for other people . . . Gujerati peasants when they speak of themselves conceive of a hell or some sort of heaven. It is when they speak of others, when they are looking for some wider theory to explain the grief, sorrow and misfortune of others, that they have recourse to the theory of rebirth.

But other people, I suspect, are those beyond the circle of greatest intimacy. I speak with diffidence here, but it was not my impression that the idea that a much loved mother or spouse has been reincarnated in some unknown form has much imaginative reality. Rather, those by whose deaths one is touched most deeply are assumed to inhabit a different world in a form which bears a close resemblance to the one in which we had known them. It is as though, to plagiarise from Proust, they were travelling abroad.

In comparison with ethnography from other parts of India – as well as other parts of the world – certain aspects of this data stand out. Take Srinivas's classic account of the Coorgs. The original founder of the Coorg *okka* ('joint family') is the focus of special ritual attention (1965:159–60). When a Coorg ancestor possesses a Banna oracle, he displays all the personal idiosyncracies with which he was associated in life. If, for example, 'the ancestor had a game leg, the oracle limps about . . .' (p. 164). As well as communicating with their ancestors through an oracle, the Coorgs commonly build them shrines, where they may be represented in the form of small figurines, or their presence signalled by some personal possession like a walking stick or small sword (Srinivas 1965:160–1)[19]

The Banaras mortuary rituals, by contrast, display total disinterest in the descent line's founder. The focus of ritual attention is merely a small fragment of that line, and there is no concern with its origins. It is possibly significant here that the Coorg *okka* exists in theoretical perpetuity supported by a corporately owned estate which should never be partitioned. In the context with which I am concerned, by contrast, the coparcenary body rarely extends beyond those descended from a common great-grandfather. The constant re-definition of relevant ancestry is at least consistent with a constant re-definition of the property-holding corporation.

In contemporary Banaras – as in ancient Brahmanism (Malamoud 1982) – the complete obliteration of the physical remains of the deceased is accompanied by an almost equally radical effacement of his personal characteristics and biography. No place is made in the mortuary rites for a celebration of his individual achievements; no eulogies are delivered in praise of his particular virtues, and no recognition is given to the passing of a unique life. Assigned the role of sacrificial victim, he reproduces the prototypical sacrifice from which creation proceeded. In so doing he acts in a world which is beyond time and to which his personal biography is a complete irrelevance. The events of life are erased in the interests of creating a picture of timeless recurrence. As with the Balinese, the depersonalisation of the person goes hand in hand with the detemporalisation of time (Geertz 1975).

Though the ancestors with whom I am indirectly acquainted may reveal their own idiosyncratic personalities when they appear to reprimand or advise their descendants in dreams, and to some extent when they are embodied in the Brahman *purohit* on the twelfth day after death, they are on the whole represented as rather faceless and stereotypical creatures. It is ghosts rather than ancestors whose specific biography and personal characteristics demand recognition (pp. 229ff). Almost standardised links in a chain of descent, an ancestor's social existence is rather short lived. No shrine, monument or other material object preserves his memory. During the rituals he is of course materially embodied in the *pinds*. But it is principally people rather than things that represent the dead: the Mahabrahman, the family priest and of course the chief mourner himself. In tangible bodily form, however, an *ancestor's* one reappearance in the world of the living is in the person of the priest at the time of *sajja dan*. By contrast with the Coorg situation, and unlike ghosts, ancestors do not make a habit of possessing the living.

There are, of course, exceptions to the general rule that the dead are never enshrined. Many memorials are dedicated to *satis*; but it is remarkable, as I have already observed (p. 52), how little these memorials evoke of the specific biographies of the women to whom they are dedicated. Elaborate mausoleums are also sometimes erected over the grave of a celebrated ascetic, shrines are dedicated to a 'hero-ghost' (*bir*), and stone images set up for a *brahm* – the particularly powerful spirit of a Brahman who has died a 'bad death'. But as we shall see (chapter 8), the entombed ascetic is not 'really' dead; and he is certainly not an ancestor. Nor of course are *birs* or *brahms*, who are merely forms of 'super-ghost'. Stuck in the limbo of *pret*-hood, incapable of further refinement and transformation but possessors of a dangerously volatile power, the best thing to do is to fix them in stone.

6.6 Digestion and transformation

I hope to have shown that one recurrent theme which runs throughout the ritual sequence I have reviewed is that of ingesting and digesting the deceased. ✝ In what follows I try to make sense of this at first sight puzzling symbolism.

The place to begin, I believe, is with the preoccupation of Brahmanical thought with the processes of recycling and transformation. The doctrine of *samsara*, according to which each unliberated soul is endlessly reincarnated according to its karmic balance in one of the 840,000 forms of life, provides one example. A concern with circulation is clearly also apparent in the way in which the Brahmans conceive of their own place in the order of things. Just as the Brahman as priest must at all costs pass on the gifts he receives in *dan* unless he is to rot with the sins of the donor, so the Brahman as teacher is enjoined to transmit his knowledge on pain of a similar penalty.[20] But more than a passive agent of transmission, the Brahman is an agent of transformation who is likened to the philosopher's stone that turns base metal into gold, or to the Ganges that absorbs the city's sewerage and transforms it into holy water. In this role he is identified with fire and *kusha* grass. In ritual contexts a blade of *kusha* is commonly made to stand in for a Brahman; while in accepting the food of *shraddh* the Brahman replaces the fire that transmits oblations to the gods (Kane 1973:4:349). He works this alchemy above all by eating the food of the gods and ancestors, and by 'digesting' the offerings made to them. 'The Brahman's stomach is like a letter-box', they say. Fire in general – and his digestive fire in particular – is 'the postman of the gods': their 'mouth' and their 'messenger' (*dev-dut*), and 'the link of exchange' (*adan-pradan ki kari*) between humans and deities. Other castes may of course also be seen as passing on substances which they have transformed; but it is the Brahmans who most explicitly elaborate their role in these terms. It is after all largely they who have articulated the theory of the system, and they who straddle the crucial boundary between the mundane world of men and the transcendent world of the gods, effecting transformations between the two.

This Brahmanical preoccupation with keeping that which has been received in general circulation is echoed in mythology. The myth associated with the feast of *Anant Chaturdashi*, for example, tells the story of the sage Kondal's search for an explanation of the terrible misfortunes which afflicted him. Lord Vishnu advised him that the answer lay with Anant – himself a form of Vishnu whose name means 'without end'. In the course of his almost endless search for the deity, Kondal made enquiries of many beings. None was able to help him, but all added a question of their own which they desired Kondal to put to the god. The cow, for example, wanted to know why her calf did not receive her milk, the mango tree why her fruit was infested with maggots when ripe, and two separate tanks wished to know why their waters continually overflowed one into the other. The answers which Vishnu provided when he eventually revealed himself as Anant are instructive. In her previous life the cow was the earth which swallowed up some of the seeds which were planted in it without yielding forth their fruit, the mango tree was a Brahman who did not pass on his knowledge, and the two tanks were married sisters who gave *dan* only to each other.

It is, of course, obvious that the mortuary rites are crucially concerned with the proper transformation of the ghost into an ancestor, and with the proper recycling of the soul. Related to this, I suggest, is the fact that during mourning the normally bounded physical body must be left free of constraint. The chief mourner's body is the vehicle of the ghost, and its unboundedness represents a capacity for metamorphosis. Also significant here is that both the *pind*, and the food served for the symbolic Brahmans, are typically of rice boiled in diluted milk, which is known as *pak* – a term which the dictionaries translate as 'cooking' or 'digestion'. Being boiled they belong to the category of *kachcha* food. The word *kachcha* suggests incompleteness, lack of fixity, and hence a potential for transformation. It is these qualities which make such food particularly capable of creating bodily substance. It is therefore wholly appropriate that it should figure so prominently in the offerings made to the departed (Beliappa and Kaushik n.d.)

Such food, moreover, would rate as a 'light diet' which stimulates the 'fire of the stomach' (*jatharagni*), which in turn effects the process of digestion (cf.

Tabor 1981). So just as food is transmitted to the gods by being offered into the sacrificial fire, and the corpse by being offered into the fire of cremation, so the deceased and the food which will sustain him are transmitted by being offered into the gastric fires of the Brahman and chief mourner. There is even perhaps a sense in which the symbolic ingestion of the deceased, his consignment to the fire of digestion, re-plays the burning – or as Malamoud (1975) would have it the cooking – of the corpse on the cremation pyre.

The rites of the twelfth day correspond to the deceased's arrival at his destination after twelve months. The residue of his sins will now be *'burned'* away by the punishment he endures at the hand of Yamraj. At the level of the rite, he is at this point submitted to the digestive fires of the Brahmans, who 'eat for his salvation'. It is tempting to conclude that it is this ritual act which actually accomplishes the final moral purification of the deceased, the fire of the Brahman's stomach being the fire by which Yamraj incinerates the remaining sin – an interpretation consistent with the fact that it is explicitly said that in the act of eating the diners assimilate the sins of the departed.

Another angle on all this would be to consider the fact that the 'gross' outer body is consumed by the fires of cremation; that on the eleventh day (when the *pret* has just acquired a new arm-length body) the impure Funeral-priests are expected to eat an offering which represents the substance of the deceased, and that the pure Brahmans who attend the feast which follows the rite through which the deceased is reborn as an ancestor are again said to partake of the dead man. Finally, some of the textual sources relate how the body which he now acquires and through which he experiences the joys of heaven or the torments of hell is eaten by deformed and hideous demons before his soul is reincarnated on earth (O'Flaherty 1980b:17). In short, it would seem that each time the soul acquires a new body, the old one is 'eaten' – which is to say that it is consumed *and transformed* by the fires of digestion. Not only transformed, but also perhaps at certain points reincorporated, as for example when one of the *sapindikaran pinds* is consumed in order to produce a son.

Digestion, indigestion (*ajiran*) and constipation (*kabz*) strike the outsider as something of an obsession in Banarasi Brahman culture. Even the most prim of people may volunteer a graphic account of the state of their bowels in the course of a casual conversation. In the practice of Ayurvedic medicine, the vast majority of illnesses seem to be attributed to a malfunction of the digestive process (cf. Tabor 1981), and to the consumption of impure or stale (*basi*) food. The bowels should be evacuated first thing in the morning before consuming any food, and the need to do so at any other time of the day is commented on with concern tinged with disapproval. This distate seems to stem above all from the idea of mixing fresh food with food which has lain rotting in the stomach.

Whether gifts, knowledge or food, that which is retained rots, festers and corrupts the body; and here it is clearly the digestion of food which provides the root metaphor. Irregular exchange at the level of the social order is often represented and conceptualised in terms of a biological model of digestive malfunction. Bribes may be readily 'eaten', but, like *dan*, they are not so readily 'digested'; and as we have seen (pp. 122ff), one of the most persistently cited characteristics of money derived from such sources is that it cannot be productively invested. Like impure food which causes dysentery and which flows through the body without nourishment to it, such money passes through the hands of those who accept it without sustaining them or promoting their welfare. Most striking of all, however, is the way in which my informants would sometimes describe the likely death of a Brahman who fails to pass on in *dan* what he receives in *dan*. Such reprobates are apt to die vomiting excrement. A more revoltingly graphic image of improper circulation is hard to imagine.

What I am suggesting, then, is that physiological processes offer themselves as a 'model' for the more general concern with circulation and transformation. The crucial point about digestion is that it is a double process which distils the good and usable part of food out of the bad and unusable part. The first produces blood, semen and vigour in the body, while the second is expelled. I can put the matter no better than one of Cantlie's (1981:53) informants: '. . . you get butter only from the good portions of milk, not the impurities. Again when the milk is boiled, the impurities are burnt out and you get ghee. Blood is like ghee.' Or again in the words of the *Caraka Samhita*, one of the foremost texts on the theory and practice of Ayurvedic medicine, food which is subjected to the fire of digestion is

> converted into two kinds of substances within the body. These are: 1) the desirable or nourishing ones (*prasada*), which is called *rasa* (or organic sap) and 2) the impure ones or waste products (*mala*), which is called excrement or *kitta*.
> From the excrement (*kitta*) are formed the following: sweat, urine, faeces, *vayu*, *pitta*, *kapha*, the dirty things excreted through the eyes, ear, nose, mouth, hair follicles and genital organs . . .
> From the foods transformed into the nourishing substance are formed all the desirable body constituents like *rasa*, blood, flesh, fat, bone marrow, semen . . .
> (quoted in Chattopadhyaya 1977:78)

I once spent some hours at a shrine where an initiate exorcist was undergoing possession. The purpose was to bring the evil spirits who possessed him under control and to convert them into helpful and beneficent tutelaries. The deity of the shrine (Bhut Nath Bhairav) would 'digest' these spirits, I was told, enabling the initiate to retain the good while he absorbed the evil. It was his bowels which would separate the benevolent from the bad.

In the same kind of way, I argue, the digestive process provides an analogy for what should happen at death. By eating the deceased, the impure waste – his sins – are expelled, while his pure essence is distilled and in some sense perhaps retained by the social body. But given that he is translated by the digestive fires to another world, in *what* sense is he retained? Just as the good part of food is refined into semen or uterine blood, the source of life, so the properly recycled ancestor becomes the source of progeny and sustenance. What the rites have distilled can now nourish the living.

6.7 On the impurity of death

That death occasions severe impurity is clear enough. But why it should do so, the kind of pollution it causes, the way in which the regime of mourning helps to eliminate that pollution, and the range of people who are effected by it, are all far less straightforward matters.

In his study of the Coorgs, Srinivas (1965:104) postulated a basic continuity between the concept of purity as it relates 'to permanent features of the social structure like caste' and as it occurs 'in certain non-structural contexts' (like death). Dumont went further. The impurity of the Untouchable and the impurity of birth, death or menstruation are of the same kind (1959:18–9). 'Ancient literature confirms that temporary and permanent impurity are *identical in nature*' (1970a:47, emphasis added).

In reaction to this, Das (1982:148) has expressed her 'discomfort at identifying these as constituting a single type', and has suggested that 'the existence of many lexical items to express different types of impurity points to the need for examining them separately in the first instance'. The thrust of her general argument, however, suggests something far stronger. In essence, the opposition between purity and pollution is a specific cultural idiom for a more general opposition between incorporation and marginality. 'The rules of impurity basically serve as a metaphor for liminality' (1976:252). Pollution is occasioned by birth and death because the new-born and the deceased are marginal to the ordered categories; because the social world is experienced as being 'disarticulated' from the cosmic order. Caste impurity, which does not readily fit such a model, is held to be something distinct – as is indicated by the distinct terms which are used to describe it.

In the abstract, my Banarasi *Brahman* informants were disposed (perhaps predisposed) to endorse this conclusion with enthusiasm. *Sutak* is a generic term for states of temporary impurity: for the cosmic pollution caused by an eclipse, and for the pollution of birth, menstruation and death. It is of an entirely different order, I was repeatedly told, from caste pollution. There is a *yonigat bhed* – 'a species difference' – between them. While it is true that even a Brahman chief mourner becomes temporarily untouchable, this does not for the time make him anything like a Leather-worker. Though both might be described as *ashuddh*, one could not possibly say that the disability of the Leather-worker stemmed from the *sutak* of his caste.

But life is complicated. The Mahabrahmans regularly attribute the degraded status of their caste to the fact that they participate in the death pollution of their patrons by virtue of representing the ghosts of the moribund (pp. 75ff); and it is an inescapable fact that his caste-fellows' contact with the chief mourner is restricted in very much the same way as their contact with persons of inferior caste. When I pointed this out, and naïvely insisted on being told *why* the two types of impurity should be regarded as different, conversation invariably collapsed in mutual incomprehension and frustration.

What did emerge from these interrogations, however, is that there is also 'a night and day difference' between the *sutak* of birth and death. Someone who is suffering from birth pollution cannot eat with, or even touch, a caste fellow afflicted by *maran ashauch* (the impurity of death). It is *not* as though the two types of impurity put them on a par. Birth pollution is commonly distinguished as *vriddhi sutak* – 'the *sutak* of increase'. The obvious reference to the increase of the family does not appear to be the only one. I was several times told that while death pollution diminishes day by day, the impurity of birth increases until it is finally spent. Birth pollution does not involve a literal untouchability, does not afflict kin belonging to different households, and – apart from mother and child – the only disability it imposes on those who are affected concerns the worship of the gods. The reason given for its lesser severity is that merit (*punya*) is generated by the event which brings it about. Death pollution, by contrast, is also known as *patak* – a word which the dictionaries gloss as 'sin' or 'misdeed'.

On the other hand, both these 'types' of impurity are not only kinds of *sutak*, but both are also brought about by the – one might say purposeful, even violent – separation of bodies (cf. Inden and Nicholas 1977:102–3). Death pollution is triggered at the point at which the vital breath evacuates the body, which, according to one theory at least (pp. 180ff), is the point at which the chief mourner cracks open the cranium as the corpse lies burning on the pyre. Birth pollution is triggered by cutting the umbilical cord.

The reasonable, if anondyne, conclusion seems to be that there are both differences and similarities between the permanent impurity of caste and the temporary impurity of *sutak*, and also within this category between the pollution of birth and death. Neither 'identical in nature', nor is there a clear-cut distinction between them. We are dealing with 'fuzzy concepts' that overlap in complex ways, and the search for definitive meanings – of the sort that impurity is 'really' a matter of liminality – seems to be misguided. Misguided, as I have argued elsewhere (Parry 1991), because many everyday concepts do not have firm edges and fixed lexicon-like meanings such that it is possible to specifiy any one set of defining features shared by all of its instances (Aitchison 1987:45; cf. Smith 1988). While it is perhaps plausible to suggest that the *sutak* of death is a way of speaking about a 'disarticulation' between the social and cosmic orders, it is rather less easy to see how this applies to menstrual pollution. Rather than sharing a set of defining features, different instances of impurity are more probably characterised only by the 'family resemblances' between them, and we should rather ask ourselves Wittgenstein's (1958:66–7) question about 'the proceedings we call "games". I mean board-games, card-games, ball-games, Olympic games, and so on. What is common to them all?' The answer, of course, is that there is no common factor, and that the category consists only of 'a complicated network of similarities overlapping and criss-crossing'.

If the relationship between different 'types' of pollution is hard to pin down, it is no easier to specify why death is supposed to cause it, or how the regime of mourning helps to get rid of it. The corpse itself is often represented as a major source of impurity, and I have been told that merely by touching it three days of *sutak* 'become attached'. The problem, however, is that if cremation is a sacrifice, how can the offering be so unworthy? The solution is to deny the difficulty. The corpse is an object of great sacredness. So from where on this theory does pollution derive? From 'the sin of burning the body hairs' and the violence perpetrated on the deceased at the rite of *kapal kriya*. I once encountered a party of mourners at Manikarnika *ghat* who had come with the corpse of a Rajput neighbour who had fallen on hard times and had died without an heir. The body was immersed in the river, and when I enquired why I was told that there was nobody ready to accept 'the fault of burning'. Consistent with all this is the fact that at the time of lighting the pyre the chief mourner should pray to be forgiven for the sin he is committing, that it is he who will suffer the most intense pollution, and that it is often claimed that no pollution is incurred until the corpse (or its effigy) is cremated (p. 181). If there is no cremation, there is no impurity.

According to a third discourse, however, the pollution of death afflicts the survivors by virtue of the body particles they share with the deceased, and regardless of whether they had any contact with the corpse or how it was disposed of. The contagion of death seeps as it were along the arteries of bodily connection. These shared body particles are to some extent given by birth, but are also sustained or created by food. It is almost as if they remain inert unless activated by feeding, for only the mother observes death pollution for a child who dies before it has eaten its first grains, or – as some people put it – before it has cut teeth with which to masticate. Moreover, the parents of a married daughter are only afflicted by birth pollution if her child is delivered in their own home while 'she is eating their grains'. 'They catch it', my informants say, 'from eating and drinking.'

The theory that death pollution is a consequence of 'the sin of burning the body hairs' is all of a piece with the view that the regime of mourning is essentially a regime of atonement in which 'the one who gave fire' plays the part of principal penitent. But more than expiation, my informants also describe it as a kind of austerity. As Dumont (1971a) and Das (1982:126) have both noticed, the chief mourner is required to resemble an ascetic. This Das interprets in terms of the liminality of both statuses. But there is, I think, more to it than that. It is by taking on the role of the ascetic that the chief mourner is able to accomplish his purpose. As Sita Maharaj explained, 'power (*shakti*) comes from his renunciation (*tyag*) and austerities (*tapasya*) and it is by means of this power that the (ghost's) body is constructed'. Not so much a passive submission to pollution, mourning is a positive programme of control that enables the *karta*, or 'doer', to do what a man has to do: give birth to his father. It is wholly appropriate then that the Coorgs should use 'the Vedic word denoting ascetic observances preliminary to sacrifice . . . for mourning, and even death pollution' (Dumont 1959).

As other informants represent it, it is the role of the *brahmcharya* – rather than that of the ascetic – that the chief mourner really assumes. *Brahmcharya* is the first of the four *ashrams*, the four theoretical stages of the male life-cycle – the stage of celibate studentship. Since it is only at the turban-tying rite which follows *sapindikaran* that a man finally achieves full adulthood, it seems symbolically appropriate that in the preceding sequence he should be seen as submitting himself to the preparatory discipline of *brahmcharya*. It is also perhaps significant that according to textual sources the celibate student has a greater immunity from the pollution of death than those in the 'householder' stage (Orenstein 1968:120).

The purpose of mourning is also explained as 'a demonstration of sorrow' (*shok pradarshan*), and as a kind of quarantine imposed by pollution. With time this pollution seems to dwindle of its own accord. But there is also possibly some idea that the regime of mourning actively reduces it. By becoming a temporary renouncer, the chief mourner weakens the ties of connectedness which bind him to the world of social relationships. His asceticism, in other words, may be construed as diminishing the consubstantiality he shares with the deceased. No salt should be added to the food which he eats for the *pret*. To accept someone's salt is to accept that one is bound to them.

The idea that degrees of bodily connectedness determine the degree of death pollution, and hence the duration of mourning, is at any rate central to both textual and popular theory. Stated baldly, and building largely on Orenstein (1970a),[21] I believe that the elaborate rules about the duration of mourning laid down in the *Shastrik* texts are informed by three consistent principles. The first is that people of lesser purity and spiritual power are *more* closely bound to each other (and therefore more polluted by the death of one of their connections) than their betters. The second is that if there is a difference in status between them, the inferior connection is almost invariably represented as being more closely bound to the superior than the latter is to him. The inferior is therefore more polluted by the death of a superior than the other way about. The rider to this – and the third principle – is that bodily connectedness is not immutably given at birth, but can be diminished, enhanced or even created by one's actions (cf. Mines 1989).

Consistent with the first principle is the much quoted formula that Brahmans are liberated from death pollution after only ten days, Kshatriyas after twelve, Vaishyas after fifteen and Shudras after thirty – as shown in bold on Table 9 which is reproduced from Mines. The purer and more knowledgeable the Brahman, the less pollution he suffers. According to some texts, for

Table 9. *The duration of mourning for connections of different* varna *(after Mines, 1989)*

| | | Varna of survivor | | | |
		Brahman	Kshatriya	Vaishya	Shudra
	Brahman	**10**	10	10	10
Varna	Kshatriya	6	**12**	12	12
of	Vaishya	3	6	**15**	15
deceased	Shudra	1	3	6	**30**

example, a Brahman who knows the Vedas and keeps the sacred fire is polluted by birth and death for only a single day; one who is learned in the Vedas but does not keep the sacred fire is polluted for three days, while one without either qualification is impure for the full ten days (Orenstein 1968:118). Again, somebody who is engaged in an important ritual and who is in a state of exceptionally heightened sacredness is impervious to the pollution of birth and death (Orenstein 1970b:26).

Consistent with the second principle is the ruling that – assuming hypergamous unions between members of different *varnas* – a person of lower *varna* mourns for a *sapinda* relative of higher *varna* for considerably longer than the latter mourns for him. The facts are again recorded in Table 9. A Shudra is enjoined to mourn for a Brahman kinsman for ten days, a Kshatriya kinsman for twelve and a Vaishya for fifteen – as though he were himself a member of the *varna* of the deceased. But on *his* death, the Brahman relative is polluted for only one day, the Kshatriya for three and the Vaishya for six. Though it is true that the pollution incurred on the death of *any* relative of different *varna* is less than that one incurs for a member of one's own, the difference between, as it were, looking upwards and downwards, is obvious. The lower is more closely connected to the higher than the higher is to him. Echoes of this principle sound throughout the contemporary ethnographic record: the death of a really important person commonly occasions a more lengthy period of mourning; and – with the exception of a husband mourning his wife – a senior may not be expected to mourn for juniors with the same intensity as the latter must do for him (e.g. Srinivas 1965:110–12; Parry 1979:141–2).

The third principle (as also the second) is illustrated by the ruling that the death of a *nirguna* Brahman – a Brahman without learning or piety – occasions only three nights' pollution, instead of the standard ten (Orenstein 1970a). It is as if his fallen state has eroded and enfeebled the bond of consubstantiality which connects him with his more fastidious kinsmen, and his death is consequently of lesser moment to them. Those who have been outcasted are not of course mourned at all. Nor, according to many texts, does a 'bad death' pollute the survivors (Pandey 1969:273; Orenstein 1970b:32), such a death being testimony to the bad karma of its victim, and thus of the distance which separates him from his more worthy relatives.

While these instances suggest that bio-genetic relatedness may be attenuated by behaviour, the rules regarding children are consistent with the premise that it may increase over time. The death of a small child occasions little or no impurity; and children themselves seem to be little affected by the death of a kinsman. In contemporary Banaras, for example, a Brahman boy who has yet to acquire his sacred thread is not generally required to be tonsured at the purification rites of the tenth day. His own death occasions only a restricted (three-day) period of incapacity, as does that of an unmarried daughter. It is as if growing up involves growing into relationships of shared substance. Nurtured by their food, refined and perfected through ritual, bodily connections with one's kin are as much a potential to be realised as an immutable fact of nature. It is perhaps in this light that we should understand my informants' otherwise somewhat puzzling claim that – by contrast with death pollution – the impurity of birth increases up to the point at which it is finally terminated. As the baby is slowly incorporated within the social world, it becomes more closely related to others, and hence more capable of polluting (and being polluted by) them. In this context it is surely significant that of the four *ashrams*, it is only the 'householder' who incurs the full period of incapacity (Orenstein 1968; 1970a:1363). It is during this stage of one's life that one is most fully involved in the world of interdependence and relationship.

Birth into a specific group is not therefore a sufficient, nor even perhaps a necessary, condition for shared bodily relationships. That it is not a sufficient condition is suggested by the fact that a man is *not* polluted by the death of his infant son or daughter, who from the point of view of the requirements of mourning is treated almost as a stranger. That it is not a necessary condition is suggested by the fact that one is enjoined to mourn for various superiors with whom there is no question of a kinship connection given by birth. Thus a student incurs pollution on the death of his *guru*, a servant on the death of his master (Srinivas 1965:41) and a subject on the death of his king – though the converse does not apply (Mines 1989).

According to Dumont (1959:35), 'the interdependence of high and low is not only observable in behaviour; it is also interiorized as the fundamental belief'. As I see it, however, the crucial lesson to be learned from all this is at some variance with Dumont's statement. The lower acknowledges – even asserts – its solidarity and interdependence with its superiors; but the latter as far as possible dissociate themselves from their inferiors and pretend to a phantasmagorical independence from them. Connections of inferior status are related to the higher to an extent that the higher are not related to them. Superiority is autonomy from the world of 'gross' substance. Here it is clearly the renouncer who stands for the ideal (and he of course is completely immune to the pollution of death). The pattern is one we have encountered before (pp. 152ff) – and will encounter again (pp. 245ff). What the uncontrolled grief expected of women reveals, I have argued, is their bondage to the ephemeral world of bodily connectedness and social relationships, and hence their inferiority to men.

But all this poses a problem. 'There is little doubt', writes Orenstein (1970a:1365), 'that the *shastris* considered women to be less pure than men' and that women 'were believed to be more intimately involved with life processes . . .'. We would therefore expect a woman to be more polluted by the death of a male kinsman than a man by that of a female. This is not, however, the case. How are we to account for this paradoxical fact? Orenstein's own solution is, I think, plausible: 'the code-writers were forced to conceive of women as having unattenuated kinship ties to their kinsmen, for . . . it is through their bodies that caste purity is maintained' (p. 1366). Following Mines (1989:126) one could also perhaps say that transactions create substance, that 'spouses are the most intimate and intensive . . . of mutual transactors', and that the ideology therefore demands that they should be treated identically.[22] Any differentiation would at any rate undermine the dogma that at marriage they are made 'one flesh' and that a wife is her husband's *adhangani* – is 'one half of his body'. Repressed for these reasons in relation to the duration of mourning, it is as if gender hierarchy must be vigorously reasserted in the way in which sorrow is expressed – this 'proving' that women are after all more bound to the manifest world.

As to *who* is polluted by death, the normative case is provided by the demise of a householder when the surviving connections are equal in status to the deceased. If these conditions are met, the full rigours of mourning are conventionally enjoined on all *agnates* who share a common ancestor not more than seven generations removed – that is, on all those descended in the male line from the great-grandfather of the great-grandfather. In this context, then, the *sapinda* group is an essentially agnatic unit. Maternal relatives are subject only to minor – and non-obligatory – mourning of shorter duration (Dumont 1983:7).

In contemporary Banaras there is much uncertainty, even at the level of the rules, over the range of kin who are rendered impure. According to one formula, those who share, in the male line, a common ancestor with the deceased not more than seven generations removed are impure for the full ten days, while those who share a common ancestor between seven and fourteen generations removed are polluted for three nights. According to another, which derives from the *Garuda Purana*, the duration of impurity decreases by steps with genealogical distance up to the tenth generation, when one is purified merely by taking a bath. In this scheme it is only those who share a common great-grandfather who incur the full period of incapacity. In my experience, it is in fact this limited range of agnates who would normally be those who are tonsured on the tenth day. Beyond it the observance of any degree of mourning is largely a matter of individual inclination and the importance of the deceased. In the maternal line, few people would regard themselves as affected by the death of a relative more remote than the mother's brother or maternal grandparents, and for them only three days of impurity is admitted. The same degree of mourning is observed for a married daughter and her children. What is more, affinal kin (both immediate wife-givers and receivers) are sometimes included – the husband of a sister or daughter, for example, and the brother and parents of a wife.

While most of this is broadly consistent with the rules laid down in the texts, other *Shastrik* prescriptions have only a tenuous relationship to present-day practice. Though my priestly informants regularly invoke the theory that members of different *varnas* are polluted for different numbers of days, all castes regard themselves as more or less pure after the tenth. I say 'more or less' because higher castes do not perform 'the work of the gods' until after *sapindikaran*. Amongst the low castes, however, all the restrictions of mourning terminate on the tenth day. In this instance at least, the theory which holds that the low are more polluted by death than the high is thus subverted by practice.

The *theory* itself is, however, very much present; and the basic premise which underlies it appears in the form of juniors following a more stringent regime of mourning for their seniors that the latter observe for them, and in the tendency for persons of superior quality to be treated as if they suffer less pollution as survivors and cause more on their deaths. Disciples mourn their *guru*, but he does not mourn for them. The fundemental asymmetry in the relationship between higher and lower which we find in the texts thus leaves its mark on present-day practice. But as I hope to show in the next chapter, this asymmetry emerges even more clearly in the ideas and practices surrounding possession by the spirits of those who have died a 'bad death'.

Plate 9 Over the ten days following cremation, the chief mourner offers water into the water-pot dwelling of the ghost in order 'to cool it down'. (Photograph by Margaret Dickinson.)

Plate 10 *Vrishotsarg* (literally, 'bull sacrifice') is performed on the eleventh day after death to help the deceased's soul on its journey to the 'Abode of the Ancestors'. It must cross the terrifying Vaiturni river, flowing with blood and other foul substances. The chief mourner (pictured here) holds onto the Funeral-priest who in turn holds onto the tail of a calf given at the ritual. Together they cross the Vaiturni, represented by a trench filled with water and red powder. (Author's photograph.)

Plate 11 A chief mourner prepares the sixteen rice-ball offerings which sustain the deceased on his year-long journey to the 'Abode of the Ancestors'. (Author's photograph.)

Plate 12 A Marwari chief mourner (with tonsured head), his household priest and the family Barber (in background) at the *sapindikaran* ritual held on the twelfth day after death. At the bottom of the picture is the elongated *pind* rice-ball that represents the body of the ghost, and the three round rice-balls which represent his three immediate lineal ascendants. The chief mourner will cut the ghost's 'body' into three parts and merge them with the *pind*-bodies of the three ancestors. (Author's photograph.)

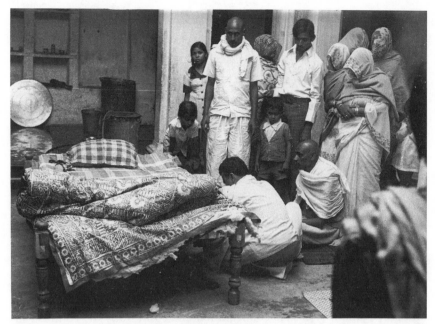

Plate 13 Part of the gift of *sajja dan* to be given to the Marwari chief mourner's household priest on the twelfth day. (Author's photograph.)

Plate 14 Recognising the heirs. The Marwari chief mourner has had a turban tied in recognition of his succession as household head, and all three brothers have been given caps by their mother's brother. (Author's photograph.)

7

Spirit possession as 'superstition'

7.1 Propositions

Those who die a 'good death' are cremated. Cremation, as we have seen, is a sacrificial ritual which not only results in the rebirth of the sacrifier but is also a more generalised source of life and fertility, even of cosmic renewal. As a consequence the mortuary rites are replete with the symbolism of parturition and propagation, of cosmic conflagration and cosmogony. By contrast, the corpses of those who die a 'bad death' are, in theory at least, immersed and such deaths are apt to result in a *blockage* of biological and material reproduction. This last finding emerges most clearly from case material on misfortunes attributed to the ghosts of those whose deaths were 'untimely'.

While the principal focus of the previous two chapters has been on the world of Brahmanical ritual, much of the data on spirit possession presented in this chapter relates to beliefs and practices which are not considered to be scripturally sanctioned, and which the public rhetoric of the Brahmans is prone to disparage. In line with the argument with which I concluded the last chapter, its central analytical claim is that while the inferior cult of the exorcist acknowledges its dependence on the superior cult of the Brahman priest, the latter lays claim to a complete autonomy from the former.

More precisely, I argue that the data on spirit affliction supports four related propositions. The first is that, so far from constituting a kind of resistance on the mystical plane to the oppression and subordination experienced by the socially disadvantaged, as I. M. Lewis (1971) has suggested, what is most striking about the spirit possession I encountered is the way in which it reproduces and legitimates hierarchy (cf. Prakash 1986). Secondly, inferiority in this hierarchy is represented – *pace* Dumont (1970a) – as being based as much on ignorance and superstition as on impurity.

My third claim relates to the question of 'levels' in Hinduism. For writers like Srinivas (1965) and Marriott (1955), 'popular' Hinduism is best seen as a syncretistic amalgam of elements culled from two distinct (if not in practice entirely separate) traditions – 'great' and 'little', 'Sanskritic' and 'non-Sanskritic'. Hinduism on the ground should be understood in terms of the interpenetration of these two levels. This general approach was severely criticised by Dumont and Pocock (1959) who argued that it deals only with isolated and disembodied elements rather than with the relations between them, and that the sociologist's first task is to look at how the elements fit together to form a coherent system of meaning. Dumont's fundamental proposition was that the same structural relations are reiterated at both the textual and the popular level which therefore constitute homologous or isomorphic structures, related as the 'general idea and the local working out of that idea' (Dumont and Pocock 1957:25). Moreover, the fundamental principle which underlies the social order also organises the religious sphere. Just as there can be no pure castes without impure ones, so it is with deities. We are in a structural world where everything exists only in relation to its opposite. Hence the worship of impure deities does not constitute a lower or separate 'level' or 'tradition' of Hinduism which has somehow yet to be assimilated to a more universal or Sanskritic mainstream. It is rather an inescapable corollary of the worship of pure deities. Hinduism on the ground is not conceptually separable into different elements; nor for the villagers themselves are there two traditions but simply one, say Dumont and Pocock (1957:40) in criticism of Marriott who implies otherwise; 'the idea of two levels is an invention of the anthropologist', Tambiah (1970:371) confidently concludes.

Too confidently, I believe, for my informants make a crucial distinction between those beliefs and practices which they consider to be *shastrik* and those which they consider to be *laukik* – roughly a distinction between that which is textually sanctioned and that which is not (pp. 193–4). The *shastrik* elements are *pramanik* ('proven') and unquestionably authoritative, and in their interpretation the Brahman is pre-eminent. By contrast, the *laukik* is ephemeral, a mere matter of local usage to be discarded if it offends against contemporary canons of good sense. Disputes over the propriety of this or that ritual practice invariably revolve around the question of whether it is *shastric* or *laukik* and, though there is much disagreement on what belongs to which category, the distinction itself is not in question and has great ideological salience (cf. pp. 46ff). In my experience, then, the religious universe *is* widely visualised as being composed of elements taken from two conceptually separable traditions. Further, and as I hope to demonstrate here, the beliefs and practices which are held to belong to the lower level are open to a good deal of sceptical scrutiny and may even be dismissed as 'mere superstition'.

I claim therefore that, seen from the *participants'* point of view, the facts are on Marriott's side: we are *not* dealing with a seamless whole. But what my data also suggest is that Dumont's insistence on a degree of homogeneity between the two levels is *objectively* correct. Though the superior castes may not recognise – or wish to acknowledge – that the 'non-Sanskritic' rites of the lower orders are merely a variation on a more distinguished and prestigious Sanskritic theme (Dumont and Pocock 1959:45), in the case I discuss this is clearly so. My third proposition, then, is that the question of whether the different 'levels' in Hinduism represent different 'traditions' (in the manner of Marriott), or constitute homologous structures and the local working out of a general idea (in the manner of Dumont), is at least partly a matter of perspective – theirs and ours, participants' and observers'.

In anthropology the distinction between 'religion' and 'superstition' went out with the dodo – for which we might be entitled to breathe a deep sigh of relief were it not for the fact that for our informants it is often alive and well. Modern scholarly squeamishness has tended to obscure this crucial sociological fact. I have to admit, however, that my claim that much of what I describe is liable to be derided as 'sheer superstition' by the higher castes is at some variance with the conventional wisdom which denies that 'traditional' Hinduism has any such notion (e.g. Chaudhuri 1979:19), and which emphasises the tolerant catholicism of the Hindu world view where the beliefs and practices of others are accepted as valid, if inferior (e.g. Pocock 1973). I must also admit that I am far from confident that the English word 'superstition' can be precisely matched by any equivalent term from the traditional Hindu lexicon. In modern Hindi a reasonable approximation would be *andhvisvas* – literally 'blind faith'; but this is a nineteenth century neologism which was originally used to impugn the importance and morality of what it described, but not its existence. It was only subsequently that the word acquired this additional sense (Bharati 1970).

Despite these difficulties I believe that the notion of 'superstition' – both in its older sense of something which is opposed to religion by its excess and lack of authoritative textual sanction (Belmont 1982), and in its modern sense of something which has no reality – does convey the attitude which the Brahmans widely purport to hold towards spirit possession. If this is right, then some important consequences follow for our understanding of Hindu ideology – and this brings me to my fourth proposition in which I align myself with Fuller (1988). For Dumont and Pocock the relationship between the so-called 'pure' and 'impure' cults is one of complementarity and symbiosis. This is true, but only partially so, for there is a significant asymmetry here. The inferior cult places itself in a relationship of hierarchical complementarity to the superior cult, as these writers suppose and as I will show. But at the same time the superior cult repudiates the beliefs and practices of the inferior as 'mere superstition', allowing its practitioners to construct in ritual a world in which they are no longer dependent on their inferiors. Once more, the lower recognises its dependence on the higher, but not vice versa, as is consistent with the autonomous ideal of the ascetic with which the Brahman has been forced to align himself (Heesterman 1985).

7.2 Ghosts, victims and exorcists

Though the purpose of the mortuary rites is to convert a marginal and malevolent ghost into a benevolent ancestor, those who died a 'bad death' are unlikely to make this transition easily. For their salvation the Sanskritic tradition prescribes the supplementary rite of *Narayani bali* (pp. 200ff), but this is held to be particularly difficult to perform, and its efficacy is often impaired by the inadequacy of its execution or by the sheer burden of bad karma accumulated by the deceased. In any event those who die a 'bad death' are liable to get stuck in the limbo of *pret*-hood on a long-term basis – maybe 30,000 years in a tough case. Not surprisingly such spirits are apt to draw attention to their miserable lot by molesting the living in the hope of coercing them to take measures to alleviate their plight.

Ghosts and ancestors are in many ways opposed. By liberating the latter from their 'ghostly condition' (*pret-yoni*) and helping them to attain a 'good state' after death, the living win the blessings of the ancestors by which they confer material prosperity and – above all – the increase of their descent line. The ancestors, then, are persistently associated with the material and biological reproduction of those they have left behind. Ghostly affliction, by contrast, represents an equally persistent *threat* to reproduction, for the commonest symptoms of possession are barrenness, miscarriages, still-births, the death of infants and the fact that although the family earns well the money can never be put to productive use and never yields sufficiency. In thirty-two of the seventy-one cases for which I have adequate information, the principal reason cited for seeking the help of an exorcist was a problem of this order. Given this close association between ghosts and gynaecological problems it is entirely appropriate that the city's sacred tank of Pishach Mochan, to which many victims resort in order to rid themselves finally of unwanted ghosts, is also the site of a major fair at which women bathe in order to cure their infertility.[1]

A second contrast between ghosts and ancestors is that, as far as the ancestors go, none of my informants was inclined to question their existence or their capacity to intervene in the affairs of their descendants. Yet paradoxically, actual good fortune is rather rarely explained in terms of their intervention. There is nothing theoretical, however, about the *mis*fortunes attributed to ghosts and many people devote considerable material resources to appeasing them. Yet ghostly possession and propitiation are widely viewed with frank scepticism, and of the whole battery of possible causes of present suffering (bad *karma*, inauspicious astrological conjunctions, the anger of the deities and so on), diagnoses in terms of spirit affliction are the most open to dispute. Nor are misgivings confined to the matter of whether this or that victim is really possessed or is merely shamming, for some informants rate all exorcists as charlatans, claim that ghosts do not really possess the living and dismiss the whole phenomenon as *dhong* ('deceit' or 'trickery'), *kapol-kalpit* ('fabricated') or *banavati* ('made up'). Such scepticism is most commonly and stridently expressed by the men of the highest castes, though it cannot be said that they have a complete monopoly on doubt (cf. Cohn 1954:242). For my benefit at least, even some of the exorcists themselves acknowledged or affected a profound cynicism, referring to their exorcisms as 'hocus-pocus' (*prapanch*) or as 'merely a way of making a living' (*keval khana kamane ka dhang*). So while the vast majority of my informants gave me the impression of being basically secure in their convictions about the nature of the gods and ancestors and the proper means of approaching them, in the case of ghosts there is far less confidence.

The relative immunity from scepticism which the ancestors enjoy is, of course, partly explained by the fact that it is hard to gainsay an assertion about the ultimate source of good fortune and few would wish to do so; whereas there is far greater scope for the development of doubt when specific misfortunes are attributed to a specified ghost, and when the affliction persists despite the appropriate propitiation. Practical reason may also promote scepticism, for when an affliction is put down to a ghost belonging to another household within the community there is likely to be a good deal of pressure on that household to bear a substantial share of the not inconsiderable costs of the exorcism, and their pecuniary interests clearly encourage them to voice their doubts publicly. Even more important, however, is that spirit possession is – as we shall see – a predominantly low-caste malady, and one which is particularly likely to afflict low-caste *rural women*; and that the curative rituals they undergo are *not* considered to be authenticated by the Sanskritic tradition. Unsanctioned by Brahmanical authority, the whole phenomenon is for a significant minority a matter of mere superstition: an aberration of credulous yokels, hysterical exhibitionist females and cynical imposters – at least, that is, until misfortune strikes.

Though nobody can list them all, it is conventionally said that there are sixty-four varieties of *bhut-pret* (the generic term for malevolent ghosts), just as there are sixty-four sorts of bad death. These different kinds of ghosts have different characteristics, are the products of different kinds of 'bad death' or are the spirits of different kinds of people, and need to be handled in different ways. An *akash kamini* (literally, 'a lustful woman of the sky'), for example, is said to be the spirit of a woman of Acrobat caste (Nat) who had met her death by falling off a tight-rope (cf. Crooke 1926:142). Amongst female ghosts, however, the most abundant are the *bhavani* (the spirits of young virgins), *churail* (the spirits of barren women, or of those who have died in pregnancy or childbirth) and the *mari* (widely described as a specifically Untouchable and unusually malicious variant). Such ghosts are especially likely to cause gynaecological problems and are often credited with 'binding up' the fertility of women or causing miscarriages. They tend, as a consequence, to be accompanied by one or more *marua* – the spirits of the young children and aborted foetuses they have destroyed.

In fact, not all spirits are unambiguously evil. Those who died a violent death in a just cause become *birs* (or *daityas*), and some *birs* act as the *dih* or guardian of a village or city neighbourhood, and control the activities of lesser spirits within that territory. Their aid may therefore be invoked in the course of exorcism. They do not, however, have jurisdiction over Muslim spirits; and here the exorcist (whatever his religion) will enlist the help of a Muslim *Sayyad*, or of one of the *Panchon pir* ('the five Islamic saints').

This catalogue of spirits could go on and on; but I shall content myself with referring briefly to two other particularly prominent varieties. The first is that of an Untouchable Leather-worker – a Chamar – who dies bearing a grudge for ill-treatment received at the hands of a caste superior. The oppressor, or his progeny, then suffers from *Chamar dosh* (the 'fault' or 'sin' of the Chamar) and is afflicted by the deceased who can only be called off through the intercession of the Leather-workers' deity (Chamar *devata*). The crucial point is that this entails offerings on the victim's behalf which *must* be made by a living Chamar, who charges handsomely for a service held to be rendered only at grave personal risk.

Now it certainly seems that the notion of *Chamar dosh* conforms with the thesis that spirit possession is really an oblique aggressive strategy by which the weak and the exploited get back at those who oppress them. But in fact this conclusion should not be drawn too easily – partly because everybody recognises that the most likely oppressors are the least likely victims of malevolent possession, but mainly because the importance of such ideas pales almost into insignificance when compared to the prominence of certain other ideas about ghosts which appear to uphold the hierarchical order.

The *brahm*, for example, is the vengeful spirit of a Brahman who has died a bad death; the more ritually fastidious he was in life, the more powerful and dangerous his ghost. One who died in a state of resentment over some misappropriation of his property is especially dangerous, and cases in which the victim's family suffers on account of some debt outstanding to a Brahman at the time of his death are common. The most ferocious *brahms* of all are the spirits of those who fasted to death in revenge for some offence against them. *Brahms* are one of the commonest sources of ghostly affliction, and are probably the most dangerous – left to run rampant they will decimate a whole descent line in a matter of months. Some say that they can never be induced to leave until they have finished the job; others that although they cannot be successfully dealt with by a low-caste exorcist, a *panda* or tantrik can cause such a spirit 'to sit down'. Consistent with the non-violence appropriate to a Brahman it is sometimes claimed that the *brahm* does not himself kill or maim his victims, but merely issues orders for the other spirits who constitute his retinue to do so. He is at any rate a pure vegetarian and does not accept alcoholic libations. He should be presented with wooden sandals (for the strictest Brahmans refuse to wear leather shoes), an ascetic's water-pot (*kamandal*), a sacred thread, a *dhoti*, and other offerings appropriate to his caste status; and should theoretically be honoured with fire sacrifices and the repetition of *mantras*. *Brahms* are often pacified by providing them with a stone image in which to reside. Many of these are installed along the *Panch-kosi* pilgrimage route during 'the fortnight of the ancestors', when in subsequent years offerings of Ganges water and uncooked rice will be made to them.

It might, I recognise, be argued that the extraordinary malevolence and power attributed to such spirits is an expression of the resentment which the lower castes feel towards their hierarchical superiors. But it is surely clear that such notions can only serve to entrench Brahmanical authority, rather than redressing in some measure the balance of power. Given that Bhumihar Brahmans are the dominant caste in a great many villages of this region, ideas about their capacity to exact even a posthumous vengeance must presumably lend some support to their ability to command their subordinates.

As the retinue of the *brahm* and the infant cohort of the female *mari* suggests, ghosts tend to hunt in packs. 'One pret', people say, 'comes on top of another' – partly because one bad death in the family leads to another, and partly because ghosts congregate like vultures wherever there look to be pickings. As a result the majority of victims become the vehicle of more than one spirit. Four or five is by no means uncommon, and I have recorded up to eleven. In such a case the exorcist must correctly identify the 'root' (*jar*) – that is, the original instigator of the attack – before he can successfully treat the problem. This propensity for spirit affliction to emanate from several different sources at once provides scope for a certain amount of secondary elaboration which helps to protect the diagnosis from falsification. A treatment fails, not because the exorcist was incompetent or wrong, but because one of the subsidiary ghosts had managed to take cover and evade discovery.

Ghostly attack is closely associated with liminal states and times. Ghosts are particularly active between midnight and three in the morning, on *amavasya* days and during eclipses. There are three periods in the year which are associated with intensified activity towards the dead, and in particular towards those who have died a 'bad death': 'the fortnight of the ancestors' and the dark fortnights of *Paush* (Dec-Jan) and *Chaitra* (March-April). All three are in important respects periods of calendrical or seasonal transition. Eclipses and *amavasyas* which fall during these periods are doubly liminal and therefore doubly suitable for performing exorcism rituals.

Bhut-pret are repelled by iron, fire and bright lights. As Sita Maharaj observed without the slightest trace of irony, 'in the cities the ghosts have all run away from the electric lighting'. Conversely they are attracted towards certain substances – like cloves and cardamom – which therefore have a prominent role in exorcism rituals. But above all, evil spirits are strongly drawn towards blood, excrement, putrescent corpses and other forms of impurity. Pregant and menstruating women, mothers in labour and those who have recently given birth are particularly vulnerable – as is anybody who goes out at night to defecate in the open. It is all very well for the upper classes to scoff, I was told, but those with flush toilets are out of the firing line.

There is, of course, more to it than modern plumbing – the general point being that that the least pure are the most vulnerable. It is this, of course, which is held to account for the fact that the lower castes, and in particular their womenfolk, are the most prone to possession. My data suggests that in something of the order of 70 per cent of cases the principal victim is female, while in over 80 per cent of cases she or he belongs to one of the Untouchable or clean Shudra castes. Such susceptibility testifies not only to a lack of purity, but also to a lack of spiritual power – my male Brahman informants attributing their own relative immunity to the spiritual force they acquire through their performance of the daily rituals of *sandhya*,[2] and to their command of the *gayatri mantra*,[3] the recitation of which is enough to put any ghostly assailant to flight. What is more, it is only the high castes who perform the whole sequence of mortuary rites prescribed by the texts, and it is therefore such families who are least likely to spawn a ghost. The afflicted, then, are the victims of their own ignorance, carelessness and impurity; and their affliction only goes to prove their real worth.

As some of the sceptics would see it, the correct interpretation is rather different, though the general message remains the same. Possession is a manifestation of ignorance and superstition, an interpretation which confirms the enlightened in a conviction of their own superiority. Women are not only superstitious and ignorant but prone to hysteria, and are manipulative creatures given to duplicity and the 'sixteen arts'. A ghost gets them when they don't get their way – an insight reached independently of I. M. Lewis, and shared by at least some of women themselves.

> EXORCIST (interrogating ghost):'Who are you and why are you troubling this person?'
> GHOST:'I will not tell you.'
> EXORCIST:'I beg you. I touch your feet. Please let her alone. Big people give *sukh* [happiness] not *dukh* [trouble]. So why do you torment her?'
> GHOST: 'I will not go. I am not doing any harm. All her children are alright. They are all eating and earning. I have been here a long time. I did not come today.'
> WOMAN PASSER-BY (derisively): 'You take a stick to her and see if it does not go!'

Some of my informants, however, seemed to have anticipated Wilson (1967) rather than Lewis: spirit possession is as much about rivalry *between* women as it is about 'the war between the sexes'. That at least was how a close relative of the main protagonists interpreted the following case. When Vishvanath, a Joshi Brahman, remarried in Jaunpur after the death of his first wife, the latter's spirit began to afflict his new bride – a common enough pattern. A tantric was called in; but his cure proved short-lived and the ghost reappeared. At this point Vishvanath's elder brother's wife also started to get possessed, the second spirit announcing its identity as 'the goddess of the household' and declaring that the sister-in-law's possession was a fraud. A violent scene ensued between the two supernatural beings, this culminating with the one

which was afflicting Vishvanath's wife admitting personation and claiming
to be in reality the spirit (*jinn*) of a Muslim wrestler from Jaunpur. Since
ghosts regularly assume a false identity in order to evade capture, nobody
could be quite sure that this claim was as frivolous as the last had apparently
proved.

Given that ghosts of the opposite sex are commonly supposed to enjoy a
carnal relationship with their victims and to destroy all desire for their spouse,
it is clear that possession by the ilk of a beefy Muslim wrestler may be an
unconscious way in which a woman tells her husband something about his
marital performance. Since ghosts tend to afflict their own, a female victim
may even by implication be consorting with her husband's deceased father –
which would also be one in the eye for her mother-in-law. Following this line
of thought, we can speculate that here we perhaps have another reason why
the highest castes are so reluctant publicly to attribute misfortune to spirit
affliction. Even in a mystical form, adultery is not something they can
generally bring themselves to acknowledge. More generally, and by contrast
with the comparative restraint of most Brahmanical ritual and its discrete
suppression of the more unseemly details of the problem it addresses,
exorcism typically involves not only a loss of bodily and emotional control,
 but also a quite public laundering of the family's dirty linen: tales of domestic
violence, sexual inadequacy, murderous intentions and mystical revenge. At
least when it concerns one's own, high-caste respectability combines with
masculine pride to favour a decent reticence on such matters and a lofty
disdain towards rituals which expose them to the general gaze.

Moreover, their manipulative aspect is hard to miss. One day at Pishach
Mochan I encountered a young man in frenzied possession – a rare occurrence
at this stage of the treatment. He had come, along with his father's brother's
sons, to 'seat' the *brahm* which had been plaguing their family for years. This
was the ghost of an elderly Brahman whose land they had cultivated on
tenancy, and to which they had acquired title as a result of recent legislation.
Their subsequent affliction was their landlord's posthumous revenge. Now,
after many troubled years, the problem had been properly diagnosed and
apparently brought under control, and they had come to Banaras for the final
pacification of their tormentor. But what emerged from the young man's
sudden and unexpected possession was that the land in question was about to
be partitioned, that the possessed man was dissatisfied with his share, and that
the ghost refused to be 'seated' until the matter was equitably settled.

More generally, however, ghosts are likely to prove most troublesome to
their own family and lineage. The reason for this is that they want action to
alleviate their miserable lot, and it is their agnates who have an absolute duty
to perform the appropriate but costly rituals which this entails – as well as the
greatest pragmatic interest in doing so. Others are likely to call in an exorcist
merely to send the spirit elsewhere. As this suggests, stranger ghosts
sometimes prove to have been deliberately dispatched by an exorcist in the pay

of one's enemies. In the long run though, a ghost eventually returns to its source – its own lineage of origin.

More immediately, it is, as we have seen (pp. 128–9), common for ghosts to travel between affinally related households in the same direction as women and gifts, passing from wife-givers to wife-takers and then perhaps to *their* wife-takers. Sometimes it is said that they were sent out of pure malevolence; sometimes that they followed the affinal prestations of their own volition. In either event a history of spirit affliction in the family may prove a major obstacle in negotiating subsequent marriages; and this is one reason why the wife-givers are extremely reluctant to acknowledge any responsibility in the matter. Another is that they are expected to pay for the exorcism, take the ghost back and arrange for it to be expensively 'seated' at the sacred tank of Pishach Mochan or some other equivalent site. In the first instance, then, they are likely to repudiate the diagnosis as misconceived, or even as maliciously inspired. But if their affines persist in holding them responsible, they will employ their own exorcist to confirm the diagnosis, or even, it is alleged, to capture the offending spirit and hide it away so that the wife-takers will not be able to substantiate their charge when challenged to do so in the presence of arbitrators. My case histories suggest that quarrels between affines over the ghosts which are supposed to have passed between them rather commonly escalate to the point at which the two households refuse to have anything further to do with each other.

This idea that evil influences are transferred at marriage is often resoundingly validated by experience, since for many people marriage does indeed initiate a period of conflict and disruption within the domestic group as the interests of the newly formed conjugal family assert themselves against those of the joint household as a whole. It seems plausible, then, to see in these beliefs about spirit possession a recognition on a mystical plane of a common experience that is a product of the normal developmental cycle of the domestic group. It is also perhaps significant that these ghosts are said to attach themselves to the affinal prestations. Since the size of the gifts is a persistent source of bitter conflict between in-laws, it is not surprising that they should also be represented as a source of supernatural danger. Since they should flow asymmetrically from wife-givers to wife-receivers, we find once again (pp. 130ff) that a mystical menace surrounds exchanges which are inherently unbalanced.

'A *pret*-obstacle', as the aphorism has it, 'destroys sexual attraction (*rati*), affection (*priti*) and wealth (Lakshmi)'; though in fact any misfortune, however trivial, may be seen as evidence that one has been 'caught' by a ghost; and a series of concurrent ones is strong grounds for suspecting their mischief. 'In the low castes', my high-caste informants will say, 'even a headache is caused by the spirits.' Sometimes the *bhut-pret* will 'ride' with its victim, using him or her as a vehicle for making known its desires. Often, however, it will disguise its presence and remain mute for years. Possession does not therefore necessarily manifest itself in trance-like states of dissociation.

When it does so, the victim to whom the ghost has 'attached itself' (*lagna*) 'manifests possession' (*habuana*), 'plays' (*khelna*), 'sways to and fro' (*jhumna*) and 'becomes hyperactive' or 'feverish' (*harkat/hararat hona*). By contrast with these verb forms appropriate to involuntary and uncontrollable possession, 'the rider comes' (*svari ana*) to the exorcist who is master *of* – rather than being mastered *by* – evil spirits. While the victim is a 'sick person' (*rogi*) or a 'troubled one' (*dukhiya*), he is 'one with qualities' (*guni*), a 'knowledgeable one' (*jankar*) or simply a 'craftsman' (*karigar*). Most generally, however, exorcists are known by the terms *ojha* or *sokha*, or by the compound *ojha-sokha*. Despite this elison, the specialists themselves draw distinction here. The *ojha* lures and entraps the ghosts, while the *sokha* supervises his efforts and is the real expert in identification. Both are seen as being *in principle* quite distinct from a tantric – for though he too may act as an exorcist, his methods and powers derive from an authoritative textual source and his clientele consequently consists of a better class of person. In practice, however, one man's tantric tends to be another man's *ojha*.

Leaving the tantrics aside, nearly all exorcists are male, the vast majority are of middle-ranking or low caste, many come from families with some tradition of exorcistic healing, and some of those patronised by Hindu patients are Muslims. Exorcism is a part-time speciality (consultations generally being held on a Sunday and a Tuesday), though for the successful it is a regular and substantial source of income. Many exorcists claim to have started in the profession when they themselves were recovering from an affliction.

Ramraj, for example, was originally afflicted by a spirit which – taking the form of a pie-dog – had attacked him one night as he was crossing a bridge in Calcutta. Unable to eat, and afflicted by symptoms like those of leprosy, he consulted a number of exorcists – though none was able to identify his assailant. Eventually however the spirit declared himself, and told of the manner of his death. Major Phillips Takes Lincoln was a British army officer visiting India on leave when he had been murdered by his hosts. Though now in a subdued and benevolent form, the major continues to possess Ramraj, and enables him to identify the ghosts which afflict his patients. Though himself a vegetarian and a smoker only of country cigarettes, when the major is upon him Ramraj demands meat, beer and virginia tobacco, and speaks of course in Sandhurst English – or so I was told, the major proving somewhat tight-lipped in my company.

But contrary to what this might lead one to suppose, the illness which begins the career of many an exorcist is not seen as a strict calling, and the spirit which then afflicted him does not usually become his tutelary, or only remains so until a higher power can be persuaded to replace it. Most exorcists claim to command the aid of beings superior to a British officer and gentlemen – occasionally of a deified hero who acts as a territorial guardian, but more often from one or more of the goddesses of the Sanskritic tradition: Kali, Durga or Kamrup Kamacha Devi for instance. It is through her power that he is able to summons the guilty ghosts, and it is into her custody that he commits them until their identity and demands can be properly established.

7.3 Panna *ojha*

Panna *ojha* is a man of commanding presence in his mid-sixties. Despite his ochre renouncer's robes, Panna is a householder. By caste a Potter (Kumhar), he lives in a village some five or six miles from the centre of the city. Most of his patients see him on the verandah of his house, on one side of which is a raised platform which contains a shrine to the goddesses Durga and Sitala, and a square sacrificial fire-pit into the ash of which several ascetics' tongs and tridents are stuck. During his consultations Panna sits imposingly on the platform, with his patients – generally in family groups – at his feet below him. His sessions begin with an elaborate act of worship for his tutelary deities and a lengthy reading from various sacred texts (the *Hanuman Chalisa* and the eighteenth chapter of the *Gita* for example).

Most of his patients know that they should bring with them a quantity of rice, and this they put down on the platform along with an initial diagnostic fee (*nagrani*) of Rs. 20. Panna begins by asking for a brief account of the problem, and then divides the rice into a series of separate piles, one for each immediately plausible cause of the affliction: the planets, the gods, the ghosts, sorcery or organic illness for example. These are all identified with a specific pile, and one of the patient's party is asked to pick one of the piles without telling Panna which it is. He then invokes the powers of the various deities who guide him, takes a pair of tongs from the fire-pit, bangs them down on one of the piles as instructed by his tutelary, and looks to the patient's representative for confirmation that this was the one selected. At this stage it always is of course, for he invariably chooses the ghosts or sorcery, and nobody would come to him if they didn't already suspect one or the other – or probably both. If he has picked the ghosts' pile, he will then subdivide this according to their possible provenance: one for an agnatic ghost, one for an affinal ghost and one for a stranger. The same procedure is repeated five or six times, all the while honing in on a particular answer and all the while picking up crucial clues about where to look from the comments of the family members.

At various stages he enters into more direct communication with his tutelary deities, who come and go throughout the session taking turns of duty – now Kali, now Jalpa Devi, now Baba Bholenath (Shiva) himself. Breaking into song he addresses the deity whose 'shadow falls' upon him: 'Hey, Adi Shakti Mai . . . the root of the ghost – where does it come from?' And through Panna the goddess replies: 'In his lineage somebody began and then abandoned the worship of the Emperor of Mecca-Medina; and there is a *bhavani* from the wife's parents house. It is coming from the north-east corner.'

In comparison with most exorcists, Panna's clientele is somewhat atypically up-market. By way of example, I take one morning in April 1983 when he dealt with the following cases.

1. The first was that of a Brahman priest from one of the big Banaras temples who had come with his wife and their twelve-year-old son who was continually ill. It emerged that three ghosts were involved, and in a somewhat scolding tone Panna expressed his surprise that the family of a priest who was always worshipping the deities should have succumbed to their malevolence. They had been sent by agnates with whom the family were engaged in a long-running property dispute. One of these ghosts was a *brahm*, and the priest protested that this was impossible since his brother had recently taken their ancestors to Gaya. But the objection was brusquely dismissed. Though Gaya is an infallible source of salvation for ancestors, said Panna, a *brahm* will only be 'seated' at a place of its own choosing. It would moreover have been necessary to perform various supplementary rituals at Pret-shila in Gaya in order to convert it into an ancestor. Having satisfied – or at least silenced – the father, Panna turned his attention to the son, who was given sacrificial ash to swallow and smear on his forehead, and who was told never to enter – far less to eat in – the house of the offending agnates. Before going to bed he should be careful to wash his hands and feet, and to recite the *Hanuman Chalisa*. The *brahm* they would seat in 'the fortnight of the ancestors', and in the meantime the boy should come back to him after two or three weeks.

2. The next case involved a man of Water-carrier caste (Kahar) who runs a small shop in the heart of the city, his wife and their two small children. Their eldest son had recently died in his sleep, and their little girl was always ill and did not respond to medical treatment. At first Panna thought that he could see that the wife had had two mothers-in-law; and though not quite right, it turned out that he was pretty close for the husband immediately volunteered that his *chachi* (FyBW) used to live with them and that now they had nothing more to do with each other. The reason for this was that he had inherited (or at least taken control of) the property which had belonged to his *chachi*'s parents. But it was not he – cross-questioning revealed – who had performed the mortuary rites. 'You took from them', asked Panna severely, 'but gave nothing at all? So it is from the *nanihal* [the mother's parents house] that the *bhut* have come.' It soon became clear, however, that they had not come of their accord. The aunt had employed an exorcist who had sent an *Aughar Mashan* – the ghost of an Aghori ascetic who had died while performing his terrible austerities on the cremation ground (chapter 8) – to afflict them. It was this spirit which had caused the death of their son, an earlier miscarriage and the death of two other infants to whom they were closely related. The immediate task, said Panna, was to take these four *marua* to be 'seated' at Pishach Mochan; and to go to Manikarnika *ghat* to offer liquor and marijuana to the Aghori ascetics who live there, and to Shiva as the Lord of the Cremation Ground. These offerings would temporarily appease the *Aughar Mashan*, but they would not be able to deal with it properly until they

could perform a fire sacrifice during *Nauratra* ('the nine nights of the goddess').

3. Next Panna turned to a young and highly distraught schoolmistress who had travelled alone from a small bazaar town about 40 miles away. Her sick father was being arraigned on a false charge of embezzlement, and her husband did not love or provide for her. The problem, she thought, lay with her parents-in-law who had employed some magical means to alienate her husband's affections. Panna lit some camphor, incinerated a clove in the flame while muttering a '*mantra*' under his breath, and cut three lemons in half as a *bali* (sacrifice). The young woman was given some ash and told that she would have to wait until that afternoon for further treatment.

4. The fourth case was that of a couple in late middle age. The husband ran a carpet business, and the problem was that although it was reasonably successful their expenditure always out-stripped their income. More immediately, since his marriage their son no longer held them in proper regard, and their daughter-in-law had just run off to her parents' house after they had rebuked her for corrupting the boy. A Muslim *jinn*, and the spirit of a (Dandi Svami) Vaishnavite ascetic whom they had acquired along with the house they had recently purchased, turned out to be responsible (the former being specifically blamed for their financial problems). The Dandi Svami was to be pacified by making a shrine for him in one corner of their house; but the *jinn* would have to be 'seated' at the shrine of some Muslim saint.

5. There were eight ghosts which afflicted the low-caste family of four brothers whose turn it now was. Again they had unaccountable problems balancing the books, but the chief trouble lay with a possessed daughter who made all their lives a misery. The details of the various sources of the affliction turned out to be extremely complicated, and here I shall only report what was said about one of the ghosts involved. This was a *brahm* which had been deliberately sent along with the wife of one of the brothers at the time of her marriage. It was this ghost which was the chief tormentor of her husband's brother's daughter; and it was this set of affines with whom relations were already particularly strained.

Panna's recommendation was that they should entrap the ghost in the effigy of a *brahm*, which they would then take to the wife-giving village from which it had originated. Here they would make it various offerings, instruct it to torment those who had sent it 'until horses sprout horns' and to 'eat the sons, not follow the married daughters'. They would then bury it in a hole adjacent to the shrine of the village's guardian deity (*dih*). The bottom of the hole was to be layered with earth taken from the far bank of the Ganges; the effigy was to be put in a pot full of Ganges water with a lid on top, and the hole filled in with earth taken from the Banaras side of the river. They would then make offerings to the village protector who would ensure that the ghost remained firmly confined within its own territorial jurisdiction.

All this was received somewhat cautiously, and – despite Panna's assurances – one of the brothers persisted in the objection that the exorcists of their affinal village (who had enough to answer for already) would simply send the spirit back. Nor did any of this promise the immediate relief they so desperately needed, for there were still seven other ghosts to consider. They had already tried several different exorcists, they revealed, but none to much effect. Panna patiently explained that the only realistic solution was to pick the ghosts off one by one, and that if they dealt with the 'heaviest' first, the others would prove easier meat. Not entirely convinced, the brothers then suggested that he should share the job with two other experts of their choosing. But Panna was adamant: 'I only blow [spirits away] alone.'

6. All this was punctuated from the back of the verandah by cries of 'elephant, elephant, elephant . . . I will not go . . . I will not go'. This came from the ghost possessing a Goldsmith woman who had arrived with her anxious husband shortly before. Panna broke off the previous consultation to question the spirit, though this proved a predictably futile exercise for the ghost was characteristically evasive. Panna then drew a circle on the ground before which he spread out a handful of cloves, and called on the net of Indra and the Emperor of Delhi – the latter to deal with any Muslim assailant – to catch the spirits tormenting his patient. After a couple of minutes he announced that two of the cloves now had ghosts adhering to them. These he placed in the circle and burnt in a camphor flame. The husband was told to take his by now subdued wife home, make various offerings to the goddess, give the patient a 'Compose' tablet – a mild sedative available across the counter in any Indian pharmacy – and return with her the next day.

7. The final case involved a man of Milkman (Ahir) caste, whose childless wife was suffering from severe menstrual bleeding. The source of the problem was provisionally identified as a ghost belonging to her mother's father's house.

7.4 The tomb of Bahadur the martyr

Having been from one exorcist like Panna to another, and having found that their problems persist, many lower-caste Hindus are tempted to try the tomb (*muzar*) of the Muslim martyr Baba Bahadur Shahid, which is located on the periphery of the city. As a martyr, Bahadur Shahid was of course himself supposedly the victim of a bad death[4] (as were the deified ghosts who preside at Hindu shrines like Pishach Mochan). Every Thursday maybe four or five hundred people gather in the courtyard which surrounds the tomb, and of these I would guess that perhaps two-thirds are Hindus. (It is by contrast striking that Muslim patients hardly ever arrive at Pishach Mochan.) The suspected victim of malevolent possession is accompanied by one or more family members; and the notion is that the Baba will eventually coerce the ghost into an admission of its true identity and will take it into his protective custody. But in order to effect a complete and lasting cure it is necessary for the supplicant to attend the shrine on forty consecutive Thursdays.

First, however, active possession must be induced. In order to do this any bound hair is loosened; the patient is sat facing the shrine, is made to drink some of the water with which the martyr's sarcophagus has been bathed at the celebration which is held to mark the anniversary of his death (*urs*), and some incense which has been smouldering on his tomb is held under the patient's nostrils. She will then start to sway – at first gently – as the spirit comes upon her. After some time the possession will grow more violent and the victim gyrates vigorously from the hips, or rocks to and fro as she thumps her hands on the ground in front of her or claps them over her head. Some paw the earth and roll in the dust towards the shrine. Others stand windmilling their arms, or hop up and down. When the ghost is about to leave, the patient runs or skips across the courtyard and stands outside the shrine, taking leave from its occupant. But neither ghosts nor women can enter it.

Hopefully the afflicting spirit will after a few visits start to speak. Probably at first it will merely complain of its discomfort. 'I am burning . . . I am burning. That water is poisoning me.' Sometimes it is defiant ('I have great power *Baba* and I will not tell you'); sometimes penitent ('great is my fault, *Baba*'); sometimes transparently mendacious (I am a Chamar and with me is an Englishman'). At this stage those who had accompanied the patient will start to question the spirit, though at the beginning it is almost sure to dissimulate – this dissimulation being, I believe, an essential feature of the whole process. The ghost initially provides a whole battery of possible identities which are interminably argued over between visits by the family who between them gradually construct the most compelling and acceptable account of the problem, an account in which the victim (or rather the ghost) generally acquiesces, but may refine, on subsequent visits. But others too have a hand in the process, for over the weeks a considerable cameraderie is built up between those who attend regularly, and members of other parties will gather round to watch the progress, offer advice, help with the interrogation or ask questions in the hope that the ghost will shed light on their own problem – for just sometimes a helpful spirit will appear. Occasionally the victim does not or cannot enter possession, perhaps (as we might see it) because he or she is a very young child or an imbecile who cannot understand what is required. In such an eventuality a woman of the family or a neighbour who is known for the ease with which she embodies spirits will be brought along, and – through the martyr's grace – will get possessed by a cooperative ghost who will give truthful answers to the questions put to it. But most ghosts are incorrigeable liars, and it is only after many visits that they will acknowledge defeat, declare their real identity and agree to be bound over to the Baba's safe-keeping. Sometimes, of course, they claim to have been sent; and on three occasions I saw blows exchanged in the courtyard over accusations levelled at one of the accompanying party.

Though it is true that those Hindus who take their problems to Bahadur Shahid for the time being at least escape the clutches of the Brahmans who would otherwise preside over the 'seating' of their ghosts at shrines like Pishach Mochan, they do not escape their scorn. That the victims of ghostly attack should search for a cure at the shrine of some obscure Muslim martyr merely confirms in 'respectable' Hindu eyes the inferiority and marginality of possession activities. (And nor of course do they gain any credibility in the eyes of orthodox or middle-class Muslims for whom the solutions they seek are equally irrefutable evidence of the superstition in which they are mired.)

7.5 Seating a ghost at Pishach Mochan

In most cases, however, a Hindu exorcist does succeed in diagnosing and – at least temporarily – controlling a spirit attack. Having done so he will sooner or later decide that it is time to 'seat' the ghosts at the sacred tank of Pishach Mochan (or perhaps at the shrine of Vindyachal Devi in Mirzapur or at Harsu Brahm in the village of Chayanpur). *Pishach* is a 'ghost' or 'demonic being', so Pishach Mochan would translate as either 'salvation *from* ghosts' or 'salvation *of* ghosts'. Both these meanings are implied by what happens when the ghosts are successfully installed at the tank, for both victims and ghosts are released from their suffering.

The tank is surrounded on two sides by flights of stone steps, at the top of which are a number of temples. These are owned by several families of Brahman *pandas* (in this context 'temple-priests'), and are extremely big business for at peak periods they are visited by many thousands of exorcists and their clients, of pilgrims *en route* to Gaya, and of mourners performing the Sanskritic rites associated with a 'bad death'.

Of these Brahmanical rituals, the one which is invariably performed at Pishach Mochan and which is of some relevance here is *tripindi shraddh*. Its purpose is to liberate a troublesome spirit from the ghostly state in which it is stuck, despite perhaps the prior performance of *Narayani bali* and other rituals designed to alleviate the effects of a 'bad' death (pp. 200–1). In such cases, *tripindi shraddh* is, as it were, the rite of last resort. Properly performed it can take up to seven or eight hours, and the details of the ritual sequence are extremely complex. All that need concern us here is that the central part of the rite consists of an offering of three *pinds* (balls of rice or flour). Each of these stands for one of the three possible human dispositions, or *gunas*: *sattvik* (ascetic, tranquil and pacific), *rajsik* (refined and luxurious) and *tamsik* (coarse and brutal). The three *pinds* are thus designed to satisfy a ghost of *any* character. Three Brahmans are appointed to represent the three possible kinds of spirit, which during the course of the ritual are homologised with the gods Brahma, Vishnu and Rudra (a fierce form of Shiva).[5]

When an exorcist comes to 'seat' a ghost at Pishach Mochan, he is normally accompanied both by male representatives of the victim's family and by one or generally two professional colleagues whom he brings along to certify his work. As the Sanskritic rite requires three Brahmans, its 'non-Sanskritic' variant commonly seems to require three exorcists. In a typical case the one who presides would probably first draw a circle on the ground with a balsam flower (*gulmenhdi*), into which he invokes his tutelary deity. He will then pick up a clove, placing it on the back of his hand or may be holding it in front of his face between his two extended forefingers. This is a trap for the ghost which he will summon through the power of his tutelary deity which now possesses him. He shudders, snatches in the air, hisses through clenched teeth, smacks his lips, snorts like a pig, growls like a dog, strains as though severely constipated, smells his hand and periodically exclaims 'Let me fuck your mother! You still wandering here . . . get away. Look out . . . catch it, catch it.' When the *pret* has successfully been lured onto the clove he puts it into the circle and his colleague checks that the ghost has really come by using another clove like a magnet to pick it up. A lemon or a nutmeg is then cut in half as a sacrificial offering (*bali*) to the ghost, the life it contains substituting for that of the victim. If there is more than one ghost afflicting the patient, then the same procedure is repeated for each.

Having caught your ghost, you summon your *panda*. Though almost to a man the Brahmans of Pishach Mochan affect a total scorn for all these proceedings, the *panda* (who has of course already had a word on the side with the exorcist) puts his hand on the cloves in the circle and confirms that they contain this or that ghost. This is preparatory to a *pind* offering over which he is about to preside. But first a price must be agreed, and the *pandas* drive a hard bargain, the payments they extract commonly representing many months income for the afflicted family. Though almost all the victims are quite innocent about any financial arrangement between *pandas* and exorcists, the latter in fact collect half this fee, for the *pandas* of course depend on the exorcists for such business to come their way.

PANDA (studying the cloves in the circle):'Do you see it? One of them is your *marua*. There is also a *bhavani*. She is very old. Tell me if I am not right? You will have to offer two *pinds*. It is not possible with just one.'

EXORCIST:'Yes, yes. They are both demanding separate *pinds*.'

PATIENT'S UNCLE (suspiciously):'How old is the *bhavani*?'

PANDA:'That's not my job. I'll just do the one *pind* if you like.' (Touches cloves again). 'There is a *bhavani* there for sure. She will sit but it will cost you Rs. 200.'

PATIENT:'We can pay Rs. 40. We are very poor.'

PANDA:'So you are poor and you want to get me a bad reputation. You want the work done but you don't want to pay.'

PATIENT'S FATHER folds his hands in supplication:'We are under your protection *panda ji*.'

PANDA:'Alright. Don't shove a stick up my arse.'

EXORCIST (to whom they appealed for support):'What can I do? You hear what *panda ji* says. How can you get it done cheaper. If it is not done properly we will have to come back.'

PANDA:'OK. You can give me Rs. 10 less.'

PATIENT'S UNCLE:'Please do it for Rs. 40.'

PANDA:'For Rs. 40 I will do one of them.'
EXORCIST (alarmed):'No, no. It is a matter of doing both.'
PANDA:'This is not *dan* or *dakshina*. For that you can go to Dashashvamedh *ghat*
    . . . You won't get anywhere by folding your hands. I can do that too.' (Stalks off
    in apparent irritation and attends to another party.)
PATIENT'S FATHER (to exorcist):'Those people over there have seven spirits and
    the *panda* is only asking Rs. 60.'
EXORCIST:'Yes, but only one of them is a heavy *brahm*.'
PATIENT'S FATHER:'Alright, so we add another Rs 15.'
EXORCIST:'In that case go and talk to the *panda*.'
PANDA (reappearing):'You say I should take less? You want to ruin me? Alright, but
    I will have to make it up from somebody else.'

Having settled the fee, the *panda* presides over an extremely crude,
simplified and abbreviated version of the Sanskritic *tripindi shraddh* ritual to
which I have just referred. But the Brahmans avoid describing it as such,
though that is plainly what it is, while the exorcists generally have only the
haziest idea of the Sanskritic model, or of the meaning of the three *pinds*
offered to each ghost. Along with each of these the *panda* disinterestedly
garbles off in local dialect what passes for a '*mantra*', which the patient's
representative desperately tries to repeat:

> Forgotten or omitted, known or unknown, mother's mother or mother's father,
> wife's mother or wife's father, whoever drowned in water, fell from a tree, was
> burned by fire, was bitten by a snake, was killed in battle or who is in the form of a
> ghost, who gives trouble, puts obstacles in our way or appears in our dreams, we fall
> at your feet and beg your benediction. Becoming by the light of this sacred place a
> deity for seven births, reside in the precincts of Kashi.

The three *pinds* are then merged into one, and the clove containing the *pret* is
buried within it.

Various offerings appropriate to the species of ghost which is being 'seated'
are now presented at one or more of the little images which surround the tank;
the exorcists cut lemons or nutmegs as a thank-offering to their tutelaries, and
light a row of five or six little pieces of camphor, scratching a line on the
ground between them with a knife. It is said that this marks the separation
between the good and bad supernatural beings, and that if the flames merge
into each other the problem has not been properly resolved. Sometimes the
ghost is literally nailed to one of the trees which surround the tank; sometimes
its tongue is cut out to prevent it uttering again – a precaution I have seen acted
by the exorcist biting through a strand of *kusha* grass which hangs from the
mouth of the victim.

The patient's representative then touches the *panda*'s feet, receives his
blessing and goes off to immerse the *pind* and bathe himself in the stagnant
water of the tank. Meanwhile the exorcist disappears to make an offering to
the presiding deity of the shrine, though he also finds time to collect his money.
Before they leave, the party may obtain a certificate from the *panda*
guaranteeing the efficacy of the ritual:

'The case of patient Horilal was seated at Pishach Mochan. It is therefore sorted out. If the cure proves false or incomplete the matter should be brought before the *panda* and the exorcist. If the complaint proves justified it will be done again at no extra charge; otherwise the complainant will be charged double'
Signed: Amarnath Upardhayaya (*panda*)
Panna Lal (*ojha*)

7.6 On 'levels' and hierarchy

What I find particularly striking about these proceedings is the way in which the Brahman priests are apt to deny them any legitimacy whatever. Yet it is I think clear that the offering of three *pinds* at the end of the exorcism ritual is, as Dumont would have it, 'in some way homogenous' with what they regard as the authentic Sanskritic rite of *tripindi shraddh* (vague though this formulation is), and that *we* – the observers – can legitimately see them as related as the 'general idea and the local working out of that idea'. But the crucial point is that that is *not* the way in which the participants themselves present it. The exorcists are largely unconscious of the continuity between the two rites, and if the *pandas* are aware of it they are not letting on, for this would invest exorcism with a spurious legitimacy. *Both* Dumont and Marriott are therefore correct. To the outside observer a homogeneity between the two levels manifestly exists; but for the participants themselves what is most salient is their heterogeneity.

It is, of course, this perceived discontinuity which allows the Brahman to regard the rites of exorcism with a cynicism which can hardly discourage his rapacity. But clearly such rapacity is only possible in a world in which there are others more credulous – and this endless interplay between cynicism and credulity deserves emphasis in any account of the phenomenon.

I once spent a morning on the roof of one of the Pishach Mochan temples with a party of three exorcists and their four patients. The latter consisted of two Leather-worker brothers and their deceased brother's wife; and a Potter called Nand Kishore from the same village. The Leather-workers, it emerged, had been suffering from a spirit affliction for many years, one of the symptoms of which was their continual quarrelling. Pattu, the younger of the two brothers, had himself acquired some expertise in dealing with ghosts, though during a pause in the early part of the proceedings he told me that he had little faith in Pishach Mochan and was only there under family duress.

When some little while later the exorcists claimed to have summoned the first of their ghosts, Pattu insisted on examining the clove for himself and discovered that no spirit had yet alighted. The exorcists were forced to begin all over again, and again they failed. The third time Pattu conceded that a ghost had indeed arrived, but claimed that it belonged to his brother's widow and was nothing to do with him. It was only half an hour later that he capitulated and acknowledged that their ghosts had come, though at first he refused to offer the increasingly irate *panda* more than Rs. 30 for seating them.

Eventually, under pressure from his brother and sister-in-law, he grudgingly acquiesced in accepting responsibility for a third share of a payment of Rs. 225.

The exorcists could now turn their attention to Nand Kishore, the Potter. Presumably impressed by Pattu's fastidiousness, Nand Kishore invited him to check that his spirits had really come. They had not; and nor did they at the next five or six attempts. Things seemed to have reached an impasse and everybody took a break during which the enraged *panda* stormed off downstairs, followed shortly after by Pattu. When business resumed it was clear that there had been a sudden breakthrough. Pattu confirmed that the spirits had at last arrived, though among them was something nobody had expected – unmistakable evidence of *Chamar dosh*, the affliction caused by the spirit of an aggrieved Leather-worker and removed only by the intercession of one of its caste-fellows. The problem was serious since it is mandatory to remove this kind of 'ghost-obstacle' before the others will budge; and Pattu was candid that it would of course cost. I do not know exactly what proportion of the Rs. 500 which Nand Kishore paid over to the *panda* found its way back into Pattu's pocket, but I am confident that he more than covered his costs on the day out.

I am not, of course, in a position to gauge the *extent* of Pattu's scepticism, nor even that of the *pandas* themselves. But with regard to the latter it is possible to say in broad terms where it stops. For them the problem with exorcism is emphatically not a problem with 'magic' in general since by almost any definition many of the Sanskritic rites over which they are proud to preside over have a 'magical' character. Nor certainly is it a rejection of the possibility of supernatural beings embodying themselves in a human vehicle, for there are many contexts in which a priest or an ascetic is supposed to homologise his own body with that of a deity or ancestor. Nor is it the *existence* of ghosts which is denied; it is rather their capacity to molest the living, or sometimes their capacity to afflict those with a decent modicum of purity and spiritual power. Alternatively scepticism may focus on the exorcist: either his power over *prets* is flatly rejected; or his power is admitted, but his inclination to use it for the benefit of his clients is denied. Like the ghosts they command, exorcists are inveterate cheats and liars, and the world would be a better place without them. Not only do my high-caste informants give different grounds for their incredulity, but the same individual is likely to switch promiscuously between them. At one moment he denies that ghostly affliction has any objective reality; at the next he seems to be saying that it is wrong to 'believe in' exorcism in the Old Testament sense of having 'faith' or 'putting one's trust in' it. And despite his strident disdain he sometimes proves willing, at least as a final resort, to swallow his misgivings in the face of misfortune. A further paradox is that – on the principle that it takes one to catch one – the main deities enshrined at Pishach Mochan, the run of village protectors and some of the supernatural beings who act as tutelaries to the exorcist, are themselves held to be reformed ghosts, yet for the *pandas* their power is not in question (cf. Dumont 1986a:349).

What they all dispute, however, is the legitimacy and efficacy of the rites over which they and the exorcists jointly preside. In Pocock's (1973) comfortable picture of the tolerant catholicism of the traditional Indian world view, the Brahman gives credence to, and patronises, the impure cult even though he will not officiate at its rituals. But in the situation I have described more or less the opposite is true. Provided the price is right, the *panda* is pleased enough to preside over the ritual culmination of an exorcism, though he is generally unwilling to give it much credence. As far as he is concerned, the exorcisms in which he participates are a contemptible aberration. Yet for the exorcists and the victims the whole procedure must be authenticated by the Brahman's authority and it is only by performing a pale imitation of the Sanskritic rite of *tripindi shraddh* that the ghost is finally laid. As with the set of ideas which accounts for who gets possessed in the first place, the hierarchical order is thus resoundingly validated by the tenets of those it demeans.

This situation has, I believe, some important implications for our picture of Hindu ideology. In Dumont's view, this ideology presupposes that the 'pure' and the 'impure' cults (and similarly priesthood and possession) exist in a relationship of complementarity and interdependence mirroring the complementarity and interdependence which exists between castes. But the first thing which is striking about the situation I have described is that the inferior cult is degraded as much on account of its unenlightenment as on account of its impurity, suggesting that the opposition between knowledge and ignorance is quite as significant a structuring principle as the opposition between purity and pollution. What is equally striking, however, is that the Sanskritic rite can exist without exorcism; but exorcism can only be brought to a successful conclusion with the aid of a Brahman and a version of the rituals over which he presides. It is therefore tempting to conclude that the complementarity between superior and inferior which Dumont stresses is an intransitive relationship which exists only from the inferior's point of view. The ritualistic universe of the Brahman can pretend to an autonomy impossible for their inferiors. The higher can dispense with the lower; but the converse does not apply – an asymmetry which might also be illustrated from *varna* theory, according to which the higher power includes the lower and can legitimately assume its functions, but not vice versa: ' . . . the Vaishya is dependent on the Kshatriya and Brahmin, the Kshatriya is dependent on the Brahmin and the Brahmin is dependent on no one' (Marglin 1977).

In all justice it must be said that Dumont (1970b:40) himself appears to recognise this Brahmanical quest for autonomy when he writes in his paper on world renunciation that 'the complementarities of common religious practice become blurred and indistinct when we move to the level of Brahmanic practice . . . [while] in Brahmanic theory they tend to disappear altogether'. What he neglects to point out, however, is that the logical corollary of this is

that his stress on complementarity is essentially a view *from the bottom up* –
strange irony for a writer who is routinely charged with purveying a
Brahmanical view of Hindu ideology! Even in its mature formulation, the real
referent of Dumont's model of the hierarchical world of caste is the world with
which he began: that of the Pramalai Kallar. Moffat (1979) is therefore in
error to claim, in Dumont's defence, that 'the most remarkable feature of the
"view from the bottom" is its identity with . . . the view from the top'; but he is
right to conclude that in their religious practice the low castes 'continually
reproduce among themselves the ideology necessary for the legitimization of
the social system of structured inequality'.

PART IV

The end of death

8

Asceticism and the conquest of death

8.1 Getting back to the beginning

If, for the householder, a good death is an act of sacrificial renunciation which results in the regeneration of self, time and cosmos, the paradox is that the proper aim of the real renouncer is to escape from this endless cycle. The corollary of rebirth is the relentless recurrence of death, and the renewal of life is a renewal of suffering. Before creation there was only *Brahman*, a state of timeless and undifferentiated unity. Cosmogony proceeded by a process of progressive differentiation from this primeval protoplasm, duality emerging out of non-duality (pp. 13–14). The ultimate quest of the ascetic is to recapture this primordial state of non-differentiation and to re-establish the unity of opposites which existed before the world began. By abolishing duality he aims to abolish duration and death.

The discipline of *yoga* is, as Eliade (1969; 1976) has shown, directed at precisely this goal. By his physical postures the yogi subjugates his body and renders it immobile; by concentrating on a single object he frees his mind from the flux of events and arrests mental process; and by slowing down and eventually stopping his breath 'he stops the activities of the senses and severs the connection between the mind and external sensory objects' (Gupta 1979:168). Sexual intercourse may be converted into a discipline in which the semen is immobilised by the practice of *coitus reservatus*, or its normal direction of flow reversed by reabsorbing it into the penis after ejaculation. By thus controlling his body he acquires magical powers (*siddhis*) by which he may defy nature and control the world. But above all, the yogi's immobilisation of mind, body, breath and semen represents an attempt to return to what Eliade describes as a 'primordial motionless Unity'; and to attain *samadhi*, a timeless state of non-duality in which there is neither birth nor death nor any experience of differentiation.

This suspension of time and conquest of death is, as I understand it, the aim of the ascetic regime of a small sect of renouncers known as Aghoris who are intimately associated with death, corpses and the cremation ground, and on whom this chapter focuses. To most Hindus this regime seems – and is

251

undoubtedly intended to seem – outlandish and shocking; and by comparison with the practices of other ascetic orders it is certainly aberrant. But what I hope to show is that both the theological premise on which their practice is founded, and the goal to which it is directed, are thoroughly conventional. In classical monistic theory, every soul is identical with the Absolute Being; all category distinctions are a product of illusion (*maya*), and behind all polarities there is an ultimate unity. What is peculiar to the Aghoris, as Eliade (1969:296) perceived, is a particularly literal working-out of this monistic doctrine through a discipline which insists on a concrete experience of the identity of opposites, and on a material realisation of the unity between them. It is a matter of a kind of externalised fulfilment of what is more orthodoxly interpreted as a purely internal quest.

We have repeatedly encountered the idea that ascetic austerities are a source of creative power. By virtue of the terrible austerities which will finally liberate him from the world, the Aghori is held to acquire the capacity to defy the ordinary laws which govern it, and to confer life and fertility on those who remain within it. Properly oriented towards an escape from the world, renunciation generates a power that can be put to use inside it.

At the outset I should acknowledge that – for reasons which will become obvious – there are many gaps in my data relating to the Aghoris, and should explicitly state that I have not personally witnessed many of the secret performances with which they are associated. What needs to be kept firmly in mind then is that at various points the account relates, not so much to what these ascetics actually do, as to what they say they do and what other people believe them to do. But whether fact or fantasy, the practises with which they are credited seem to be informed by a perfectly coherent logic, and it is with the ideas which underlie these practices that I am chiefly concerned.

Although there are many similarities of regime, and perhaps also a direct historical connection, between the Aghoris and the skull-carrying Kapalikas of certain late Sanskrit texts (Lorenzen 1972), they themselves trace the foundation of their order to an ascetic called Kina ('rancour') Ram, whom they claim as an incarnation of Shiva, and who is supposed to have died (or rather 'taken *samadhi*') in the second half of the eighteenth century when he was nearly 150 years old. The *ashram* (or 'monastic refuge') Kina Ram founded in Banaras (which is also the site of his tomb) is one of the most important centres of the sect, though only one or two ascetics actually live there. Each of the succeeding *mahants* ('abbots') of this *ashram* is supposed to be an *avatar* of (Shiva's *avatar*) Kina Ram; the present incumbent being reckoned as the twelfth in line.[1]

At the time of my fieldwork there were probably no more than fifteen Aghori ascetics permanently or semi-permanently resident in Banaras and its immediate environs,[2] but others from elsewhere congregate at Kina Ram's *ashram* during the festivals of *Lolark Chhath* and *Guru-Purnima*.[3] The evidence suggests that at the end of the last century their numbers were several times greater – Barrow (1893:215) gives an estimate of between one and two hundred – though it is very unlikely that they were ever a numerically significant element in the ascetic population of the city. Their hold on the popular imagination is, however, out of all proportion to their numbers, and some Aghoris acquire a substantial following of lay devotees. Recruitment to the sect is theoretically open to both sexes and to all castes. In practice, however, all the ascetics I knew or knew of were male and of clean caste origin (though some of their devotees were female).[4] The discipline of the Aghori is 'the discipline of the left hand' (*vam panthi sadhana*). He performs austerities at, and may live on, the burning *ghats*. Morinis (1984:187) describes how one ascetic on the Tarapith cremation ground 'had built an entire wall of his hut out of skulls using mud as mortar'. The Aghori may go naked or clothe himself in a shroud taken from a corpse, wear a necklace of bones around his neck and his hair in matted locks. His eyes are conventionally described as burning red, like live coals, his whole demeanour is awesome, and in speech he is stereotypically brusque, churlish and foul-mouthed.

Rumour persistently associates the Aghoris with human sacrifice. What is certain is that during the British raj more than one Aghori was executed for the crime (Barrow 1893:208); and that in more recent times the *Guardian* newspaper (6 March 1980) reported the death in police custody of an old ascetic who was living on a south Indian cremation ground and who was suspected of the sacrifice of five children whose blood he collected in bottles for the performance of rituals by which he sought to attain immortality. What we can never know, however, is whether these ascetics were genuinely guilty of the crimes of which they were accused, or whether they themselves were the victims of popular convictions about the behaviour of those who follow their path.

This path is supposed to include the rite of *shav-sadhana*, in which the ascetic seats himself on the torso of a corpse to worship. By means of this worship he is able to gain an absolute control over the deceased's spirit, through which he communicates with other ghostly beings.[5] The Aghori sleeps over a model bier (made from the remnants of a real one), smears his body with ash from the pyres, cooks his food on wood pilfered from them[6] and consumes it out of the human skull which is his constant companion and alms-bowl, and which he should ideally have taken himself from a corpse acquired at the cremation ground. One of my ascetic informants rather shamefacedly admitted to having obtained his from a hospital morgue, though he claims to have taken precautions to ensure that it was a skull of the right type. It belonged, he says, to a young man of Merchant caste who had died from snake-bite. Another who lived for some time at Manikarnika *ghat* during the course of my fieldwork is, however, remembered as having acquired his in the approved manner by retrieving the corpse from the river, and one of my informants claims to have unwittingly lent him the knife with which he performed the operation. Before eating I have seen this ascetic offer the food it contained to a dog, thus converting it into the 'polluted leavings' (*jutha*) of the most debased of animals, and one which is also – like the ideal Aghori – a scavenger living off the carrion of the cremation ground.[7] The 'true' Aghori is entirely indifferent to what he consumes, drinks not only liquor but urine, and eats not only meat but excrement, vomit and the putrid flesh of corpses.[8]

I myself have been present when an Aghori drank what was said to be the urine of a dog, and swallowed what was undoubtedly ash from a cremation pyre. With regard to necrophagy, all I can say with complete assurance is that they readily own to the practice, that as far as my lay informants are concerned the matter is not in question, and that several of them claim to have seen an Aghori eating corpse flesh. One highly revered ascetic has hung a large portrait of himself in the leprosy hospital which he founded, in which he is shown sitting cross-legged on a corpse, a bottle of liquor in one hand while in the other is a morsel of flesh which he is raising to his lips. Apart from its very existence, the interesting thing about the painting is that the corpse which he is devouring appears to be his own. Another ascetic informant insisted that the crucial point about the corpse on which the Aghori sits to worship is its identity to his own body.

Starting with *Dabistan*, a sixteenth-century Persian source (cited by Barrow 1893 and Crooke 1928), the historical records treat necrophagy as an indisputable fact and provide several supposedly eye-witness accounts of the practice, though some of these are far from credible. The narrator of *The revelations of an orderly* (a semi-fictional work published in Banaras in 1848) claims, for example, that: 'I once saw a wretch of this fraternity eating the head of a putrid corpse, and as I passed he howled and pointed to me; and then scooped out the eyes and ate them before me.' Another nineteenth-century British account claims that 'near Benares they are not unusually seen floating down the river on a corpse, and feeding upon its flesh' (Moor quoted in Oman 1903:166); while according to a third, the drunken Aghori 'will seize hold of corpses that drift to the banks of the river and bite off bits of its flesh . . . (Barrow 1893:206). Or again, Tod (1839:84) reports that 'one of the Deora chiefs told me that . . . when conveying the body of his brother to be burnt, one of these monsters crossed the path of the funeral procession, and begged to have the corpse, saying that it 'would make excellent *chatni*, or condiment".

What would seem to be more serious witness to the practice is provided by the series of prosecutions which followed the special legislation passed by the British to ban – as Crooke (1928) phrased it – 'the habit of cannibalism'. One Aghori, for example, who was tried in Ghazipur in 1862

> was found carrying the remains of a putrid corpse along a public road. He was throwing the brains from the skull on the ground and the stench of the corpse greatly distracted the people. Here and there he placed the corpse on shop boards and on the ground. Separating pieces of flesh from the bones he ate them and insisted on begging. (Barrow 1893)

The defendant later admitted that 'he ate corpses whenever he found them' (p. 209). Convictions were also obtained in subsequent prosecutions brought before the courts in Rohtak in 1882, and in Dehra Dun and Berhampore in 1884. In one of these cases the accused testified that 'he frequently ate human flesh when hungry' (p. 210); while the newspaper report of a further incident asserts that it forms 'the staple of their food' (*The Tribune* (Lahore), 29 November 1898, cited in Oman 1903:165).

None of these reports can be taken entirely at face value. One reason for this is that some of them are plainly motivated, and have more to do with the politics of British administration than they have to do with the empirical facts of the case. Although written in fictional form, *The revelations of an orderly* were for example clearly intended to be read as an account of daily reality, and their real purpose seems to have been to provide a damning indictment of an impotent and corrupt local administration.[9] Nor can the ascetics' confessions in court be regarded as beyond suspicion. Quite apart from the very real possibility of police duress, the hallmark of a 'real' Aghori is that he consumes the flesh of corpses, and any acknowledged failure to do so is an admission of inadequacy.

Certainly the claim that it forms 'a staple of their food' must always have been remote from any reality, and I am convinced that if necrophagy is indeed practised by any of the Aghoris I encountered, it is an irregular – perhaps even a once-off – affair, performed in a ritual manner at night during certain phases of the moon (associated with Shiva).[10] Details of the precise ritual procedure surrounding such an event are supposed to be secret, and there is a considerable discrepancy between the accounts I was given. Some said that the consumption should ideally be preceded by an act of intercourse on the cremation ground; others that having eaten the flesh the ascetic should cremate the remains of the corpse and smear his body with the ashes. But almost everybody agrees that, after eating, the real Aghori will use his powers to restore the deceased to life (cf. Barrow 1893:221; Balfour 1897:345–6), and that the flesh he consumes should be that of a person who has died a 'bad death'.

This association recurs in the notion that the skull which the Aghori carries should have belonged to the victim of an 'untimely death', as should the corpse on which he sits to meditate (cf. Morinis 1984:188). The preference is not just a question of the practical consideration that, since such corpses are immersed, their remains are the ones most likely to be available. It is also a matter of the power which resides in such skulls, which is said to render even the most virulent of poisons innocuous. That of a Teli (Oil-presser) or of a Mahajan (Trader) who has died a 'bad death' is especially prized. Traders are said to be sharp and cunning and their skulls are therefore particularly powerful.[11] With the proper *mantras* an Aghori can get his skull to fetch and carry for him, or cause it to fight with another. It is as if life resides in the skull itself, only waiting to be activated by one who knows the proper incantations.

It is because the vital breath of a person who has died a bad death has not been released from his cranium by the rite of *kapal kriya* that his skull remains a repository of potential power.

Like other sects with a close affinity to Tantrism, the Aghoris perform (or at least claim to perform) the secret rite of *chakra-puja* involving the ritual use of the so-called 'five Ms' (*panchanmakara*): *mans* (meat), *machhli* (fish), *madya* (liquor) and *mudra* (in this context parched grain or kidney beans) and *maithun* (sexual intercourse). A group of male adepts, accompanied by one or more female partners, sit in a circle. The woman is worshipped as a manifestation of the goddess and is offered the food and drink which is subsequently consumed by the males who feed each other. The first four 'Ms' all possess aphrodisiac qualities and thus lead towards the fifth – in which the adept and his partner incarnate Shiva and his consort united in *coitus reservatus*. As far as my subsequent argument is concerned, the crucial point is that the female partner should ideally be a prostitute or a woman of one of the lowest castes; and she should also be menstruating at the time and thus doubly polluted. But what is also significant is that the sexual intercourse which is supposed to occur is a calculated repudiation of procreation. Not only is the semen witheld, but the act takes place at a time when the female partner is infertile. Moreover, she is preferably a prostitute: the one class of women who have a 'professional hostility' to fertility and who provide the perfect 'symbol of *barren* eroticism' (Shulman's (1980:261–2) apt phraseology; my emphasis). Consistent with the discussion of Aghori aims which follows, the act of ritual copulation thus reveals a rejection of reproduction, and identifies the male adept with Shiva locked in a union with his opposed aspect which is both without end and without issue. It is a sexual pairing rid of its normal consequences: progeny and death (the latter being commonly used in popular speech as a metaphor for ejaculation, and being caused by a failure to retain the semen).

This liason between the Aghori and the prostitute recurs in several other contexts. The prostitutes of the city not only visit the burning *ghats* to worship Shiva there in his form as Lord of the Cremation Ground, but are invited to dance in his honour at his temple's annual festival at Manikarnika *ghat*. Each year on the festival of *Lolark Chhath* they also used to come to sing and dance at the tomb of Kina Ram (though the practice was abandoned in the late fifties after a serious disturbance among the university students). Moreover, it is said that the bed of a prostitute is equivalent to a cremation ground in that it is an equally proper place for an Aghori to perform his *sadhana* (ritual practice).

By his various observances the Aghori acquires *siddhis*, or supernatural powers, which give him mastery over the phenomenal world and the ability to read thoughts. One apparently common sign of his magical abilities is that he can make water flow from the dry locks of his matted hair. If he is sufficiently accomplished he can cure the sick, raise the dead and control malevolent ghosts. He can expand or contract his body to any size or weight, fly through the air, appear in two places at once, conjure up the dead and leave his body and enter into another. All this, of course, is exactly what one might predict from the Aghori's dealings with corpses and bodily emissions, for – as Douglas (1966) pointed out – that which is anomalous and marginal is not only the focus of pollution and danger, but also the source of extraordinary power.

While *siddhis* may, of course, be won by ascetics who follow quite different kinds of regime, it is widely believed that they are acquired more quickly and more fully by those who pursue the path of the Aghori. This path, however, is more difficult and dangerous than that which is followed by other orders; and one whose discipline is inadequate, who is overtaken by fear during his austerities, or who fails to retain his semen during *chakra-puja*, pays the penalty of madness and death (cf. Carstairs 1957:232). He then becomes an *Aughar-mashan*, one of the most recalcitrant and tenacious of malevolent ghosts.

The association between madness and the Aghori is not, however, an entirely straightforward one. The genuine Aghori, it is acknowledged, is – almost by definition – likely to seem demented to ordinary mortals, and is apt to talk in a way which they cannot comprehend. But this is merely evidence of his divine nature and of the fact that he has succeeded in homologising himself with Shiva, who is himself somewhat touched by a kind of divine insanity, and with Lord Bhairav, one of whose manifestations in Banaras is as *Unmat* ('mad') Bhairav. Moreover complete lucidity is not the best policy for one who shuns the world and does not wish to be endlessly importuned for spiritual guidance. But while there may be an element of both divine and calculated madness in an authentic ascetic, it is also recognised that some Aghoris are simply insane in the medical sense. Their affliction, however, is generally attributed to a failure of nerve or an insufficiently fastidious attention to detail during the performance of such dangerously powerful rites, rather than to any notion that their attraction to these practices suggests that they were unbalanced already.

By virtue of his magical powers, the Aghori who has, in the local idiom, 'arrived' (*pahunche hue*), is likely to attract a large lay following who bring their pragmatic problems to him for solution. Baba Bhagvan Ram, the most celebrated Aghori in Banaras (and probably in the whole of north India), has for example a wide circle of committed devotees. Most of them are high caste,[12] and many are members of the professional middle class. Two other Aghoris I knew also had a significant, if less extensive, middle-class following. Even in the presence of an ascetic other than their guru, the humility of such devotees – who would in other contexts brook no trifling with their dignity – is really remarkable, and can even extend to cleaning up his excrement.

Although motives are hard to be confident about, for what it is worth I record my strong impression that what attracts many of these people to the Aghori's following are the *siddhis* which he is believed to have obtained and which he may be induced to use on their behalf in an insecure and competitive world. In many instances their discipleship seems to date from a period of grave personal crisis: an investigation for corruption, a business failure, or the looming prospect of providing a suitable dowry for several unmarried daughters for example. As at least some of these middle-class devotees themselves represent it, however, the initial appeal of the Aghori's message was rather the egalitarian social ethic he preaches, and about which I shall shortly say more. But in some of these cases I rather cynically suspected that the key to the ascetic's success lay in teachings which could be seen as 'progressive' and 'modern', and which could therefore serve to legitimise a more shamefaced and surreptitious concern to tap the source of a fabulous supernatural power.

The paradox of the situation, however, is that in order to gain and maintain a reputation as an ascetic worthy of the name, the laity require miracles as evidence of his attainments; yet the brash display of such powers is regarded with equivocation for it testifies to an incomplete spiritual development. While proof that he has taken the first step, it demonstrates that he has gone no further, for the one who has really 'arrived' is the one who scorns to indulge the laity with such trifles, who is indifferent to reputation, and who pursues his own salvation with a complete disdain for the world. In order to attain his ultimate quest for immunity from death, a double renunciation is necessary: first a renunciation of the world and then a renunciation of the powers that are thereby acquired (cf. Eliade 1969:89, 1976:106–7).

The man-in-the-world, however, remains thirsty for miracles and his compromise is the ascetic who is seen to work wonders – as it were, under the counter and in spite of himself – while denying his capacity to do so. It is not uncommon, in my experience, for one ascetic to be disparaged by the followers of another on the grounds that he is a mere performer of supernatural tricks.[13] But at the same time the follower feels obliged to justify the claims he makes for his own guru by reference to a personal experience of the marvels he can accomplish. Did he not witness, or even himself benefit from, this or that miraculous cure? Was he not actually with his guru in Banaras when the latter was unmistakably sighted in Allahabad? The fact that the ascetic himself disclaims such reports merely confirms his spiritual authenticity.

Transcending the world and the *siddhis* he thereby achieves, there comes a point at which the ascetic can dispense with the austerities from which his accomplishments derive. Having really 'arrived', his *sadhana* is now superfluous, and he can begin to distance himself from the more dramatic aspects of Aghori discipline. That at least is the path along which Baba Bhagvan Ram appears to have travelled, and since he has taken effective control of its management, Kina Ram's *ashram* has become an increasingly 'domesticated' and respectable institution which has lost much of the sinister awe with which it was regarded in the days of its former *mahant*. It has as it were (and as several informants expressed it) become progressively 'Vaishnavised' – a trend which has no doubt been encouraged by the Baba's rapidly expanding middle-class following which now extends into the expatriate Indian community.

The curse of an Aghori is particularly terrible and virtually irrevocable. The food of the accursed may turn to excrement as he raises it to his lips, or his heir may die. When a filthy Aghori dressed in the rotting skin of a fresh-water porpoise was, some generations ago, refused admission to the Maharaja of Banaras's palace during the performance of a magnificent *yagya*, the sacrificial offerings became immediately infested with maggots and the sacrifice had to be abandoned. As a result of this incident, the Maharaja's line has continually failed to produce heirs, and has been forced to perpetuate itself by adoption; while the curse also stipulated that any Aghori who henceforth accepted food from the palace would be afflicted by a fistula in the anus (*bhagandar*). When the late *mahant* of Kina Ram's *ashram* was at last induced to revoke the curse and eat from the royal kitchen, the Maharani immediately conceived a son – but the *mahant* himself succumbed to the foretold disorder.

For the development of my theme the story is particularly instructive in two ways. The first is that it draws our attention to the fact that the curse of an Aghori, and – as we shall see – his blessing too, is as often as not concerned with reproduction and fertility. But what is also significant is that the exclusion of the ascetic from the Maharaja's *yagya* appears to be merely a transposition of the well-known mythological incident in which Shiva is excluded from the sacrifice of his father-in-law, Daksha, on the pretext that he is a naked skull-carrying Kapalika (O'Flaherty 1976:278), the sectarian precursor of the Aghori. But Shiva is essential to the sacrifice if the evil it unleashes is to be mastered (Biardeau 1976:96). Denied his share, he spoils the whole event and precipitates a disaster of cosmic proportions. Though the scale of our story is admittedly more modest, it is not difficult to see that the Aghori is merely playing the role which was written for Shiva – as well he might, for as we shall find he aspires to be Shiva.

The blessing of an Aghori is as beneficent as his curse is awesome. By it he may confer inordinate riches, restore the mad, cure the incurable or bestow fertility on the barren. In order to conceive a child, both Hindu and Muslim couples go in large numbers to Kina Ram's *ashram*, where they visit his tomb, bathe in the tank of Krimi Kund ('the tank of worms')[14] and take ash from the sacred fire which is fuelled by wood brought from the cremation pyres and which is a form of the goddess Hinglaj Devi. The tank is the one beside which Kina Ram performed his austerities – thus again making a direct link between *tapas* and the powers of creation. The same procedure should ideally be repeated on five consecutive Sundays or five consecutive Tuesdays, days of the week which are special not only to Kina Ram but also to the god Bhairav. An identical procedure will cure children of the wasting disease of *sukhandi rog* which is caused by a barren woman touching or casting her shadow on the child immediately after she has bathed at the end of her period.[15] She will then conceive but the child will start to 'dry up' (*sukhna*) and wither away.

An Aghori's blessing is characteristically given by violent man-handling and abusing its recipient. Bhim Baba, for example, used to live on the verandah of the City Post Office, stark naked, morosely silent, and generally surrounded by a crowd of onlookers and devotees. Every so often, as if infuriated, he would lumber to his feet (for he was massively fat) seize a small earthenware pot and hurl it with a roar into the crowd. The fortunate target of his missile could leave assured that his problem was about to be solved or his aspirations met (cf. Morinis 1984:177; Barrow 1893:226).[16] It is said that on festival occasions Kina Ram would throw his urine on the crowds by way of blessing. Indeed the bodily emissions of an Aghori are charged with a special potency and have miraculous medicinal qualities. I was, for example, told how a jeep which had run out of petrol had run perfectly well on the urine of the Aghori who was travelling in it; and how a phial of this substance had cured the grave illness of the sister of one of this ascetic's middle-class devotees. I have also heard it claimed that a lay follower may be initiated by the guru by placing a drop of his semen on the disciple's tongue; while Barrow (1893:241) cites an eye-witness report of the initiation of an ascetic at which the preceptor filled a skull with his urine which was then used to moisten the novitiate's head before it was tonsured.

Now my informants continually stress that as a result of his *sadhana* the truly accomplished Aghori does not die. He realises the state of non-duality I referred to earlier; he 'takes *samadhi*', and enters into a perpetual cataleptic condition of suspended animation or deep meditation. His body is arranged (if necessary by breaking the spine) in a meditational posture (known as *padmasan*), sitting cross-legged with his up-turned palms resting on his knees. He is then placed in a box which, in Banaras, is buried in the grounds of Kina Ram's *ashram* (and which is everywhere oriented towards the north). Unlike the householder, or ascetics of most other orders, his skull is not smashed to release the 'vital breath'. A small shrine containing the phallic emblem of Shiva is erected over the site of the grave, the emblem transmitting to the worshipper the power emanating from the ascetic's subterranean meditation.

By entering *samadhi* (the term refers to his tomb as well as to his condition within it) which he is represented as doing by conscious desire at a time of his choosing, the ascetic unequivocally escapes the normal consequences of death: the severance of the connection between body and soul, the corruption of the body and the transmigration of the soul. Provided that he has 'taken *samadhi*' while still alive (*jivit-samadhi*), rather than being 'given' it after death, his body is immune to putrescence and decay although it remains entombed for thousands of years. It is still the occasional habitation of his soul, which wanders the three *loks* (of heaven, earth and the netherworld) assuming any bodily form it chooses and changing from one to another at will. The real ideological stress is here, rather than on the incorruption of the particular body he inhabited before he took *samadhi*. Endless stories nevertheless testify to a conviction that the body of the model ascetic is perfectly and perpetually preserved in its tomb; and it is widely believed that this body is at times animated by his peripatetic soul which may be brought back to its former shell in an instant by the fervent prayers of the devotee.

A *samadhi* (in the sense of tomb) which is reanimated by the presence of the soul is described as a *jagrit-samadhi* ('awakened *samadhi*'). Baba Bhagvan Ram's disciples credit him with thus 'awakening' the occupants of every one of the fifty *samadhis* within the precincts of Kina Ram's *ashram* since he took over its effective management; and this makes it possible to induce them to take a more direct hand in the affairs of men. As for himself, Bhagvan Ram denies the appeal of heaven, where – as he wryly informed me – 'all the celestial nymphs (*apsaras*) are now old ladies'. His intention is rather to spend eternity 'watching and waiting' here on earth within easy reach of ordinary mortals. It is out of compassion for the sufferings of humanity that such an ascetic denies himself the final bliss of complete dissolution into *Brahman*, for once he is finally liberated 'who will give the sermons?'

But what exactly is the connection between the discipline I have described and this conquest of death? One preliminary observation here is that Aghori ideology, if not always their practice, insists that members of the order do not solicit alms. This relates to the familiar South Asian contradiction that, while the ascetic is enjoined to remain completely independent of the material and social order, he must necessarily depend on the gifts of the householder in order to support himself, and can therefore never entirely escape from the lay world. Aghori practice may be seen as one radical solution to this dilemma. His loincloth is a shroud, his fuel the charred wood of the pyres, his food human refuse. By scavenging from the dead (who have no further use for what he takes), the Aghori escapes the clutches of the living, and in theory at least realises the ascetic ideal of complete autonomy.

We may also note that the Aghori's vigil on the cremation ground may be represented as an unblinking meditation on the classic Hindu themes of the transience of existence and the inevitability of mortal suffering. 'Surrounded by death in the place of death, those aspects of reality that end in the fires of the cremation ground become distasteful . . . attachment to the world and the ego is cut and union with Shiva, the conqueror of death, is sought' (Kinsley 1977:100). Like ascetics of other orders, the Aghori aspires to die to the phenomenal world, to undergo the 'Death that conquers death', and to exist on earth as an exemplar of the living dead. But what makes him different from others is that he pushes this symbolism to its logical limits.

The theological line which the Aghoris themselves most forcefully stress, however, is the notion that everything in creation partakes of *parmatma*, the Supreme Being, and that therefore all category distinctions belong merely to the world of superficial appearances, and there is no essential difference between the divine and the human, or between the pure and the polluted. As

Lal Baba represented his own spiritual quest to me, it is to become like that ideal Aghori, the sun, whose rays illuminate everything indiscriminately and yet remain undefiled by the excrement they touch.

The doctrine that the essence of all things is the same may clearly be taken to imply a radical devaluation of the caste hierarchy, since from this point of view there is no fundamental difference between the Untouchable and the Brahman. What is less obvious, however, is whether this teaching is one which relates only – as Dumont's (1970a and b) model would suggest – to the ascetic (caste is irrelevant for *him* but not for the world at large), or whether the Aghori's devaluation of the social order is to be interpreted as a message for *all* men. My Aghori informants themselves were not altogether unequivocal on the matter, sometimes denying to caste any relevance whatsoever, while at others presenting equality as a matter of the *religious* truth of the enlightened rather than as the appropriate goal of social policy. This lack of clarity is perhaps only to be expected, since for them the central concern is with dissolving the barrier between god and man (or more precisely between Shiva and the individual ascetic himself), rather than with tearing down that which divides men from each other.

It is, however, clear that the *social* implications of Aghori doctrine are far absent from the teachings of Baba Bhagvan Ram, their most illustrious representative in Banaras, who has derived from its religious truth a this-worldly ethic of equality and community service – though I concede the possibility that this may be a modern re-working of the renouncer's message. The *ashram* Bhagvan Ram founded just across the river from Banaras includes a hospice for lepers, primary school, dispensary, post office and printing press. Amongst his circle of followers inter-caste marriage is positively encouraged. But within the egalitarian order which he would have his disciples realise, unquestioned authority remains with the guru, whose teachings are not without a streak of ambivalence. While caste may be dismissed as a conspiracy of the powerful, the vow by which his male devotees should offer their daughters in marriage leaves considerable doubt about the equality of the sexes within marriage,[17] and the doctrine of karma is not in question. But though lepers are paying the price of past wickedness, this does not give others the right to exclude them from society.

If, however obliquely, Aghori doctrine poses questions about the ultimate legitimacy of the social order, there is a rather different way in which their practice reinforces this message of doubt. In orthodox caste society, polluting contacts between castes must be eliminated in order to preserve the boundaries of the group, for which, as Douglas (1966) argues, the boundaries of the body often serve as a metaphor. The Aghoris inversion of the same symbols of body margins implies exactly the opposite message. With the destruction of boundaries implied by the consumption of flesh, excrement and so on, goes an affirmation of the irrelevance of caste boundaries. Coming at the issue in a more general way suggested by Turner (1969), we might also note the relationship which exists between liminal states, the suspension of the hierarchical structure of everyday life, and a stress on a vision of an unhierarchised and undifferentiated humanity. By contrast with that of the initiand in tribal society, the Aghori's liminality is permanent – and it is also of a somewhat extreme character. It is hardly surprising, then, that he should represent something of the equality which is generally associated with those liminal to the routinely ordered structure.

Perhaps the most striking aspect of the data, however, is the remarkable similarity between the character assumed by the Aghori and the person of Shiva. Indeed the description of Shiva given by his disapproving father-in-law perfectly fits the stereotype of the Aghori.

> He roams about in dreadful cemeteries, attended by hosts of goblins and spirits, like a mad man, naked, with dishevelled hair, laughing, weeping, bathed in ashes of funeral piles, wearing a garland of skulls and ornaments of human bones, insane, beloved of the insane, the lord of beings whose nature is essentially darkness. (Briggs 1938:153)

The epithet *aughar* by which the Aghori is widely known and which implies uncouth carefreeness, is one of the names of the god. As the Ganges falls from heaven to earth through the matted locks of Shiva, the Aghori makes water miraculously flow from his hair. Like Shiva, who ingested the poison which emerged from the Churning of the Oceans and thereby allowed creation to proceed, the Aghori is a swallower of poison who liberates the blocked-up fertility of women. Like his prototype he is addicted to narcotics, is master of evil spirits, is touched with madness and his most salient characteristic is his moodiness. He is *arbhangi*: one who follows his whims with truculent intransigence. He adorns his body with the ornaments of Shiva, plays Shiva's part as spoiler of the sacrifice when denied admission to it, is greeted in a way appropriate to the god with cries of *Bom, Bom* or *Har Har Mahadev*, and indeed claims and is acknowledged to be Shiva. So, for example, the *mahants* of the Kina Ram *ashram* are explicitly said to be his *avatars*. In the rite of *chakra-puja*, the Aghori becomes the Lord of Forgetfulness wrapped in a deathless embrace with his consort, while his necrophagy on the cremation ground may be seen as an act of communion in which he ingests Shiva (represented by the corpse), and thus re-creates his consubstantiality with him. The skull he carries associates him with Shiva's manifestation as the terrifying god Bhairav who – to atone for the sin of chopping off Brahma's fifth head – was condemned to wander the earth 'as an Aghori' with a skull stuck fast to his hand. Dogs, which like the Aghori scavenge off the cremation ground, are his familiars – as they are of Bhairav in whose temples they wander freely. The special days for visiting these temples are the same as those for visiting Kina Ram's *ashram*; the god too blesses his worshippers in the form of a (token) beating delivered by his priests, and in ritual intercourse the Aghori's female partner is often identified as his consort, Bhairavi. In short, as

Lorenzen (1972:80) has shown, the ascetic homologises himself with the god and acquires some of his divine powers and attributes.[18] Above all, like Shiva – the Great Ascetic and Destroyer of the Universe whose emblem is the erect phallus and whose sexual transports shake the cosmos – he transcends the duality by uniting opposites within his own person, and thereby acquires Shiva's role as *Mahamritunja*, the 'Conqueror of Death', who amongst the gods is the only one who survives the dissolution of the cosmos and who is truly indestructible (*avinashi*).

This, it seems to me, is the crux of the matter. The theme of inversion and the coincidence of opposites runs throughout the material I have presented. The ascetic becomes the consort of the prostitute, the menstruating prostitute becomes the goddess, beating a blessing, the cremation ground a place of worship, a skull the food-bowl, excrement and putrid flesh become food, and pollution becomes indistinguishable from purity. Duality is abolished, polarities are combined,[19] and the Aghori thus recaptures the primordial state of non-differentiation. He passes out of the world of creation and destruction and into an existence which is beyond time.[20] So while I have argued that the mortuary rites of the householder represent a re-creation of the deceased, a renewal of time and the regeneration of the cosmos, I am arguing here that by embracing death and pollution, by systematically combining opposites, the Aghori aims to suspend time, to get off the roundabout and to enter an eternal state of *samadhi* in which death has no menace. As this book began with the atemporal and undifferentiated void which existed before the world was created, my ethnographic description ends here with the ascetic's attempt to return to this void, and thereby to escape from death after death after death.

8.2 Hierarchy, complementarity and ascetic autonomy: some concluding remarks on salvation and society

All that remains is to try to draw out more explicitly a central strand in my analysis that has to do with the relationship between the renouncer's quest for salvation and the hierarchical values of the world he abandons.

Hierarchy: 'rule or dominion over holy things' (SOED). As Dumont (1970a:65) emphasised, 'the original sense of the term concerned religious ranking'. For Dumont, hierarchy is inseparable from holism, the valorisation of the social whole rather than the human individual. It is 'the *principle by which the elements of a whole are ranked in relation to the whole*, it being understood that in the majority of societies it is religion which provides the view of the whole, and that ranking will thus be religious in nature' (1970a:66, original emphasis). In the modern West, by contrast, 'religion, as an *all-embracing* principle, has been replaced by individualism . . .' (1971b:33).

In any holistic society there is assumed to be some overarching value in terms of which the whole is ordered, and everything else is as far as possible expressed. Those who are held to incarnate this value most fully are accorded the highest status, represent the whole, and thus 'encompass' the rest of the social order. As an illustration of this relationship of hierarchical encompass-ment, we are invited to consider God's creation of Eve out of Adam's spare rib. From an undifferentiated being, the prototype of 'mankind', Adam becomes male as opposed to female. 'There could not be', says Dumont (1971a:69), 'a more pictorial symbolism of the normative subordination of women to men', nor a better illustration of a hierarchical relationship. Man encompasses woman who derives from *a part* of him, and represents the species in relation to God and the animals. The hierarchical superior thus encompasses what is in a sense both complementary and contrary to himself.

As this example suggests, hierarchy is also represented as inseparable from complementarity. In 'traditional' India, the encompassing principle is held to be the opposition between purity and pollution. Both conceptually and practically, the pure can only exist in relation to the impure: 'society is a totality made up of two unequal but complementary parts' (1970a:55). And just as there can be no pure castes without impure ones, so it is with the deities and cults devoted to them (e.g. Dumont 1970c, chapter 2). In Hinduism the concept of the divine, like the concept of caste, is a relational one, and

> belief in the gods is . . . subject to an overriding belief in the necessary coexistence of opposites, in the complementary relationship of the pure and impure. The religion of the gods is secondary; the religion of caste is fundamental . . . The interdepen-dence of high and low is not only observable in behaviour; it is also interiorized as the fundamental belief. (Dumont 1959:34–5)

What much of my discussion has suggested, however, is that this seemingly self-evident bracketing of the notions of hierarchy and complementarity is rather more problematic than is generally recognised. Part of the problem derives, I believe, from an over-stark opposition between the householder and the renouncer. While the former is held to inhabit a world 'of strict interdependence, in which the individual is ignored', the latter 'puts an end to interdependence and inaugurates the individual' (1970a:185). Consistent with the 'yawning gap' (1986b:26) which separates these persons goes an equally sharp break between their goals. Salvation is seen as opposed to the *trivarga* – the three *worldly* goals of human existence: the moral order of *dharma*, the politico-economic domain of *artha* and the sensual pleasures of *kama* – and is said to be 'fatal' to them (1970b:44). But if salvation is superior to the *trivarga*, it is hard to see why it should not be said to encompass them, as the *dharmic* realm of the Brahman is said to encompass the politico-economic realm of the king. And in fact, of course, there is a great deal of evidence that renunciation does provide a pervasive language in terms of which these other domains are ordered (e.g. Das 1981: Shah 1981; Davis 1986). If, to put it more pointedly, the renouncer represents the autonomous individual, and if (as Dumont 1970b, chapter 2, also argues) his teachings have really been the principal source of ideological innovation in the world he has left behind him, it is surely to be expected that these teachings will have a potentially subversive impact on the cultural recognition of complementarity.

In an important discussion of the Hindu pantheon in South India, Fuller (1988) has argued that the interdependence between high and low is a rather lop-sided one. The cult of the village deities acknowledges their solidarity with, and dependence on, the higher Sanskritic deities; but in their major temples the rituals and representations surrounding the latter 'symbolise a different – and imaginary – world in which the complementary inferior on whom the status of the superior depends and with whom there must always be a relationship is eliminated' (p. 33). These Sanskritic deities stand, Fuller argues, for a Brahmanical ideal in which relationships with inferiors are as far as possible denied; while through the cult of the village deities the largely low-caste worshippers express their acceptance of a relationship of hierarchical interdependence with those at the top of the hierarchy. 'When such a model issues from the religion of inferiors, instead of superiors', he says (p. 35), 'the legitimation of hierarchy surely attains its apogee.'

In line with Fuller's analysis, a good deal of the ethnographic data I have presented appears to be informed by a pervasive assumption that relative superiority implies relative autonomy, with the corollary that inferiors depend on their superiors to an extent that the latter do not depend on them. We have, for example, encountered this principle in our discussion of the *Shastrik* mourning regulations which presuppose that the pollution of death seeps through the body particles which the mourners share with the deceased. When there is a difference of status between them, the lower are held to be more closely related to their superiors than the latter are to them, and are therefore more polluted by their deaths. The closeness of the relationship between superiors and inferiors is not, in other words, conceived to be a symmetrical one (pp. 218ff). Again, in the context of spirit possession (pp. 245ff), we have seen that the 'impure cult' presided over by the low-caste exorcist authenticates itself by reference to, and acknowledges it dependence on, the 'pure' cult over which the Brahman priest presides. The Brahmanical rituals designed to pacify the spirits of the malevolent dead, by contrast, have no need whatever of the 'impure cult', which the priests deride as ignorant 'superstition'. The lower depends on the higher, but the converse does not apply.

Something of this pattern is also found in the way in which the legitimate expression of sorrow is structured by gender (pp. 152ff). While men are required to display restraint and a calm submission to the inevitability of death, women are expected to give way to immoderate and uncontrollable grief, in which they reveal their inability to come to terms with the deceased's passing and their reluctance to relinquish the corpse. What this dramatically demonstrates, I argue, is that women are more bound to the world of social and bodily relationships then men, and are therefore inferior to them. Even in the midst of their grief, hierarchy is once more legitimated by the actions of those it subordinates.

While in Brahmanical theory a couple may be required to offer sacrifice together, the wife is a strictly subordinate partner to be replaced in case of need by *kusa* grass (Kane 1974:2:368; Leslie 1989:139; cf. Ojha 1981:258). Though a priest may be rendered religiously incapable by the death of his spouse, he can always remarry (e.g. Fuller 1984:30); and, by definition, a man who renounces the world in pursuit of the highest spiritual goals must do so without a wife. Women, by contrast, have little religious independence (Kane 1974:2:367, 558); the rejection of their right to sacrifice is 'almost unanimous' in the later texts, and they are often held to be ineligible to renounce the world (Leslie 1989:108, 139). 'By a girl, by a young woman or even an aged one', says Manu (5:147–8), 'nothing must be done independently, even in her own house. In childhood a female must be subject to her father, in youth to her husband, when her lord is dead, to her sons; a woman must never be independent.' On the death of her husband, the 'true wife' may even be expected to immolate herself on his pyre, and those that survive as widows theoretically inhabit a kind of twilight zone suspended between life and death. Though it is true that women are embodiments of *shakti*, of divine power or energy, in the absence of a male counterpart that power is both dangerous and destructive. While the superior can pretend to autonomy, the inferior is dependent on the superior to make safe, auspicious and beneficent its *own* powers and capacities – a rule which applies as much to kings in relation to Brahmans[21] as it does to women in relation to men.

Though he does not develop its implications for his general thesis, and as we have already noted (p. 247), Dumont (1970b:40) himself seems to recognise this asymmetry in his essay on world renunciation when he speaks of 'the complementarities of common religious practice becoming blurred and indistinct when we move to the level of Brahmanic practice' and tending 'to disappear altogether' at the level of Brahmanic theory (cf. 1970b:63). In various recensions of that theory, the highest power in the universe is *Brahman*, the all-pervasive Absolute Being into which the renouncer may aspire to become absorbed, and which subsumes all dualities within itself and therefore contains the whole of the rest of creation. Here the divine is plainly no longer a relational concept. Though it is an odd-sounding label to apply to such an abstract entity, in Dumont's terms *Brahman* is divinity in a purely 'substantialised' form. Its existence does not, that is, depend on anything outside itself. Those who move towards it, move up in the hierarchy of created beings, and progressively out of the social world of interdependence and relationship.

Asymmetry also appears to be implicit in the very definition of hierarchy as a relationship of 'encompassment' in which the higher subsumes or contains the lower within itself. Since the superior encompasses the capacities of the inferior, it would seem to have no absolute need of others to represent them. Banaras itself makes the point. Since it englobes the rest of space there is no need for its people to make pilgrimages to other sacred centres, for these are contained within it.

At the level of the social order, *Shastrik* theory associates each *varna* with a specific form of power, the superior encompassing the inferior (Marglin 1977). Thus the all-embracing mystic power of the Brahmans endows them with the ability to control the cosmos through their knowledge of the Vedic texts and the science of sacrifice. Subsumed within this power is both dominion over the earth and human beings (the function of the Kshatriya), and dominion over cattle and production (the function of the Vaishya). But the converse does not of course apply: the Kshatriya cannot pretend to the cosmic power of the Brahman, and the Vaishya cannot pretend to the capacities of either. So while the texts allow the Brahman to assume the temporal power of the Kshatriya in times of distress (or to perform the duties of the Vaishya), there are no circumstances in which the lower can legitimately arrogate to themselves the functions of the higher. Again, the six conventionally enumerated duties of the Brahman are to study and teach the Veda, to sacrifice and to preside over the sacrifices of others, and to give and receive gifts. By contrast, the duties of the Kshatriya are to study, offer sacrifice and make gifts. In each of these examples, then, the higher is more complete, and therefore less reliant on others, than the lower. Relative superiority implies relative autonomy. The human apogee is clearly the renouncer, and it seems evident that the asymmetry I have sought to identify bears witness to the influence his message acquires in the world he has renounced.

Now I am not trying to argue that renunciation should be regarded as the 'encompassing' value in Dumont's (1970b:154) sense of being *the* predominant ideology in terms of which all other aspects of social life are as far as possible expressed. It seems to me impossible to identify such *a* value; and in relation to Dumont's theory I am struck by the fact that in Banaras religious status is apt to cloak itself in the language of dominance, rather than dominance expressing itself in the language of purity (pp. 109–10).

Nor am I claiming that complementarity is simply a matter of inescapable social reality, and that it remains unrecognised at the ideological level. As the much-quoted saying has it, 'Shiv[a] without Shakti [his consort] is a corpse (*shav*).' Interdependence, in other words, is not merely a matter of pragmatic fact. It is also acknowledged in ideology. Dumont (1970a:92) was, it seems to me, right in claiming that the division of labour between castes 'is oriented towards the needs of the whole'. My point is simply that there is another level at which this social imperative of mutual dependence is denied; that if hierarchy is a matter of encompassment then a repudiation of complementarity is an open possibility (since the superior subsumes *within itself* the powers and capacities of its inferiors), and that it is the prestige and influence of the renouncer's message which gives this possibility real ideological salience.

Further, the relationship between that message and hierarchy itself is profoundly ambiguous. On the one hand the renouncer relativises the caste order by declaring it inconsequential to his ultimate quest for salvation. It is demoted, as Dumont (1970a:190) put it, from 'religious truth to a purely social fact'. While he may not deny its mandate over the man-in-the-world – though some renouncers do just that (pp. 261–2) – he certainly relativises it. But if the argument I have been making is correct, then the teachings of those who have left the world behind them have been appropriated by those who remain within it as another language for legitimating hierarchy, which now becomes a matter of relative autonomy. If, as Béteille (1986) has cogently argued, the relationship between individualism and equality is contingent, rather than the necessary one which Dumont (1970a) postulates, what this suggests is that the same might also be true of the relationship between holism and hierarchy. When the superior denies his dependence on the inferior, the valorisation of the social whole has certainly clearly gone by the board.[22]

But given that social reality demands otherwise, for whom does this ideological denial have any real resonance? As my example of the expression of grief should suggest, I believe that the basic premise that inferiors are more enmeshed in the transient world of relationship is a pervasive one. But it is I think clear that the contradiction between having both to affirm and to deny interdependence with others is most acute for the Brahmans. As Das (1982) has elegantly demonstrated, the Brahman is represented as a householder in relation to the renouncer, and a renouncer in relation to the householder. He is both inside and outside the world, and it is therefore not surprising that his ideology should most sharply reveal a basic ambivalence towards it.

Brahmanical ambivalence about the world of interdependence is perhaps nowhere more clearly illustrated than in the ideology of the gift. The religious gift – the gift of *dan* – is said to be a surrogate for asceticism appropriate to the debased epoch in which we now live. Its orientation is not to this world but the next, and the donor must on no account receive any kind of worldly reciprocation for it. The theory, in short, denies the world of social interdependence by denying the moral norm of reciprocity on which that world must be based. The gift is geared to salvation, and salvation turns its back on society and disregards its basic axioms. It is this, I have argued, that largely accounts for the moral ambiguity that surrounds it (pp. 130ff).

Though there is certainly a tension – even a contradiction – between the values of asceticism which have so strongly influenced the ideology of the Brahman and the premium which even he places on material acquisition, their co-existence should not perhaps surprise us. Worldliness and other-worldliness would seem to be part of the same complex of ideas in that renunciation must draw at least part of its ideological force from a propensity to value the world highly. Avidity and asceticism may even reinforce each other. The true gift is an act of abandonment, a *renunciation* of the donor's hard-earned surplus. But the pilgrim's renunciation is generally encouraged by priestly cajolery that may sometimes amount to extortion. The ideology of the generous donor who gives without counting the cost, and the grasping recipient who exploits it for personal gain, are two sides of the same coin (pp. 119ff).

In its attitude to the world, even asceticism itself is somewhat Janus-faced. Ideally conceived as a voluntary relinquishment of life, death is repeatedly represented as a kind of renunciation. But it is also imaged as sacrifice. Though the two symbols are closely associated, the ultimate aim of renunciation is conventionally understood to be liberation from the endless cycle of rebirths, while sacrifice is a pre-eminently creative act through which the sacrifier – and even the cosmos – is reborn. The simple conclusion that sacrifice is concerned with keeping the wheel of creation in motion, renunciation with escaping from it, is however too simple. Like sacrifice, asceticism also unleashes an extraordinary creative potency. The dead are burned at the very spot where Vishnu burned with the fire of the austerities through which he engendered the cosmos (pp. 11ff), and it seems clear that their own 'austerities' are a way of regenerating it (pp. 30ff). One construction which is put on the ascetic regime which the chief mourner observes in the period following cremation is that through it he accumulates the power to create a new body for the deceased (pp. 217–18). But perhaps the most vivid example is provided by the fearful austerities of the Aghori, austerities that give him the power to confer fecundity on the householder (p. 259).

The symbol of asceticism thus points in two opposite directions at once. It offers a route of escape from the world, yet it generates a power that is necessary to sustain it. The renouncer transcends, or even rejects, worldly hierarchy, yet the values he represents are set to work in its service. These values coexist with, and may even entrench, a cupidity which is entirely antithetical to them. Even within itself, asceticism seems to embody what Heesterman (1985) describes as 'the inner conflict' of the Hindu tradition – an irresolvable tension between salvation and society, a tension which pervades the ethnography I have provided.

But perhaps not only the Hindu tradition(s)? Though in different degree, a deeply uneasy relationship between the ultimate goals of religious striving and the social order is, I would argue, common to all of the major world religions. At first sight it is at any rate tempting to draw a distinction between those systems of thought in which there is a radical distinction between this world and the other world, and those in which they are represented as being broadly homologous. Take Evans-Pritchard's account of Nuer conceptions of the after-life – such as they are, for the Nuer are notably vague on the topic. 'General opinion', however, is that the dead 'live a life like that they lived when they were on earth amid their cattle and dung fires in villages and camps' (1956:159). In salvation religions, by contrast, there is a complete antithesis between the world of human existence and a transcendent world which is entirely free from suffering, misery and death. From such a perspective life in this world is plainly devalued, and movements of ascetic withdrawal from it are clearly a logical development.

It is, of course, undeniable that the salvation religions differ greatly in the attitude they take to the world; and the contrast between Indian and

Judaeo-Christian traditions has often been commented on. In 'orthodox' Theravada Buddhism, only those who renounce the world can aspire to salvation, and the laity are left with the lesser religious goal of achieving a better rebirth. In Hinduism this opposition between life in the world and the quest for freedom from the cycle of rebirths is rather less stark in that various traditions allow for alternative paths to salvation – the path of devotion, for example, or the doctrine that all who die in Banaras automatically attain 'liberation'. In the dominant orthodoxy, however, renunciation remains a requirement. In Christianity, by contrast – though there have been those, like St Bernard, who saw the cloister as the only sure route to salvation (Lawrence 1984:154) – the gates of heaven have in theory always been open to those who remained in the world, and the kind of radical split between the spiritual goals of the monk and the layman that is characteristic of Theravada Buddhism is absent (Reynolds 1980). Since salvation is to be obtained within it, the world is less radically devalued. As Troeltsch (1931) clearly shows, however, the attitudes of the pre-Reformation Church to the social order nevertheless remained ones of extreme ambivalence.

Ambivalence is not, however, a monopoly of the world religions, though it is in them that it is surely most strongly marked. The posthumous fate of the Nuer notwithstanding, some kind of tension between the image of an ideal order, and society as it actually exists, is certainly a far more general phenomenon. On the basis of Fortune's (1963) data, for example, Bloch and I have argued that in their mortuary practices the Dobuan islanders (of Melanesia) construct an idealised world in which the members of the matrilineage are at last freed from the aggravating flux of life imposed on them by the pattern of alternating residence, in which the generations succeed each other without the frightening and dangerous necessity of having to depend on sorcerous affines, and from which exchange with outsiders has been eliminated (Bloch and Parry 1982:27–30). What we have here, then, is a set of representations which also repudiates the interdependencies on which society is, and must be, based.

I invoke the example to suggest that the strain towards an ideological denial of complementarity which I have stressed in the Indian context may be part of a much wider picture. From the whole Durkheimian tradition we are well used to thinking of the world of the sacred as replicating the social order and as rendering it apparently inviolable and immune to change. But the other side of the coin is that in order to achieve this latter result the sacred domain must in part be constructed in antithesis to the world of everyday life, and that it therefore suggests possibilities which are profoundly unsettling to it. At the same time as it sacralises the social order, to a greater or lesser extent the sacred almost inevitably puts it in question.

Notes

1 Through 'divine eyes'

1 I refer here primarily to the so-called *mahatmya* literature. The defining feature of this genre of Sanskrit texts is that they laud the incomparable superiority of a particular place (deity or time) over all others, and specify (with often mathematical precision) the bounteous 'fruits' to be obtained by performing the rituals associated with it. *Mahatmyas* of Kashi are found in a number of *Puranas*, but by far the most extensive and widely cited is the *Kashi khanda*, a portion of the *Skanda Purana*. The dating of such works is notoriously uncertain, though it seems likely that the *Kashi khanda* acquired something close to its present shape around the mid-thirteenth century AD (see Eck 1980 and 1983:347–9). *Mahatmyas* are not, however, immutably ossified in the form of their original composition. Not only is it unlikely that there ever was *a* single original, but such texts are open to constant 'revision and interpolation in order to bring them into line with changes in topography and patterns of worship' (Entwistle 1987:228; cf. Parry 1985). Like many others of the genre, the *Kashi khanda* takes the form of a dialogue. It is told as it was originally recounted by Shiva to the goddess Parvati.

   Unless otherwise stated, my citations from the *Kashi khanda* are from Baikunthnath Upadhyay's summary, commentary and translation into Hindi. Separate chapters of the work are put out as small pamphlets which are available throughout the city, and are bought and read by large numbers of pilgrims. Reference is also made to the *Kashi mahima prakash*, a brief vernacular digest of the same text. The Sanskrit sources have been exhaustively treated by Eck (1983). Though my own account overlaps with Eck's at a number of points, and has been influenced by some of her formulations, its central thesis is quite distinct. While many of the ideas about the city which are reported in this chapter have a textual pedigree, I should emphasise that the vast majority of them are also very much part of the oral tradition of those who live and work on the *ghats*.

2 On the *Kashi khanda*, see note 1 above. The *Shiva Purana* provides a variant on this cosmogonic account (cited in Eck 1983:243).

3 My informants speak of *Brahm*, but their understandings of this entity are so close to the classical concept of *Brahman* that I feel justified in substituting this term. The Stutleys gloss it as an '"all-pervading, self-existent power" . . . "invisible, ungraspable, eternal, without qualities, it is the imperishable source of all things" . . . It is the "falling together" and hence unification of all opposites' (Stutley and Stutley 1977:49–50).

4 The distance of 5 *kos* (about 10 miles), which the name of the pilgrimage suggests, refers to the notional radius of the circle rather than its circumference (Eck 1978).

5 Similar claims are made for other sacred centres (e.g. Vidyarthi 1961:117).

6 *Man changa to kathauti men Ganga; man pakka to paikhane men Makka.*

7 *Pan* is betel-leaf. The leaf is folded into an envelope containing betel-nut, lime, tobacco (optional) and other condiments. Many Banarasis chew it constantly, and taking *pan* together is a key symbol of friendly social relations. Meet an acquaintance on the street, and – whatever one's hurry – politeness almost demands that one of you say, 'please come, please eat *pan*'. For the foreign anthropologist this is something of a hazard of fieldwork in the city, for not only is *pan* an acquired taste, and spitting out the scarlet juice with seemly aim an art to be mastered, it is also a constant reminder of one's linguistic imperfections. It can be as hard to articulate, and as hard to follow, as a conversation between two people with lemons in their mouths.

8 There is no general agreement on the form of the *mantra*, though the favourite theory is that it consists of the sacred syllable 'Aum', or the name of Ram. It is certainly something short, for as Anant Maharaj explained, 'God does not have much time to waste. There is a lot of other work to be done.'

9 See, for example, Dimmitt and Van Buitenen 1978:273–86.

10 See, for example, Chandler's (1910:3–5) vivid story of 'a notoriously evil-liver, and a consumer of cow's flesh' being loaded onto the Banaras train in Calcutta when he was close to death. As everybody predicted, he failed to make it.

11 Cf. Morinis (1984:297) who interprets the Hindu variant of this idea in terms of a conception of pilgrimage as an allegorical journey of the soul to God. 'If the geographical journey to the abode of the deity is taken as an allegory for the passage of the soul through life to God, then the termination of the allegorical journey at the earthly shrine invokes the idea of the completion of the soul's life passage. This suggestion explains why many sacred texts place a value on death in the pilgrimage centre (when the reality and the allegory coincide) . . .'

2 A profane perspective

1 At the 1971 and 1981 censuses the Municipal Council area had a population of 583,856 and 708,647 respectively. This compares with a 1901 figure of 215,223. The 1981 figure for the 'Varanasi Urban Agglomeration' was 816,369. Today it is over a million.

2 I do not, of course, intend to imply that the *character* of this conflict has remained unchanged over the past two centuries – merely to draw attention to its existence.

3 These events have most recently been discussed in detail in Freitag 1989a:19ff.

4 In the case of those pilgrims who arrive by rail in carriages specially chartered by a pilgrim-tour operator, it is possible to quantify this with some precision. According to the station-master's statistics at Varanasi Cantonment station, in 1976 245 such carriages (each with an official capacity of 76) had spent an average of 31 hours and 24 minutes in the station sidings!

5 *Aj*, 3 May 1979.

6 This correspondence was opened in *Aj* on 24 April 1979 by a planted request for information from 'a searcher', and ran on throughout May. See also *Sanmarg* for the same period.

7 *Aj*, 15 May 1979.

8 *Aj*, 18 May 1979.

9 *Aj*, 17 May 1979.

10 It is perhaps worth noting that in the holy city of Gaya the main cremation ground is more or less adjacent to Vishnupad, the city's most important temple. Not only is Vishnu's footprint its chief object of veneration, but this is what the name of the temple actually means.

11 I base this assertion partly on the testimony of the *Narada Purana* (cited earlier), and partly on other circumstantial evidence – the report, for example, that Raja Balwant Singh of Banaras was cremated at the *ghat* in 1770 (that is, five years *before* the supposed date of the Kasmiri Mal incident) (*All About Benares*, 1918:50).

12 House of Commons Parliamentary Papers for 1825 record 160 *satis* in Banaras and Allahabad between 1815 and 1823, as compared with a figure of 561 for Ghazipur and Gorakhpur (quoted in Mukhopadhyay 1957:108).

13 Of these, 251 went to Kashi-labh Mukti Bhavan; 283 to Ganga-labh Bhavan, and 24 to Manikarnika-Seva Ashram. Statistical information is derived from the hospice registers.

14 For Kashi-labh Mukti Bhavan I have figures for seven years between 1958 and 1976. Over this period 885 patients arrived in the hospice, not one of whom is identifiable by caste name as an Untouchable.

15 The last two statements are based on the 251 cases at Kashi-labh Mukti Bhavan.

16 In two cases I have not been able to identify the districts recorded.

17 Seven from Maharashtra, two from Bengal and one from Delhi.

18 One from Nepal and one from the UK. In addition fourteen corpses are recorded as having come from districts which I have not been able to identify, making up the total of 10,018.

19 Though it is true that Jaunpur and Azamgarh are more populous than Ghazipur and Mirzapur, the difference is small in comparison with the difference between the rates at which these districts dispatch corpses to Banaras. At the 1971 census, Jaunpur had a population of roughly 2 million, Azamgarh of 2.86 million, Ghazipur of 1.53 million and Mirzapur of 1.54 million. In 1970–1, Jaunpur contributed 56 per cent of all outsider corpses cremated in Banaras, and Ghazipur only 0.6 per cent (cf. Table 3).

20 In the mid-1950s the village of 'Senapur' in the southeast of Jaunpur district was 2 miles from an all-weather road to Banaras (28 miles away). Planalp (1956:596) reports that nobody from the village had been taken there to die for the past seventeen years, and that even formerly the practice had been uncommon. To ensure 'the least expense and trouble to the family' when the decision to go had been taken, 'a Mishra Brahman skilled in predicting the time of death by feeling the pulse was called'.

21 Numerically at least, the dominant caste in Jaunpur, Ghazipur and Rohtas (Shahabad) is the same – the relatively low-caste Ahir-herdsmen (with respectively 13 per cent, 16 per cent and 14 per cent of the total population of the district). The most numerous caste in the weakly represented district of Allahabad is the Brahmans (11 per cent); and in the relatively well-represented districts of Azamgarh and Mirzapur, untouchable Chamar-leatherworkers (20 per cent and 13 per cent respectively). In Azamgarh, Rajputs are second in numerical strength with 19 per cent of the population; in Mirzapur Brahmans with 9 per cent (Schwartzberg 1968, based on the 1931 census – the last in which caste populations were recorded).

22 The year 1918 had particularly high mortality. There were 104,287 registered deaths in the district, a rate of 90.4 per 1,000. This compares with a 1917 figure of 41,287 and a rate of 35.7 (UP Sanitary Reports for 1917–18). My cremation-*ghat* statistics cover the period between 1 April 1917 and 31 March 1918. I have

made the rough and ready assumption that three-quarters of the 1917 Jaunpur total can be assigned to this period, and one-quarter of the 1918 total (probably an over-estimate since most of the excess mortality due to the influenza pandemic was concentrated in the later part of the year). I have further assumed that Hindus died at a rate proportionate to their share of the population (89–90 per cent). On these figures, around 1.9 per cent of Jaunpur Hindu corpses were taken to Banaras. But since some deaths were never registered, this must be regarded as an upper limit. Unfortunately, there are no remotely plausible figures for the number of deaths in Jaunpur in 1976–7. My estimate is based on a UP death rate of 20.5 in 1976 and 19.1 in 1977 (Sample Registration System), on a crude population figure for the district of 2.25 million, and on the assumption that 89–90 per cent were Hindus. This gives a figure of between 13.6 and 14.7 per cent of Jaunpur Hindu corpses being brought to Banaras. I am much indebted to Tim Dyson for help with this point.

23 The principal reason for keeping this record, I suspect, has to do with the operation of the Mahabrahman share system, discussed on pp. 75ff below. The Mahabrahmans rely on these records to identify the mourners they will serve at the tenth and eleventh day rituals, and the (Dom) municipal clerk receives a fee for supplying such information. Since there are always Mahabrahmans present at Manikarnika, they have no need of others to collect it for them.

24 1948–9, 1956–7, 1966–7, 1969–70 and 1976–7.

25 According to the 1981 census, 18.12 per cent of the population of Banaras district was of 'Scheduled Caste'. For Azamgarh, Jaunpur and Ghazipur, the figures are 24.82, 21.44 and 20.59 respectively.

26 In just over 5 per cent of the entries, the mourners had either refused to specify their caste, or had supplied caste names which I have not been able to identify.

27 1937–8, 1948–9, 1956–7, 1966–7 and 1976–7.

28 See, for example, *The Sunday Times*, 18 July 1986.

29 I am extremely grateful to Sara Ahmed and Marianna Caixeiro for generously sharing information with me on the new crematorium.

30 Though the mourners save money, they are unlikely to save much time. Though a 'traditional' cremation takes 3 to 5 hours, while the 'machine' incinerates a corpse in 60 to 90 minutes, for the latter they may be required to queue for up to 12 hours. There is also, of course, the risk of a prolonged power-failure mid-way through – not a negligible one at certain times of the year in Banaras.

31 While there is always a municipal clerk on duty at the two cremation grounds without whose certificate the Doms will refuse to cremate, those who dispose of corpses from other *ghats* are supposed to report to the Municipal Corporation within three days. Especially when the death is of a small child, many people neglect to do so.

32 This was at the time of the 1977 Pryag *Kumb Mela*.

3 Shares and chicanery

1 Discussion of the exorcists and the temple-priests of the sacred tank of Pishach Mochan, who control the spirits of those who have died a 'bad death' and whose activities are located away from the river front, is deferred to chapter 7.

2 The Kathmandu daily, *Rising Nepal*, records that much the same procedures were followed on the death of King Mahendra in 1972, though in keeping with the spirit of the times the Mahabrahman was allowed to return to the capital after three days. Even amongst Nepali commoners this specialist is required to consume some of the bone residue of the deceased (Toffin 1987).

3 Sherring (1872:35) reports that 'no other Brahman will touch a Maha-Brahman. Should he by chance do so, he must bathe, and wash his clothes.'

4 *Ke ka bhagya hoyen Mahabrahman duari par aye.*

5 On the death of a member of one of the Punjabi Funeral-priest families, a local Mahabrahman accepted the offerings – though my informants were divided about the propriety of this. Some saw it as unexceptionable since these Punjabi priests are really 'good' Brahmans; others objected on the grounds that they are really Mahabrahmans, and that one Mahabrahman has no right to accept gifts on the death of another.

6 Based on my 1976–7 observations, this would be as large a number as he could reasonably expect. The arithmetic is that out of an average of seventy-three corpses which were brought each day to the two cremation *ghats* where he and his servants keep watch, only about twenty-two (30 per cent) would be from within the city area, and thus his potential clients. Of these about half are likely to be excluded because they are Untouchables or world renouncers, *jajman* of the Bengali, Maharashtrian or Punjabi Funeral-priests, or because they have been surreptitiously siphoned off by a member of his own community (probably one of his own employees), or are completely indigent. One of my informants, however, claims that he once derived as many as forty *jajman* from a single *pari*; while I have seen several *paris* from which not a single *jajman* who would make gifts on the tenth or eleventh day resulted.

7 This figure is based on 1976–7 observations, and at that time would have roughly represented the average monthly earnings of a day-labourer, and was higher than the monthly wage of a domestic servant. Sterling equivalent figures are, of course, problematic not only because of the enormous disparity in purchasing power, but also because of dramatic fluctuations in the exchange rate falling to below Rs. 15 to £1 in 1976–7 and rising to over Rs. 55 in 1992.

8 The four original ancestors are named. The fifth is known only as Panchuan Bakhra – 'Fifth Share' – but is conceived to have been a real historical figure.

9 The lunar month is divided into a dark and a bright fortnight of approximately fifteen days each. The term *pachchh* is a corruption of the standard Hindi word for fortnight.

10 The question of whether priestly rights can be freely sold (for example in execution of a decree) has proved a delicate legal issue. Legal precedent established by the British courts makes the matter contingent on whether the priest can be said to occupy an office which could not be transferred to somebody incompetent to perform it. When, for example, temple offerings are received by somebody who does not actually perform the worship himself, rights could be transferred without restriction (e.g. Nand Kumar Datt v. Ganesh Das, *Indian Law Reports* (ILR), 1936 Allahabad, vol. 58, p. 457). The courts held that Mahabrahmans do occupy an office and receive offerings on account of performing a service. Though their rights could be mortgaged to another Mahabrahman, it was not therefore possible to enforce a sale in execution of a decree when the purchaser was incompetent to perform the office (see, Durga Prasad v. Sahmbhu, *ILR*, 1919 Allahabad, vol. 41, p. 656).

11 A *damri* is an archaic unit of currency. There were 8 *damris* in one *paisa*, and a forty-day *pari* could be described as an 8 *damri* or 1 *paisa pari*.

12 The principal must in theory be repaid within sixty years if the *pari* is not to be ceded outright to the creditor. In practice, I find it difficult to imagine that a *pari* could be successfully reclaimed after more than fifteen or twenty years.

13 This is much less likely to happen with *pachchh*, for, unlike *pari*, *pachchh* rights always recur on a particular day of the fortnight. If you have *pachchh* on the first day of the bright fortnight of one month, you will go on having it on the same day at two and a half, five, seven and a half or ten monthly intervals (depending on the extent of subdivision). In the case of rights which recur after two and a half months, and after seven and a half months, the fortnights will alternate (i.e. the next turn will be on the first day of the *dark* fortnight). In the case of five and ten month rights, both the day and the fortnight remain the same.

14 When Bihari's father came to Banaras as a young man at the beginning of this century from his village in Jaunpur district, he did not apparently own any *pari* at all. The family's meteoric rise from rags to riches appears to be the fruit of the series of highly irregular unions he contracted with rich widows, combined with a somewhat factious and violent disposition.

15 Many rural people regard Tuesdays and Sundays as inauspicious for the performance of *shraddh*. If the tenth or eleventh day falls on one of these days the rituals appropriate to it will be combined with those of the subsequent day. This of course substantially affects the profits of the *pachchh*-holder. According to Planalp (1956:623–4), the problem relates to making gifts to the Mahabrahman on a Tuesday or Sunday lest another death in the family should occur. There is no restriction on other parts of the ritual sequence.

16 They may also take their cue from the amount of 'tax' paid to the Dom.

17 For example, Punjabi Khatris and Aggarwals, Gujerati Brahmans, Marwaris, Bengalis and Kashmiris.

18 This tax is also paid when a surrogate corpse is cremated as part of the *putla vidhan* ritual.

19 *The Sunday Times* for 13 July 1986 gives a figure of £700 per day, which – even allowing for inflation – seems quite implausible from my own observations. Though it is true that for most Banarasis the Dom raja's riches are beyond the dreams of avarice, they are grossly inflated in this and other journalistic accounts. (See also *India Today*, 15 March 1983 and *Dharam Yug*, 4 May 1975).

20 A more detailed account is provided in Kaushik 1979.

21 At the time of my 1992 visit, six out of twenty-one crematorium employees were Doms.

22 This is the case, for example, with Marwaris and Punjabi Khatris.

23 I was told that this service is generally requested by people from Arrah district and Ranchi in Bihar, and by certain Banarasi merchant castes.

24 Vidyarthi (1961:84) records that the Pandas of Gaya have a similar system for allocating the duties of shrine priest at the famous Vishnupad temple.

25 Ghora *ghat*, from which a considerable number of predominantly low-caste corpses are immersed.

26 Of these, ghee and *tulsi* (basil) are said to be the most important. The full complement includes the *ashtgandh* ('the eight odours') – of which the best known are sandalwood, camphor, resin (*ral*), incense (*dhup*) and ghee – and the *dashang*, which consist of barley, parched lotus seeds (*makhana*), sesame seed, rice, ghee, birch bark (*bojpattra*), gum resin (*gugul*), molasses (*gur*), incense and 'five fruits' (*panchmeva*) which generally include coconut, date and a nut called *chiraunji*.

27 If the shop with *pari* is temporarily closed, one of the others can supply the *kapal kriya* goods, though these will then be replaced by the right-holder and the money split half and half. In the face of some hostility, a fourth shop was opened on the *ghat* during the course of my fieldwork. Though he had so far resisted it, its owner

was under strong pressure to take a place in the rota. Of the three shops which do belong to the ring, one has *pari* for two days in each cycle (whereas the other two shops have only one day). The explanation which is always offered for this is that the profits from one of these days are devoted to off-setting the cost of offering worship at, and maintaining, the Shamshan Nath temple on the *ghat*, the temple dedicated to Siva as the Lord of the Cremation Ground.

28 By April 1992 the rate was Rs. 62 per maund.

29 One maund is 37.3 kg.

30 *Dainik Jagran*, 2 May 1992. I am indebted to Marianna Caixeiro for drawing my attention to this item.

31 The fact that the priest has rights to all *jajman* from a given area (or caste) contrasts, of course, with Wiser's (1936) classic account of *jajmani* relationships where the bond is conceived of as one between the specialist and the various *households* of his patrons.

32 See, for example, Dwarka Nath Misser and others v. Rampertab Misser and others, *Calcutta Law Journal*, 13, 1911, 449; Narayan Lal Gupta v. Chulhan Lal Gupta, *Calcutta Law Journal*, 15, 1912; *All India Reporter* (*AIR*), 1917, Patna 37; Suraj Prasad v. Ganesh Ram, *Allahabad Law Journal Reports* (*ALJR*), 19, 1921.

33 Bansi Lal and others v. Kanhaiya and others, *Allahabad Law Journal Reports*, 18, 1920; also reported in *AIR* 1921, Allahabad 374 and in *ILR*, 1920, 43, All. 159. See also Ram Chander and others v. Chhabbu Lal, *AIR* 1923, All. 350(B).

34 If indeed they ever existed. It is possible that nine is a conventional number and was modelled on the *Naupatti Sabha*, an association of the nine leading merchant families of the city in the eighteenth century (Bayly 1983:177–8; Freitag 1989a:24). Certainly no informant provides the same list of names for the extinct lines.

35 Elderly *Nau kul sardar* talk of a time when some (or all?) of those families who now regard themselves as *Hazar bhai* would have been known as *Chapparband* or *Tidiya pandas*. Literally, *chapparbandi* are 'wages paid for thatching work', but in the Banaras region of the late eighteenth century the term referred to a kind of occupancy tenant (Mishra 1975:72). *Tidiya* means 'locust'. Today neither label has much currency or any real sociological significance.

36 Though for reasons which I explore on pp. 122ff below, the latter are somewhat reluctant to marry them.

37 I am grateful to Peter van der Veer for providing me with this individual's real name, without which I could not have put this information together.

38 Though I do not know the state of Gajanand's relations with the *Lal Mohriya panda* of Pryag, I do know that one of the latter's daughters is married into a *Nau kul* family in Banaras who have sided against him in his long-running feud with Anjaninandan Mishra, and who themselves have a bitter dispute over *jajmani* rights with the family of Dhunman *panda*. (They too claim an interest in the Bihar district of Hazaribagh). It was allegedly as a consequence of this conflict that the previous incumbent of the *Nau kul gaddi* lost his life in a sulphuric acid attack in the mid-1950s. A further significant detail is that this family are also Banaras's chief *tirath- purohits* for Orissa, and that the other daughter of the *Lal Mohriya panda* of Pryag is married to that city's chief *panda* for the same area. In other words, the main *pandas* for Orissa in the two centres are married to two sisters. See Figure 2.

39 They are concentrated in the south of the city (in the vicinity of Harishchandra *ghat*).

40 In Gaya, by contrast, there is no such separation. The Gayawal are both *tirath-purohits* and right-holders in the Vishnupad temple (Vidyarthi 1961:8). Nor

in Banaras is the division of labour between *pandas* and Mahabrahmans contested, as it appears to be in Hardwar where the latter claim the right to act as pilgrimage-priests for the lower castes (Jameson 1976).

41 My source for the 1821 judgement is Nevill (1909:70). In Suraj Prasad v. Ganesh Ram and others (*ALJR*, 19, 1921) it was similarly held that the *ghatiya* has no legal entitlement to receive 'alms' on the *ghats*. Pt. Chandrabali and others v. Gangoli and others (Civil Appeal No. 4 of 1944 in the Court of the Civil Judge, Benares) dealt with a case brought by a *ghatiya* against a group of *Hazar bhai* who had allegedly seized by force half of the offerings he had just received from a pilgrim. Dismissing the case, the judge ruled that the Gangaputras 'have been in exclusive enjoyment of the special prerogative to receive *dan*', and recorded his view that while they are concerned with 'the sublime process of the salvation of the soul', the *ghatiyas*' duties merely arise 'out of baser duties confined to worldly comforts of body and belongings'. It is for this reason that a *ghatiya* can be female, though the Gangaputra has to be male. In an earlier hearing of the same case (Original suit no. 443 of 1942), the City Munsif had arrived at a more ethnographically plausible conclusion: *dan* is a charitable gift made for the spiritual fruit it bears and of one's own accord. It is not a remuneration for any particular service or function performed by the priest or *panda*, for which *dakshina* is paid. The *ghatiyas* are entitled to the second but not the first.

42 The physical assertiveness required of a *gumashta* encourages many *tirath-purohits* to employ Ahirs. Amongst the *dalals* I have even encountered one or two Muslims.

43 In this context the category Gangaputra included both the *Nau kul* and *Hazar bhai*. The Magistrate's order referred to many previous disputes at the station, and to the challenge recently mounted by the Joshi Brahmans to their exclusive rights. He therefore gave instructions that the latter should be required to file a list of their agents with the police, who would issue badges without which no *gumashta* would be allowed to enter the station. For a number of reasons (detailed later), the Gangaputras have, however, been consistently hostile to the administration's repeated proposals to licence their agents. In 1916 one Krishna Lal deliberately courted arrest by going on the platform at Moghul Sarai without a permit. In his appeal against conviction he was represented before the Allahabad High Court by Jawaharlal Nehru, the order was declared to be *ultra vires* and the conviction was set aside (Emperor v. Krishna Lal, *ILR*, 39, 1916).

44 The *pandas* of other north Indian sacred centres are also well known for their dedication to wrestling and body-building. On the Chaubes of Mathura, for example, see Bharati 1963:138; Entwistle 1987:6–7; Lynch 1990).

45 Sarda Kunwar v. Gajanand and others, *ILR*, 64, 1942, Allahabad.

46 The case against Anjaninandan must, I think, have been finally dropped. Of the twelve who had been taken into police custody, six were acquitted for want of sufficient evidence, five (including Anjaninandan's two sisters' husbands) were sentenced to transportation for life, and the one who allegedly dealt the fatal blow was sentenced to death. On appeal (Criminal Appeal no. 16 of 1949 in the High Court of Judicature at Allahabad), this last conviction was set aside, as was that of one of the sisters' husbands – on the grounds that he had been the chief mourner at his father's *dasvan* and the court could not believe that he would have participated in a brawl on such a solemn occasion. Special leave to appeal to the Supreme Court on behalf of the remaining four was granted on 21 May 1952.

47 Sherring (1872:38) describes the Bhanreriya as 'by profession a prognosticator of coming events' who accepts the *dan* of Saturn (*Shani*), and serves as a pilgrim guide.

Today they almost invariably describe themselves as Joshis – from *jyotishi*, an astrologer. Their standing and role in the pilgrimage complex of Ayodhya is very similar, and has been well described by van der Veer (1988:230ff).

48 Today more and more pilgrims stay in independent *dharamshalas* or modern hotels rather than with their traditional *pandas*, and are consequently far less susceptible to the latter's control.

49 This proposal goes back to the District Magistrate's order of 1903 (see note 43). It was again actively canvassed in the early 1970s.

50 Vidyarthi's evidence for their decline in Gaya is unconvincing. Based on statistics collected by the Lodging House Committee, his figures ignore – amongst others – all those who arrive by road (1961:97).

51 Without a *gamcha* the *panda*'s *gumashta* or Joshi is almost undressed. It is a kind of multi-purpose scarf or towel, generally slung over the shoulder, and used for mopping one's brow, drying oneself after bathing, or covering one's head against the sun and face against the dust.

52 *Virya pradhanta hai.* I first became aware of this early on in my fieldwork when people repeatedly asked me to explain why my young daughter's hair was so blond when my own was comparatively dark. I was at first puzzled by their knowing smiles when I pointed out that my wife was also fair. The naivety of my answer merely confirmed, as I later realised, the wisdom conventional on the *ghats* – that European women are so promiscuous that nobody truly knows the identity of their father (which is why Westerners see no point in performing *shraddh* to their ancestors). When the penny dropped, I took to fielding the question with the explanation that in childhood my own hair had also been blond – an answer accepted without the previous nudges and winks.

53 As many as one in four of the couples shown on some of the genealogies I collected for the least prestigious priestly communities were by orthodox Brahmanical standards irregular. Even amongst the *tirath-purohits* such relationships are far from unknown.

54 A *surehtin* or *rakhail*, as opposed to a *byauta* who has been accepted with due ceremony as 'the gift of a virgin' (*kanya dan*).

55 *Shudra ka ann khane se buddhi palat jati hai. Jainsa khave ann vainsa hove man.*

56 In 1978 an elderly Bihari pilgrim was killed when she was butted into a well in the Vishvanath temple by a cow. The *pandas* helped to retrieve the body, and then returned to business as usual. No attempt was made to purify the temple. It is not entirely obvious whether we should see this as testifying to the impossibility of polluting it, to the *pandas*' cynical disregard of such considerations, or to a combination of the two.

57 I was myself accommodated by *pandas* on visits to Gaya and Pushkar.

58 Though my suggestion is that one of the ideological assumptions underlying the *Kali-varjas* is that the only appropriate response to the threat of disorder is the imposition of stricter control, it is of course clear that the theory also serves to legitimise innovation. Vedic precepts are acknowledged as supremely authoritative, while following them is prohibited in an epoch so debased (cf. Kane 1973:3:967; Srinivasan 1980; Parry 1985).

59 For a critique of this theory, see Parry 1979:74–6.

60 See, for example, Fuller 1984; Good 1989; Bose, Patnaik and Ray 1958; Vidyarthi 1961:84; Chaudhuri 1981 and Morinis 1984:142ff, 183ff. While the typical pattern appears to be a *pari* system for public worship, the right to perform private worship for the individual devotee is allocated on various bases. In the Minakshi temple in

Madurai, for example, such worship is conducted by whichever priest is on hand (Fuller 1984:98ff); while Chaudhuri (1981:40ff) discusses a Bengali example in which the priests act on behalf of worshippers and pilgrims with whom they have long-term *jajmani* relations.

4 Giving, receiving and bargaining over gifts

1 *Apujya ko pujne se durbhiksh parta hai.*

2 Cf. Heesterman (1985) who notes that 'the highest Brahman is a *srotriya*, one learned in the Veda (*sruti*), who does not accept gifts' (p. 37) and that 'the preeminence of the brahmin is not based on his priesthood, but on his being the exponent of the values of renunciation' (p. 44).

3 The terms *pap* and *dosh* are used in this context. But the most common term here is the Sanskritised Hindi word *prayashchitt*. In literary usage this normally has the sense of 'expiation' or 'atonement' performed by the sinner. But in the colloquial usage of the Banaras sacred specialists it unquestionably has the additional sense of the 'sin' which is expiated, and is used interchangeably with *pap* and *dosh*.

4 Instructed by the priest, the *jajman* recites the exact time of the donation (*yuga*, year, month, fortnight, day), the particular astrological conjunction under which the gift is being made, the place (from the continent of Jambudvipa down to the name of the *tirath*), the donor's name and *gotra*, the purpose of the gift and to whom the merit should accrue, and the name of its recipient. Precisely what is being given (Rs. 51, a cow, an umbrella) is then specified and the *jajman* concludes by separating himself from the gift by declaring, 'I give to you' (see Bakker 1984:156).

5 There is also the adage that 'the learning of the priesthood lasts two generations; the wealth three' (*do pusht panditai; tin pusht daulat*).

6 Cf. Entwistle 1987:7 who reports that the Chaubes of Mathura utilise their profits from the pilgrimage business in money-lending.

7 With the exception of sesame (*til*), all these things are distinguished by their high value; but others of equal worth are not generally mentioned. I am only able to offer a series of more or less *ad hoc* explanations for the items regarded as a particular peril. Elephants, for example, are pre-eminently associated with royalty, and the textual sources endlessly emphasise how the gifts of the king represent a special danger to the Brahman. Sesame, I was told, should be included amongst the worst kinds of *dan* because it is given in the name of the deceased, and in the expectation that each grain prolongs his or her residence in heaven by a day. Since it is associated with funeral and *shraddh* rituals, and is explicitly given in exchange (*badle men*), it is an especially 'bad *dan*' (*kudan*). A number of textual sources also roundly condemn its *sale* as equivalent to merchandising one's ancestors (Nath 1987:139), and it is perhaps partly for this reason that Banarasi Brahmans regard Oil-pressers (*Telis*) as a particularly inauspicious caste (cf. Parry 1991).

8 I do not of course deny that the bride is also represented as Laksmi, the goddess of wealth, who brings prosperity, fertility and increase to her husband's line. What I do wish to claim, however, is that in addition to this more comforting and better-known side of the picture, there is also a discourse in which the most salient feature of affinal prestations is that they are threatening and hazardous in a way which invites direct comparison with the gift to the priest.

9 Both Heesterman (1959:241) and Malamoud (1976:162ff) are therefore correct – *dakshina* is both a 'gift' and a 'fee'. The 'fee' element, however, should perhaps be thought of as rather more like the payment a patient makes to a pyschoanalyst than to a physician or dentist. The efficacy of the services provided is held to be

contingent on the satisfactory settlement of the account.

10 There appears to be some regional variation here. In van der Veer's (1988:208) Ayodhya data this kind of ambiguity does not appear to exist. *Samgita* is the 'small gift which is said to make up for any deficiency in the central gift'; *dakshina* is simply a fee for ritual services.

11 This is accomplished by the *sankalp* – the pouring of water into the hand of the recipient (cf. Nath 1987:218; Trautmann 1981:287; see also note 4 above).

12 As I hope I have demonstrated in the previous section, the *form* which that problem takes is of course culturally specific.

13 Cf. Bouglé (1971:58–60) who locates 'the decisive reason' for the Brahman *varna*'s superiority and 'the deep source of its privileges' in the role of its priestly representatives at the sacrifice.

14 With regard to the kind of bargaining I describe here, the priests generally use the verb *manga* ('to demand' or 'claim') rather than *saudebaji karna* ('to haggle'). I have, however, heard this second verb used of their negotiations.

5 The last sacrifice

1 It is sometimes said that although you can repay your debt to your father by performing his mortuary rites, you can never entirely discharge your debt to your mother 'because the father just went, and having sowed his seed went away. The mother kept it for nine months and then raised it.'

2 Even more common, however, is the notion that the son's son's son is the 'replica' – indeed the repetition of – his father's father's father. See p. 205.

3 Gorer's thesis that the elaborate rituals of mourning in Victorian Britain provided the bereaved with the therapeutic opportunity of expressing their grief, and that the decline of these rituals has made death all the harder to bear, is echoed in much popular theorising about the unprecedented trauma of bereavement in contemporary society. In a pointed critique of Gorer's argument, Cannadine (1981:191) has suggested that it is equally likely that the Victorian celebration of death was 'not so much a golden age of effective psychological support as a bonanza of commercial exploitation'; was of more benefit to the undertaker than to the widow, more a means of asserting status than assuaging sorrow, and more a source of financial anxiety than of emotional solace. The implied corollary – that a greater degree of cultural explicitness about death, its elaborate ritualisation, and the structured expressions of emotion demanded of the bereaved, provide 'traditional' societies with a more effective means of coping with grief – seems to me to be open in the present instance to similar objections, to belittle the strength of human attachments, and to refuse to take the *content* of the ideology seriously. As I argue below, the Hindu celebration of a 'good death' only makes sense in the context of highly elaborated ideas about 'bad death' – ideas in which it might be difficult to discover much solace.

4 For comparative examples from outside India, see Wilson 1939, and Huntington and Metcalf 1979:34ff, 74, 102ff.

5 The qualification is necessary. Fuller (1984:30), for example, reports that a priest in the Minakshi temple in Madurai can only perform the public worship so long as he has a living wife. Unlike his widow, however, he can of course regain his 'completeness' by remarrying.

6 Alternatively, *sumrityu* or *sukal mrityu*. These terms are, however, far less commonly heard than that for a 'bad' or 'untimely' death (*akal mritu*).

7 According to Aiyangar (1913:16), certain texts recommend that after death 'the

right side of the body should be ripped open in order to make the entrails nishpurisha, free from excrement . . .'

8 Despite this theory, *sapindikaran* is in fact normally performed by whoever takes the role of chief mourner in the absence of a son.

9 Cf. Danforth 1982:39 for a comparative example.

10 But the term *durmaran* – literally, 'bad death' – is also used.

11 For a helpful discussion of the Birs of Banaras, see Coccari (1986, 1989).

12 In the extreme instance of a leper, even the ghost-body which the deceased acquires subsequently would appear to be ineradicably contaminated. It is at any rate forbidden to merge this body with those of the ancestors at the twelfth day ritual of *sapindikaran*.

13 Though I have also heard smallpox rated as bad death, its classification as such is felt to be problematic since the victim is said to have been possessed by the goddess Sitala.

14 My informants' formula is that one day of Shiva is equivalent to 100 years of Vishnu; one day of Vishnu to 100 years of Brahma and one day of Brahma to 100 human years.

15 The *mantra* was revealed to Lord Vishnu by Shiva himself as a boon for his devotion. The story is well known. Vishnu was worshipping Shiva by reciting his thousand names and offering a flower for each. In order to test him, Shiva used his power of illusion to conceal one of the flowers; whereupon Vishnu unhesitatingly plucked out one of his lotus-like eyes to complete the offering.

16 His sovereignty over heaven threatened by Krishna's popularity, Indra sent rain clouds to destroy people and herds. Krishna afforded them shelter by holding the mountain over them for seven days.

17 The low boredom threshold of the gods is as much our problem as theirs. When I asked why there is so much evil in the world when the gods are so powerful, Anant Maharaj explained: 'How else would the world continue (*srishti kainse chalegi*)? If everybody went to heaven, then what? It's all God's show (*tamasha*). Why do you go to the cinema? To amuse himself God also wants some entertainment.'

18 It is of course also the case that the chastity and devotion of his *wife* may protect a man from a premature end. The exemplary instance is the well-known story of Savitri whose husband, Satyavan, had been claimed by Yamraj after they had been married a year. By doggedly importuning Yamraj wherever he went, Savitri not only managed to win back her husband's life, but also the sight of her blind parents-in-law and the kingdom of which they had been wrongfully deprived.

19 My previous experience had suggested that yellow saris may sometimes be offered to the Ganges, not with the intention of preventing a bad death, but rather of counteracting the evil effects of one which has already occurred. When Annu, a young woman of Toy-maker caste (Kharadi), did not conceive during the first few years of her marriage, the problem was put down to the resentful ghost of her deceased grandmother (*dadi*). A feast consisting of *puris* and vegetables was spread out by a yellow sari, and a vow (*manauti*) was taken to make subsequent offerings if the deceased would leave them in peace. A *Satyanarayan katha* (a recitation celebrating Lord Vishnu's benevolence) was then performed, and the yellow sari taken in procession to the Ganges. Shortly afterwards Annu did indeed conceive.

20 The relationship between the concepts of *pran* and *atma* is discussed on pp. 180–1.

21 Cf. Das (1985:188–9) who also notes the ambivalence: sometimes the body is likened to a temple, at others it is seen as an ephemeral object of disgust. This she associates with the distinction between the body as 'a system of moral relations'

and the body as a 'biological substance', ritual striving to substitute the first definition for the second.

22 The standard formula is that, traced through the father, one has common body particles with those with whom one shares an ancestor not more than seven generations removed, and traced through the mother not more than five generations removed. In the context of mourning, however, this theory is modified to become a purely agnatic one (see pp. 221–1).

23 It is, by contrast, regarded as auspicious to dream of a corpse.

24 According to the *Garuda Purana* this final gift should also include sesame (the sweat of Vishnu which satisfies demons and removes sins), iron (which prevents the soul from being chastised by the terrible iron implements of Yamraj), gold (which satisfies Brahma and the other gods, and frees the deceased from its ghostly form), cotton and salt (which eliminates fear of Yamraj and his messengers), grains (which please the officials who look after the east, west and north entrances to his city), and land (which expiates even the sin of brahmanicide).

25 Alternatively, *Anant nam satya hai* or *Hari bol, Hari bol* ('say the name of Hari'). Anant and Hari are also names of Vishnu.

26 I speak of Banaras. Elsewhere the bones will be collected on the day after cremation, and the last of the six will be made on that day.

27 In fact, however, all six offerings are commonly made as the corpse lies on the pyre in a rite presided over by the Mahabrahman. They are placed on its mouth, heart, navel, genitals and two arm-pits. In many cases these offerings are dispensed with altogether.

28 The chief mourner should face south, and his sacred thread should hang in the *apsavya* position from his right shoulder over the left side of his body.

29 In some communities all the sons of the deceased are tonsured, as is the corpse itself.

30 Though the priests agree that this is the 'correct' procedure, some people make only three circumambulations, while south Indians usually go round in the inauspicious anti-clockwise direction.

31 I am indebted to Sara Ahmed and Marianna Caixeiro for this information.

32 Amongst Doms, whose womenfolk attend the cremation, the widow is presented at the time of bathing with 'the saris of widowhood' (*rand sarion*) which she will wear over the year to come. These are given by close affinal relatives, and she is required to put them on there and then, one on top of the other.

33 This is the case amongst the Maharashtrian and certain south Indian communities resident in Banaras. The purification consists in notionally bathing the corpse 108 times. In practice this is accomplished by pouring water over it through a sieve, the shower effect of which is taken to constitute a multitude of separate purifications.

34 Their insistence does not, however, entirely square with the procedures laid down in at least some of the manuals. The *Shraddha Parijat*, for example, prescribes the recitation of the *Purusha Sukta* at the time of collecting the bones (*asthi sinchaya*) on the day after cremation. This Rig-Vedic hymn recounts the prototypical sacrifice of the cosmic giant Purusha (Prajapati).

35 A sister's husband (*jija*) is similarly – if less vehemently – excluded.

36 Before the corpse is taken into the new crematorium at Harishchandra *ghat*, it is apparently common for the chief mourner similarly to circumambulate and touch it with fire.

37 The only exception of which I am aware consists of those rare cases in which an ascetic is buried. It is perhaps significant, however, that ideologically the interred

ascetic is not properly dead. He exists in a state of suspended animation known as *samadhi* (pp. 260–1).

38 The Rajasthani dictionary makes the connection with fertility, if not with masculinity, still more explicit by listing 'womb' and 'menstrual blood' as possible meanings of *phul*. Pregnancy can be described as 'flowering' (Gold 1988:79). An association between (actual) flowers and bone relics is again illustrated by many stories told in Banaras about opening the tomb of some great ascetic. All that it is found to contain are some sweet-smelling flowers.

6 Ghosts into ancestors

1 In the textual tradition the term is not generally applied to the rituals of the first ten days.

2 *Khoa* of cow's milk, rather than buffalo's, should be used for the preparation of *pinds*.

3 The third set of sixteen is omitted altogther; but of the second set one *pind* is normally given. This is tacked on to the tenth day offerings and is food for the *pret*. Of the first sixteen, it is those known as the ten 'body-*pinds*' which are regarded as really essential.

4 Conventionally defined as their *pattidar*, those with whom they share common property interests.

5 Failing that, three should be offered on the third day, four on the seventh and three on the tenth.

6 Fasting does not necessarily entail a complete abstention from food, but rather the avoidance of all *cultivated* grains and all food to which salt has been added. Cultivated grain (and more especially rice) is the prototypical food, and abstention from food is above all an abstention from grain. As the term itself suggests, *phalahar* typically consists of fruit, which is particularly appropriate to the ascetic because he has renounced his domestic hearth and in theory cannot cook for himself. But the category also includes *wild* rice (*teni chaval*) and wild vegetables, as well as preparations made from the flour of water-chestnuts (which are rated as a kind of cereal), or to which naturally occurring rock salt (*sendha namak*) has been added. The crux of the matter is that *phalahar* excludes all crops cultivated by the plough. This correlates, I suspect, with the fact that ploughing is represented as an act of violence against the earth and the insect life it harbours, thereby rendering such food uncongenial to the highest spiritual states.

7 An exception is made for rock salt. See note 6.

8 Upper garments, I was several times told, should button so that they do not have to be pulled over the head – a notion which is possibly correlated with the idea that sin resides in the hair.

9 According to Crooke (1926:94), 'the popular belief is that this is done in order that the animal may carry away with him the sins of the dead man or the contagion of death, like the cow in Vedic ritual which was intended for sacrifice and was released'. My own informants never spontaneously volunteered this explanation, but when put to them they readily endorsed it.

10 My informants were adamant that there is a clear distinction between *yagya* and *bali* – though none was able to specify it. Contextual evidence seems to suggest that it more or less matches Hubert and Mauss's (1964) distinction between sacrifices of 'sacralisation' (where the primary objective is to tap into the power of the 'good sacred') and 'de-sacralisation' (where the primary objective is to get rid of a state of 'bad sacredness').

11 The ritual of offering consists of a complex sequence of actions, many of which are common to a number of different types of *shraddh* (cf. note 14 below and chapter 7 note 5). In this instance, the broad outlines are as follows. The presiding priest should sit facing north and the chief mourner facing south. A 'lamp of protection' (*raksha-dip*) is lit, and the ritual dedication of the rite (*sankalp*) is recited. Invoking the sacred waters of the *tiraths*, the chief mourner purifies himself and the paraphernalia of the ritual. The space of the ritual is closed and protected by scattering mustard seeds (*digbandhan*). Some remaining seeds are parcelled into a betel-leaf with a piece of *kusha* grass, and inserted at the waist into a fold of the chief mourner's loin-cloth to protect him during the ritual (*nivi-bandhan*). A place for the ghost to sit (*asan*) is now established and various offerings made on it. The *pret* is invoked, receives offerings and *dan* of several kinds is promised in its name. Bhusvami (the Lord of the Earth), a Brahman (represented by *kusha* grass) and *vikira* (the spirit of any member of the family who has died a 'bad death' and who remains in the limbo of *pret*-hood) are then fed.

Having requested the presiding priest's permission to proceed, the chief mourner makes an altar of sand, draws a line on it from north to south with the root of a *kusha* grass, passes a flame over this line, and puts a strand of *kusha* grass down on the altar. On this he offers the *pind* of the *pret*, wiping away any grains which remain stuck to his hand with a piece of *kusha*. At the beginning and end of this sequence he turns towards the east, moves his sacred thread onto his left shoulder and invokes the power of Vishnu. He now does *puja* (worship) to the *pret* by offering threads, fragrance, rice, flowers, incense, light, betel-nut, food and drink to the *pind*. At the end of this sequence he smells the *pind*, worships Vishnu and the Brahman, burns the *kusha* grass on which the *pind* had been offered, recites the *visarjan mantra* which closes the rite, extinguishes 'the lamp of protection' and immerses the *pind* in the river or tank.

12 Because smelling is a kind of consumption equivalent to eating, one should never smell flowers which are to be offered to the gods. They would become *jutha*, a term which generally refers to saliva-polluted left-overs. Though it would normally be eaten, *prasad* – the food offering consecrated by a deity and returned to the worshipper – confers the grace of the deity merely by smelling it.

13 If an intercalary month occurs in that particular year, an extra *pind* is added to the sequence of sixteen. By the same token, 390 diminutive *pinds* would be given.

14 *Sapindikaran* is an extremely elaborate and complex ritual which may last for several hours. Though it is impossible to do justice to the details in a brief space, the standard sequence would consist of the following principal phases (which may be compared with my outline of the eleventh day offering in note 10 above, and with the *tripindi shraddh* offering described in chapter 7 note 5).

Five Brahmans (generally represented by *kusha* grass) are invited to represent the *pret*, his three lineal ascendants and the Vishvadevas, and water is offered for washing their feet (*padargh*). The chief mourner washes his own, and sips water from the palm of his hand as an act of internal self-purification (*achaman*). He next provides a 'seat' (*asan*) for the Vishvadeva Brahman, and then for the three ancestral Brahmans. Having lighted 'the lamp of protection' (*raksha-dip*), he purifies himself and the ritual paraphernalia, and closes and protects the space of the ritual by scattering mustard seeds (*digbandhan*), inserting the residue in a fold of his *dhoti* to protect himself (*nivi-bandhan*). The Vishvadevas are invoked (*avahan*) and worshipped (by being offered perfume, flowers, incense and so forth). Food is offered to Bhusvami (the Lord of the Earth) and then to the Vishvadevas. 'Seats' are now provided for the Brahman representative of the ghost and the ancestors. Each time he has completed some service for the *pret*, the chief mourner should purify himself by sipping water from his palm before he provides the same service for the ancestors. The ancestors, but not the *pret* (who appears to come of its own accord), are then invoked. Water is offered into a leaf-cup for the *pret*, and this water is then mixed with water in the cups of the ancestors (*jal miloni*). The representative Brahmans are worshipped, fed and offered water with which to swill out their mouths. Offerings are made to the *vikira* (those who have got stuck in the limbo of *pret*-hood).

Two altars are now prepared out of sand – one for the *pret* to the west of one for the three ancestors. *Kusha* grass is used to draw a line between the two and fire is moved over this line. The waters of various *tiraths* are called upon to purify the altars. Strands of *kusha* are put down to serve as a 'seat' for the four *pinds*, which are now prepared and presented. The grains which adhere to the chief mourner's hand are brushed off with the roots of *kusha* grass. These are an offering to the father, father's father and great-grandfather of the chief mourner's great-grandfather. Water is offered onto the *pinds*; and the chief mourner inhales from the north and exhales over each *pind* in the south. At this point he extracts the mustard seeds from the waist of his loin-cloth. He then worships the three ancestral *pinds* by making them offerings of flowers, incense, etc. A little rice which has been left over from making the *pinds* is offered onto them. The *pret*'s *pind* is now cut into three portions which are merged with the three ancestral *pinds* (which may in turn be merged into one). On asking the priest whether the work has been done, he is told that it has been well done. He smells the *pinds*, asks the priest's permission to remove them, and draws the symbols of Vishnu's conch and discus on the altars before destroying them. He then dispatches the Vishvadevas and the ancestors to their proper realms (*visarjan*), receives the blessing of the presiding priest, extinguishes the lamp of protection, immerses the *pinds*, bathes, changes his sacred thread and puts on fresh clothes. This is followed by the worship of Ganesh and the presentation of the *sajja dan*, as described in the running text.

15 These four *pinds* are in addition to the three sets of sixteen, so that the whole sequence is said to consist of fifty-two *pind* offerings.
16 My phrasing here is deliberately cautious. The reason is that in Hindu theory the essence of sacrifice is a deliberate act of abandonment or renunciation. It is not entirely clear that the *sapindikaran* ritual implies such an act.
17 I was often told that shaving is prohibited as a precaution against cutting oneself, for this would render one ineligible to perform *shraddh*.
18 Some people say that these restrictions apply throughout the full fortnight only to those whose fathers have died. If one's mother is dead, but one's father is still alive, they apply only up until the time when one has performed her individual *shraddh*.
19 It is perhaps significant that Srinivas's evidence seems to suggest that in those areas where the ancestors have shrines, they do not manifest themselves through oracles; and conversely, where there are oracles there are no shrines (1965:161–2).
20 Cf. Stevenson (1920:228) who records that religious instruction is included within the general category of *dan*.
21 Orenstein's pioneering work (1965b, 1968, 1970a and b) on the logic of *Shastrik* purity regulations has, in my view, been treated a little ungenerously by Tambiah (1973) and Mines (1989) who cover much of the same ground and who recapitulate some of his fundamental insights. What is of particular relevance here is that both of these writers in effect endorse his conclusion that the relationship between higher

and lower is one of *asymmetrical* dependence in which the inferior is held to be more closely related to the superior than the latter is to him.

22 While Mines offers her solution as an alternative to Orenstein's, it is not clear to me why they should be regarded as incompatible.

7 Spirit possession as 'superstition'

1 This is held on the fourteenth day of *Agahan* (November-December), and commemorates the demonic *pishach* who – on the compassionate advice of the sage Valmiki – had first obtained salvation by bathing in the tank. In his previous life a Brahman, he had become a *pishach* because he had accepted *dan* in a place of pilgrimage. The fair is known as *lota-bhanta. Lota* is from *lotna* ('to roll over'), for the *pishach* had rolled over in the mud of the tank as its water shrank from his hideous sins. *Bhanta* is an aubergine, which is what those who bathe on that day should offer to the tank. Aubergines are regarded as overtly phallic, and the word *bhanta* almost shades into obscenity.

2 For a description of *sandhya* rituals, see Stevenson 1920:210.

3 The *gayatri mantra* is taught to the twice-born initiate at the time of his investiture with the sacred thread.

4 Hardly anything seems to be recalled about Bahadur Shahid's historical identity; and I was told that his tomb has only become the focus of possession activities within the last twenty-five years.

5 More specifically, *tripindi shraddh* consists in establishing three 'shrine-pots' in the names of the three deities with whom the three types of ghost are identified, feeding and honouring real or symbolic Brahmans who represent these ghosts, and the offering of three *pinds*. The pot dedicated to Brahma, who is represented by a minute silver image, is surmounted by a white flag. The *sattvik pret* is identified with Brahma, and will receive a *pind* made of barley. The Brahman who represents it should be fed sweets and *puris* (a kind of bread prepared by frying), and should receive a cow as *dan*. The *rajsik pret* is equated with Vishnu, who is represented by a tiny golden image and whose pot is decorated with a red flag. The *pind* which is offered to it is of rice, and its Brahman representative is fed horse-bean lentils (*urad*) and *khir*, and should be given clothes in *dan*. The third pot with a black flag is dedicated to Rudra who is represented by a copper image. The *tamsik pret*, who is offered a *pind* made of sesame seeds, is associated with Rudra. Its Brahman representative is fed on *urad* and *khichri* (pulse and rice boiled up together), and should be presented with shoes, an umbrella and a small straw sitting-mat.

The ritual opens with preliminary rites of purification and protection more or less identical to those described for the eleventh and twelfth day offerings (chapter 6 notes 11 and 14). Water is charged with power by the recitation of *mantras*, and this water is used to sanctify the *jajman*'s body, the paraphernalia of the *shraddh* and the ground on which it is performed. The *sankalp* to dedicate the performance is recited, and the three 'shrine-pots' are established and given offerings. 'Seats' are now prepared for the three Brahmans who represent the three ghosts, and offerings are made to each of their places. Reminiscent of the *sapindikaran* ritual, the *sankalps* suggest that the three *prets* are located in different cosmic layers. Food is offered to Bhusvami ('the Lord of the Earth') and then to the three Brahmans. The *jajman* prepares three altars, draws a line on each with *kusha* grass, moves fire over this line and then puts a strand of *kusha* down on it. The three *pinds* are now offered onto these *kushas*. The *jajman* inhales from the north and exhales over the *pinds* in the south, and then makes various offerings to them. He now offers *tarpan* (libations) to Vishnu in the form of Saligram and to the other three spirits. As he does so he is instructed to repeat a lengthy verse in which he announces that his offering is intended for all in the descent lines (*vansh*) of the father and mother who are in the form a *pret*, who were killed by a lion, burned by fire, died without sons, who were mad or had killed a Brahman. The *pinds* are immersed in the tank; the *kusha* grass on which they were offered is burnt and gifts are made to the presiding priest(s) and to the *panda* of the Pishach Mochan temple. The main image of the temple, dedicated to the original *Brahmrakshas* who obtained salvation at the tank, is worshipped and garlanded; and in some cases the *jajman* looks at his reflection in a bowl of oil which is given away to the Barber.

8 Asceticism and the conquest of death

1 Siddartha Gautam Ram was installed in February 1978, at the age of nine. Though I do not know about the present situation, by 1983 he himself had not yet gone to live in the *ashram*, but remained with his *guru* – Baba Bhagvan Ram – in the compound of the refuge for lepers which the latter founded. It is said that he was given to Baba Bhagvan Ram to raise after the latter had fructified the formerly infertile union of the boy's parents. While the young *mahant* is described as an incarnation of Kina Ram, and hence of Shiva himself, Bhagvan Ram is held to be an incarnation of the god's *shakti* (his active female aspect), and more particularly of the goddess Sarveshvari (the consort of Shiva as the Lord of All).

2 I personally encountered twelve, but with only eight of them did I have any but the most fleeting contact. Although some Aghoris spend a significant amount of time on pilgrimage (in particular to Pryag, Pashupatinath in Nepal and Kamakhya in Assam), most appear to have a home base, and none that I came across was rigorously peripatetic.

3 *Guru Purnima* falls on the full-moon day of the month of *Asadh* (June-July) and is a traditional time for paying formal respects to one's guru. The more spectacular occasion, however, is *Lolark Chhath* which is celebrated on the sixth day of the bright fortnight of *Bhadon/Bhadrapad* (August-September). An enormous fair is held at the tank of the sun, known as *Lolark Kund*, the waters of which provide a cure for both leprosy and human infertility. (This set of associations between the sun, leprosy and fertility recurs in a number of different contexts.) On *Lolark Chhath*, however, it is the affliction of barrenness which receives the greatest stress, and thousands of childless couples come to bathe in the tank. The festival is also said to fall on the anniversary of a well-known incident when Kina Ram gave an infertile and therefore greatly distressed Brahman woman the blessing of the birth of three sons in the three following years by beating her three times with a stick. (I discuss the violent nature of Aghori blessings later on in the text.) According to the legend, she was a servant of Svami Tulsidas (though in reality it is not certain that the historical Kina Ram had even been born by the time of Tulsidas's death). After consulting with Lord Ram, Tulisdas had told her that it was not in her fate to conceive. As we shall see, fertility may also be procured by bathing in the tank of Krimi Kund, which is situated inside the compound of Kina Ram's *ashram*, and by subsequently visiting his tomb. On the day of *Lolark Chhath* many couples undergo both remedies. It was also then that the prostitutes of the city used to come to sing and dance at the *ashram* in honour of Kina Ram (see pp. 256ff).

4 A female ascetic who lived in Banaras until her death around 1970 is said to have been an Aghori, and is certainly described as performing the ritual practices which are the hallmark of the order. Vidyarthi, Saraswati and Jha (1979:220–4) record an

interview with a householder-ascetic who lives with his wife and who claims to be an Aghori, while Sinha and Saraswati (1978:145–6) provide a brief account of an Aghori couple who live together as Shiva and Parvati. All those I knew had completely renounced family life, though the *guru* of one of my ascetic informants was a householder. (See also Barrow 1893:224.)

5 According to the descriptions I was given, the corpse is held fast during *shav-sadhana* by a silken thread, which binds its wrist or ankle to a stake in the ground. It is then surrounded by a protective circle, within which the evil spirits of the cremation ground cannot penetrate, and outside of which are placed meat and liquor for them to consume. These spirits will try to engage the adept in a dialogue which he must at all costs resist. Provided that he is sufficiently resolute, they will eventually tire and accept the offerings he has left for them. This is a sign that his austerities will be rewarded. The corpse's mouth will relax, allowing the Aghori to feed it a tiny quantity of *khir*. He will subsequently decapitate it in order to acquire the skull, or cut a bone from the spine, and finally immerse its remains in the river. This is followed by a period of severe ascetic restraint which completes his mastery over the deceased's spirit.

6 In theory Kina Ram's *ashram* has the right to claim five unburnt logs and 5 *paisa* for every pyre lit at the nearby cremation ground at Harishchandra *ghat*. In practice all that is actually collected is some charred wood from the pyres. This is not only used for cooking but also for maintaining the sacred fire which is the embodiment of the goddess Hinglaj Devi (a manifestation of Agni) who came to dwell with Kina Ram in Banaras after he had visited her shrine in Baluchistan.

7 Dogs are also the attendants (*gan*) of Shiva in his form as the terrifying Lord Bhairav.

8 In the ritual language of the Aghori, liquor is known as *daru* or more commonly as *dudhva*, urine as *amari pan* and excrement as *bajri*. *Daru* means medicine or simply liquor; *dudhva* would seem to relate to the standard Hindi *dudh*, 'milk'; and *amari pan* to *amrit*, 'nectar of immortality'. I do not know what, if anything, *bajri* means outside this context.

9 See, for example, the *Calcutta Review*'s commentary on the orderly's revelations, published along with selections from them (1849:11:318–96).

10 The night most closely associated with such practices is *chaturdashi*, which is also known as *Mahakal ratri* – the night of Shiva as the destructive Lord of Time. *Chaturdashi* is the penultimate (lunar) day of the dark fortnight of the Hindu month, and is an inauspicious time during which Vedic study is proscribed (cf. Kane 1974:2:395). It immediately precedes the even more inauspicious day of *amavasya* when ghosts are abroad and easy to contact. The *chaturdashi* which falls in the month of *Phalgun* (February-March) is the day of the festival of *Shivratri*, which celebrates Shiva's marriage and is one of the most important days for visiting his temples.

11 Why Oil-pressers should be preferred is more obscure. One explanation I was offered is that their work is proverbially dirty. Others said that – like Traders – they are particularly intelligent, while a third view held the opposite, and claimed that consequently their skulls are easy to control. It is probably significant that Oil-pressers are regarded as an inauspicious caste.

12 The magnetism of the Aghori ascetic for many high-caste householders was reported as early as the first half of the nineteenth century. 'In the holy city [of Banaras], many Brahmans, Kshatris, and high Sudras, take instruction from this sage [the *mahant* of Kina Ram *ashram*]; but do not venture to imitate his manners'

(Martin 1838:2:492). The same source notes that 'the Rajas and their chief relations have a strong hankering after their doctrine'.

13 More damning still is the accusation that he uses his *siddhis* for material gain. Whether the magical powers in question are those of the Aghori, or those of the old woman who knows a charm for curing piles, in the long term they are completely incompatible with the accumulation of profit, which leads to their inexorable decline.

14 Some informants claim that Krimi Kund is a bastardisation of the correct name Krin Kund. *Krin* is the 'seed' *mantra* of the goddess Kali.

15 *Sukhandi rog* is also cured by visiting Aughar Nath ka Takiya, which is in another part of the city and which contains the tombs of several Aghoris.

16 A photograph of Bhim Baba (who died before my fieldwork started) and a light-hearted account of a brief encounter with him and another Aghori are given in Newby (1966:228–34). A special edition of the popular Hindi magazine *Nutan Kahaniyan* (Allahabad, June 1977) was devoted to stories of miraculous encounters with Aghoris. One of the articles is a profile of Bhim Baba and provides a vivid description of his method of blessing (which is almost identical to accounts I was given). This source also contains an account of Bhim Baba's origins which has extremely wide currency in the city: he was a judge who renounced the world and became an Aghori after having to deal with a case in which he was obliged to administer a manifestly unjust law. On a brief visit to Kathmandu I was able to track down Bhim Baba's younger brother who gave me a different story. The family are Maharashtrian Karade Brahmans who settled in Nepal when their father obtained an appointment at the Pashupatinath temple through the good offices of th *raj-purohit*. Bhim Baba was apparently in continual conflict with his somewhat disciplinarian father, refused to study, and finally left home (completely naked) after a quarrel in which his father reproached his ingratitude for years of parental support. He was never employed, far less a judge.

17 'Oh Shiva this daughter in the form of energy, I am offering to you to be used for the satisfaction of your holy desires and for the benefit of society – that is for breeding to such a progeny (*sic*) as may be useful for humanity, without any restriction of caste, creed or nationality' (cited in a pamphlet entitled *An introduction to Shri Sarveshwari Samooh*, published by the Awadhoot Bhagwan Ram Kust Sewa Ashram).

18 The Aghoris' identification with Shiva does not, of course, make them unique. The same might be said of many other Shaiva ascetics and even of Shaiva priests. What is again unusual about the present case is the means rather than the end, and perhaps also the aspect of Shiva with which they choose to identify.

19 One obvious symbol of this merging of opposites is the androgyne; and it is perhaps significant that Baba Bhagvan Ram – despite his unambiguously masculine physique – has assumed a somewhat androgynous character. He is said to be an incarnation of a female deity (see note 1 above), is represented as a swollen-breasted goddess in a picture kept in a shrine within the *ashram* he founded, and is said to appear sometimes before his followers in a sari.

20 In a number of respects all this invites comparison with the annual pilgrimage of the Huichol Indians to the Wirkuta desert, where all the separations of profane life are obliterated and everything is done backwards in order to effect a return to the time of creation (Myerhoff 1978). One crucial difference, of course, is the Aghori's reversal is a life-long commitment rather than a temporary phase in the annual round. Unlike the Gogo rituals of purification described by Rigby (1968), his

inversions are not merely aimed at going back to the beginning of things so that
time may start again, but rather at arresting time altogether.

21 It will be evident from this that I do not subscribe to the 'neo-Hocartian'
revisionism of Dirks (1987), according to whom the superiority of the Brahman
was a product of the emasculation of kingship brought about by the British.
Discussion of this issue is, however, best deferred to a subsequent publication.

22 If alternatively one were to insist that *by definition* hierarchy is inseparable from
holism, and if my argument is correct, then the claim that 'traditional' India
provides social science with its most privileged instance of the hierarchical ordering
of society is severely compromised. In asserting their autonomy from inferiors, the
superior repudiates 'hierarchy' (in that sense of the term).

References

Abbott, J. 1932. *The keys of power: a study of Indian ritual and belief*. London: Methuen and Co.

Aitchison, Jean. 1987. *Words in the mind: an introduction to the mental lexicon*. Oxford: Basil Blackwall Ltd.

Aiyangar, B. N. 1913. 'Funeral ceremonies'. *Quarterly Journal of the Mythic Society*, 4:13–25.

Aiyar, K. V. Rangaswami. 1941. Introduction to *Krtyakalpataru of Bhatta Laksmidhara*, vol. 5, *Danakhanda*. Baroda: Gaekwad's Oriental Series 91.

Alexander, J. and P. Alexander. 1987. 'Striking a bargain in Javanese markets'. *Man* (n.s.) 22, 1:42–68.

All about Benares. 1918. Benares: K. S. Muthiah and Co.

Altekar, A. S. 1947. *Benares and Sarnath: past and present*. Varanasi: Banaras Hindu University.

Arnold, David. 1989. 'The ecology and cosmology of disease in the Banaras region'. In S. B. Freitag (ed.), *Culture and power in Banaras: community, performance and environment, 1800–1980*: 246–67. Berkeley: University of California Press.

Babb, L. A. 1975. *The divine hierarchy: popular Hinduism in central India*. New York: Columbia University Press.

Bakker, Hans. 1984. *Ayodhya: the history of Ayodhya from the 7th century B.C. to the middle of the 18th century, its development into a sacred centre with special reference to the 'Ayodhyamahatmya' and to the worship of Rama according to the 'Agastyasamhita'*. Groningen: University of Groningen.

Balfour, H. 1897. 'The life-history of an Aghori fakir'. *Journal of the Anthropological Institute* (London), 26:340–57.

Barrow, H. W. 1893. 'On Aghoris and Aghoripanthis'. *Journal of the Anthropological Society of Bombay*, 3:197–251.

Bayly, C. A. 1981. 'From ritual to ceremony: death ritual and society in Hindu north India since 1600'. In Joachim Whaley (ed.), *Mirrors of mortality: studies in the social history of death*: 154–86. London: Europa Publications Ltd.

1983. *Rulers, townsmen and bazaars: north Indian society in the age of British expansion, 1770–1870*. Cambridge: Cambridge University Press.

Beck, B. E. F. 1976. 'The symbolic merger of body, space and cosmos in Hindu Tamil Nadu'. *Contributions to Indian Sociology* (n.s.), 10, 2:213–43.

Beliappa, J. and M. Kaushik. n.d. 'The food of well-being'. Paper prepared for the ACLS-SSRC Joint Committee on South Asia (Sub-committee on South Asian

Political Economy – Project II).

Belmont, Nicole. 1982. 'Superstition and popular religion in Western Societies'. In M. Izard and P. Smith (eds.), *Between belief and transgression: structuralist essays in religion, history and myth* (trans J. Leavitt): 9–33. Chicago: The University of Chicago Press.

Béteille, A. 1986. 'Individualism and equality'. *Current Anthropology*, 27, 2:121–34.

Bharadwaj, S. M. 1973. *Hindu places of pilgrimage in India: a study in cultural geography*. Berkeley: University of California Press.

Bharati, Agehananda. 1963. 'Pilgrimage in the Indian tradition'. *History of Religions*, 3, 1:135–67.

1970. 'The use of 'superstition' as an anti-traditional device in urban Hinduism'. *Contributions to Indian Sociology* (n.s.), 4:36–49.

Biardeau, M. 1971. 'Etudes de mythologie hindoue (III): 1. Cosmogonies puraniques'. *Bulletin de l'Ecole Française d'Extrême-Orient*, 58:17–89.

1976. 'Le sacrifice dans l'Hindouisme'. In M. Biardeau and C. Malamoud, *Le Sacrifice dans l'Inde ancienne*: 7–154. Paris: Presses Universitaires de France (Bibliothèque de l'école des hautes études, sciences religieuses, vol. 79).

Bloch, M. and J. P. Parry. 1982. 'Introduction: death and the regeneration of life'. In M. Bloch and J. Parry (eds.), *Death and the Regeneration of Life*: 1–44. Cambridge: Cambridge University Press.

Bose, N. K., N. Patnaik and A. K. Ray. 1958. 'Organization of services in the temple of Lingaraj in Bhubaneswar'. *Journal of the Asiatic Society*, 22, 2:85–129.

Bouglé, C. 1971. *Essays on the caste system by Celestin Bouglé* (trans. D. F. Pocock). Cambridge: Cambridge University Press.

Briggs, G. W. 1938. *Gorakhnath and the Kanphata yogis*. Calcutta: YMCA Publishing House.

Cannadine, D. 1981. 'War and death, grief and mourning in modern Britain'. In Joachim Whaley (ed.), *Mirrors of mortality: studies in the social history of death*: 187–242. London: Europa Publications Ltd.

Cantlie, A. 1981. 'The moral significance of food among Assamese Hindus'. In A. C. Mayer (ed.), *Culture and morality: essays in honour of Christoph von Furer-Haimendorf*: 42–62. Delhi: Oxford University Press.

Cape, C. P. n.d. *Benares: the stronghold of Hinduism*. London: Robert Culley.

Carstairs, G. M. 1957. *The twice-born: a study of a community of high-caste Hindus*. London: The Hogarth Press.

Chandler, E. 1910. *The mantle of the east*. Edinburgh and London: William Blackwood and Sons.

Chattopadhyaya, D. 1977. *Science and society in ancient India*. Calcutta: Research India Publications.

Chattopadhyaya, Kshatresachandra. 1937. 'Religious suicide at Prayag'. *Journal of the U.P. Historical Society* 10:65–79.

Chaudhuri, Buddhadeb. 1981. *The Bakeshwar temple: a study on continuity and change*. Delhi: Inter-India Publications.

Chaudhuri, N. C. 1970. *To live or not to live: an essay on living happily with others*. New Delhi: Orient Paperbacks.

1979. *Hinduism: a religion to live by*. London: Chatto and Windus.

Coccari, Diane M. 1986. 'The Bir Babas of Banaras: an analysis of a folk deity in north Indian Hinduism'. Ph.D. thesis (South Asian language and literature). University of Wisconsin-Madison.

1989. 'Protection and identity: Banaras's Bir Babas as neighborhood guardian deities'. In S. B. Freitag (ed.), *Culture and power in Banaras: community, performance, and environment, 1800–1980*: 130–46. Berkeley: University of California Press.

Cohn, B. S. 1954. 'The Camars of Senapur: a study of the changing status of a depressed caste'. Ph.D. thesis. Cornell University. (University Microfilms International, Ann Arbor, 1979.)

1962. 'Political systems in eighteenth century India: the Banaras region'. *Journal of the American Oriental Society*, 82, 3:312–20.

1964. 'The role of the Gosains in the economy of eighteenth and nineteenth century upper India'. *Indian Economic and Social History Review*, 1, 4:175–82.

Coomaraswamy, A. K. 1941. 'Atmayajna: self-sacrifice'. *Harvard Journal of Asiatic Studies*, 6:358–98.

Crooke, W. 1926. *Religion and folklore of northern India*. London: Oxford University Press.

1928. 'Aghori'. In J. Hastings (ed.), *Encyclopedia of religion and ethics*, 1:210–13. New York.

Danforth, L. M. 1982. *The death rituals of rural Greece*. Princeton: Princeton University Press.

Daniel, E. V. 1984. *Fluid signs: being a person the Tamil way*. Berkeley: University of California Press.

Das, Veena. 1976. 'The uses of liminality: society and cosmos in Hinduism'. *Contributions to Indian Sociology* (n.s.), 10, 2:245–63.

1981. 'Kāma in the scheme of puruṣārthas: the story of Rama'. *Contributions to Indian Sociology* (n.s.), 15, 1–2:183–203.

1982. *Structure and cognition: aspects of Hindu caste and ritual* (second edition). Delhi: Oxford University Press.

1985. 'Paradigms of body symbolism: an analysis of selected themes in Hindu culture'. In R. Burghart and A. Cantlie (eds.), *Indian religion*: 180–207. London: Curzon Press.

1986. 'The work of mourning: death in a Punjabi family'. In M. I. White and S. Pollak (eds.), *The cultural transition*: 179–210. Boston: Routledge and Kegan Paul.

Das, Veena and J. S. Uberoi. 1971. 'The elementary structure of caste'. *Contributions to Indian Sociology* (n.s.), 5:33–43.

Dave, J. H. 1959. *Immortal India*, vol. 2. Bombay: Bharatiya Vidya Bhavan.

Davis, R. H. 1986. 'Way of life'. *Contributions to Indian Sociology* (n.s.), 20, 1:135–48.

Davis, W. G. 1973. *Social relations in a Philippine market*. Berkeley: University of California Press.

Dewey, A. 1962. *Peasant marketing in Java*. New York: Free Press of Glencoe.

Dimmitt, C. and J. A. B. van Buitenen. 1978. *Classical Hindu mythology: a reader in the Sanskrit Puranas*. Philadelphia: Temple University Press.

Dirks, N. B. 1987. *The hollow crown: ethnohistory of an Indian kingdom*. Cambridge: Cambridge University Press.

Douglas, Mary. 1966. *Purity and danger: an analysis of concepts of pollution and taboo*. London: Routledge and Kegan Paul.

Dubois, Abbé J. A. 1968 (1816). *Hindu manners, customs and ceremonies*. Oxford: Clarendon Press.

Dumont, L. 1959. 'Pure and impure'. *Contributions to Indian Sociology*, 3:9–39.

1970a. *Homo hierarchicus: the caste system and its implicatons*. London: Weidenfeld and Nicholson.

1970b. *Religion, politics and history in India*. Paris: Mouton.

1971a. 'On putative hierarchy and some allergies to it'. *Contributions to Indian Sociology* (n.s.), 5:58–78.

1971b. 'Religion, politics and society in the individualistic universe'. *Proceedings of the Royal Anthropological Institute for 1970*: 31–41.

1983. 'The debt to ancestors and the category of *sapinda*'. In C. Malamoud (ed.), *Debt and debtors*: 1–19. Delhi: Vikas Publishing House.

1986a. *A South Indian subcaste: social organization and religion of the Pramalai Kallar* (trans. M. Moffat and A. Morton). Delhi: Oxford University Press.

1986b. *Essays on individualism: modern ideology in anthropological perspective*. Chicago: Chicago University Press.

Dumont, L. and D. F. Pocock. 1957. 'Village studies'. *Contributions to Indian Sociology*, 1:23–41.

1959. 'On different aspects or levels in Hinduism'. *Contributions to Indian Sociology*, 3:40–54.

Eck, D. 1978. 'Kashi, city and symbol'. *Purana*, 20, 2:169–92.

1980. 'A survey of the Sanskrit sources for the study of Varanasi'. *Purana*, 22, 1:81–101.

1983. *Banaras: city of light*. London: Routledge and Kegan Paul.

Egnor, M. T. 1983. 'Death and nurturance in Indian systems of healing'. *Social Science and Medicine*, 17, 14:935–45.

Eliade, M. 1959. *The sacred and the profane: the nature of religion*. New York: Harcourt Brace Jovanovich.

1965. *The myth of the eternal return*. Princeton: Princeton University Press (Bollingen Series XLVI).

1969. *Yoga: immortality and freedom*. Princeton: Princeton University Press (Bollingen Series LVI).

1976. *Patanjali and yoga*. New York: Schocken Books.

Entwistle, A. W. 1987. *Braj: centre of Krishna pilgrimage*. Groningen: Egbert Forsten.

Epstein, T. S. 1967. 'Productive efficiency and customary systems of rewards in rural south India'. In R. Firth (ed.), *Themes in economic anthropology*: 229–52. London: Tavistock Publications.

Evans-Pritchard, E. E. 1956. *Nuer religion*. Oxford: Clarendon Press.

Evison, Gillian. 1989. 'Indian death rituals: the enactment of ambivalence'. D.Phil. thesis. The University of Oxford.

Fanselow, F. S. 1990. 'The bazaar economy: or how bizarre is the bazaar really?' *Man*, 25, 2:250–65.

Firth, R. 1966. *Malay fishermen: their peasant economy* (second edition). London: Routledge and Kegan Paul.

Fortnightly Reports. United Provinces: Governor's situation reports for the years . . . (India Office Library, London).

Fortune, R. 1963. *Sorcerers of Dobu: the social anthropology of the Dobu islanders of the Western Pacific*. London: Routledge and Kegan Paul.

Freitag, S. B. 1989a. *Collective action and community: public arenas and the emergence of communalism in north India*. Berkeley: University of California Press.

Freitag, S. B. (ed.). *1989b. Culture and power in Banaras: community, performance and environment, 1800–1980*. Berkeley: University of California Press.

Fuller, C. J. 1984. *Servants of the goddess: the priests of a south Indian temple*. Cambridge: Cambridge University Press.

1988. 'The Hindu pantheon and the legitimation of hierarchy'. *Man* (n.s.), 23:19–39.

1989. 'Misconceiving the grain heap'. In J. Parry and M. Bloch (eds.), *Money and the morality of exchange*: 33–93. Cambridge: Cambridge University Press.

Gaborieau, M. 1977. 'Systèmes traditionnels des échanges de services spécialisés contre rémunération dans une localité du Népal Central'. *Purusartha*, 3:3–70.

Garuda Purana. n.d. With Hindi commentary by Sudama Misr Shastri. Varanasi: Bombay Pushtak Bhandar.

Geertz, C. 1975. 'Person, time, and conduct in Bali'. In C. Geertz, *The interpretation of cultures*: 360–411. London: Hutchinson.

1978. 'Suq: the bazaar economy in Sefrou'. In C. Geertz, H. Geertz and L. Rosen (eds.), *Meaning and order in Moroccan society*: 123–313. Cambridge: Cambridge University Press.

Gold, Ann G. 1988. *Fruitful journeys: the ways of Rajasthani pilgrims*. Berkeley: University of California Press.

Good, Anthony. 1989. 'Law, legitimacy, and the hereditary rights of Tamil temple priests'. *Modern Asian Studies*, 23, 2:233–57.

Gorer, G. 1965. *Death, grief and mourning in contemporary Britain*. New York: Doubleday.

Goudriaan, T. 1979. 'Introduction, history and philosophy'. In S. Gupta, D. J. Hoens and T. Goudriaan, *Hindu tantrism*: 3–67. Leiden: E. J. Brill (Handbuch der Orientalistik).

Gouldner, A. W. 1960. 'The norm of reciprocity'. *American Sociological Review*, 25:161–78.

Greaves, Edward. 1909. *Kashi the city illustrious, or Benares*. Allahabad: The Indian Press.

Gupta, S. 1979. 'Modes of worship and meditation'. In S. Gupta, D. J. Hoens and T. Goudriaan, *Hindu tantrism*: 121–85. Leiden: E. J. Brill (Handbuch der Orientalistik).

Harper, E. B. 1959. 'Two systems of economic exchange in village India'. *American Anthropologist*, 61:760–78.

Heber, (Bishop) Reginald. 1861. *Narrative of a journey through the upper provinces of India* (2 vols.). London: John Murray.

Heesterman, J. C. 1959. 'Reflections on the significance of the daksina'. *Indo-Iranian Journal*, 3:241–58.

1962. 'Vratya and sacrifice'. *Indo-Iranian Journal*, 6:1–37.

1971. 'Priesthood and the Brahmin'. *Contributions to Indian Sociology* (n.s.), 5:43–7.

1985. *The inner conflict of tradition: essays in Indian ritual, kingship and society*. Chicago: University of Chicago Press.

Heitler, R. 1972. 'The Varanasi House Tax Hartal of 1810–11'. *Indian Economic and Social History Review* 10, 3:239–57.

Herrenschmidt, O. 1978. 'A qui profite le crime? Cherchez le sacrifiant'. *L'Homme*, 18, 1–2:7–18.

1979. 'Sacrifice symbolique ou sacrifice efficace'. In M. Izard and P. Smith (eds.), *La Fonction symbolique*: 24–42. Paris: Editions Gallimard.

Hertz, R. 1960. *Death and the right hand* (trans. R. and C. Needham). London: Cohen and West.

Hocart, A. M. 1950. *Caste: a comparative study*. London: Methuen and Co. Ltd.

Hubert, H. and M. Mauss. 1964. *Sacrifice: its nature and function* (trans. W. D. Halls). London: Cohen and West.

Huntington, R. and P. Metcalf. 1979. *Celebrations of death: the anthropology of mortuary ritual*. Cambridge: Cambridge University Press.

Inden, R. B. and R. W. Nicholas. 1977. *Kinship in Bengali culture*. Chicago: University of Chicago Press.

Jameson, A. S. 1976. 'Gangaguru: the public and private life of a Brahman community of north India'. D.Phil. thesis. University of Oxford.

Kaelber, W. O. 1976. '"Tapas", birth and spiritual rebirth in the Veda'. *History of Religions*, 15:343–86.

1978. 'The "dramatic" element in Brahmanic initiation: symbols of death, danger and difficult passage'. *History of Religions*, 18:54–76.

Kakar, Sudhir. 1982. *Shamans, mystics and doctors: a psychological enquiry into India and its healing traditions*. Boston: Beacon Press.

Kane, P. V. 1973. *History of Dharmasastra*, vols. 3 and 4. Poona: Bhandarkar Oriental Research Institute.

1974. *History of Dharmasastra*, vol. 2. Poona: Bhandarkar Oriental Research Institute.

Kapur, Anuradha. 1985. 'Actors, pilgrims, kings, and gods: the Ramlila at Ramnagar'. *Contributions to Indian Sociology* (n.s.), 19, 1:57–74.

(Shri) Kashi Khanda. n.d. Compiled and rendered into Hindi by Baikunthnath Upadhyay. Varanasi: Shri Bhragu Prakashan.

Kashi mahima prakash. Compiled by Kashinath Jha. Varanasi: Master Kheladilal and Sons.

Kaushik, Meena. 1979. 'Religion and social structure: a case study of the Doms of Banaras'. Ph.D. thesis. University of Delhi.

Kennedy, James. 1884. *Life and work in Benares and Kumaon 1839–1877*. London: T. Fisher Unwin.

Khuri, F. I. 1968. 'The etiquette of bargaining in the Middle East'. *American Anthropologist* 70:698–706.

Kinsley, D. R. 1977. '"The death that conquers death": dying to the world in medieval Hinduism'. In E. Reynolds and E. H. Waugh (eds.), *Religious encounters with death: insights from the history and anthropology of religion*: 97–108. University Park, Pa. and London: Pennsylvania State University Press.

Knipe, D. M. 1975. *In the image of fire: vedic experience of heat*. Delhi: Motilal Banarasidass.

1977. '*Sapindikarana*: the Hindu rite of entry into heaven'. In E. Reynolds and E. H. Waugh (eds.), *Religious encounters with death: insights from the history and anthropology of religion*: 111–24. University Park, Pa. and London: Pennsylvania State University Press.

Kolenda, P. M. 1967. 'Toward a model of the Hindu *jajmani* system'. In G. Dalton (ed.), *Tribal and peasant economies*: 285–332. Garden City, NY: American Museum of Natural History.

Kolff, D. H. A. 1971. 'Sannyasi trader-soldiers'. *Indian Economic and Social History Review* 8:213–18.

Kumar, Nita. 1988. *The artisans of Banaras: popular culture and identity, 1880–1986*. Princeton: Princeton University Press.

Law, B. C. 1926. *The law of the gift in British India*. Calcutta: Eastern Law House.

Lawrence, C. H. 1984. *Medieval monasticism: forms of religious life in Western Europe in the Middle Ages*. London: Longman.

Leach, E. R. 1976. *Culture and communication: the logic by which symbols are connected*. Cambridge: Cambridge University Press.

Leslie, I. J. 1989. *The perfect wife: the orthodox Hindu woman according to the 'Stridharmapaddhati' of Tryambakayajvan*. Delhi: Oxford University Press.

1991. 'Suttee or sati: victim or victor?' In I. J. Leslie (ed.), *Roles and rituals for Hindu women*: 175–91. London: Pinter Publishers.

Leuchtag, E. 1958. *With a king in the clouds*. London: Hutchinson.

Lévi, S. 1898. *La doctrine du sacrifice dans les Brahmanas*. Paris: Bibliothèque de l'école des hautes études, sciences religieuses, 11.

Lévi-Strauss, C. 1973. 'Introduction à l'œuvre de Marcel Mauss'. In M. Mauss, *Sociologie et anthropologie*: 9–52. Paris: Presses Universitaires de France.

Levin, M. 1930. 'Mummification and cremation in India'. *Man*, 30:29–34, 44–8, 64–6.

Lewis, I. M. 1971. *Ecstatic religion: an anthropological study of spirit possession and shamanism*. Harmondsworth: Penguin Books.

Lorenzen, D. N. 1972. *The Kapalikas and Kalamukhas: two lost Saivite sects*. Berkeley: University of California Press.

Lutgendorf, Philip. 1989. 'Ram's story in Shiva's city: public arenas and private patronage'. In S. B. Freitag (ed.), *Culture and power in Banaras: community, performance and environment, 1800–1980*: 34–61. Berkeley: University of California Press.

Lynch, O. M. 1990. 'Mastram: emotion and passion among Mathura's Chaubes'. In O. Lynch (ed.), *Divine passions: the social construction of emotion in India*: 91–115. Delhi: Oxford University Press.

Madan, T. N. 1987. *Non-renunciation: themes and interpretations of Hindu culture*. Delhi: Oxford University Press.

Malamoud, C. 1972. 'Observations sur la notion de "reste" dans le brahmanisme'. *Wiener Zeitschrift für die Kunde Sudasiens* 17:6–26.

1975. 'Cuire le monde'. *Puruśartha: Recherches de Sciences Sociales sur l'Asie du Sud*, 1:91–135.

1976. 'Terminer le sacrifice: remarques sur les honoraires rituels dans le brahmanisme'. In. M. Biardeau and C. Malamoud *Le Sacrifice dans l'Inde ancienne*: 155–204. Paris: Presses Universitaires de France (Bibliotèque de l'école des hautes études, sciences religieuses, 79).

1981. 'On the rhetoric and semantics of purusartha'. *Contributions to Indian Sociology* (n.s.), 15, 1 and 2:33–54.

1982. 'Les Morts sans visage'. In G. Gnoli and J.-P. Vernant (eds.), *La Mort, les morts dans les sociétés anciennes*: 441–53. Paris: Cambridge University Press and Editions de la Maison des Sciences de l'Homme.

1983. 'The theology of debt in Brahmanism'. In C. Malamoud (ed.), *Debt and debtors*: 21–4. Delhi: Vikas Publishing House.

Malinowski, B. 1922. *Argonauts of the western Pacific: an account of native enterprise and adventure in the archipelagoes of Melanesian New Guinea*. London: Routledge and Kegan Paul.

1926. *Crime and custom in savage society*. London: Kegan Paul, Trench, Trubner and Co., Ltd.

The Laws of Manu. Translated from Sanskrit into English by Georg Buhler, 1886. (Sacred Books of the East Series, 25), Oxford: Clarendon Press.

Marglin, F. A. 1977. 'Power, purity and pollution: aspects of the caste system reconsidered'. *Contributions to Indian Sociology* (n.s.), 11, 2:245–70.

Marriott, McKim. 1955. 'Little communities in an indigenous civilization'. In M. Marriott (ed.), *Village India: studies in the little community*: 175–227. Chicago: University of Chicago Press.

1968. 'Caste ranking and food transactions: a matrix analysis'. In M. Singer and B.

S. Cohn (eds.), *Structure and change in Indian society*: 133–71. Chicago: Aldine Publishing Co.

1969. Review of L. Dumont: *Homo hierarchicus, essai sur le système des castes*. *American Anthropologist*, 7:1,166–75.

1976. 'Hindu transactions: diversity without dualism'. In B. Kapferer (ed.), *Transaction and meaning: directions in the anthropology of exchange and symbolic behaviour*: 109–42. Philadelphia: Institute for the Study of Human Issues.

Marriott, McKim and R. Inden. 1977. 'Toward an ethnosociology of South Asian caste systems'. In K. David (ed.) *The new wind: changing identities in South Asia*: 227–38. The Hague: Mouton.

Martin, M. 1838. *The history, topography, and statistics of Eastern India*. London: W. H. Allen and Co.

Mauss, M. 1966. *The gift: forms and functions of exchange in archaic societies* (trans. I. Cunnison). London: Cohen and West.

Mehrotra, R. R. 1977. *Sociology of secret languages*. Simla: Indian Institute of Advanced Study.

Mines, Diane P. 1989. 'Hindu periods of death "impurity"'. *Contributions to Indian Sociology* (n.s.), 23, 1:103–30.

Mishra, Kamala Prasad. 1975. *Banaras in transition (1738–1795): a socio-economic study*. New Delhi: Munshiram Manoharlal.

Moffat, M. 1979. 'Harijan religion: consensus at the bottom of caste'. *American Ethnologist*, 6, 2:244–60.

Monier-Williams, M. 1883. *Religious thought and life in India*. London: John Murray.

Morinis, E. A. 1984. *Pilgrimage in the Hindu tradition: a case study of West Bengal*. Delhi: Oxford University Press.

Mukhopadhyay, Amitabha. 1957. 'Sati as a social institution in Bengal'. *Bengal Past and Present*, 76:99–115.

Myerhoff, B. G. 1978. 'Return to Wirikuta: ritual reversal and symbolic continuity on the Peyote hunt of the Huichol Indians'. In B. A. Babcock (ed.), *The reversible world: symbolic inversion in art and society*: 225–39. Ithaca: Cornell University Press.

Nanda, Serena. 1989. *Neither men nor women: the Hijras of India*. Belmont, Calif.: Wadsworth Publishing Co.

Nath, Vijay. 1987. *Dana: gift system in ancient India (c. 600 BC. – c. AD. 300): a socio-economic perspective*. Delhi: Munshiram Manoharlal.

Neale, W. C. 1957. 'Reciprocity and redistribution in the Indian village: sequel to some notable discussions'. In K. Polanyi, C. M. Arensberg and W. H. Pearson (eds.), *Trade and markets in the early empires*: 218–36. Glencoe: Free Press.

Nevill, H. R. 1909. *Benares: a gazetteer* (vol. 26 of the District Gazetteers of the United Provinces of Agra and Oudh). Allahabad: Government Press, United Provinces.

Newby, E. 1966. *Slowly down the Ganges*. London: Hodder and Stoughton.

O'Flaherty, W. D. 1973. *Asceticism and eroticism in the mythology of Siva*. London: Oxford University Press.

1976. *The origins of evil in Hindu mythology*. Berkeley: University of California Press.

1980a. *Women, androgynes and other mythical beasts*. Chicago: University of Chicago Press.

1980b. 'Karma and rebirth in the Vedas and Puranas'. In W. D. O'Flaherty (ed.), *Karma and rebirth in classical Indian traditions*: 3–37. Berkeley: University of California Press.

O'Hanlon, M. 1983. 'Handsome is as handsome does: display and betrayal in the Wahgi'. *Oceania*, 53, 4:317–33.

Ojha, C. 1981. 'Feminine asceticism in Hinduism: its tradition and present condition'. *Man in India*, 61, 3:254–85.

Oman, J. C. 1903. *The mystics, ascetics, and saints of India: a study of sadhuism, with an account of the Yogis, Sanyasis, Bairagis, and other strange Hindu sectarians.* London: T. Fisher Unwin.

Opler, Morris and Rudra Datt Singh. 1950. 'The division of labor in an Indian village'. In Carleton S. Coon (ed.), *A reader in general anthropology*: 464–96. London: Jonathan Cape.

Orenstein, H. 1965a. *Gaon: conflict and cohesion in an Indian village.* Princeton: Princeton University Press.

1965b. 'The structure of Hindu caste values: a preliminary study of hierarchy and ritual defilement'. *Ethnology*, 4:1–15.

1968. 'Toward a grammar of defilement in Hindu sacred law'. In M. Singer and B. S. Cohn (eds.), *Structure and change in Indian society*: 115–31. Chicago: Aldine Publishing Co.

1970a. 'Death and kinship in Hinduism: structural and functional interpretations'. *American Anthropologist*, 72:1,357–77.

1970b. 'Logical congruence in Hindu sacred law: another interpretation'. *Contributions to Indian Sociology* (n.s.), 4:22–35.

Pandey, Raj Bali. 1969. *Hindu samskaras: socio-religious study of the Hindu sacraments.* Delhi: Motilal Banarasidass.

Parry, J. P. 1979. *Caste and kinship in Kangra.* London: Routledge and Kegan Paul.

1985. 'The Brahmanical tradition and the technology of the intellect'. In J. Overing (ed.) *Reason and morality*: 200–25. London: Tavistock Publications.

1986. 'The *gift*, the Indian gift and the "Indian gift"'. *Man*, 21, 3:453–73.

1989. 'On the moral perils of exchange'. In J. Parry and M. Bloch (eds.), *Money and the morality of exchange*: 64–93. Cambridge: Cambridge University Press.

1991. 'The Hindu lexicographer? A note on auspiciousness and purity'. *Contributions to Indian Sociology* (n.s.), 25, 2:267–85.

Peggs, James. 1848. 'Exposure of the sick on the banks of the Ganges'. *Calcutta Review*, 10.20:404–36.

Planalp, J. 1956. 'Religious life and values in a north Indian village'. Doctoral dissertation presented to the Faculty of the Graduate School of Cornell University. (Ann Arbor: University Microfilms).

Pocock, D. F. 1973. *Mind, body and wealth: a study of belief and practice in an Indian village.* Oxford: Basil Blackwell.

Polanyi, Karl. 1957. 'The economy as instituted process'. In K. Polanyi, C. M. Arensberg and W. H. Pearson (eds.), *Trade and markets in the early empires*: 243–70. Glencoe: Free Press.

Prakash, Gyan. 'Reproducing inequality: spirit cults and labour relations in colonial eastern India'. *Modern Asian Studies*, 20, 2:209–30.

Pret Manjari (Samvat 2032. Compiled by Sudama Misr Shastri and revised by Mannalal Abhimanyu.) Varanasi: Bombay Pushtak Bhandar.

Prinsep, James. 1831. *Benares illustrated.* London.

Raheja, Gloria G. 1988. *The poison in the gift: ritual, prestation, and the dominant caste in a north Indian village.* Chicago: University of Chicago Press.

Randeria, Shalini. 1989. 'Carrion and corpses: conflict in categorizing untouchability in Gujerat'. *European Journal of Sociology*, 30:171–91.

(The) Revelations of an orderly (by Paunchkouri Khan [pseudonym] 1848.) Benares: Recorder Press (selections reprinted in *Calcutta Review* 1849, 11:348–96).

Reynolds, F. 1980. 'Contrasting modes of action: a comparative study of Buddhist and Christian ethics'. *History of Religions*, 20:128–46.

Rigby, P. 1968. 'Some Gogo rituals of "purification": an essay on social and moral categories'. In E. R. Leach (ed.), *Dialectic in practical religion*: 153–78. Cambridge: Cambridge University Press (Cambridge Papers in Social Anthropology 5).

Sahlins, M. 1972. 'On the sociology of primitive exchange'. In M. Sahlins, *Stone age economics*: 185–275. Chicago: Aldine, Atherton Inc.

  1976. *Culture and practical reason*. Chicago: University of Chicago Press.

  1978. 'Culture as protein and profit'. *The New York Review of Books*, November 23, pp. 45–53.

Saraswati, Baidyanath. 1975. *Kashi: myth and reality of a classical cultural tradition*. Simla: Indian Institute of Advanced Study.

  1985. 'The Kashivasi widows'. *Man in India*, 62, 2:107–20.

Schwartzberg, J. E. 1968, 'Caste regions of the north India plain'. In M. Singer and B. S. Cohn (eds.), *Structure and change in Indian society*: 81–113. Chicago: Aldine Publishing Company.

Scott, J. C. 1976. *The moral economy of the peasant: rebellion and subsistence in southeast Asia*. New Haven: Yale University Press.

Selections from the vernacular newspapers of the North Western Provinces for the years . . . Allahabad: Government Press.

Sen, Rajani Ranjan. 1912. *The holy city (Benares)*. Chittagong: Minto Press.

Shah, K. J. 1981. 'Of artha and the Arthasastra'. *Contributions to Indian Sociology* (n.s.), 15, 1–2:55–73.

Sharma, Miriam. 1978. *The politics of inequality: competition and control in an Indian village*. The University Press of Hawaii.

Shastri, D. R. 1963. *Origin and development of the rituals of ancestor worship in India*. Calcutta: Bookland Pvt. Ltd.

Sherring, M. A. 1975 (1868). *Benares: the sacred city of the Hindus*. Delhi: B.R. Publishing Corporation.

  1872. *Hindu tribes and castes as represented in Benares*. London: Trubner and Co.

Shraddh Parijat. n.d. Compiled by Rudradatt Pathak. Gaya: Shri Vishnu Prakashanam.

Shulman, D. D. 1980. *Tamil temple myths: sacrifice and divine marriage in the South Indian Saiva tradition*. Princeton: Princeton University Press.

  1985. 'Kingship and prestation in south Indian myth and epic'. *Asian and African Studies*, 19:93–117.

Singh, Ram Bachan. 1973. *Varanasi: ek paramparagat nagar*. Varanasi: Bharatiya Vidya Prakashan.

Singh, Rana P. B. 1986. 'Siva's universe in Varanasi'. In T. P. Verma, D. P. Singh and J. S. Mishra (eds.), *Varanasi through the ages*:303–11. Varanasi: Bharatiya Itihas Sankalan Samiti (Publication No. 4).

Singh, R. L. 1955. *Banaras: a study in urban geography*. Banaras: Nand Kishore.

Sinha, Surajit and Baidyanath Saraswati. 1978. *Ascetics of Kashi: an anthropological exploration*. Varanasi: N. K. Bose Memorial Foundation.

Smith, Brian K. 1989. *Reflections on resemblance, ritual and religion*. Oxford: Oxford University Press.

Smith, E. E. 1988. 'Concepts and thought'. In R. J. Sternberg and E. E. Smith (eds.),

The psychology of human thought: 19–49. Cambridge: Cambridge University Press.

Smith, Vincent A. 1958. *The Oxford History of India*. Oxford: Oxford University Press.

Srinivas, M. N. 1965. *Religion and society among the Coorgs of South India*. London: Asia Publishing House.

Srinivasan, A. 1980. 'Order and event in Puranic myth: an analysis of four myths from the Bhagavata Purana'. *Contributions to Indian sociology* (n.s.), 14, 2:195–212.

Stevenson, Sinclair. 1920. *The rites of the twice-born*. London: Oxford University Press.

Stirrat, R. L. 1988. *On the beach: fishermen, fishwives and fishtraders in post-colonial Lanka*. Delhi: Hindustan Publishing Corporation.

Strathern, M. 1979. 'The self in self-decoration'. *Oceania*, 44, 4:241–57.

Stutley, Margaret and James. 1977. *A dictionary of Hinduism*. London: Routledge and Kegan Paul.

Sukul, Kubernath. 1974. *Varanasi down the ages*. Varanasi: Kameshwar Nath Shukul.

1977. *Varanasi vaibhav*. Patna: Bihar Rashtrabhasha Parishad.

Tabor, D. C. 1981. 'Ripe and unripe: concepts of health and sickness in Ayurvedic medicine'. *Social Science and Medicine*, 15B:439–55.

Tambiah, S. J. 1970. *Buddhism and the spirit cults in north-east Thailand*. Cambridge: Cambridge University Press.

1973. 'From varna to caste through mixed unions'. In Jack Goody (ed.), *The character of kinship*: 191–229. Cambridge: Cambridge University Press.

Tawney, R. H. 1972. *Religion and the rise of capitalism*. London: Penguin Books.

Tod, Lt. Col. J. 1839. *Travels in western India*. London: W. H. Allen.

Toffin, G. 1987. 'Funeral priests and the caste system in the Kathmandu valley'. In Neils Gutschow and Axel Michaels (eds.), *Heritage of the Kathmandu valley*: 217–33. VGH Wissenschaftsverlag: St Augustin.

1990. Hiérarchie et idéologie du don dans le monde indien'. *L'Homme*, 30, 2:130–42.

Trautmann, T. R. 1981. *Dravidian kinship*. Cambridge: Cambridge University Press.

Troeltsch, E. 1931. *The social teaching of the Christian churches* (vol. 1). London: George Allen and Unwin Ltd.

Turner, Victor. 1969. *The ritual process: structure and anti-structure*. Chicago: Aldine Publishing Co.

1974. 'Pilgrimage as social process'. In V. Turner, *Dramas, fields and metaphors: symbolic action in human society*: 166–230. Ithaca: Cornell University Press.

1975. 'Death and the dead in the pilgrimage process'. In M. West and M. Whisson (eds.), *Religion and social change in southern Africa*: 107–27. Cape Town: David Philip.

1977. 'Sacrifice as quintessential process, prophylaxis or abandonment'. *History of Religions*, 16, 3:189–215.

van Baal, J. 1975. *Reciprocity and the position of women: anthropological papers*. Assen: van Gorcum.

van der Veer, P. 1985. 'Brahmans: their purity and their poverty. On the changing values of brahman priests in Ayodhya'. *Contributions to Indian Sociology* (n.s.), 19, 2:303–21.

1988. *Gods on earth: the management of religious experience and identity in a north Indian pilgrimage centre*. London: The Athlone Press.

Vidyarthi, L. P. 1961. *The sacred complex of Hindu Gaya*. Bombay: Asia Publishing House.

Vidyarthi, L. P., B. N. Saraswati and Makhan Jha. 1979. *The sacred complex of Kashi*.

Delhi: Concept Publishing House.

Wilson, G. 1939. 'Nyakusa conventions of burial'. *Bantu Studies*, 13:1–31.

Wilson, P. J. 1967. 'Status ambiguity and spirit possession'. *Man* (n.s.), 2, 3:366–78.

Wirth, Louis. 1975 (1938). 'Urbanism as a way of life'. In John Friedl and Loel J. Chrisman (eds.), *City ways: a selective reader in urban anthropology*: 26–45. New York: Thomas Y. Crowell.

Wiser, W. H. 1936. *The Hindu jajmani system*. Lucknow: Lucknow Publishing House.

Wittgenstein, L. 1958. *Philosophical investigations* (trans. G. E. M. Anscombe). Oxford: Basil Blackwell.

Yang, Anand A. 1987. 'The many faces of sati in the early nineteenth century'. *Manushi* 1987:26–9.

Zaehner, R. C. 1962. *Hinduism*. London: Oxford University Press.

Index